# Modern Pension Plans

## PRINCIPLES AND PRACTICES

# Modern Pension Plans

## PRINCIPLES AND PRACTICES

........................................................................

BY

## HUGH O'NEILL

*Pension Consultant*

*New York*
**PRENTICE-HALL, INC.**
*1947*

# Preface

..................................................................................

THE MAJOR PURPOSE OF THIS BOOK IS TO PRESENT A NON-TECHNI-
cal description and explanation of the various means and methods of operating modern pension plans, and of the basic provisions
of such plans.

Past experience proves that employers, whether public or private,
who undertake to establish and operate pension plans must adhere
to certain principles and practices if financial or other difficulties
are to be avoided. Obviously it is to the interests of an employer
to operate a pension plan which is technically and financially sound;
his employees are even more concerned in having a plan of such
character. The book, therefore, while developing the subject matter in a manner that should be useful to an employer in establishing
a new pension plan, as well as in evaluating any he may now have
in operation, also will enable an employee to appraise the nature
of his prospective or present pension coverage. Furthermore, the
book will be of value to those several groups—life underwriters,
attorneys, accountants, trust officers, and industrial relations specialists—who are called upon to render advice in connection with
pension plans.

It may be well to point out that while this book, among other
things, purports to indicate what an employer *may* do in developing a pension plan, and in some cases what he should avoid, it does
not presume to tell him what he *should* do. This qualification is
important. A pension plan must be designed in relation to an
employer's *particular* circumstances, and by the employer working
in concert with the necessary technical advisers. Not in contra-
diction of the foregoing, but as a possible guide for an employer
seeking the type of plan which might prove suitable to his situation,
there appears in the final chapter a survey of 612 pension plans
established within recent years.

The author wishes to make grateful acknowledgment for help-
ful suggestions, both general and technical, received in the development of the book. To the several thousand corporate officials,

v

without whose courtesy and cooperation the pension survey previously mentioned would not have been possible, he likewise extends his thanks and appreciation.

HUGH O'NEILL

*New York City*
*October, 1946*

# Contents

# CHAPTER I

## The Case for Pensions

•••••••••••••••••••••••••••••••••••••••••••••••••••••••••••••••••••••••••••

THE ABILITY OF MODERN INDUSTRY TO PRODUCE A TREMENDOUS quantity of goods with great rapidity is an accepted fact. The recent unprecedented increase in the productivity of industry may be attributed largely to technological improvements in machine design and to the unification of production through large-scale enterprise. While the technical and functional aspects of production have been the object of intense research, less attention has been given to the human factors that likewise affect production.

It is apparent that if the entire personnel of an organization stops work, production will cease. Less apparent, though the entire personnel may be at work, are the stresses, strains, and discontentments among the employees that may slow up production. The causative factors may be simple or complex; the individuals affected may be few or many. There may be involved such an easily remedied thing as the condition of the drinking water, or, more serious, a dissatisfaction with wage differentials within a shop, or, even more difficult of adjustment, a differential between one shop and another. At any rate, production costs will tend to rise unless the factors that slow up production are recognized and eliminated. To the extent that they are subject to the control of the employer, and not all are, a study designed to eliminate these factors constitutes a job of industrial relations.

Industrial relations, using the term with particular reference to employer-employee relations, have reached only in recent years a status that is recognized in some quarters as having a function equally important with other phases of production. In numerous large enterprises this recognition has taken the form of delegating to an executive officer, such as a vice-president, the responsibility for the formulation and the carrying out of an industrial relations program for the organization. The purpose of such a program is to aid production by improving employer-employee relations, through the use of the most suitable means and methods. Industrial relations thus take account of the human equation in production, with a consciousness that technology alone is not a complete answer to sustained production and lowered costs.

Among the means which may be utilized under an industrial relations program to promote better employer-employee relationships is a sound pension plan. By a sound pension plan is meant, in general, a plan that is characterized by a definite system for retiring aged or superannuated employees, and one which is adequately and properly financed to achieve its purposes. While in the past decade there has been an increasing use of pension plans of this character, the number actually in operation is relatively small when measured against the total number of business establishments. With specific reference to corporations there are about 500,000 of them actually engaged in business and industry.[1] Among these are to be found the bulk of the pension plans now operating, but it is unlikely that there are in existence more than 7,500 separate plans. It is important to note that a great majority of these plans, possibly ninety-five per cent, has been established in the last ten years.[2]

It would be a tribute to the newly developed science of industrial relations if this recent growth in pension plans could be credited to its activities. This growth, however, must be explained largely in the light of other factors, later to be discussed. Among employers conducting small or medium-sized enterprises, there still exists widespread uncertainty as to whether a pension plan is applicable to their organizations. This uncertainty expresses itself in such questions, direct or implied, as: whose interests are served under a pension plan; what reasons may be advanced to justify the establishment of a plan; what does a pension plan cost and who pays for it? The remainder of this chapter will be directed to a discussion of these and allied questions.

## I. WHOSE PENSION PLAN?

It is common usage to speak of pension plans—as well as of group life, accident and health plans, and others—as employee-benefit plans. Used as a conventional phrase by those who clearly understand the purpose of such plans, it is perhaps tolerable. The

---

[1] *Economic Almanac for 1945-46*, p. 143; National Industrial Conference Board, New York, N. Y.

[2] "How the Commissioner Handles Pension Plans," by Norman D. Cann, Deputy Commissioner of Internal Revenue, Washington, D. C., *National Association of Cost Accountant's Bulletin*, July 15, 1945.

average employer, however, seems to believe that so-called employee-benefit plans are literally such; that beneficially his, the
employer's, interests are not involved. His failure to recognize
that pension plans, and allied plans, are instruments of management or *employer*-benefit plans has helped heavily to retard their
adoption.

The question as to whose interests are served by pension plans
may be illuminated partly by the attitude labor leaders have taken.
A violent denunciation of private pension plans by Samuel Gompers, made years ago, constitutes an extreme labor view. The gist
of his statement was that pension plans were established to dis-
courage union organization; that they sought to reduce labor turnover where wages and working conditions were unsatisfactory,
through the promise of a pension that the worker might never receive because of the loss of his job or his premature death; and that
pension plans in general were intended to chain employees to their
jobs.

While similar expressions by other labor leaders have followed
that of Gompers, the hostility of national labor leaders to private
pension plans seems to have been modified by the old-age benefits
provided by Social Security.[3] Thereunder, the mobility of the
worker is unimpaired, for he generally loses no previously earned
benefits if his employment is temporarily interrupted or actually
terminated; consequently the allegiance of an employee to a particular employer (as against a trade union) which might be obtained through a private pension plan is presumed to be minimized.
For the most part, labor unions seem neutral today toward pension
plans, with some evidence that certain unions may seek to obtain
pension coverage through collective bargaining. The attitude of a
labor union, presumably, will be dependent on the specific terms of
a pension plan, such as, whether the plan vests the pension benefits; that is, whether it specifies the return to an employee of a
proportionate share of pension benefits accrued, if his services
should terminate before normal retirement.

It is true in any case that, historically, labor has not been uncertain in its appraisal of private pension plans but has regarded them
as instruments of management. While the official labor viewpoint

---

[3] Inquiries were directed by the writer to the headquarters of the two major labor
unions in the United States, the American Federation of Labor (AFL) and the
Congress of Industrial Organizations (CIO). The official policy of both seems to
be a "hands-off" one, each leaving it to its affiliates or associated unions to develop
or determine, each for itself, a policy toward private pension plans.

may not necessarily typify the attitude of the rank and file of its members, nor of the clerical and supervisory employees, nevertheless it has been observed that pension plans seldom have been requested by employees. In short, where pension plans have been established they have been brought about by the employer, or in the case of large corporations, by the top management group.

## II.  ADVANTAGES IN PENSION PLANS

It has been remarked previously that a pension plan constitutes a means, used in industrial relations, to improve employer-employee relationships. A pension plan is not the only instrument, however, which may be used to bring about this highly desirable result; and the benefits to an employer of a pension plan must be related to his financial outlays if the plan is to be justified as a business procedure.

It has been claimed at different times that pension plans provide the employer with a means of accomplishing the following objectives: provision of relief for the needy and aged employee; encouragement of continuity of service; improvement of morale; reduction or elimination of strikes and labor trouble; increase of employee loyalty; attraction of new employees; creation of good will in the community; increase in output per worker; reduction of labor turnover; securing of payroll relief; reward for long service, and opening of avenues of promotion. It is highly doubtful if any pension plan of itself ever realized or could be made to realize all of these purposes. Nor is it necessary to contend that a pension plan should do so, any more than it might be held that a particular machine in an industrial plant is useless because it is incapable of performing the entire manufacturing process. A pension plan is *one* of the instruments available to an employer which may be expected to bring him certain benefits. It may solve some of his industrial relations problems, but it is not a panacea for all of them. Certain of the more fundamental advantages that may be expected to accrue to the employer from adoption of a pension plan will be examined.

### A.  Effect on Labor Turnover

The term *labor turnover* refers to the fact that normally employees are added to and separated from the payroll of an employer in the course of his operations. A certain amount of such turnover is unavoidable in any organization as a consequence of deaths and disability among employees, and also from necessary elimination of the incompetent and inefficient workers. With allowance for this, labor turnover rates may show wide variations. They differ as between industries; between enterprises in the same industry; as between skilled and unskilled workers; and between workers on an hourly wage and those on salary. Also, turnover rates differ as between employees of differing age, sex, and race.

There is common agreement that excessive or abnormal turnover among employees is uneconomical. It is deleterious in its effects on the morale of the personnel, and otherwise is costly to the employer. While the effect on morale is not easily measured, the costs which are incurred in hiring and training a new employee are ascertainable; also the costs which may have accrued from lost production before a new employee is recruited. These costs will vary in accordance with the degree of skill required to perform the vacated job, and its importance in production. Again, it is mostly the larger employers who have an accurate knowledge of their labor turnover costs. The small employer, while he may have an approximate idea of his turnover rate, rarely has any knowledge of his turnover costs.

Generalizations about the effect of pension plans on labor turnover are difficult to formulate. The evidence available consists largely of the statistically unsupported opinion of employers, obtained through questionnaires. The samples of these opinions, obtained from time to time, also are small, principally because the number of pension plans that have been in operation for any length of time is likewise small. The opinions of employers on the effect of pension plans on labor turnover, moreover, are expressed usually in terms of the general effect of pension plans in their organizations, rather than in terms of detailed information relative to the effect on different age, sex, or occupational groups or on employees at different levels of compensation.

The opinion of employers, in any case, ranges from the view that pension plans are very effective in reducing turnover, to the view that small value attaches to them. Many employers are unable to evaluate their pension plans as to effects on turnover, and they have stated as much. The conservative opinion would seem to demand a qualified viewpoint of pension plans in relation to their effect on labor turnover. These qualifications would relate mainly to the nature of an industry; the composition of the working force of a particular enterprise; the adequacy of the wage or salary scale maintained; the existence of other employee-benefit plans; and the liberality of the pension plan itself. In other words, a careful analysis of the particular conditions existent in an enterprise, preceding the adoption of a pension plan, is essential for predictive purposes; also such an analysis is necessary if any reliable conclusions are to be reached as to the effect on turnover after the introduction of the pension plan. Furthermore, the terms and provisions of the plan itself, such as the amount of benefits provided and the length of service required before the granting of benefits, may be expected to prove important in influencing turnover results.

## B. Retirement of Superannuated Employees

The essential purpose of a pension plan is the retirement of the superannuated or aged employee. In almost any business, established for twenty or thirty years, whose personnel has numbered consistently ten employees and upward, there are certain to be some aged employees. Among these, a few may be completely efficient, but more likely most of them are semi-efficient, and therefore are a drag on production. In addition, because wages and salaries of employees tend to rise as the length of their service increases, particularly in the case of employees among the clerical, supervisory, and managerial groups, the compensation of the superannuated employee is often far out of line with the value of his services.

It is these consequences of superannuation—inefficiency and overpayment for services rendered—that largely justify the establishment of pension plans. Neither the argument that the employer has a social obligation, nor humanitarian considerations, seem necessary in developing the case for pensions. To specialists in the field of pension planning, it is a frequent experience to find organizations that have stagnated because of excessive numbers of superannuated employees in the personnel. It should be added that, proportionately, superannuated employees are more likely to be found in the management group than among the rank and file of workers. To the extent that this is true of the management, the effects of inefficiency and overpayment for services obviously are more deleterious to the business in a relative sense than when superannuation is confined to the personnel with less responsibilities, and of a lower wage and salary scale.

An employer with superannuated employees, and without a pension plan, usually is not in a position to solve his problem in a satisfactory way. The method of discharging them arbitrarily is theoretically possible, but actually impractical. First of all, if the business is located in a small community, the elimination of aged employees arbitrarily without regard to their needs or circumstances might create local ill will. Another possible result might be a drying-up of the local labor supply. Furthermore, damage to the morale of the remaining employees would certainly occur, with restlessness, disaffection, and downright disloyalty to the employer following in the wake of such a policy. For businesses located in large industrial centers, considerations of public ill will and the effect on the labor supply might not be deterrents to an arbitrary policy of discharge, although considerations of the morale factor would still remain. It is of interest to observe, in passing, that many large-scale enterprises whose operations are national in scope, after having adopted a pension plan, have made capital of the fact both among employees and in public relations.

An alternative procedure to that of arbitrary discharge, in lieu of a pension plan, would be to informally retire superannuated employees by monthly payments from operating income, or by purchase of annuities from an insurance company when employees reach retirement age. Each method has been tried, mostly by the larger corporations, but has proved unsatisfactory. For the small employer the monthly payments from operating income for retirement benefits, which normally tend to rise from year to year, ultimately would become a financial drain that he could ill afford; and the financial outlay required for the outright purchase of annuities also is apt to be too expensive for him.

The usual procedure, followed by employers with superannuated employees, but without pension plans, is to adopt a mixed policy. Some employees are laid off, if it is found they have accumulated anything for themselves; others are given lump sums to help them out, or are paid small monthly allowances; still others are retained on the payroll, inefficient as they may be, although, in some cases, they may be shifted to a job where, though they may not assist production, they cannot impede it. This mixed policy, viewed as a business matter, and strictly from the employer's interests, is no better and probably worse than the policy of arbitrary discharge. It does not satisfy the superannuated employees who are retired, because either there is discrimination in benefits provided or the benefits are totally inadequate to their needs; nor does it rid the employer completely of the inefficient, for he undoubtedly will retain some on the payroll.

An employer, loaded with any considerable number of super-annuated employees, frequently is conscious of his problem, in the sense that he feels something should be done about it. With no adequate solution available, such as would be found in a pension plan, and rarely with a precise idea of the costs of retention of the superannuated, he temporizes. Nothing is done, other than to follow the policies outlined above.

A pension plan unquestionably is a means of removing or retiring the superannuated employee on a basis satisfactory to employer and employee alike. The fundamental issue is the cost of such a plan to the employer. There are differing views as to pension costs (ignoring for the present the matter of what the costs will be), particularly as they relate to the question of who ultimately pays the costs. They will be stated, with some comment.

## III. WHO PAYS FOR PENSION?

### A. Equalization Theory

One view of costs holds that the employer's outlay for a pension plan will be offset by measurable gains or savings, and, in addition, that there will be intangible benefits, such as improved employee morale, community good will, and so forth. The measurable gains will arise from reduced labor turnover, payroll savings, and increased efficiency. For economy in reference, we have termed this the equalization theory.

The difficulty in evaluating the effects on labor turnover, and therefore the possible savings, already has been indicated. It is likely that if the claims for savings from this source were moderate, they would obtain greater credence, and they could be substantiated more readily, in fact. For example, both experience and logic support the belief that pension plans have little, if any, influence in reducing turnover among younger employees; and that among the older employees, those over fifty, stability normally exists regardless of pension plans. A pension at sixty-five for a youth of twenty-five or thirty is considered too remote to be a stabilizing factor. The older employees, except among top executives, usually have had their mobility reduced anyway by the lack of opportunity to shift jobs. The influence of a pension plan on labor turnover, therefore, is apt to be greatest, so far as age alone is considered, among those employees in the age-group of thirty to forty-five. Inasmuch as this group is likely to be highly trained and the most efficient, elimination of turnover among them could make for significant economy in operations.

Payroll savings come about as a result of the replacement of the inefficient, superannuated, and overpaid employees by younger men. The immediate gains achieved by this procedure are evident. Normally, a replacement of an older employee can be made at a lower wage or salary; or one and one-half to two employees may be used to fill the vacated job at no increased wage or salary cost. Reduction in costs thus would arise from both payroll savings and increased efficiency, or at least from the latter.

There normally develops, from the removal of the superannuated, the opportunity of promotion for younger men, with a corresponding effect on their morale. This is an intangible benefit. The restlessness that may be engendered among younger employees, however, by the retention of superannuated employees, because there is no practical way to dispose of them, may become unhealthy. It may not affect turnover, but employee morale may be impaired to the extent that the chances for promotion are limited or deferred by retention of the superannuated; thus indifference may result among the younger employees with a consequent impairment of efficiency.

If, by use of a pension plan, the employer actually realizes the gains, as outlined, his costs, or financial outlays, may be absorbed or more than offset. That this substantially will be the result is the belief of students of pensions, of many employers with pension plans, and of numerous industrial relations specialists.

## B. Employer Pays

At the other extreme to the view that pension costs are absorbed, or more than offset, by the benefits of the pension plan, is the theory which conceives of them as strictly additional labor costs. Those holding this view reject the idea that pensions pay for themselves. They feel that the advocates of pension plans overstate their case. They believe that the outlays for pension plans are nothing less than additional costs of production, the assumption of which, if passed on to the consumer, would impair the competitive position of the enterprise, or, if not passed on, would have to be absorbed through reduced returns on the invested capital. Furthermore, they are in fairly general agreement that pension plans are paternalistic and make for unjustifiable dependence of the workers on the employer.

This view on who pays for pensions is perhaps most prevalent among the stock-holding interests, particularly where management and stock ownership are separated. The management group, perhaps because they are closer to the operations of the business, are more inclined to take the position that the costs are equalized. The weight of opinion, in any case, is opposed to the conception that an employer's pension outlays constitute true costs to him, that is, are not offset in some measure by gains realized from the pension plan.

### C. Consumer Pays

The belief that the consumer pays for the costs of pension plans is not widespread. Those who take this stand, however, contend that, whatever the pension costs may be, they are, like other costs of production, passed on to the consumer. In their opinion, therefore, it is not essential to take account of the benefits that may flow to the employer, or to consider whether the pension plan increases costs, so long as the consumer can be made to pay them.

It is possible, assuming that outlays for pensions result in increased labor costs, that an industry, having a monopoly or a semi-monopoly, could pass them on to the consumer. If pension costs are absorbed, as believed by those who adopt the equalization theory, there then would occur a free gain to that enterprise which could pass them on to the consumer.

### D. Employee Pays

Those who maintain that an employer's outlays for pension plans are not costs to him, but actually are absorbed by his employees, regard the employer's payments to a pension plan as *deferred wages*. Under this theory, the incidence of cost is placed on neither the employer nor consumer, but on the employee. This is brought about in time through a lowering of wages or salaries, or through the maintenance of a given scale which, in the absence of a pension plan, would have been increased. The following statements set forth this view:

The notion that in the free pension system the beneficiary gets something for nothing is an illusion. There is no free pension where the question of pension and wages are involved together. In the course of a limited number of years such pensions will be adjusted to the salary or wage scale. Under such conditions all salaries will be affected, while only a minority will get pensions.[4]

---

[4] Pritchett, Henry S., *13th Annual Report,* Carnegie Foundation for the Advancement of Teaching, 1918, p. 21.

Also see: "The Social Philosophy of Pensions," Carnegie Foundation for the Advancement of Teaching, Bulletin No. 25, 1930, p. 14.

Again:

The real incidence of the cost of a retirement system in the case of employees who enter the service after the establishment of the system is placed by economic forces on the employee. The benefits offered by the system become part of the compensation for the services rendered.[5]

The idea that the cost of pensions falls on employees, or in other words is a deferred wage, has long been in controversy. It has been argued by those who hold to the equalization theory that the costs are absorbed, and neither employer nor employee pays; that is, the gains, through increased efficiency, reduction in labor turnover, and improvement in morale, pay the costs. The contention that the consumer pays for them likewise is offered in contravention; or else that the stockholders pay the pension bill. Finally, the statement is made, in lieu of anything else, that it cannot be proved that pension payments constitute deferred wages, and the matter is left there.

The resistance to the idea that pensions are deferred wages is possibly explained by certain major consequences that might be expected to result, if this conception obtained wide acceptance. First of all, if the employer's contributions to a pension plan were to come out, ultimately, from the employees' salaries or wages, the corollary would be that pension plans should be completely contractual. In other words, the employees would be entitled to demand a guarantee of the pension payments at normal retirement age, and a proportionate benefit if, for any reason, employment were to be terminated prior to retirement. Secondly, the employees could insist rightfully that the pension plan be properly and adequately financed, and that the pension funds be invested with every safeguard taken against possible impairment. A third possible consequence would be that the employees might request representation in the management of the pension fund.

It is a fact, as discussed in the following chapter, that the majority of pension plans, established in this country up to almost 1930, were not contractual, and were haphazardly financed. Also, employee representation, while perhaps not necessarily vital to the bona fide administration of a pension plan, was absent in the early pension plans.

The inference that pension payments were deferred wages in the

[5] Meriam, Lewis, *Principles Governing the Retirement of Public Employees*, D. Appleton & Co., New York, N. Y., 1918, p. 388.

early pension plans, however, does not necessarily follow. It has been argued that industries which were first to introduce pension plans or systems, worthy of the name, were in an expansion period and usually were capable of meeting the pension bill out of profits, without having to reduce salaries or wages to meet the costs, assuming no equalization occurred. Also, as pensions were, in their early development, thought of as gratuities (as still seems to be implied in the phrase *reward for service*), no particular relationship between pension costs and the bill for wages and salaries was clearly distinguished.

### 1. Employer Aspects

The logic of the conception that pension costs ultimately will be defrayed by the employees seems inexorable, however, under certain sets of circumstances. One such would relate to the terms of the pension plan: if it were properly funded by regular annual contributions; if the pension benefits were contractual or guaranteed; and the extent to which vesting (severance) benefits were granted on termination of employment. The other circumstances would be the extent to which a given enterprise, exposed to free competition, would find it necessary to make every effort to reduce or shift costs, either as a means of earning a fair return on its capital, or simply to survive. The ability of employees to resist, or avoid paying for their own pensions under the given circumstances, would perhaps be neither more nor less than the bargaining power they possessed, in relation to direct compensation received in the pay envelope.

Whether in the economic future there will develop a general consciousness among employers that their financial outlays for pension plans are essentially a part of compensation, that is, deferred wages, remains to be seen. There is already recognition of this fact by some employers at least. One large national corporation reported a few years ago that the rate of wage dividends to employees, paid for years, had been reduced. It was stated that the reduction was to assist in meeting the annual contributions to the pension plan. Also many organizations which, over the years, have paid bonuses to the management group have, in recent years, shifted some or all such bonuses into pension plans.

The acceptance of the idea that an employer's outlays for a pension plan constitute deferred wages, and that therefore the pension plan actually is supported by the employees, may be a desirable development. In the first place, it disposes of the unsound, but commonly held, notion that pensions are a gratuity and constitute a benevolence of the employer. The fact is that there exist very few enterprises which could afford to make continuous gifts to employees in the amounts necessary to support a pension plan and long remain in business. Secondly, it focuses the attention of the employer on the utility of pension plans as instruments of management, whereby he obtains certain benefits, possibly at no increased cost to himself. In other words, if the benefits of reduced labor turnover, of payroll relief through retirement of the superannuated, and of improvement in morale are realized, and if the contributions to the plan are in fact deferred wages, the employer makes a clear gain for which the employees pay.

It is true that pension plans necessarily would have to be constructed so as to be completely contractual, if the deferred wage concept of pensions were to be accepted. Also vesting, an allowance to the employee of a proportionate share of the employer's contributions to the plan if the former should terminate employment before retirement, would largely have to be allowed. However, most of the pension plans, established in recent years, are contractual in fact anyway; also partial or complete vesting of the employer's contributions to the pension plan is increasingly customary, at least in those plans underwritten by insurance companies. Such being the case, it would appear that there has occurred in actual practice an acceptance of the deferred wage concept, although theoretical disagreement as to its validity may continue to persist.

The actual provisions of contemporary pension plans, however, while apparently reflecting acceptance by employers of the deferred wage concept, probably cannot be so interpreted for several reasons. The plans created in the past five years represent a large majority of all pension plans in operation. Their establishment was motivated largely by tax considerations, rather than by an understanding of the fundamental advantages obtained by the employer, or by any appreciation of the possibility that employees might pay the pension bill in the form of deferred wages. Also in designing new pension plans, or revising older ones, it has been necessary to meet certain requirements as set forth in the Federal law and in the regulations of the Treasury Department, if tax advantages are to be obtained. The latter require that a pension plan be completely contractual (although the vesting of benefits in the case of termination of employment prior to normal retirement is left to the employer), and that, if the entire plan should be terminated, distribution of the assets of the plan must be made among the employee beneficiaries of the plan. In other words, a sizable proportion of pension plans have been established without particular reference to the basic advantages to be obtained by the employer; also, in their construction, plans have been influenced by the law, rather than by any appreciation by employers that their payments may be in the nature of a deferred wage. Experience with employers confirms the latter conclusions. It is uncommon to find employers who fully appreciate that their financial outlays for pension plans may be equalized or absorbed; and even less common to encounter one who conceives of the costs of a pension bill as part of employee compensation, or deferred wages.

## 2. Employee Aspects

If pensions constitute deferred wages and the plans produce the benefits previously discussed, the employer who neglects to establish a plan obviously ignores a useful means of reducing costs. But what of the employees? Will they object to paying for their own pensions? Is there anything in the deferred wage concept that should be regarded as objectionable, so far as they are concerned? The answer to both questions would seem to be in the negative, provided the pension plans are completely contractual, and are non-discriminatory in their benefits, and also that they provide for partial or complete vesting, and for a pro-rata distribution of the accrued pension benefits to the employees if the plan should be terminated.

The employer and the employee have a joint interest in reducing costs, although it is true the employee may not be as conscious of the fact as the employer. The reason why special emphasis has been placed thus far on the advantages of pension plans to the employer is that, in general, he has been slow to grasp the utility of pension plans as a means of reducing costs. Complementary to this, however, is the fact that the interests of the employee may simultaneously be served. The retirement of superannuated and inefficient employees, while it reduces the costs to the employer, likewise opens the way to promotions for the remaining employees. Also, to the extent that turnover is reduced and general efficiency is promoted by a pension plan, such reductions in costs enable an enterprise to maintain its competitive position. Employees with any considerable length of service clearly have a stake in the survival of the business itself. For older employees whose mobility has been reduced by age, as well as for others whose services may have to be terminated before retirement, a modern pension plan, fully contractual and with liberal vesting provisions, is a source of security. If it is true that the employees pay for this security in the form of deferred wages, they nevertheless have, by collective action, served their own interests through the instrumentality of a pension plan. So far as the willingness of employees to pay some of the costs of their own pensions is concerned, this has already been proved by use of the contributory principle.

### E.  Non-contributory and Contributory Principle

A pension plan to which the employer alone contributes is described sometimes as non-contributory; a plan to which the employees contribute is described as contributory. The purpose of employee contributions has been mainly to reduce costs to the employer. Other reasons adduced for such contributions are that thereby employee interest is engendered, thrift promoted, and paternalism minimized.

The use of the contributory principle came rather late in the development of pension plans in this country, and never received universal application. It was felt by some that, if contributions were received from employees, representation in the management or administration of the pension fund would have to be granted. This was not always considered as desirable. Others believed that, inasmuch as the contributions of employees should be returned to them on termination of their employment before retirement, no important reduction in costs would result. The requirement of contributions from employees, therefore, seemed superfluous. The cultivation of thrift among employees, while admittedly desirable, could be achieved by other methods.

The use of the contributory principle perhaps would have been extended further except for the deductions from salaries and wages brought about by Federal Social Security taxes, State unemployment taxes, and later by the withholding provision in the collection of income taxes. The withholding tax made it apparent that an employee's contribution to a pension plan was made after taxes had been levied on his wage or salary, whereas the employer's contribution was made before taxes. The employer, that is, may deduct, as expense, his contributions to the plan; the employee may not. Because of the difficulty of making further salary deductions, in addition to those already mentioned, a substantial number of the new pension plans, established since about 1941, have been non-contributory in character.

Independent of the above considerations, the merit of contributory plans remains in question as a practical matter. Only a small minority of employees live, or remain in the employ of a particular employer, until retirement age. If an employee's contributions, plus interest thereon, are returned to him upon severance of employment before retirement, no particular gain accrues to the employer. It is true that an employee may have accumulated, at the time of severance of employment, a fund he otherwise might not have had. This might be important to an employer, perhaps, in relieving him from payment of a dismissal wage, or severance pay, as is provided in some industries. The employee contributions would also reduce financial outlays of the employer, by the amount of such contributions. Insofar as the outlays for a pension plan represent true costs to the employer, there might be some reduction in cost to him from the contributions of the employees who actually were to be retired.

There is always the possibility that an employer will fail to persuade sufficient numbers of his employees to contribute, to make a pension plan possible or practical. It cannot be lost sight of that the essential purpose of a pension plan is to retire the superannuated. Those employees who elect not to contribute and thus remain out of a plan might prove later to be the superannuated, with no funds accumulated with which to retire them.

There is a further practical consideration for the employer; that the adoption of a contributory plan may lead to a request for increases in wages or salaries by employees, to offset the amount of their contributions. There are, in addition, mechanical difficulties to be encountered in obtaining contributions from employees on an equitable basis. The usual method is to collect from employees a flat percentage of their wage or salary. Differences in age, as well as in levels of compensation, create a problem of adjusting contributions so that each employee pays no more than is proper in relation to service, salary, and the pension benefits provided. The best of formulae, worked out to preserve equitable treatment of employees in respect to their contributions, fail to obtain complete equality. Finally, there are administrative costs connected with the maintenance and handling of contributory pension plans, not necessarily associated with non-contributory ones. These costs arise in the keeping of separate employee accounts, deductions from the wage or salary of each participating employee, and extra computations.

On the theoretical side, that is, if contributions to pension plans are regarded and treated as deferred wages, direct contributions by employees would seem to be superfluous. If the payments to a pension plan by the employer ultimately become a part of compensation, the wages or salaries of employees will be adjusted in time to absorb such payments. The extent to which such adjustments will take place will depend on the numerous factors which generally affect levels of compensation.

A further result of recognizing the employer's payments to pension plans as deferred wages would be to make the distinction of *non-contributory* and *contributory* somewhat meaningless. At least it would be inaccurate to describe a pension plan, in which the employees actually pay the bill, as a non-contributory plan simply because, as a matter of mechanics, the employer issued his check for the necessary payments to support the plan. The employer's role would continue to be a vital one, both in establishing a plan, and in administrative and supervisory ways. His relation to the pension plan, however, would assume more the aspect of fiscal agent for the employees. Such a relationship does in no way obviate the advantages the employer might expect to obtain; nor does it impair the conclusion that the employees have obtained security through their collective action under the mechanism of a pension plan.

## IV. THE PROBLEM OF ACCUMULATION

There have occurred several developments in recent years, the social and economic consequences of which have yet to be fully reflected, which appear significant in relation to pension plans. One of these is the decline in interest rates; the other is the rise in personal income taxes. An illustration of the impact of these two developments will elucidate the point.

*1929.* To highlight the matter, we shall consider the year to be 1929, and examine the outlook of an individual whom we will call A, who proposes to retire at age 65. He is now age 40, married, has two children, and is earning a salary of $10,000 a year. We shall further assume A's earnings will be constant at $10,000 until he retires.

It is possible, and frequently assumed by budget, life-insurance, and other financial advisers, that such an individual can save 30% of his annual income, or $3,000. *A*'s income tax is nominal,[6] so broadly there remains a balance of $7,000, which enables him to maintain standards of living proper to his station and satisfactory to himself. *A* thus assumes that he can save $3,000 each year after payment of income taxes.

It is possible for *A* to invest on a safe basis at 5% interest.[7] Traditionally, such a rate of return has been possible for years; in fact 5½% to 6% is thought by substantial numbers of investors not to carry excessive risks. The problem of compounding interest may present a difficulty, if high-grade bonds are selected as a medium for accumulation, although some banks are paying 5% on savings deposits. The $3,000 annual savings which will accumulate from now until *A* is sixty-five, at 5% interest, will amount to $146,000. Again using a 5% return on the accumulated capital, *A* may look forward to a retirement income of $7,300 a year. His personal pension, so to speak, which will result from his accumulated savings thus will be equal to approximately three-quarters of his earned income of $10,000 a year.[8] The adequacy of such an income for *A* and his wife, after his children are raised, is apparent.

*1945.* Now let us examine the outlook of *B* in 1945, likewise earning a salary of $10,000 a year. He too is age 40, married, with two children. His objective also is retirement at 65. As with *A*, it is assumed that there will be no increases in salary before retirement. What will *B* be able to accumulate toward retirement at 65?

---

[6] For example:

*1929*

| | | |
|---|---:|---:|
| Income............................................... | | $10,000.00 |
| Less Deductions...................................... | | 500.00 |
| | | $ 9,500.00 |
| Less Personal Exemption..................... | $3,500.00 | |
| Credit for Dependents...................... | 800.00 | 4,300.00 |
| | | $ 5,200.00 |
| Normal Tax ($4,000 at .5%; $1,200 at 2%)............................ | | $44.00 |
| Surtax................................................................. | | NONE |
| Less Earned Income Credit............................................ | | 11.00 |
| TOTAL TAX........................ | | $33.00 |

[7] See page 68.

[8] It perhaps should be emphasized that the discussion is based on *A*'s *outlook* in 1929; later developments to come will modify this outlook.

First of all, it is assumed B needs to maintain about the same living standards that A had in 1929. A, it will be recalled, with practically no income taxes, after saving $3,000, had a spendable income of approximately $7,000 with which to maintain himself and his family. With a similar amount B can achieve about the same standards in 1945; the purchasing power of his dollars, at least, is about the same as in 1929.[9]  B, however, in 1945 has an income tax of about $2,000 to meet.[10]  Of a $3,000 surplus above expenditures for living, income taxes therefore absorb about $2,000, leaving B $1,000 a year to invest, as against the $3,000 which remained to A in 1929. Furthermore, B finds that, instead of a 5% return on his savings, he can expect no more than 3%.[11]  B thus begins his accumulation program, as contrasted with that of A, with his possible annual savings cut two-thirds, from $3,000 to $1,000, and his expected interest rate of return reduced 40%—from 5% to 3%. If B pursues his program, saving a $1,000 yearly and compounding it at 3%, he will accumulate a fund of approximately $37,000 at 65. A 3% return on this amount will provide a retirement income of $1,100 a year. The comparative status of A, with a retirement income of $7,300 a year at 65, and of B, with $1,100 a year, needs no elaboration.

The comparison given, it is recognized, is an approximate one and if elaborated in detail would call for minor modifications. It serves the purpose, however, of dramatizing an indisputable fact. The individual earning a salary of $10,000 in 1945, faced a new and

---

[9] Cost of living in the United States (Index: 1923 = 100) in 1929: 100.1; in 1945: 106.3; National Industrial Conference Board, New York, N. Y. This index measures the cost of living for the lower-income groups, so perhaps is not entirely applicable; however, in a general way it serves our purpose.

[10] For example:

| 1945 | | |
|---|---|---|
| Income.......................................... | $10,000.00 | |
| Less Deductions................................. | 500.00 | |
| | $ 9,500.00 | |
| Normal Tax at 3%............................... | | $  270.00ª |
| Net Income..................................... | $ 9,500.00 | |
| Surtax Exemption............................... | 2,000.00 | |
| | $ 7,500.00 | |
| Surtax on $7,500................................ | | 1,810.00 |
| TOTAL TAX.......... | | $2,080.00 |

ª A $500 deduction is allowed in computing the Normal Tax, thus: $9,000 × 3% = $270.
[11] See page 68.

difficult problem of accumulation as a consequence of reduced interest rates and increased personal income taxes. It could be argued, of course, that future conditions might change for the better in respect to either interest returns or income taxes,[12] and thus minimize for *B* the difficulties of accumulation. It is true that conditions might alter for the better, but, on the other hand, the reverse might occur. In any case, *B* is obliged to start his program under given conditions; he cannot make assumptions that might turn out to be gratuitous.

As *B* contemplates his problem certain things will become apparent to him. One of them, with which we are concerned only indirectly, is that, if he had plans for starting a business of his own by saving sufficient capital, they may never be realized. Another is that the probabilities are unlikely that he can accumulate a substantial estate, as was possible for his forebears. Finally, he will contemplate with dismay the fact that a conservative investment program will acquire for him only a nominal $100 monthly income at 65. These hard facts spell general social and economic consequences that lie beyond this discussion. However, *B* obviously must seek some solution which will safeguard his own future security when he is no longer a producer. One of the solutions is for *B* to make use of the annuity principle, either personally, or through the mechanism of a pension plan established by his employer.

## V. THE ANNUITY PRINCIPLE

### A. Personal Use

In the older European economies, particularly in France and England, annuities as a means of maximizing income have had long and extensive use. In the United States employment of annuities to any significant extent by investors, who sought both security of principal and maximum returns, began about 1930. A technical discussion of annuities, as well as their recent growth in this country, is given in succeeding chapters, so no extensive elaboration is necessary here. In general, however, an expanding use of annuities, referring to those largely underwritten by insurance companies appears to be associated with a long-term decline of interest

---

[12] The 1946 Revenue Act gave some income tax relief to *B*, but insufficient to relieve his dilemma. It should be noted that the allowance to *B* of a 3% compound interest return is probably too liberal; also in the illustration no income taxes were levied on *B*'s interest earnings.

rates on high-grade investments.  As the productivity of dollars invested in securities decreases, as represented by interest yielded by government bonds, first-grade corporate securities, and the issues of States and municipalities, the individual investor is forced to alternative mediums with higher returns.  A major alternative for those who seek security of principal, and also certainty of current or future income, is found in the annuity.

Annuities are obtainable in a number of forms.  There are those which pay an immediate income that continues for the balance of the lifetime of one or more persons; or those which pay for a limited period only.  There also are those which pay an income at some future date, with the purchase price for the annuity payable in installments in advance of the date at which the income is to commence.  The income yielded by an annuity will vary in respect to the type purchased, the age and sex of the annuitant, and, to a slight extent, will be dependent on rate differences between insurance companies.

As an example of the productivity of an annuity a male age 65 can currently obtain a return of from 7% to 8% of the purchase price.  The amount of the return will be mainly dependent on the form of the annuity purchased; that is, whether it provides that the income cease upon the death of the purchaser, contains a refund provision, or continues for a limited time to a stipulated beneficiary thereafter.  It is obvious that, as compared with a 3% return, the owner of an annuity of this character has more than doubled his income.  The underlying reasons for such a phenomenal increase in the productivity of the investor's dollars are relatively simple, although often misunderstood.

It is sometimes stated that the purchaser of an annuity gambles on how long he will live, the implication being that, if he lives long, there will be a profit, and, if he does not, there will be a loss.  This is a confused conception of the principles of annuities.  To gamble in the literal sense signifies the creation of a risk where none existed previously, such as occurs in any game of chance.  Also in such games there are no economic benefits created, the so-called winner merely winding up with the assets of the loser.  The economic justification of annuities is that, among a group of individuals, certain of them must augment the returns on their accumulated capital to maintain existence or the standard of living they believe to be necessary.  The selection of any other investment method than annuities to accomplish this, where the income would equal that of annuities, normally would involve risks fatal to assume. The individual who believes he can provide his own annuity by consuming his principal and earned interest, takes the risk that he may live longer than expected and become penniless before death occurs.

It is a characteristic of annuities that they relieve the individual of risks he cannot assume, while at the same time they provide needed or desired income. The individual who purchases an annuity and dies shortly thereafter without having lived to receive payments equal to his purchase price, cannot be said to have suffered a loss. To so believe is equivalent to believing that one who purchases a loaf of bread and consumes it has suffered a loss to the extent of its cost. The consumption of capital, which occurs in annuities based on the probabilities of living or dying, is parallel. By group action, individuals obtain through annuities an income adequate for their maintenance or needs while living. Neither those, in the group possessed of annuities, who die "early" or who "live long" can be said to have sustained a loss or made a gain. In either case they have consumed their "loaf of bread," necessary to their survival or to the maintenance of a desired living standard.

We return to B who, we pointed out, can look forward to an annual income of $1,100 a year at 65 after having invested $1,000 a year at 3%. What will the use of annuities do for him? If annuity rates remain unchanged twenty-five years hence, and if he then has in hand $37,000 (the accumulation of $1,000 yearly earning 3%), B could obtain a life income of about $2,900 a year. This is more than two and one-half times the realizable income at 3% on $37,000, and thus B's position income-wise is much more favorable. However, it provides no estate for B's wife. In the case of A, it will be recalled, his anticipated income would have been $7,300 from interest alone, and at death his wife would have received a $146,000 estate. B, therefore, to protect his wife, must purchase a type of annuity which will maintain her if she survives him. This he can do. Assuming that they are of the same age, the income from a joint and survivor annuity will amount approximately to $2,000 a year, payable so long as either B or his wife lives.

While the annual income from an annuity is greater when purchased for B individually ($2,900, an increase of more than 250% over the realizable income from interest only, $1,100) it is less when a joint and survivor annuity is secured for him and his wife.

But even in the latter case the increase in income approximates 100%, sufficient to prevent B's living standards from falling to what would be almost a subsistence level relative to his previously earned income. The prospect for B of a retirement income of about $2,000 a year at 65 for himself and his wife, while it promises security, does not offer much more. It is true that a Social Security benefit of about $1,000 a year may be payable to B and his wife when they are 65, which would restore the joint income to $3,000 a year. This amount, however, would still be $4,300 under the theoretically possible income of $7,300 which A and his wife could have looked forward to in 1929.

## B.  Pension Use

It is not within the control of B to make use of the annuity principle through a pension plan unless his employer establishes one. In case one is established, the value of B's compensation from the point of view of accumulation may be increased, because whatever amounts are paid into the pension plan by the employer for B's benefit normally will constitute non-taxable income to B. The effect of this tax exemption will be illustrated. To do so we will make several assumptions: (1) that B's salary is increased to $11,000; (2) that B's salary remains at $10,000, but an additional $1,000 is paid into a pension plan for his benefit; (3) that B's salary is reduced from $10,000 to $9,000, and $1,000 is paid into a pension plan to retire him at 65.

### 1.  Direct Salary Increase

It is well known that personal income taxes are progressively more severe as income rises, and that the top dollars of income are taxed most heavily. In the present case a salary increase of $1,000, paid directly to B, leaves him $650 after taxes. In short, B will have to pay a $350 tax on the $1,000 salary increase. If he pursues the policy of investing this $650 at 3% to age 65 it will amount to about $24,000. This sum, added to the $37,000 we have already indicated that he could accumulate, totals $61,000. A return of 3% on this sum would raise his income about $700 to a total of $1,800 a year, from interest alone. If B makes personal use of the annuity principle he could obtain at 65, based on present annuity rates, a life income, for himself only, of about $4,800 a year; for his wife and himself, of about $3,400 a year.

## 2. Pension Plan Increase

Instead of a direct increase of $1,000 in $B$'s compensation let us assume that he continues to receive $10,000 a year, but that an additional $1,000 is paid to a pension plan for his benefit. Normally this $1,000 is currently non-taxable income to $B$. If this amount is annually compounded at 3% in the pension plan until $B$ is 65, its value will be $37,000 as compared with the $24,000 in the previous case in which he receives a $1,000 direct salary increase. Translated into interest income at 3%, $B$ receives $1,100 a year from the pension fund as against the $700 income, as outlined in the previous case. There has been an increase in the capital accumulated by use of the pension plan, as well as in interest income, of about 50%. As compared with the results from a direct salary increase, $B$ now has a total interest income of about $2,200 a year; $1,100 interest income from his personal savings, and $1,100 from the pension fund. If the accumulations, both in and out of the pension fund, are converted to annuity income, $B$ will receive approximately $5,800 a year, and $B$ and his wife about $4,100.

It is clear that the productivity of $1,000 deposited annually in a pension plan, which ultimately accrues for $B$'s benefit, is substantially greater than that of $1,000 added to current income. Inasmuch as $B$ is accumulating funds to retire at age 65, it is to his advantage that the $1,000, which might have been paid to him currently, be paid instead to the pension fund. It is assumed, of course, that the pension fund is soundly invested, the benefits are fully vested, and the plan is completely contractual. Aside from the increased value which the $1,000 salary increase has attained through having been paid to the pension plan, $B$ likewise has been relieved of the problem of investing it.

## 3. Salary Reduction and Pension Plan

Thus far we have shown the financial results if $B$ receives a direct salary increase, from $10,000 to $11,000, and also if his salary remains constant but $1,000 is paid to a pension fund. It may be, however, that $B$'s employer feels that, in paying him $10,000, it is all the job is worth. He may not be in a position to promote $B$ to a higher salaried job. Also, for general reasons of economy, it may not be feasible for the employer to increase $B$'s salary by $1,000, either directly or through the medium of a pension plan. It is conceivable, however, that $B$, not wishing to seek a new position, but definitely being interested in his ultimate security, might consent to a reduction in current salary if a pension plan were to be established. If the value of his compensation would be increased in this way, or as we are discussing it, if the total amount of his long-term savings and the income thereon would be enhanced, *B* would perhaps have nothing to lose, and something to gain.

What would *B*'s accumulations or retirement income amount to if he received $9,000 in direct compensation, and $1,000 were placed in a pension fund for his benefit? *B*'s income tax on a $9,000 salary would be about $1,750,[13] as compared with $2,080 when his salary was $10,000. Thus his income tax would be reduced by $330.[14] Under the pension plan, however, the $1,000 which *B* formerly accumulated himself would be set aside for him. By accepting a salary reduction *B* would improve his position to the extent of having $330 a year more to accumulate. The value of this at age 65, compounded at 3%, is equal to something over $12,000. In this example, *B*'s income at 65 from interest on his personal accumulations of $12,000 and from the pension fund ($37,000) would be about $1,500 a year; his capital accumulation approximately $49,000. This compares with $1,100 a year if his salary remained at $10,000. Annuity income to *B* would be $3,800; to his wife and himself about $2,700; as compared with $2,900 and $2,000 respectively if his salary had remained at $10,000. *B* has improved his position somewhat by taking a salary cut.

The value of compensation higher than $10,000 a year would of course show greater relative gains if the top $1,000 of income

---

[13] *1945*

| | | |
|---|---|---|
| Income............................................ | $9,000.00 | |
| Less Deductions................................... | 500.00 | |
| | $8,500.00 | |
| Normal Tax at 3%................................. | | $ 240.00* |
| Net Income....................................... | $8,500.00 | |
| Surtax Exemption................................. | 2,000.00 | |
| | $6,500.00 | |
| Surtax on $6,500................................. | | 1,510.00 |
| TOTAL TAX.......... | | $1,750.00 |

* A $500 deduction is allowed in computing the Normal Tax, thus: $8,000 × 3% = $240.00.

[14] It will be noted that *B* was shown as actually paying about $2,000 income tax before a salary reduction (page 19), or $80 less than the computed tax shown in the footnote on page 19. *B*'s income tax, therefore, is here similarly reduced $80.

were placed in a pension plan. This would be true both relatively and in an absolute sense, because of the progressive nature of income taxes.

To better visualize the outlook of $A$ in 1929, and the possibilities for $B$ in 1945, the preceding analysis is summarized in several tables below.

*Table I.* To restate the premises: $A$, age 40, earns a salary of $10,000 in 1929; he pays nominal income taxes, saves $3,000 a year, and assumes that he may compound it at 5%, to retire at age 65. He is married with two children. He expends $7,000 for living expenses. $B$, age 40 in 1945, is of the same family status, likewise earns a salary of $10,000. He pays $2,000 income taxes, also expends $7,000 for living, and saves $1,000 a year and assumes that he may compound it at 3%, to retire at 65. The estates at death of both $A$ and $B$ are shown without deductions for taxes or administration costs.

TABLE I

RELATIVE OUTLOOKS OF $A$ AND $B$

|  | 1929—A |  | 1945—B |
| --- | --- | --- | --- |
| Salary...................... | $ 10,000 | Salary...................... | $10,000 |
| Capital Accumulated (ages 40 to 65)..................... | 146,000 | Capital Accumulated (ages 40 to 65).................... | 37,000 |
| Annual Income at Retirement (Interest at 5%).......... | 7,300 | Annual Income at Retirement (Interest at 3%).......... | 1,100 |
| Social Security Annual Income | NONE | Social Security Annual Income | 1,000 |
| Estate at Death After Age 65 | $146,000 | Estate at Death After Age 65 | $37,000[a] |

[a] If $B$'s wife should survive him she would also receive monthly Social Security income payments until her death, equal to three-quarters of $B$'s primary benefit, or about $500 a year.

*Table II.* This table summarizes and contrasts the income $B$ would expect to receive at 65 on his then accumulated capital from (I) interest alone, (II) personally making use of the annuity principle, (III) using the annuity principle through a pension plan, after accepting a salary reduction of $1,000. From ages 40 to 65, whether $B$ accumulates his capital personally or through a pension plan, it is assumed it will be compounded at 3% interest. The salary in the first and second instance is assumed to remain at $10,000; in the third, it is assumed that $B$ will receive a salary of $9,000 and that $1,000 will be contributed to a pension plan. Illustration of the results of an increase in $B$'s compensation of $1,000, both with and without introduction of a pension plan, is omitted. The effects in such case may be referred to in the discussion on pages 23 and 24.

## TABLE II

### Several Outlooks of B—1945

|  | I<br>Interest<br>Only | II<br>Annuity<br>Personal<br>Use | III<br>Annuity<br>Pension<br>Plan |
|---|---|---|---|
| Salary.................................... | $10,000 | $10,000 | $ 9,000 |
| Capital Accumulated at 3% (ages 40 to 65).. | 37,000 | 37,000 | 49,000 |
| Annual Income at 65 from Accumulations... | 1,100[a] | 2,900[b] | 3,800[c] |
| Social Security Annual Income at 65........ | 1,000 | 1,000 | 1,000 |
| Estate at Death After Age 65.............. | $40,000[d] | NONE[d] | NONE[d] |

[a] Based on a 3% return.
[b] A joint and survivor annuity to pay an income to B's wife after his death would reduce this figure to $2,000. There would be no estate in the usual sense.
[c] As in (b) a joint and survivor annuity would reduce this to $2,700 for B and his wife.
[d] Plus approximately $500 Social Security annual income to wife, if latter survives B.

In conclusion it is apparent that B, to increase his capital accumulations for income purposes, will have to either (1) take the risks of speculation, (2) reduce his standard of living, (3) make use of the annuity principle personally or through his employer under a pension plan, or (4) combine all three alternatives in some degree. His conservative course would be to reduce his standards somewhat, as well as to make use of annuities. It seems probable in any case, omitting speculation, that the maintenance of his standards will eventually force him to take advantage of the annuity principle, either personally or through the mechanism of a pension plan.

## VI.  PENSION TREND[15]

The phenomenal growth of pension plans which has occurred in less than a decade raises the question of the permanency of newly established plans, as well as the probabilities of continued expansion of their use. It has been observed that numbers of pension plans were established because of the large profits and high corporate and personal taxes that accompanied World War II. The inference has been drawn, therefore, that either business recession or a decline in tax rates will lead to abandonment of many plans by employers, and consequent indifference on the part of other employers without plans toward establishing them. It is true that

---

[15] This discussion of the future status of pension plans in relation to their permanency, and to further expansion of their use, appeared more or less as given here in the Journal of Commerce, Pension and Profit Sharing Special Supplement, New York, N. Y., May 15, 1945, in an article by the writer entitled: "Pension Plans as Permanent Institutions."

rarely are pension plans established by corporations operating with a deficit, or at the break-even point. Also income taxes in recent years have been a potent motivating factor leading to the establishment of a plan. The opinion, however, that pension plans will be given up with business recession or because of a reduction in income tax rates, or for the same reason the trend to establish pension plans will suffer a major interruption, would seem to overlook fundamental long-term factors which have been affecting the American economy.

These fundamental factors relate to the shift from an agricultural to an industrial economy; to the development of large-scale enterprise as a mode of production and to changes in the methods of distribution of goods and services; to the fact that population growth is approaching stabilization, with a rise in the average age of its members. To elaborate on these factors in detail would require a separate treatise, but in their consequences they have been described as making America a mature economy. It is not necessary to accept the view that opportunity for the individual has been limited to make use of the concept of maturity; but the social, economic, and political changes which have already occurred from the operation of the above fundamental factors are apparent.

The movement of agricultural workers from the farms to the cities has been long a process and frequently commented upon. The extent of this, however, in a relatively short period is striking. In 1875 it is estimated that, of the working population, about 50% were in agricultural and 50% in the manufacturing and service industries. By 1930, only 20% were in farming, and 80% in manufacturing and the service industries.

From the turn of the century, when large-scale enterprise developed, it has come to pass that today a small percentage of approximately half a million corporations accounts for a large share of industrial production. It is expected that by 1960, or a decade or more thereafter, the population will have stabilized with a heavily increased percentage of older ages among both the population generally and those gainfully employed.

The effects generated by these vast changes became apparent to numerous observers years ago. It had become evident that a nation composed mostly of individual entrepreneurs, as represented by the farmer and the small business man, had changed to one composed largely of employees. There was every indication of an increased dependency of the workers on employers for their survival and their security. Responsibility of the family for its aged members was expected to be weakened by these changes with a consequent increase in the number of old-aged indigent. From a political aspect these economic and social changes spelled increased centralized control by the Federal government, and intervention in business affairs previously unknown. That there is an increased dependency of the worker on his employer, resulting in more central control, is signified in the Social Security Act of 1935. A further example is the unemployment insurance legislation of the Federal government.

The effect of all this on the future growth of private pension plans, and on the maintenance of existing plans, cannot be overlooked. It is doubtful, however, that the Social Security Act, as sometimes stated, would have of itself led to an increase in private pension plans. It did focus the interest of the population in general on the problem of old-age security, and lead to a stock-taking by individuals of their own retirement situation. It furthermore prompted those in the income groups earning over $3,000 to compare their benefits at 65 under the Social Security Act with the benefits of those receiving less than $3,000. It was apparent to those earning $3,000, $4,000, or $5,000 a year that $50 a month (about the maximum Social Security benefit at 65 to a single individual) would not constitute an adequate income for retirement. This fact, however, would not necessarily lead employers to establish or maintain a private pension plan for their higher paid employees. This is true despite a subsidy in the form of an income tax deduction to the employer for his payments to a pension plan. It cannot be said either that the fundamental advantages to an employer of a pension plan have been, or are, clearly enough perceived by him to provide an explanation for their recent growth, or for the continued development of pension plans in the immediate future.

If a tax subsidy to employers, and the personnel advantages accruing to them do not effectively influence, in the near future, the growth of pension plans, what will?

In our discussion of the problem of accumulation it was brought out that the decline in interest rates and the rise of personal income taxes had reduced the possible capital accumulations by an individual earning a salary of $10,000 a year. An individual in such an income bracket usually occupies an executive or managerial position. This is also true of those whose salaries are higher, as well as lower, to perhaps the $3,000 level. The problem of accumulation is similarly acute for both those in the lower and higher brackets. There is a growing realization among the managerial groups that they can no longer obtain ultimate security by the former methods of accumulation, such as were theoretically possible in 1929. As the conviction gains ground among the managerial class that interest rates may remain at low levels for a long time to come, and that high personal income taxes will continue to prevail (although modified somewhat from those of the war period), they will seek the protection of private pension plans. In other words, if the insecurity of the rank and file of workers has been alleviated by Social Security, the managerial class will likewise demand that their insecurity be relieved through employer action.

The position of the employer, when managerial pressure develops for pension coverage, can hardly be other than compliance in the long run. Inasmuch as the employer will realize some or all of the benefits expected to flow from a pension plan—especially if his contributions are deferred wages anyway—he may, at no increased cost, serve his own interests and at the same time satisfy his managerial employees. Finally, if corporate income taxes continue, there will be a further powerful motivation toward the use of pension plans. As has been indicated, a corporation's contributions to a pension plan, if reasonable in amount, and if made in accordance with the law, are a deductible expense for income tax purposes. A corporation without a pension plan may be in an anomalous position: not only might it be carrying a larger share of the tax load than those corporations with pension plans, particularly as against its competitors, but also it will fail to obtain the personnel advantages of such plans.

# CHAPTER II

# Pension Development

·······································································

PENSION PLANS IN THE UNITED STATES HAVE A SHORT HISTORY. Use of pension plans by business and industry to any significant extent began in the early years of the twentieth century. There is discernible, notwithstanding the short history of pensions, three phases in their development in terms of administration and methods of financing. These phases or periods overlapped, but in general they may be marked as follows: (1) the first period, extending from about 1900 to approximately 1925; (2) the second, from 1925 to 1942; (3) the third, from 1942 onward.[1]

The characteristics of pension plans established in these respective periods are sufficiently different to warrant a historical division in time. They are less easily classified generically. If allowance is made for the fact that the plans as established in any one of these periods, when compared to those of another period, possess similar characteristics, a further differentiation is justifiable.

The early pension plans, 1900-1925, may be classified as *company-administered* plans. Those that were established from 1925 to 1942 may be termed *insured* plans; the ones established in 1942 and onward, *insured and self-administered* plans.

## I. COMPANY-ADMINISTERED PLANS

Company-administered pension plans were established mainly prior to 1925. It was approximately that year which marked the entrance of life insurance companies into the pension field. The pension plans established thereafter, particularly those under the auspices of the insurance companies, differed markedly from the company-administered plans.

---

[1] For a detailed background of pension development up to 1932, see: Conant, Luther, *Critical Analysis of Industrial Pension Systems,* Macmillan Co., New York, N. Y., 1922; *Industrial Pensions in the United States,* National Industrial Conference Board, New York, N. Y., 1925; Latimer, Murray, *Industrial Pension Systems,* *Vol. I,* Industrial Relations Counselors, New York, N. Y., 1932.

By a company-administered pension plan is meant one in which both the administration and the financial control of the plan in whole or part is at the discretion of the employer or management. For example, on the administrative side such matters as which employees should receive a pension, when it should be paid, the amount of the pension, and how long it should run, are completely discretionary with the management. This also is true of financial aspects, such as whether reserves should be set aside to guarantee the pension benefits, promised or provided, and the method of investment of such pension reserves.

In the operation of company-administered plans, however, there developed differences both administratively and financially. The variations as between the plans in these two aspects were sufficiently distinctive to require identifying labels. Company-administered plans were described, therefore, as *discretionary, limited-contractual, informal,* or *non-contractual* plans,[2] as well as by several other names. Also, to denote the absence of employee contributions, the term contributory or non-contributory frequently was used in prefix to the above descriptive labels. The terminology has never been entirely satisfactory. In addition to being awkward and confusing, it is of limited accuracy in denoting the particular nature of a company-administered plan. A general differentiation among earlier plans—company-administered pension plans—is to describe them as either *informal* or *formal* plans.

## A. Informal Plans

A company that provides pensions to its employees on a basis that discloses no definitive policy or system, either before or after pensions begin, operates an informal pension plan. The justification for calling what essentially is a nondescript procedure, a plan, largely is because it takes some care of aged or superannuated employees. It distinguishes a company, possessed of an informal plan, from one that completely ignores pensions for aged employees. Organizations which use the informal method are usually of medium or small size in which intimate contact with employees more readily prevails. When an employee reaches the age at which he is unable to perform his usual work the problem of what to do with him arises. The employee's destiny pension-wise will depend on a number of factors. If he is in actual need a monthly

[2] See Conant, Jr., Luther, *Critical Analysis of Industrial Pension Systems,* Macmillan Co., New York, N. Y., 1922.

allowance in an amount thought adequate to sustain him will be paid, but with no guarantee as to the continuity of payments. If the employee is still in relatively good health, but not efficient at his regular job, he may "work out his pension" as a watchman or doing odd jobs at a nominal wage. If the employee has been thrifty and has accumulated some money no pension provision may be made for him. If an employee becomes superannuated in a period of financial stress or depression for the employer, he is likely to be laid off without pension benefits. As between employees, the personal regard of the employer or management for an individual may also determine whether a pension shall be paid and in what amount. The employee in any case has neither any expectation or encouragement that a pension may be paid. So far as the source of pension payments are concerned they are paid from either operating income or surplus.

It is apparent that an employee with a company operating an informal pension plan has a chance of obtaining something slightly better than nothing when the time comes for retirement. The employer is at no time in the position of having promised anything, nor is he committed in any way to the payment of a pension or continuation of it once commenced. The employer might be constrained to pay a pension to a particular employee by fear of public opinion or for the sake of the morale of his working force, or by his own humanitarian feelings. The general operation of informal plans, nevertheless, is at the complete discretion of the company in every respect.

Informal pension plans obviously provide negligible security and uncertain benefits to employees. They also present administrative and possible financial problems to the employer, in operation, because there is a lack of definite policy and of any advance financial provision for payment of pension benefits. It would seem, therefore, that informal plans would have tended to fall into disuse as better pension plans were developed. The fact is, however, that, while the informal pension plan has been referred to as an early type of plan, it has had wide-spread use even up to recent years. This has been explained in terms of the advantages that its complete flexibility and absence of pension commitments give to the employer. The informal plan, however, has also been severely criticized from the employee's viewpoint for the very reasons that are supposed to make it advantageous to the employer.

The real explanation for the extensive and even continued use of informal plans is perhaps more properly ascribable to lack of knowledge on the part of employer and employees alike. It is only in recent years that information as to improved types of pension plans has been available to employers and has had extensive circulation. Coincidentally there has also developed a fuller understanding of the nature of the pension problem.

Initial turning away from the informal method occurred first among the railroads, later among the banks, public utilities, and the larger manufacturers. The early pension plans adopted in these industries are here designated as formal plans. They were company-administered in the same manner as informal pension plans, but significant changes had occurred in the administration and the methods of financing them. It was these changes, perhaps more than any date, that mark the beginnings of industrial pension development in America.

## B. Formal Plans

### 1. Administrative Aspects

The institution of formal pension plans represented an advance over informal plans. A definite procedure was developed that governed the granting of pensions. Rules were laid down which prescribed the conditions that must be met for an employee to be entitled to a pension at retirement. These rules mainly related to the attainment of a specified age and the completion of a minimum number of years of service by an employee before any retirement benefit would be granted him. Also, the rules specified the class of employees, such as wage earners, and salaried or occupational groups, who were eligible for pensions. They frequently set forth the conditions to be observed if pension payments were to be continued after retirement. There were "behavior" clauses which might prevent the employee from working for a competitor after retirement or from working at all. Also the right to recall the pensioned employee into service if the employer needed him was another string sometimes attached to the pension payment.

The rules and conditions obtaining among formal pension plans varied, but the similarities were greater than the differences. This was true, if for no other reason than that imitation was the common thing; the railroad plans were copied by the public utilities, and so forth. A new enterprise utilized the plans of its contemporaries or even its competitors. Notwithstanding, a major difference among formal pension plans must be noted. The usual plan provided rules and regulations pertaining to qualifications for a pension, and its payment after retirement. It, however, did not guarantee a pension. The employee might have qualified for a pension of a definite amount under the rules, but had no certainty that he would receive one. It still remained discretionary with the employer or management as to whether payment would be made at retirement, or continued thereafter. In this respect the formal plan was on a par with the informal plan. The usual formal pension plan, therefore, represented an advance as to *form*. The important content for an employee, certainty of a pension and continuation thereof if he had qualified under the rules, however, was not necessarily met. The complete discretion retained by the employer or management in the operation of formal plans was so universal that they were generically described, as we have noted, as discretionary plans.[3] It was a modification of the complete discretion in some formal plans that led to the further differentiation, *limited-contractual* plans.[3] The latter modification consisted of a promise that, once an employee had been placed on pension, the payments would be continued. A contractual element was introduced, therefore, which was absent from completely discretionary plans. It was an uncommon provision, and very few formal plans so provided.

## 2. Methods of Financing

The methods of financing pensions under company-administered plans varied. The informal pension plans, which promised nothing, had no apparent need for accumulation of funds to provide pensions. Companies with formal plans which were completely discretionary, in numerous instances, likewise felt no need for accumulation of reserves from which to pay pensions. Inasmuch as there was no obligation to grant pensions, or continue them, once granted, any possible pension liability was difficult to visualize and perhaps impossible to calculate. In respect to those few plans that guaranteed a pension, once it commenced, a recognizable liability to pensioners was created but adequate reserves were seldom established.

The complete discretion of management that generally prevailed under formal pension plans, either to grant or continue pensions, therefore left the employee uncertain as to his pension ex-

---

[3] See page 32.

pectations.   This discretionary power also lulled management into
ignoring the making of financial provision for any pension liabilities
that might develop.   The employee, therefore, who was pensioned
was usually paid by the company out of operating income.   If
there occurred for the company a deficit year, pension payments
were met from surplus.   A series of deficits might lead to a modification or discontinuance of the pension payments, except where
there was a contractual obligation.   To the employees' uncertainty
of receiving a pension, there was added the additional uncertainty
as to whether the company always would be able to pay it.

The policy of meeting pension payments out of current income,
pay-as-you-go as it has been called, brought inevitable difficulties.
The administration of formal pension plans, even with complete
discretion reserved, normally resulted in pensioners on the rolls.   It
is a fact that when a company is twenty or thirty years old the rate
of additions to the pension roll begins to accelerate.   Also, for many
years after pensions first become payable, deaths among the already pensioned occur at a slower rate than the rate at which new
pensioners are added to the rolls.   The pension obligations begin,
in time, to constitute a severe drain on operating income.   As management became conscious of the financial problem of providing
pensions, some attempts were made to anticipate assumed pension
obligations by setting up reserves.   This came to be known as the
*balance-sheet* system of reserves for pensions.   While the balance-
sheet reserve method represented an improvement over the pay-as-
you-go system it too ran into difficulties.

The lack of knowledge and the limited experience with pension
plan operation that prevailed in the United States at the time of
establishment of company-administered plans may be held ac-
countable for the use of pay-as-you-go methods.   It also partially
explains the difficulties that were encountered in the use of the
balance-sheet reserve system.   In accounting, depreciation reserves
have been called ghosts of the balance sheet, implying among other
things that they are paper items rather than that they represent
liquid cash accounts.   Somewhat analogous were the balance-sheet
reserves for pensions.   They were not necessarily just bookkeeping
entries but they were usually inadequate to meet the ever mount-
ing pension liabilities.

Balance-sheet reserves, as disclosed in time, proved to be inadequate for several important reasons.   In the first place the reserves
which were set up were merely the estimates of the management.

These estimates were largely uninformed guess work, mostly made by management without consultation or advice from either insurance companies or independent actuaries, who possess the special knowledge to make accurate estimates of pension liabilities. Also the estimated reserves were not consistently increased. In highly profitable years the reserves were increased, but not in a systematized fashion relative to increases in the pension liability. Finally, the reserves were invested at the discretion of the management, not uncommonly in securities of the company itself. The pension funds could be and were impaired on occasion by a fluctuation in the company's securities.

The balance-sheet reserve system of accumulation of pension funds might have continued in use indefinitely were it not for two somewhat parallel developments. One of these concerns certain changes in the Federal law made in 1928 and thereafter, later to be discussed, and in the regulations of the Bureau of Internal Revenue governing pension plans. The other development was that the life insurance companies decided to enter the pension field. The commercial opportunity offered by the management of large pension reserves appeared attractive to them.

The handling of pension plans fitted naturally into insurance companies' operations, sales-wise, in technical aspects, and from the investment side. Furthermore, there was little competition from any other financial institutions. It is true that banks were being utilized as trustees for their pension funds by some corporations prior to the entrance of the insurance companies into the field. The use of banks, however, was limited to a small number, although they were large industrial corporations. Development of insured pension plans, as they came to be known, began about 1925. Historically, insured plans had been offered to employers a few years before this time, but it was from 1925 and thereafter that their real growth occurred.

## II. INSURED PLANS

The use of an insured pension plan undoubtedly constituted a landmark in the evolution of pensions in the United States. Further, it significantly influenced pension plans in Great Britain where experience with pension plans considerably antedated that in the United States. In this connection it is interesting to observe that very few pension plans were being operated through insurance companies in Great Britain in 1930. By 1935, however, it is estimated that over 1,000 pension plans were utilizing their services.[4] The pension plan offered to employers by the insurance companies was a definite entity in and of itself. The first type to be employed became known as the *group annuity* to distinguish it from individual annuity contracts. The latter, it must be noted, were used by some companies with formal plans to provide the pension benefits to employees when retirement actually took place; also later a pension plan known as the *individual annuity* plan was developed. The novel aspect of the group annuity plan, however, was that it enabled a company to transfer practically the entire administrative and financial responsibilities of operating a pension plan from management to the insurance companies. The growth in the use of the group annuity in the United States initially was slow but the rate accelerated rapidly after 1930.

## A.  Financial Operation

The modifying effect of the use of group annuities on pension planning was perhaps not completely recognized by business and industry, but the implications were numerous. On the financial side the insured plan substituted for pay-as-you-go and unstable balance-sheet reserve methods, accurate mathematical formulae for accumulation of pension reserves. A corporation employing a group annuity plan was required to set aside funds and in general to make yearly payments to an insurance company. These payments were in calculated amounts which, if regularly paid, would prove adequate to pay the pension benefits as provided under the plan. In addition to this actuarially sound system of accumulating pension reserves, there also was provided a highly trained investment management for the pension funds. The investment of pension funds in a corporation's own securities was not possible under a group annuity plan. The entire assets of the insurance company were substituted to guarantee the solvency of an employer's pension fund.

## B.  Administrative Characteristics

The modifications that the group annuity brought to the administrative side of pension plans were initially indirect. The formal plans were, as has been pointed out, mainly discretionary as to both the granting of pensions and their payment thereafter.

---

[4] Owen, A. D. K., "Employees' Retirement Systems in Great Britain," *International Labor Review*, July, 1935.

Likewise the group annuity plan in its early development did not guarantee necessarily a pension to a particular employee, even though a quasi-contractual right to receive a pension, once earned, perhaps existed. A contract between the employer and the insurance company exists under a group annuity plan. The general essence of the contract is that, in return for certain stipulated payments by the employer, the insurance company will pay certain benefits. The designation of who shall receive the benefits is a prerogative of the employer.

A contractual agreement by the employer to pay a pension to a specific employee if the group annuity plan should be maintained until such employee's retirement, or thereafter, was rarely an ingredient of early group annuity plans. In this respect it paralleled the non-contractual nature of company-administered plans. The lack of a contractual aspect as between the employer and the employee under the group annuity plan was perhaps an inheritance from the discretionary plans. In actual operation, however, the absence of such contractual agreement from the group annuity plan proved of nominal importance. The explanation is to be found in the structure of the group annuity plan.

The insurance companies, to formulate a group annuity plan, must know perforce for whom pensions are to be provided, at the inception of the plan. They must calculate the pension benefits relative to a definite retirement age. The age, sex, and salary of employees who will be eligible to pensions must be known to the insurance company. A formula for determining the amount of pensions must be devised at the inception of the pension plan. The employer must supply the data necessary to enable the insurance company to make the proper calculations. In furnishing the data, there naturally is supplied a list of particular employees who will be eligible for pensions. It was these requirements of the insurance company that initially implied a definite intention on the part of the employer to provide, for certain employees, a pension.

The employer, it is true, could select the employees whom he wished to pension, subject to the underwriting or pension rules of the insurance company. These rules in general provided that any group of employees would be acceptable, such as wage earners, salaried employees, occupational groups, and such. However, if the employer is to bear the entire cost of the group annuity, then all employees within a designated group must be included. If the employees are called upon to contribute to the plan, then it is necessary that at least 75 per cent of the eligible group participate in the plan.

The early group annuity plans, when finally formulated and entered into as a contract between the employer and the insurance company, might be silent as to any agreement by the employer to pay the pension benefit, prescribed in the plan, to a particular employee. The fact was, however, that, once pension benefits had been paid for or funded, there remained little reason to deprive any employee of his pension, who qualified under the rules. It was (and is) the practice under group annuity pension plans to give to an eligible employee a certificate explaining that a pension plan has been established and that he is a beneficiary. Discretion to refuse a pension payment at retirement to an employee theoretically might remain with the employer or management; practically the group annuity plan foreclosed such a possibility. In addition, the uncertainty of continuation of payment of the pension, such as existed under informal and most formal company-administered plans, was eliminated for the employee. Not only were there adequate funds available under a group annuity plan to pay pensions at retirement, but the insurance company normally made direct payment of the pension benefit to the employee.

A significant development that accompanied the introduction of group annuity plans, which perhaps more than anything eliminated discretionary aspects after the plan had become operative, was the obtaining of employee contributions. All informal, as well as most formal plans, were non-contributory. The employer bore the entire cost of the pension benefits. The group annuity plans allowed or made provision for contributions from the employees. The main purpose was to reduce the cost of pensions to the employer. The joint contributions of the employee and employer were used by the insurance company to provide the pension benefits. This circumstance—the employee contributing to the cost of his own pension—if no other, eliminated discretionary aspects from the group annuity plan. Theoretically it still was possible to deprive an employee of his pension by refunding his contributions, but such action was unlikely because of the practical limitations mentioned above, and the possible legal complications which might result.

While the insured plan, as it developed from 1925 on, brought to pension plans new administrative and financial characteristics, it left undisturbed certain major prerogatives of the employer.

The latter could, subject to the underwriting rules of the insurance companies, select the employees for whom he wished to provide pensions. He could prescribe the formula that should be used to calculate the amount of pension benefits, giving more or less to different groups of employees as his judgment dictated. He could require such contributions from employees as practical considerations seemed to make desirable. The limitations upon the employer were simply those that the insurance company found necessary for the development of a group annuity plan that was administratively feasible, economical to sell, and actuarially sound.

## III. INSURED AND SELF-ADMINISTERED PLANS

The description of pension development from 1942 onward as a period of insured and self-administered plans has its reasons. The use of the insured plan had multiplied at this time, partially because of the introduction of a relatively new type of insured pension plan. This was known as the Individual Annuity policy plan. Also the banks had begun to manifest an interest in pension plans to the extent that they were equipped to act as managers of pension funds under Self-Administered plans.[5] Again, there had been evolved an arrangement whereby an employer might use in combination an insured plan for one group of his employees and a self-administered plan for another. The distinguishing of the period of 1942 onward as one of insured and self-administered plans, however, is apposite only if account also is taken of two further developments. One was the rising tide of personal and corporate income taxes which had begun in 1940. The other was the amendment in 1942 of that section of the Internal Revenue Act which dealt with employee pension and profit-sharing plans.

### A. Individual Annuity Policy Plan

The insured plan in the form of the group annuity had been used increasingly for pension purposes after its introduction. However, it had been mostly availed of by the larger corporations. One reason for this was possibly that the insurance companies sought them as the most profitable prospects, and so directed their sales efforts. Also, however, the group annuity was available only to employers who could include fifty or more lives in their pension plans. The sales policy followed by the so-called group annuity insurance companies, plus the underwriting limits as to acceptable

[5] See Chapter VIII.

groups, led to a new development. This occurred about 1935 and involved the use of individual annuity policies, which could be placed on the life of each employee whom the employer wished included in a pension plan. These individual annuity policies could be made subject to the direct control of the employer, or they could be placed in a trust. In the latter case a trust agreement contained the provisions for implementing the terms of the pension plan. It should be noted that technically an individual annuity policy does not contain the terms of a pension plan in and of itself. It is simply an annuity policy offered by the insurance companies as an insured method of financing a pension plan; but the details of the latter are left to the employer and his advisers to formulate, and incorporate into a pension plan, and/or trust. In this latter respect the individual annuity policy plan more nearly resembles the self-administered plan, discussed below, than the group annuity. There had now become available, however, to smaller employers an insured method of financing their pension plans, although its use was not limited to small employers. This method might also be employed by large corporate enterprises.

### B. Self-administered Plan

A self-administered plan is not handled by an insurance company, but is designed by the employer and his special advisers, one of the most important of whom is the independent actuary. He[6] lays out the financial and other details of the plan, subject to the employer's approval. The pension funds that are to be accumulated are normally placed with a bank; the provisions of the plan are incorporated in a trust agreement; and the pension benefits are *contractual*. While the self-administered plan, as thus described, had a growing use before 1942, its use was confined to a small number of the large corporations in the country. The bulk of the earlier so-called self-administered plans in general lacked the contractual elements and the other characteristics of self-administered plans developed after 1942, and were essentially company-administered plans in their administrative and financial aspects.

### IV.  INCOME TAXES

The long-term factors affecting the total economy[7] (such as increasing urbanization), and the business advantages to employers

---

[6] Or a Pension Consultant.
[7] See pp. 28-29.

must essentially be looked to in explanation of pension developments in this country. A more superficial explanation is to be
found in the business expansion and the rising tax levies on employer and employee alike, which commenced in 1940.

The application of an excess profits tax by the government to
corporations, which claims 80 to 90 per cent of all earnings over
"normal," is not likely to lead to economy in business operations.
To the extent a corporation may have earnings subject to special
tax levies, it is natural to seek legitimate escape from payment.
If there is available to an employer a means by which the business,
the management, and the employees can be benefited at a negligible cost by virtue of a government tax subsidy, it is logical to expect
that such a means will be exploited. When, also, the owners and
employees of a corporation, as citizens, are taxed heavily on their
personal earnings, any plan that passes extra compensation to
them tax-free is certain to prove alluring. Inasmuch as contributions to pension plans were generally deductible by employers, and
such payments were non-taxable income to employees, they were
clearly a medium that, for the reasons mentioned above, served the
mutual interests of both.

Any corporation, long before 1942, had been allowed under the
Federal law to take, as a deduction from its income tax, contributions to a pension plan. Also employees who benefited from these
contributions were not taxed on them in the year the corporation
made the contribution. It was not, however, until the sharp rise in
personal taxes and the imposition of the excess profits tax in World
War II that the law, in a sense, was "discovered." There then took
place almost a scramble to seek the advantages offered by pension
plans.

## A.  Pre-1942

In 1942 the sections of the Internal Revenue Code relating to
pension plans were drastically revised. To understand the purpose
of the revisions, and the consequences for pension plans, some reference is necessary to the pension law and the practical interpreta-
tions thereof previous to 1942.

In the early history of the income tax laws the interest of the
Federal government in private pension plans was nominal. The
right of a corporation to take, as an income tax deduction, its actual
payments to pensioners had probably never been seriously ques-
tioned. They were treated as a deductible expense. The criteria

of deductibility for the Treasury Department were whether the pensions were a necessary and reasonable expense. If the pension payments met these tests they were in general an allowable deduction.

With the advent of the group annuity plan employers were allowed an income tax deduction for their annual payments to the insurance company. If the group annuity plan also called for lump sum payments for employee past-service benefits, in addition to the annual payments which were for future service, these were also deductible. The payments for past service, however, were usually spread over a period of years. All payments were subject to the limitation that they must be reasonable in amount. Presumably the entire payments for past service under the group annuity plan could be taken in one year, if they met the test of reasonableness.

Payments to a balance-sheet reserve, maintained by a corporation for the purpose of making provision for future pension liabilities, had never been formally authorized by law as a deductible item for income tax purposes. This situation and the appearance of the group annuity pension plan seemed to be the reasons for gradual abandonment of the use of balance-sheet reserves. The fact, that balance-sheet reserves continued to be used by corporations after the introduction of the income tax law, in itself is interesting. It suggests that, in company-administered pension plans, reserves were maintained in form rather than fact. Also it indicates that most company-administered plans operated their pension plan on a pay-as-you-go basis, charging pension payments against operating income. It is possible, although uncertain, that previous to 1928 companies operating balance-sheet reserve systems may have deducted their yearly credits to such reserves from income taxes. In 1928, however, there had apparently arisen for some companies operating balance-sheet reserve systems, the problem of securing tax deductions for reserves already accumulated. The solution was provided by an amendment to the revenue act of 1928. In brief this allowed employers who had accumulated balance-sheet reserves to transfer them to a trust, and to take a tax deduction for such payments to the trust. The deduction, however, was required to be spread over not less than ten years. It would seem that there should have resulted an increase in the use of self-administered plans as a product of the amended 1928 law. This perhaps would have been the case, had not the group annuity plan been making rapid strides. While some self-administered plans were created, companies which had changed from pay-as-you-go or balance-sheet reserve pension methods utilized group annuities. Newly established pension plans, for almost a decade after 1928, also employed group annuities.

The amendment to the 1928 revenue act partially clarified the deductibility of contributions to a trust. The law authorizing establishment of pension plans using the trust principle, however, had earlier origins. It appeared in brief form in the revenue act of 1921. It was this section of the law authorizing establishment of trusts, together with other provisions which regulated deductions of contributions thereto, that constituted the basis for the pension developments that were in full swing by 1940, and that led to the revision of the law in 1942. By 1938, the early law authorizing the use of trusts had passed through several modifications, resulting in what was known as Section 165 of the Internal Revenue Code. We quote here the portion that partially explains the developments in pension planning which occurred thereafter.

(a) Exemption From Tax.—A trust forming part of a stock bonus, pension, or profit-sharing plan of an employer for the exclusive benefit of some or all of his employees—
(1) if contributions are made to the trust by such employer, or employees, or both, for the purpose of distributing to such employees the earnings and principal of the fund accumulated by the trust in accordance with such plan, and
(2) if under the trust instrument it is impossible, at any time prior to the satisfaction of all liabilities with respect to employees under the trust, for any part of the corpus or income to be (within the taxable year or thereafter) used for, or diverted to, purposes other than for the exclusive benefit of his employees.

. . . shall not be taxable . . .

The extent of the deductions that were permissible, and the methods of taking them, were provided for in other sections of the Internal Revenue Code. A pension trust, however, was definitely, from the above, a tax-exempt entity. In summary, therefore, if an employer made contributions to an employees' trust they were generally a deductible expense; the contributions were not taxable income to the employee-beneficiaries of the trust until distributed; and any earnings accumulated on the trust funds were likewise nontaxable. A further limitation in the law was that the corpus and income of the trust could not be diverted to any other purpose, prior to the satisfaction of all liabilities with respect to the participating employees.

In the words "some or all of his employees" there was found

justification for the establishment of employees' trusts of all sorts and descriptions. The law was silent as to any definition or differentiations as between stock bonus, pension, or profit-sharing plans. Deductions for contributions to employees' trusts were governed by other provisions of the Internal Revenue Code. The usual test of deductibility was whether the contributions were reasonable in amount, and whether they constituted necessary business expenses.

Employers who had bonus plans, whereby the employees were yearly paid large sums in cash as extra compensation, were influenced to set up an employees' trust. The words *stock bonus* in the law likewise applied to cash bonuses. Key employees, officers, and others were agreeable to have bonuses paid in trust, for it was then non-taxable income to them, an increasingly important matter as income taxes rose. In order to avoid investment problems, in many cases, the individual annuity policy plan, newly come to hand, was employed. Profit-sharing plans were devised and benefits paid into trusts with arrangements similar to those of bonus trusts. Pension trusts with the definite object of providing retirement benefits were created by many smaller employers. The individual annuity policy plan fulfilled here a definite need.

In the widespread creation of employees' trusts, to obtain, if nothing else, the income tax advantages, certain results occurred. Many bonus and profit-sharing trusts were set up to benefit a few officers and stockholders of corporations. Pension trusts were created that also were limited to a handful of key employees. The amounts paid into such trusts were substantial in many cases; the benefits went to a few. The Treasury Department sought to broaden employee participation by regulation, and to define what constituted pension trusts, and what bonus and profit-sharing trusts. It likewise attempted to restrain excessive contributions to employee trusts, benefiting only a few employees, by ruling in some cases that the amounts paid were unreasonable. In the face of the multiplying number of trusts, however, the administrative and supervisory field problems, presented to the Treasury Department, apparently became insuperable. As important, if not more so, several court decisions in favor of taxpayers on the deductibility of their contributions to employees' trusts disturbed the Treasury Department. The conclusion apparently was reached by the latter that, if tax avoidance, not to mention tax evasion, on a grand scale for the benefit of selected employees, officers, and stockholders was to be prevented, a new law was needed. The existing law was amended, therefore, in 1942.

## B. 1942 and Thereafter

An examination in any detail of the provisions of the new law governing employee trusts, as amended in 1942, is beyond our scope. In general it was highly explicit in contrast to the relatively vague nature of the previous law. It provided, as had the former law, that an employees' trust should be a tax-exempt entity. Also it relieved the employee-beneficiaries from income taxes on the contributions made thereto on their behalf, as well as on the accumulated earnings of the trust, until a distribution of their interests had been made to them. The law went further, however. The words "some or all of his employees" were stricken out. In order to be a qualified trust, among other things, the law provided that employees must be selected by rules that would eliminate discrimination and use of discretion by the employer. It defined the methods of taking tax deductions for contributions to a pension trust, and limited the amounts that could be contributed to a profit-sharing trust. It specifically gave authority to the Commissioner of Internal Revenue to approve or disapprove trust plans that did not qualify under the law. In its entirety it was a comprehensive piece of legislation. There then followed a series of Treasury Department regulations which set forth additional rules necessary to be met before Treasury Department approval of a pension plan would be given.

The immediate effect of the revision of the law was to accelerate the rate at which pension plans were being established. The uncertainty and confusion that had developed, immediately preceding the revision of the law, were dispelled. The tax advantages remained, and, most important of all, there developed a greater understanding by employers of the fundamental advantages of pension plans, as a result of the wide publicity attending legislative revision of the law in 1942. A new phase in the development and extension of pension plans had begun.

# CHAPTER III

## Annuities and Their Application

••••••••••••••••••••••••••••••••••••••••••••••••••••••••••••••••••••••••••••••

## I. ANNUITIES

PENSION PAYMENTS TO EMPLOYEES ARE ANNUITIES INDEPENDENT of the type of pension plan, or of the method an employer may have adopted for making payment of retirement benefits. This is true whether an employer utilizes an insured or self-administered pension plan of the types described in this work, or employs a company-administered, pay-as-you-go plan, to provide pensions. In the latter, while the pension payments may not be commonly thought of as constituting annuities, they nevertheless are such, and also they may be classified as to type such as whether the payments are to be made throughout the life of the employee, whether they provide a death benefit, and so forth.[1] We are concerned here, however, with a discussion of the more common types of annuities as they are formally underwritten by insurance companies, and, by implication, as they may be employed by self-administered pension funds (without reference to insurance companies) to make payment of pension benefits.

### A. What Is an Annuity?

An annuity in its literal meaning, as the stem of the word suggests, consists of a series of annual money payments.[2] The recipient of these payments may be designated as the *annuitant*. The maker of the annual payments to the annuitant is identified by various terms, but for our purposes he is best described as the *underwriter*.[3]

---

[1] See page 60.

[2] Examples of annuities, other than pension payments, may be found in most installment payments, insurance premiums, payments to depreciation funds and so forth. For a broader discussion of annuities than attempted here, see Moore, Justin H., *Financial Mathematics*, Prentice-Hall, Inc., New York, N. Y., 1945.

[3] This chapter discusses annuities primarily as they are issued and underwritten by insurance companies; but it should be noted that a self-administered pension fund may employ the same types of annuities to make payment of the pension benefits, underwritten so to speak by the fund itself.

Annuity payments also may be made to an annuitant in monthly, quarterly, or semi-annual installments.

## B. Annuity Certain

If all annuities involved solely a series of annual payments to annuitants, as defined above, such payments being guaranteed even in the event of the death of the annuitants, we would have a simple set of financial transactions. An annuitant, who purchased such an annuity from a commercial underwriter, simply would look to the security or certainty of the payments and the rate of interest promised. The underwriter in turn would need only to provide a safe investment medium for the funds of the annuitant until payments were due, at an interest rate adequate to meet the promise to the annuitant, plus a margin for expenses and profit. In essence, an annuity of this character consists of a distribution of principal and/or interest, the underwriter approximating the services of a bank. When such an annuity is encountered or underwritten, it is known as an *annuity certain*, meaning that annual payments will be made for the term of years agreed upon; if the death of the recipient should occur prior to the expiration of the term the remaining payments would be made to the estate.

## C. Life Annuities

It is when we consider certain other forms of annuities that we encounter an additional element wherein annuity payments become conditional, or are made dependent, on some contingent event. Whereas the *annuity certain* involves merely a distribution of principal and/or interest, other forms of annuities in addition take into account the probabilities of life or death, of total and permanent disability, sickness, and so forth.

With a knowledge of these probabilities it is possible to construct any form of annuity as well as to calculate the rates or cost to annuity buyers. It is with those forms of annuities that involve consideration of the probabilities of life or death, or life contingencies, that we are mainly concerned.

## D. Annuity Rate Making

Commercial annuity rates or premiums, subject to the type of benefits provided, are a product of three assumptions by the rate makers or the insurance companies. These assumptions relate to (1) the probable mortality among annuitants, (2) the rate of interest that can be earned over the lifetime of the annuity contracts, and (3) the expense of transacting annuity business. If the assumptions in respect to any one or all of these items are different as between insurance companies, there normally will result a difference in the initial annuity cost to the annuity buyer. It becomes important, therefore, to understand how and why these assumptions are made.

## 1. Mortality Tables

What is a mortality table? It consists of a tabulation of mortality statistics among a group of people, and is used as a basis for determining future death rates.[4] To be of predictive value the group must be large enough to allow the law of averages to operate. For example, we know that in tossing a coin it must fall heads or tails on one throw. If we throw it three times it is possible, but unlikely, that the coin will fall three times heads or three times tails. If we toss it 1,000 times the probabilities increase that it will fall heads half the times and tails the other half, based on the assumption that the chances of its falling head or tail are equally likely. In other words a large number of trials must be made to determine what the experience will be. The same principle is involved in the formulation of a mortality table.

The mortality tables used by insurance companies are for numerous reasons not constructed from the mortality statistics of the general population. They are tables constructed from the statistics on insured lives, and thus are more representative of the mortality which may be expected among those with whom the insurance companies expect to do business.

Most of the mortality tables used in this country were constructed for the purpose of calculating insurance premiums, rather than with the idea that such tables would be used extensively for annuity rate calculations. One of the most famous of these tables is the American Experience Table of Mortality. It is presently employed for the calculation of insurance premiums by most commercial insurance companies in the country.[5] While this or any other properly constructed mortality table may be used also for

---

[4] "The mortality table has been defined as 'the instrument by means of which are measured the probabilities of life and death,'" MacLean, Joseph B., *Life Insurance,* McGraw-Hill Book Company, Inc., New York, N. Y., 1945.

[5] The Commissioners 1941 Standard Ordinary Mortality Table (see Appendix B) is in the process of superseding the American Experience Table for the computation of insurance premiums.

computing annuity rates, special annuitants' tables have come to be employed instead. The reason for this, in general, is that experience has revealed that the mortality rates among annuitants are less than among insured lives. Annuitants, as a class, are found to live longer. The implications of this fact for the insurance companies, and particularly for the buyer of annuities, will be developed through reference to extracts of two tables. It will be observed that Table III is denoted as a *mortality* table, and Table IV as an *annuity* table. This distinguishes them, however, only as to their probable uses; that is, the former normally is employed for calculation of insurance premiums, the latter for annuity rates. Theoretically either table might be used interchangeably, for both measure the probabilities of life and death.

### TABLE III
#### AMERICAN EXPERIENCE TABLE OF MORTALITY[6]

| Age | Number Living | Number Dying |
|---|---|---|
| 10 | 100,000 | 749 |
| 11 | 99,251 | 746 |
| 12 | 98,505 | 743 |
| 45 | 74,173 | 828 |
| 46 | 73,345 | 848 |
| 92 | 216 | 137 |
| 93 | 79 | 58 |
| 94 | 21 | 18 |
| 95 | 3 | 3 |

### TABLE IV
#### COMBINED ANNUITY MORTALITY TABLE[6]

| Age | | Number Living | Number Dying |
|---|---|---|---|
| Males | Females | | |
| 10 | 14 | 100,000 | 153 |
| 11 | 15 | 99,847 | 157 |
| 12 | 16 | 99,690 | 161 |
| 92 | 96 | 2,538 | 671 |
| 93 | 97 | 1,867 | 529 |
| 94 | 98 | 1,338 | 405 |
| 95 | 99 | 933 | 302 |
| 105 | 109 | 3 | 2 |
| 106 | 110 | 1 | 1 |

[6] For complete tables see Appendix B.

Table III reveals that of 100,000 insured lives age 10, a certain number are expected to die each year. At the age of 95 only three are living and it is anticipated that these will die before reaching the age of 96. In contrast, Table IV discloses (1) that of 100,000 annuitants aged 10 more will survive to the older ages, (2) that females are expected to experience the mortality rates of males four years younger, and (3) that of the male lives the last is expected to die at 106, and of the female lives, at age 110.

The possible effects on annuity rates, as between the use of the different tables, may be made apparent by a simple illustration, if we consider for the moment only mortality, and ignore the factors of interest and expense. To minimize calculations we will assume that an individual male age 92 wishes to purchase an annuity that will pay him $1,000 a year for life; the first payment due at the end of one year. In the event of death there are to be no further payments. In actuarial terminology an annuity of this kind is called an *immediate whole life annuity*.

What will the prospective annuitant have to pay for the annuity? If Table III were used by the insurance company the cost would be $476.85. For this sum the annuitant would receive $1,000 a year until death occurred. The steps in arriving at the cost of $476.85 are as follows. (a) Table III shows that 216 are living at age 92. While in practice annuities are not sold at this age by insurance companies, we must presume here that there will be issued an immediate whole life annuity to the entire group of 216. The table further shows that only 79 are living at age 93, 21 at age 94 and 3 at 95. (b) The possible payments of $1,000 a year for the whole of life to the 216 annuity buyers at age 92 is calculated thus. As stated above, assuming all payments are to be made at the end of the year, there will be paid to the 79 survivors at age 93, $79,000; to the 21 living at 94, $21,000; and $3,000 to the remaining 3 alive at 95. The sum of these payments is $103,000. (c) There were 216 annuitants at age 92, so each will pay an amount equal to $103,000, the total probable payments, divided by 216. This division gives $476.85, the amount shown above as the cost of an immediate whole life annuity which will pay $1,000 a year to a male age 92. If the insurance company collects in advance $476.85 from the 216 annuitants, it will have $103,000 on hand. This is sufficient to pay $1,000 a year to the survivors, the last of whom will die after attaining age 95, assuming the actual mortality is in accordance with the expected as shown by the table.

In the event that any of the annuitants disproved the mortality table, living beyond 96, the insurance company would still be obligated to continue payments. A loss to the company of course would be incurred, which would have to be made good from other assets. It was to avoid the possibility of such losses that Table IV, and others similar to it, were devised.

If we use Table IV to work out the same problem, namely the cost of an immediate whole life annuity of $1,000 a year to a male age 92, what will he have to pay? The answer is $2,285.26, or almost 5 times the amount required by Table III. The same steps in this calculation are involved as in Table III. However, whereas the insurance company there anticipated only $103,000 to make annuity payments for life to survivors, under Table IV the amount estimated to be needed from the 2,538 male purchasers of annuities age 92 is $5,800,000.

The difference in annuity cost as brought out through the use of these two tables is obviously striking. They were so selected in order to dramatize the effects of longevity on annuity rates. As a practical matter Table III, the American Experience Table of Mortality, has had limited use as a basis for calculation of annuity rates. It was constructed to compute insurance rates. Table IV, the Combined Annuity Table, was used until recently for annuity computations, particularly under group retirement pension plans. It, however, has been superseded by later annuity tables that take account of further increased longevity.

The effect of increased longevity among a group of annuitants is to increase the total payments that the underwriter must make to the annuitants. This is clearly seen in the above illustration. As the insurance companies accumulated experience with American annuity buyers, new tables were constructed to reflect this experience. There has been found a persistent trend among annuitants to long life. Various reasons have been offered to explain this fact. Among these are general factors, such as improved public health measures and advances in medical science. Particular factors in explanation are that healthy lives tend to buy annuities, and also, as a consequence, they apparently increase their life span through freedom from financial worry and care.

To take account of this increased longevity insurance companies periodically have revised their annuity tables with resultant increased cost to annuity buyers. These progressive revisions may be seen in Table V. The American Experience Table has been included therein to show possible extremes, but it should be noted that this table is more properly referred to as a mortality table.

The figure in parentheses appearing after the name of the table is the year in which the table was developed. Under the heading of *number living* there is shown the number out of 100,000 lives, *starting at the age of 25,* who have survived to the respective ages of 40, 60, and 70. The death rate expressed in decimal form tells what proportion of those alive at the beginning of the

TABLE V

ANNUITANTS TABLES

DEATH RATE—MALE LIVES

| Table | Age | Number Living | Death Rate |
|---|---|---|---|
| American Experience Table (1868)............ | 40 | 87,728 | .0098 |
| American Annuitants (Ultimate) (1920)...... | 40 | 92,068 | .0075 |
| Combined Annuity (1927).................. | 40 | 95,831 | .0046 |
| 1937 Standard Annuity (1937).............. | 40 | 96,257 | .0044 |
| American Experience Table (1868)........... | 60 | 65,052 | .0267 |
| American Annuitants (Ultimate) (1920)...... | 60 | 69,682 | .0257 |
| Combined Annuity (1927).................. | 60 | 76,739 | .0230 |
| 1937 Standard Annuity (1937).............. | 60 | 79,011 | .0198 |
| American Experience Table (1868)........... | 70 | 43,320 | .0620 |
| American Annuitants (Ultimate) (1920)...... | 70 | 48,156 | .0531 |
| Combined Annuity (1927).................. | 70 | 54,414 | .0508 |
| 1937 Standard Annuity (1937).............. | 70 | 59,264 | .0418 |

year are expected to die within the ensuing year. For example, under the Combined Annuity Table, of the 95,831 survivors age 40, 441 are expected to die between the age of 40 and 41. This is determined by multiplication of 95,831, the number living, by the death rate .0046, or 95,831 multiplied by .0046 equals 441, the number dying. Similarly the number dying may be calculated at other ages in accordance with the death rates respectively shown by the various tables.

It is quite evident that the greatest decline in mortality, and corresponding increase in longevity, occurred at the younger ages. As compared with the American Experience Table, the 1937 Standard Annuity Table shows a decline in the death rate at age 40 of about 55%. At the older ages, however, the disparity in death rates as shown by the tables is narrowed substantially.

The treatment of mortality and annuitants tables has purposely been simplified, and a discussion of the technical aspects involved in their construction omitted. The tables, however, do evidence the continued increase in longevity that insurance companies have experienced among annuitants. There also may be deduced that, to the extent increases in annuity rates might occur as a result, such increases in rates would be most substantial at the younger ages. This is the fact, as may be seen later when actual rate changes that have occurred in recent years are illustrated.

## 2. Interest

In the discussion of mortality the factor of interest as it affects annuity rates was ignored. It is clear, however, that a sum of money placed with an insurance company for a year or longer will earn some interest. The rate of interest that an insurance company assumes it can earn and safely guarantee to pay on annuity funds will depend on a number of circumstances. Chief among these will be its appraisal of the long term trend of interest on high grade securities, for the business of both annuities and insurance contemplates commitments to be met far in the future as well as currently.

Whatever the rate of interest promised to be paid on an annuitant's funds, the result will be a reduction in the cost of the annuity. The extent of the reduction will depend on the amount of interest actually guaranteed.

The application of interest earnings to reduce the cost of an annuity may be brought about by one of two methods, or both in combination. As the annuity funds held by an insurance company earn interest it could be added to the annuity payment, as computed above, such interest to be regarded by the annuitant as a reduction of his original cost. The other method, and the one employed, is to apply the principle of discount to the expected interest earnings. This results in an immediate reduction of the initial cost or rate to the annuitant. What is this principle of discount? And how does it operate in relation to annuities?

*Discount.* When we speak of *discount* in relation to money, borrowed or loaned, we denote a sum of money that has been reduced by an interest charge collected in advance. For example, if the sum of money to be loaned is $100.00, discounted for one year at an interest rate of 3%, the borrower would receive approximately $97.09. Conversely, if an individual places $97.09 in a bank that pays 3% interest he would have $100.00 at the end of a year.

In tabular fashion we show a *discount table* (TableVI), illustrating the effects of discounting $1.00 at various rates of interest for one or more years.

## TABLE VI

### Discount Table[7]

Present Value of $1.00 Due a Certain Number of Years Hence at
Various Rates of Interest

| Years | 2% | 3% | 3½% | 4% |
|---|---|---|---|---|
| 1 | .9804 | .9709 | .9662 | .9615 |
| 2 | .9612 | .9426 | .9335 | .9246 |
| 3 | .9423 | .9151 | .9019 | .8890 |
| 5 | .9057 | .8626 | .8420 | .8219 |
| 10 | .8203 | .7441 | .7089 | .6756 |
| 14 | .7579 | .6611 | .6178 | .5775 |
| 15 | .7430 | .6419 | .5969 | .5553 |
| 20 | .6730 | .5537 | .5026 | .4564 |

An examination of Table VI shows that as different interest rates are used there is a change in the discounted value of $1.00. If 4% is used there need be in hand $.9615 to have $1.00 at the end of one year. If the rate used is 2% there need be $.9804 to have $1.00 at the end of one year. It is also apparent that the greater the number of years for which $1.00 is to be discounted the less is needed to be in hand to accumulate $1.00. Whereas it took $.9615 at 4% to amount to $1.00 at the end of one year, there is required only $.5553 if 4% is to be earned for fifteen years.

In annuity or insurance calculations this process of discounting is frequently described in terms of *the present value of a dollar due in a certain number of years.* For example, the discounted value of $1.00 at 4% for one year is $.9615; the same thing is meant by the statement that the present value of $1.00 due in one year at 4% is $.9615. This phraseology will be used in discussing discount as it affects annuities.

*Discount and Annuities.* The operation of mortality reduces the cost of annuities, and as we have noted the higher the mortality the less annuities cost. The effect of interest earnings likewise is to decrease their cost. The reduction that will occur is dependent on the rate of interest guaranteed to annuitants by the insurance company.

The discount table, for example, shows that the present value of $1.00 due in 15 years at 4% is $.5553; in 14 years, $.5775, and in one year, $.9615. *Without* interest, the cost of an immediate life annuity under Table IV at age 92 is $2,285.26; but to show the effect of 4% interest on the annuity cost, it will be necessary

---

[7] For complete table see Appendix C.

to divide the sum of the present values of the total annual payments to be made each year by the number of original annuitants at age 92 and compare this with the cost of the immediate life annuity purchased without the assumption of interest earnings. Thus, of our group age 92 (Table IV), the insurance company must expect to pay to the 1,867 surviving annuitants at age 93 $1,000 each, or $1,867,000 (total annual payments). The present value of these payments, at age 92, is $1,867,000 × $.9615 (present value of $1.00 at 4% for one year), or $1,795,120.50. The second year there must be paid to 1,338 survivors at age 94 $1,338,000, the present value of which is $1,338,000 × $.9246, or $1,237,114.80. The sum of such present values carried out for each of 14 years to the age of 106, beyond which no further payments are expected, is divided by the original number of 2,538 annuitants at age 92 to determine each annuitant's cost. This cost, based on Table IV and 4% interest, is $2,051.93. Without interest, as previously given, the cost was $2,285.26.

It is apparent, therefore, that both the mortality (annuity) table utilized, and the rate of interest guaranteed by an insurance company have an important impact on the cost of an annuity.

## 3. Expense

An annuity premium, computed with mortality and interest taken into account, is known as a *net premium*. An insurance company, however, necessarily must collect something from an annuity buyer to cover the expense of operation of its business. To cover expenses, and also profits, something is added to the net premium. How much is added?

It would be convenient if a formula as simple as that used in the above net premium computation could be illustrated. In insurance terminology the computation of this expense is known as the problem of *loading*. It gives weight to all the elements of expense in the conduct of the business: administrative expenses; investment expenses; premium taxes; and costs of acquiring annuity business such as commissions, advertising, and so forth. When the expense, or the loading, is added to the net premium, we have what is known as the *gross premium*. To the buyer of an annuity this gross premium is the price or cost of the annuity to him.

An explanation of loading methods as used by the insurance companies is too technical to attempt here. It should be recognized, nevertheless, that the amount of it will affect the cost of annuities to the buyer. The loading charge may be different as between insurance companies issuing the same type of annuity, and will vary in relation to the age of the annuitant, kind of annuity purchased, and so forth. It can be ascertained by an annuity buyer readily enough if he knows the net premium to be charged. For example, a subtraction of the net premium from the gross premium charged for an immediate life annuity will normally disclose the amount of expense or loading included in the gross premium. In other forms of annuities the process is not so simple, but expense is similarly ascertainable.

### E.  The Three Factors

It is the operation of three factors, mortality, interest, and expense, that will determine the gross premium rates for a life annuity to the buyer. The actual rate is dependent on the annuity table employed to evaluate mortality or probabilities of survival, the assumed rate of interest earnings, and the rate of expense charged. Diverse assumptions in relation to any one of these factors will produce different annuity rates.

While all of this is true it must be recognized that in commercial annuity practice it is possible for two insurance companies, using different factors, to arrive at a similar gross annuity rate to the buyer. This could occur in several ways. Company A may use an annuity table which shows a slightly higher annuity cost, before use of interest, than the table employed by B Company. Company A, to equalize its annuity rate for competitive purposes with that of B Company, may do one of two things or both. It could guarantee a higher rate of interest than B Company, add less to the net premium for expense, or do both. There are, however, limitations as to the extent to which this practice may be carried. There is the necessity for use of an interest rate that is conservative, and there are also legal limitations on the amount of expense that may be included in the gross premiums. Notwithstanding such possible equalization of annuity rates, there do exist some differences in quoted rates for identical types of annuities. An illustration of these differences may be seen in Table VII.

An additional consideration that might affect annuity cost to the buyer is the form of annuity contract issued by an insurance company. Annuities may be issued in either of two ways, in a participating or non-participating form of contract.

### F.  Participating and Non-participating Annuities

In our computation of an immediate life annuity it was shown that the buyer's annuity cost depended on the annuity table utilized, the rate of interest guaranteed, and the amount of expense. In the issuance of an annuity to an annuitant, an insurance company may use a form of contract that provides, in addition to guaranteed annual payments, a share of any surplus earnings. This form of contract is known as a *participating* annuity. If no such provision is included it is called a *non-participating* annuity. The surplus earnings, possibly payable under a participating annuity, may arise from either or all of three sources. The death rate among annuitants may exceed what the annuity table predicts, resulting in a saving, because fewer people would have to be paid. The interest rate earned may be more than had been guaranteed; or the insurance company may find that it has collected too much for expense. The savings or excess earnings accruing to the company as a result could be returned to the annuitant as *dividends*. These dividends would increase the amount of the annual annuity payments. They could be considered by the annuitant as a reduction of original cost. Actually most annuities, at least immediate whole life annuities, are issued in a non-participating form of contract.

TABLE VII

IMMEDIATE LIFE ANNUITY—NON-PARTICIPATING RATES

Life Income Purchased by $1,000—Male Life

| | AGE | | | |
|---|---|---|---|---|
| Company | 55 | 65 | 75 | 85 |
| A...................,............ | $61.05 | $82.85 | $123.00 | $203.67 |
| B....................../..... | 59.39 | 81.27 | 121.65 | 203.55 |
| C.................,........... | 55.94 | 75.20 | 110.19 | 179.08 |

In Table VII Company A is Canadian, operating in this country. Companies B and C are American companies. The life income from Company A exceeds that paid by Company C by approximately 10% at the several ages. As between these two companies the difference may be explained by the fact that different annuity tables are used in computing the rates. Among the larger American insurance companies the current rates for non-participating immediate life annuities tend to be identical. This has occurred because of their present use of the same annuity table, guaranteed interest rate, and similar expense charges. Complete equality of rates, however, has not yet occurred, as may be observed in the different rates quoted by Companies *B* and *C*.

## G.  Types of Annuities

The immediate life annuity has been used to illustrate the basic principles of annuity computations. There are a number of other types with the same principles applied to their construction. Those described here are the ones that may be individually purchased or that may be utilized under a pension plan. Their specific application in pension plans will be developed later.

*Annuity Certain.* As previously explained, this annuity disburses principal and interest over a fixed period; payments are not contingent on survival. It is an investment contract without reference to the probabilities of living or dying. It is purchased by a single premium payment.

*Immediate Life Annuity.* This annuity pays an immediate income for life, with nothing further payable in the event of death. It also is purchased by a single premium payment.

*Temporary Life Annuity.* This annuity pays an immediate income for a stipulated number of years. In case of death before the stipulated years of payment expire nothing further is payable. It is purchased by a single premium payment.

*Deferred Life Annuity.* As the name implies, the income purchased through use of this annuity begins at a future date. In the event of death before income commences nothing is payable. At the time the annuity income commences it takes the form of a life annuity; thus if death occurs thereafter there are no further payments. This annuity may be purchased by either single or annual premium payments.

*Joint and Survivor Annuity.* This also is known as a *last survivor annuity.* It provides for annuity payments to at least two lives, so long as any of the annuitants shall live. Upon the death of the last survivor no further payments are made. It is purchased by a single premium payment; or by annual payments if income is to begin at a future date.

*Cash Refund Life Annuity.* A *refund* can theoretically be provided in any type of annuity. It is a provision by which, if the annuitant dies, there will be payable to his estate an amount which, when added to the payments already made to the time of death, will equal the purchase price of the annuity. Where it is included the annuity income is reduced to the annuitant. For a lesser income he is assured that there will be payable to his estate in the event of death an amount equal to the purchase price less what already has been paid to him. While he lives the annuitant is assured of a life income. It is essentially an immediate life annuity modified by the refund provision. Normally, it is purchased by a single premium payment.

*Annuity Certain and Continuous.* Strictly speaking this is a technical term reserved to describe a *species* of annuities. It consists of two elements. A refund provision is indicated in the words *annuity certain;* and a deferred life annuity is denoted by the words *and continuous.* As an example, an annuity certain and continuous might provide payments for ten years certain, and thereafter for life. An annuitant receiving income therefrom would have a life income immediately. If he should die before the expiration of ten years the insurance company would continue payments to his estate to complete the guaranteed ten years of payment for the *certain* period. It should be emphasized that the words *annuity certain* are descriptive of the refund portion of the annuity, with the *and continuous* denoting the deferred life annuity aspect. It is also made available with a 5, 15, or 20 year, or even with a 100 months' certain period.

## II. ANNUITIES AND PENSIONS

Our purpose here is to discuss, in a general way, the types of annuity contracts mainly employed to finance pension benefits where an insurance company is the underwriter.

We will assume that funds are being accumulated year by year by an employer to provide pension benefits to his employees at some future date. Under these conditions an employer may use insurance company annuity contracts in two major ways. First, investment of the pension funds may be made each year with an insurance company, more or less on a savings-bank basis, until the time arrives to pay pensions. An annuity then may be purchased to guarantee to an employee his pension benefit. Second, investment of the pension funds to provide pension benefits may take place through the yearly purchase of deferred life annuities. If the first method is used, that is, the pension funds are invested with an insurance company but the purchase of annuities is postponed until pensions begin, the insurance companies will make available to the employer several investment mediums. These will be in the form of investment contracts known as *retirement annuity* and *retirement income contracts*. When the time comes for the employees to retire, the pension funds, as they may have been accumulated in either of these contracts, may be automatically applied to the purchase of some type of annuity. On the other hand, if annuities are to be purchased each year as funds are accumulated, normally the employer will buy deferred life annuities. Usually these deferred life annuities will be bought by single payments, and they are referred to as *single-premium deferred life annuities*. These two methods of acquiring annuities to provide pension benefits differ fundamentally in operation. They will be explained.

## A.   Retirement Annuity Contract

The retirement annuity contract consists essentially of two contracts. One portion may be said to be an investment contract, and the other an annuity contract. The investment contract serves to provide the employer with a safe medium for the pension funds until they are needed. The annuity contract, while coupled to the investment contract, becomes operative only when the annuity rights granted therein are exercised.

In illustration we shall assume that an employer wishes to provide a pension at age 65 to a male employee who is now 55. Also we shall assume that the pension benefit is to be ten dollars a month, or $120.00 a year, at 65, for the balance of the employee's lifetime. How will the retirement annuity contract apply to this situation?

The life insurance company will sell the employer a retirement annuity contract to provide the $10.00 monthly pension at 65 for a series of annual level premium payments. The employer's main obligation is to continue these premium payments each year until his employee is 65, to obtain a $10.00 monthly pension for the latter. The insurance company on the other hand agrees to a number of things relative to both the investment of the annual payments and the payment of the $10.00 monthly life income at 65.

On the investment portion of the retirement annuity the insurance company guarantees: (1) a minimum rate of interest; (2) a principal sum or cash value if payments are stopped before the employee is 65; (3) a cash maturity value at 65 if it is desired in lieu of the monthly pension; (4) to pay a value upon the death of the employee equal at least to the amount of premiums paid; (5) usually, to loan at a rate of interest guaranteed in the contract such cash value as may have been created by the annual deposits; (6) in most contracts, to share any surplus earnings which may have arisen, if there is earned more than the minimum rate of interest guaranteed.

As to the annuity portion, the insurance company agrees: (1) to pay the monthly life income of $10.00 at 65 under an annuity certain and continuous, with a ten year certain period; (2) alternatively at 65, or previous thereto, to pay an income to the employee under (a) an annuity certain, (b) an immediate life annuity, (c) a joint and survivor life annuity, or (d) an annuity certain and continuous with either a 15 or a 20 year certain period; (3) to grant the annuities offered at guaranteed rates; (4) in some cases, and for a limited period, to share with the annuitant any surplus earnings.

The description of a retirement annuity contract as made up of two contracts, investment and annuity, is convenient to clarify its dual nature. Actually it is a unified instrument issued as one contract by an insurance company. Also it will be observed that if the privileges guaranteed under the annuity contract are exercised, an investment aspect again comes into operation. The funds out of which the annuities are to be paid must be kept invested by the insurance company and interest earned thereon. However, in our example in which a retirement annuity is purchased for an employee age 55, the period of the contract extending from age 55 to 65 is the investment phase in the traditional sense. This period is utilized for accumulation of capital. The period of annuity payments after 65 is one of liquidation of the capital accumulated. In the accumulation period, 55 to 65, no life contingencies, probabilities of living or dying, are basically involved, but they immediately enter when a distribution under annuities commences.

## B. Retirement Income Contract

All that has been said of the retirement annuity contract is likewise applicable to the retirement income contract. The latter, however, in addition to having an investment and annuity function, has a third feature. This takes the form of a life insurance benefit.

To return to our example, the employer's objective was to provide a pension to his employee of $10.00 a month at 65. He might also desire to provide for the employee's dependents in the event of the latter's premature death. If so, he can use the retirement income contract to accomplish this purpose, if his employee is insurable.[8] The death benefit at the inception of the retirement income contract for each $10.00 of monthly benefit payable at retirement usually is $1,000.00. It remains at this level until the cash value of the contract exceeds $1,000.00. Then and thereafter to age 65, the death value is equal to the cash value of the contract. In the later years of this contract the cash value normally exceeds the original insurance value of $1,000.00. If death occurs, the annuity provisions and agreements enumerated in the retirement annuity contract as available at retirement would also be applicable to the death benefits arising from the insurance feature, or to the cash value.

### C. Single-Premium Deferred Life Annuities

The nature of a single-premium deferred life annuity is easily understood if reference is made to the computation of an immediate life annuity. It involves the purchase of a life annuity to begin at some future date. When that date arrives annuity income commences. Because income is postponed from the time of purchase until a later date it is differentiated from an immediate life annuity by the word *deferred*. It is purchased usually with a single premium, as is an immediate life annuity. When income commences, payments continue until death occurs. If death occurs in the deferred period, however, there is no refund to the purchaser.

The employer who uses the single-premium deferred life annuity method to provide pensions for his employees buys a contract of a totally different character from either a retirement annuity or retirement income contract. How will it operate in relation to the employer who wishes to provide $10.00 a month at 65 to his male employee?

First of all the employer might purchase in a given year the entire $10.00 monthly pension for his employee by the use of a single-premium deferred life annuity. This would require a substantial immediate cash outlay, and it would be sharply at variance with the method of purchase used in the retirement annuity. There the employer made installment payments in the form of level annual premiums, which at 65 were in accumulated value sufficient to

---

[8] Under some circumstances issued on a non-medical basis.

provide an annuity of $10.00 a month.   It is true that the purchase of a retirement annuity contract may be made by a single payment, but normally it is made on the installment plan as illustrated.   On the contrary the purchase of a deferred life annuity is made normally by a single premium, but the *effect* of annual premiums or an installment purchase is obtained in this way.

The pension benefit at age 65 is to be $10.00 a month, and the employee is now 55.   If the employer for each of the ensuing ten years should purchase a single-premium deferred life annuity to pay $1.00 a month at 65, the pension benefit of $10.00 would have been provided.   He, therefore, instead of buying the entire pension benefit in one year, may pay for it in installments, in similar manner to the method he used with the retirement annuity.   He has in the buying process purchased ten single-premium deferred life annuity contracts, each to pay $1.00 at 65, the total of which will pay $10.00 a month.

What are some of the contractual differences and similarities as between the retirement annuity, retirement income, and the single-premium deferred life annuity?   As to their differences, the single-premium deferred life annuity contains no pure investment portion such as is found in the retirement contracts.   As a consequence, in the typical form of single-premium deferred life annuity as issued, there is no cash,[9] loan, or death value, and no life insurance feature as in the retirement income contract.   Nor is a cash maturity value made available when the employee is 65.   There is very little similarity between the retirement annuity and the single-premium deferred life annuity, except that, previous to the time annuity or pension payments commence, the insurance company in both cases accepts the employer's premiums, and therefore offers an investment service.   Also at age 65, if under retirement contracts the accumulated cash value is used to provide a life annuity, to that extent there is a parallel function with the deferred life annuity, which likewise at 65 commences to pay annuity income.   The difference in nature of the retirement annuity, the retirement income contract, and the single-premium deferred life annuity will be developed more definitively in Chapters VI and VII.

---

[9] As later discussed, a cash value under single-premium deferred life annuities may be made available to an employer under certain circumstances (p. 112).   Also it is possible to use a single-premium deferred annuity which will provide a death benefit (p. 121).   For the distinction between a single-premium deferred *life* annuity and a single-premium deferred annuity, see footnote, p. 122.

## III.  ANNUITY RATES

There exists no organized market for annuities similar to those for stocks, bonds, and commodities.  A purchaser of an annuity is like a buyer in the so-called over-the-counter security market.  He must obtain his annuity rate quotation by direct inquiry of the vendors, the insurance companies or their representatives.  The absence of an organized market is natural in that the annuity market is normally a sluggish one, rate changes occurring infrequently; although when general rate changes do occur the larger insurance companies tend to lose no time in approximating each others' quoted rates.  The absence or lack of an organized market for annuities, however, has obscured important changes in annuity rates that have occurred principally since 1930, when public interest in annuities, to any important extent, was first manifested in the United States.  It perhaps would be a matter of historical interest only to survey these changes were it not that the factors that produced them are still operative and probably have not been fully reflected in annuity rates.  The individual buyer, and certainly the employer who utilizes annuities for his pension plan, will be thereby affected.

### A.  Growth of Annuity Business

The interest in annuities displayed by the public about 1930, continuously expanding thereafter, has several explanations.  The bursting of the speculative boom in 1929 led many people to seek the ultimate in security and guaranteed returns on their capital.  Shortly thereafter there developed a downward trend in interest rates which, together with rising personal income taxes, turned the attention of large investors, seeking higher yields, to various types of annuities.  Coincidentally with this developing public interest, there also occurred an increase in the use of annuities by employers under pension plans.  The volume of annuities sold by insurance companies began to rise sharply from 1930 on.

In 1930 eight of the largest American life insurance companies reported obligations to make present and future annual annuity payments to annuitants of about $35,000,000 a year.  In 1935 these same companies reported their obligations to make present and future annual annuity payments as $110,000,000 a year.  In five years the volume had more than tripled.  Two of the largest companies included in the eight showed increases in 1935 annuity obligations of respectively fourteen and fifty times their 1930 reported figures. These extreme increases indicate that the two companies must have had in 1930 merely nominal amounts of annuity business. This fact is correct, but it also substantiates the general statement that not until after 1930 did the annuity business in the United States commence in real volume.

A side light on annuity growth that occurred in these five years is to be noted in the volume of life insurance in force at the same intervals. In 1930 there were about 114 billions of dollars of life insurance on the books of American life insurance companies. By 1935, the great economic depression had taken its toll, and life insurance in force had dropped to about 106 billions. In contrast to this decline of 8 billions of life insurance the insurance companies' obligations to make annuity payments had risen from $35,000,000 to $110,000,000. In 1940 the eight companies reported that their annuity payment obligations had risen to about $230,000,000, or double the figure for 1935. The rate of increase measured against the 1935 rate had slowed down, which was to be expected as the 1930 volume of annuities was relatively small. In terms of the decade 1930-1940, however, annuity payment obligations reported by the companies for the latter year had increased more than six times over those of 1930. Finally, since 1940 there has been no slackening in this phenomenal growth in annuity business.

In sketching the rise in volume of annuities from 1930, the figures cited were in terms of what the eight insurance companies stated to be their obligations for *annuity payments*. This means that of total annuity payment obligations, some was for payments currently being made to annuitants, and some for deferred annuity payments. While this is useful to portray annuity volume it does not indicate the amount of cash reserves the insurance companies must retain to meet their current and deferred annuity payments. For example, to state that there is an obligation for an annuity payment of $1,000 a year discloses the obligation, but nothing as to what the underwriter must have in cash or its equivalent to meet the payments. When in 1940, therefore, the eight insurance companies were obligated to make annuity payments, currently or in the future, of $230,000,000, they obviously had to maintain reserves to meet the payments. Approached from this point of view, the magnitude of growth of the annuity business in the 1930-40 decade may be further appreciated. In order to meet annuity payments of $230,000,000 a year to annuitants it was necessary for the eight insurance companies to maintain reserves of about one billion dollars. The amount of the reserves needed in 1930 probably was no more than 175 million dollars. The insurance companies not only were confronted with the problem of investing this large sum, necessary to increase their reserves, but they also were obliged to make the investment of these funds during a period of declining interest rates.

It may be coincidence, or it may partially explain the rapid growth of annuities in the 1930-40 decade, but, as interest rates declined, the volume of annuities increased. While in most enterprises an increased volume of sales usually leads to a reduction in the cost of the article, such is not the case with annuities. As has been seen, the rate of interest promised is an important element in the cost of an annuity. The rate and extent of the decline in interest yields from 1929 to 1944 are illustrated in Table VIII and the graph that follows.

## B. Decline in Interest Rates

The tabular columns in Table VIII give average yields for the respective years on U. S. Government bonds and triple-A corporate bonds. The government yields are for partially tax-exempt bonds, with maturities of 12 to 15 years and over. This partial tax-exemption is of minor significance for our purpose, which is to

TABLE VIII

COMPARATIVE YIELD OF GOVERNMENT AND CORPORATE BONDS

| U. S. GOVERNMENT BONDS | | Aaa CORPORATE BONDS | |
|---|---|---|---|
| Year | Average Yield | Year | Average Yield |
| 1929 | 3.60 | 1929 | 4.73 |
| 1930 | 3.29 | 1930 | 4.55 |
| 1931 | 3.34 | 1931 | 4.58 |
| 1932 | 3.68 | 1932 | 5.01 |
| 1933 | 3.31 | 1933 | 4.49 |
| 1934 | 3.12 | 1934 | 4.00 |
| 1935 | 2.79 | 1935 | 3.60 |
| 1936 | 2.69 | 1936 | 3.24 |
| 1937 | 2.74 | 1937 | 3.26 |
| 1938 | 2.61 | 1938 | 3.19 |
| 1939 | 2.41 | 1939 | 3.01 |
| 1940 | 2.26 | 1940 | 2.84 |
| 1941 | 2.05 | 1941 | 2.77 |
| 1942 | 2.09 | 1942 | 2.83 |
| 1943 | 1.98 | 1943 | 2.73 |
| 1944 | 1.92 | 1944 | 2.72 |
| 1945 | 1.66 | 1945 | 2.02 |

show the persistence and downward trend of interest rates on high grade securities. While the investment portfolios of insurance companies are diversified, beyond U. S. Government bonds and triple-A corporate bonds, in such things as first mortgages and state and municipal bonds, the exhibit exemplifies their general experi-

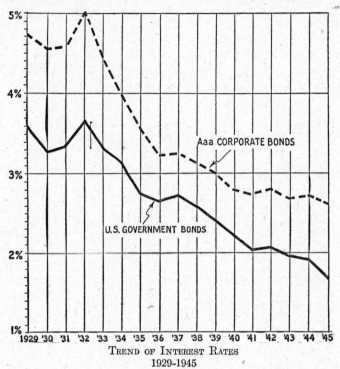

TREND OF INTEREST RATES
1929-1945

ence. The graph shown merely restates Table VIII in pictorial form. The data for government bonds are from the *Federal Reserve Bulletin;* for corporate bonds, from Moody's *Investors Service.*

## C. Trend of Annuity Rates

The period from 1930-40 was distinguished by a rapid increase in the volume of annuity business. At the same time more conservative annuity tables were adopted by the insurance companies such as the Combined Annuity and the 1937 Standard Annuity tables. These tables used in conjunction with reduced interest assumptions brought substantial increases in annuity rates.

In Tables IX-A and IX-B there are shown the rate changes which resulted. The six companies illustrated are of the largest, both as to size and in their transactions of annuity business.

Table IX-A shows the rate changes in terms of the annual income obtainable from $1,000 paid for an immediate life annuity, if bought in these companies in the year and at the age indicated. Table IX-B shows the changes for the same period in terms of the dollar cost, or the annuity rate charge for an income of $1,200 a

TABLE IX-A

IMMEDIATE LIFE ANNUITY
ANNUAL INCOME PURCHASED BY $1,000

Non-participating—Male Life

| Year | Age | Company A | Company B | Company C | Company D | Company E | Company F |
|------|-----|-----------|-----------|-----------|-----------|-----------|-----------|
| 1930 | 40........ | $ 60.73 | $ 60.74 | $ 60.74 | $ 58.90 | $ 53.97 | $ 61.35 |
|      | 65........ | 108.01 | 108.01 | 108.02 | 108.01 | 102.54 | 115.21 |
|      | 85........ | 255.29 | 255.30 | 255.26 | 255.29 | 204.29 | 223.71 |
| 1935 | 40........ | $ 54.02 | $ 54.02 | $ 54.02 | $ 54.02 | $ 54.02 | $ 54.02 |
|      | 65........ | 97.03 | 97.03 | 97.03 | 97.03 | 97.03 | 96.99 |
|      | 85........ | 229.10 | 229.10 | 229.10 | 229.10 | 229.09 | 228.83 |
| 1940 | 40........ | $ 47.11 | $ 47.11 | $ 47.11 | $ 47.11 | $ 47.11 | $ 44.88 |
|      | 65........ | 85.65 | 85.65 | 85.11 | 85.65 | 85.65 | 82.92 |
|      | 85........ | 205.80 | 205.80 | 205.80 | 205.80 | 205.80 | 201.21 |
| 1945 | 40........ | $ 40.26 | $ 43.63 | $ 40.26 | $ 40.70 | $ 43.63 | $ 40.26 |
|      | 65........ | 78.33 | 81.96 | 78.33 | 75.20 | 81.96 | 78.33 |
|      | 85........ | 196.81 | 201.33 | 196.81 | 179.08 | 201.33 | 196.81 |

TABLE IX-B

IMMEDIATE LIFE ANNUITY
ANNUITY COST OF $1,200 ANNUAL INCOME

Non-participating—Male Life

| Year | Age | Company A | Company B | Company C | Company D | Company E | Company F |
|------|-----|-----------|-----------|-----------|-----------|-----------|-----------|
| 1930 | 40 | $19,759.69 | $19,756.34 | $19,756.34 | $20,373.51 | $22,234.41 | $19,559.90 |
|      | 65 | 11,110.08 | 11,110.08 | 11,109.05 | 11,110.08 | 11,702.75 | 10,415.76 |
|      | 85 | 4,700.54 | 4,699.96 | 4,701.09 | 4,700.54 | 5,874.00 | 5,364.09 |
| 1935 | 40 | $22,213.99 | $22,213.99 | $22,213.99 | $22,213.99 | $22,213.99 | $22,213.99 |
|      | 65 | 12,367.34 | 12,367.34 | 12,367.34 | 12,367.34 | 12,367.34 | 12,372.42 |
|      | 85 | 5,237.45 | 5,237.45 | 5,237.45 | 5,237.45 | 5,238.12 | 5,245.55 |
| 1940 | 40 | $25,472.30 | $25,472.30 | $25,472.30 | $25,472.30 | $25,472.30 | $26,737.97 |
|      | 65 | 14,010.51 | 14,010.51 | 14,010.51 | 14,010.51 | 14,010.51 | 14,471.78 |
|      | 85 | 5,830.90 | 5,830.90 | 5,830.90 | 5,830.90 | 5,830.90 | 5,963.92 |
| 1945 | 40 | $29,806.03 | $27,504.01 | $29,806.03 | $29,484.03 | $27,504.01 | $29,806.03 |
|      | 65 | 15,319.92 | 14,641.29 | 15,319.92 | 15,957.45 | 14,641.29 | 15,319.92 |
|      | 85 | 6,097.25 | 5,960.36 | 6,097.25 | 6,700.92 | 5,960.36 | 6,097.25 |

year.  While the six companies are intended to be illustrative only, they typify the annuity rate changes that were made by life insurance companies as a whole.  The annuity rates for 1945 are shown on the lower part of the table to indicate further trends.

Examination of Table IX-B reveals several obvious facts.  First there will be noticed the uniformity of rates quoted by all the companies from 1930-40.  In 1930 the rates are almost the same except for Company E.  By 1935 they are almost identical at all ages.  In 1940 they are the same, except that Company F has raised its rate more than the other five companies.  The second fact is the important increase in rates disclosed.  Company A shows an increase in 1940 over 1930, of 29%, 26%, and 24% at the respective ages of 40, 65, and 85.  Company F in 1940 shows the largest increases at ages 40 and 65, of 37% and 39% respectively.  It will be noticed also that relatively, and in almost all companies, the more drastic increases occurred at age 40.  By 1945 the increases over 1930 rates by Company A were 51%, 38%, and 30% at age 40, 65, and 85.  Some lack of uniformity developed as shown in the cases of Companies B and E.  Also in the case of Company D, at age 85, the jump in rate was greater than in any of the other companies.

The main purpose of both Tables IX-A and IX-B is to illustrate the drastic decline in income and, conversely, the increase in rates to the annuity buyer.  As to the uniformity of rates, it is greater than the difference, but that a fair degree of difference is possible may be seen in the 1945 rates.  The severe increases which occurred from 1930-45 are explained by the use of a constantly reduced rate of interest and by more conservative mortality assumptions.  At the younger ages particularly, as may be seen in the greater adjustment of rates at age 40, it was found that mortality among annuitants was showing a greater relative improvement.  Annuity buyers at the younger ages through this period were constantly giving evidence of longer life than the insurance companies had assumed would be the case in formulating the annuity rates for this group.  This was true also at the older ages, but to a lesser degree.

The rate differences in 1945 as between the companies are largely due to different assumptions as to possible interest earnings.  For example, Company A and Company B were using the same annuitants table.  Company A, however, made use of a 2% interest assumption, Company B of a 2½% assumption.

## D. Future Annuity Rates

The fact that the larger insurance companies quote similar rates to buyers of non-participating immediate life annuities is a natural mathematical result, where the same annuity table and interest rate are utilized.

The use of a similar loading or expense charge, included in the annuity rate, is less easily explained. The operating expenses of insurance companies may and do show considerable deviations. So far as the annuity business of insurance companies is concerned it is possible that the total expense of this business might be approximately the same for all of the large companies. A better explanation probably is to be found in the fact that the sale of annuities during the 1930-40 period proved unprofitable to the underwriters. Despite the increased rates they probably have not as yet absorbed the annuity losses known to have been experienced on annuities issued in the 1930-40 decade. In addition, there remains uncertainty as to whether the most recent annuity rates will prove adequate or profitable. As a consequence, competition has not been keen, for there has been little incentive for companies with low expense factors to reflect them in their annuity rates.

If further rate changes in annuities are to come it seems probable, whether they are revised down or up, that the form of the annuity may be altered. Instead of using the non-participating form, as is now largely the case, annuities then would be issued on a participating basis.

The annuity buyer of a non-participating form in 1930-40 was in a buyers' market. A male age 40 paid $19,759.69 in 1930 for an annual life annuity income of $1,200. In 1945 the same annual income cost $29,806.03. In the latter case it is possible that the buyer may be obtaining his annuity at a rate that is too conservative, either as to future interest or mortality assumptions by the insurance companies. If this proves to be so, a purchaser of a non-participating annuity has no way of receiving a benefit if the insurance company in the future should earn more than it anticipated. The possible solution for the buyer is to purchase a participating annuity, if in his opinion that form will prove advantageous in future years. In a participating annuity, as in a non-participating annuity, a flat price is charged the buyer for a guaranteed annual income. The insurance company issuing a participating annuity, however, agrees to share surplus earnings with the annuitant in the form of annual dividends. Any dividends received, therefore, will increase the size of the annual income payment to the annuitant.

There already are several insurance companies that issue a participating form of life annuity. The possible advantages over a non-participating annuity must be measured by at least two considerations. One is the initial comparative rate as between the non-participating and participating forms. The second is whether the company issuing the participating form is apt to share any surplus earnings. If the comparative annuity rate for the non-participating and the participating forms is the same there is nothing to be lost in buying the latter. If a difference of any consequence exists in favor of the non-participating annuity then it becomes a problem of evaluating the possible dividends that will be paid on the participating form. The latter becomes a matter of analyzing the over-all record of the insurance company. The possibility of a share in surplus earnings as well as the amount of dividends an annuitant may receive are subject to the usual *caveat emptor* of the market place.

# CHAPTER IV

# Pension Costs

........................................................................................

T HE TRUE COSTS OF A PENSION PLAN TO AN EMPLOYER ARE REPRE-
sented by the difference between his financial outlays to maintain the plan and the savings which result from reduced labor turnover, the retirement of superannuated employees, and the increased
efficiency of personnel, all brought about through the operation of
the plan.

The determination of the true costs of a pension plan constitutes
a difficult problem in accounting. An employer's actual financial
outlays, accounting-wise, are treated as a part of the cost of wages
and salaries; or they are set up as a debit item for expense of pensions. There is no offsetting item on the credit side of the ledger.
The reason is that to measure and reduce to a money-value the
gains from reduced labor turnover, retirement of the inefficient employees, and other benefits of a pension plan may present insuperable difficulties. The variables in any employer's situation may
minimize the validity of any attempt precisely to account or place
a value on the benefits that even the employer himself may feel
have accrued from his pension plan. For example, a wage or salary
increase, given simultaneously with the introduction of a pension
plan, might obscure or invalidate any immediate conclusions as to
the effect of the plan that otherwise would appear justified. While
certain benefits, such as a reduction in labor turnover, might be immediate, on the other hand any financial gains from the retirement
of superannuated employees might not appear for many years after
the establishment of the plan. The financial outlays of the employer, in other words, might be partly offset currently by the
savings from reduced labor turnover; further offsets, however,
might be deferred until the accumulated pension funds had been
used to effect retirements, and the gains from this source had been
appraised.

74

The impossibility of predetermining the true costs has resulted in a loose, although perhaps necessary, conception of pension costs. It is customary for employers and pension consultants alike to speak of the financial outlays for pension plans as though they were *true* costs. While this conception obviously is inaccurate, if a pension plan produces a financial benefit to an employer, there must be money outlays by an employer for his pension plan in advance of any realizable benefits. The financial outlays to establish and support a pension plan, in contrast to the true costs, are more easily determinable. They may be estimated with relative accuracy. It is these probable financial outlays which will be considered herein and, in accordance with customary usage, will be referred to as the actual pension costs.

## I. ACTUARIAL PRINCIPLES

The actual costs of a pension plan of a definitive character, wherein there is an arrangement to fund pension payments due at some future time, will be affected over the lifetime of the plan by a number of factors. Chief among these will be the following: (1) the mortality rate among employees covered under the plan both before and after retirement; (2) the ages and the rates at which retirements actually take place; (3) the rate of interest earned on the pension funds; (4) the rate of withdrawal of employees from the plan; (5) the salary or wage scale of employees during the period of employment; (6) the ages and the rates at which new employees enter employment; (7) the sex of the employees and pensioners; (8) the benefits granted by the plan; (9) the methods of funding used to accumulate the pension funds; and (10) the expense of administering the pension plan.

The total effect of these various factors on actual costs may be approximately forecast. It is the function of the actuary to make a study or valuation of them as they may be expected to operate in practice either singly or in combination. The summation of his calculations will constitute the estimated costs, or the *valuation* as it is technically known. To the extent that the estimated costs are understated or overstated, they may be corrected from time to time by checking those factors which are subject to variation against actual experience, realized in operation of the pension plan. A valuation process is employed whether a pension plan is of an insured or of a self-administered character; however, the factors valuated in the case of self-administered plans may be more

numerous than those of insured plans, as will be developed later.[1]
In the following description of actuarial principles used in making
estimates of cost, that is the valuation, technical aspects other than
those necessary broadly to illustrate the process of valuation have
been avoided.

To simplify as well as to clarify the valuation process there will
be assumed a hypothetical pension plan to be funded. At the inception of the plan the employee group consists of 100 male employees, age 45. The plan provides for a definite life income benefit upon retirement at age 65. All contributions to the plan are to
be made by the employer. Other assumptions that may affect the
valuation will be considered as the explanation develops.

## A. Mortality

### 1. Before Retirement

Of the 100 male employees some may die before attaining the
retirement age of 65. It may not be essential, therefore, to make
provision for the entire 100, but only for those who survive.

Among any large group of lives selected arbitrarily deaths may
occur in due course more or less regularly. The determination of
the actual death rates of the group may be computed from statistics of mortality among the group. These statistics, tabulated as
they were in the discussion of annuities, constitute a mortality
table. A mortality table's usefulness normally is greatest if it
can be used to estimate future death rates among lives exposed to
the same influences as those from which the original statistics
were derived. If an employer, therefore, makes available to an
actuary an extended record of a large group of his employees, showing the number in his service at each age as well as the number of
deaths which have occurred among them, it may be possible for
the actuary to construct a mortality table that will be of value in
predicting the future death and survival rates among these employees. If the lack of such available data precludes this approach,
an alternative is to use one of the standard mortality tables already
constructed, and then to check periodically the actual mortality experience under the pension fund against that of the standard table.
For the purpose of this illustration we will assume that the table
selected is the 1937 Standard Annuity Table.

At age 45 the 1937 Standard Annuity Table makes the disclosure

---
[1] See Chapter VIII.

that the probability of surviving to age 65 expressed as a percentage is 75%. Of the 100 employees age 45 it is estimated there will be living at age 65, therefore, 100 × .75, or 75 employees. Thus, if mortality before retirement is taken into account it may be necessary to accumulate funds for only 75 employees. The process of making allowances for mortality is termed *discounting for mortality*. The initial pension outlays will be reduced if a mortality discount is applied in the case of any group of prospective pensioners.

## 2. After Retirement

The payment of life incomes to the 75 survivors will commence when they attain age 65. There will occur, however, a further mortality among the 75 survivors after they have been placed on the pension rolls. Death will ultimately extinguish the group and therefore the need for further pension payments. Thus the pensioned employees from the actuarial viewpoint are annuitants. Illustration of the calculation of an immediate life annuity has been given in Chapter III, both with and without the use of interest. In the situation there discussed the problem was the cost of an immediate life annuity at age 92. The discount for mortality after retirement in the present problem is solved by finding the cost of a life annuity *due*, the first payment commencing at age 65. The computation process is similar to that used for the life aged 92, the calculations required in this instance simply being extended back to age 65. A life annuity *due* is distinguished from an immediate life annuity in this characteristic. Whereas the latter makes payment to the annuitant one year from the date of purchase, the former makes its first payment at the time of purchase; and in both cases, of course, for each year the annuitant survives thereafter. If it is desired to have life annuity payments of $1.00 commence at 65, the life annuity *due* will be equal to the value of an immediate life annuity at 65, plus $1.00. Specifically, the value of a life annuity *due* to pay $1.00 annually at age 65 and thereafter, based on the 1937 Standard Annuity Table with interest at 2%, is $12.51.

Thus far we have discussed mortality before and after retirement as events which actuarially are treated separately. This may or may not be the case. A discount for mortality *before* retirement obviously would be omitted for a group of employees who had attained retirement age, since then only mortality *after* retirement would be involved. However, in the case of our 100 employees, if we assume that discounts for mortality both before and after retirement are to be taken, the principles of the deferred life annuity may be employed. The deferred life annuity simultaneously takes account of mortality prior to and after retirement.

## B.  Deferred Life Annuity

A deferred life annuity involves a method of accumulation of funds which will pay a life income commencing at some definite future date. When that date arrives the accumulated funds may be paid out in the form of a life annuity. Previous to that date, funds are accumulated at interest, but only in an amount necessary to make annuity payments to that number of a group who, according to the mortality table, will survive to such future date. *It should be noted that the annuities payable to the survivors of the group cannot be met from such funds if any other payments are made from it on behalf of the participants, such as death benefits, prior to the time the annuities are contemplated to begin.*

It has been shown that according to the 1937 Standard Annuity Table only 75 of our original 100 employees are expected to survive and to receive pensions at 65. Because of the 25 deaths which are expected to occur before retirement, less funds will be necessary to provide pensions to the survivors by the operation of this mortality. On the assumption that the pension benefits are to be funded, paid for in advance, some interest will be earned on the funds from the inception of the plan until retirements have taken place. The period of deferment in the present case is from age 45 to 65, or twenty years.

If use is made of an interest factor of 2% and the 1937 Standard Annuity Table is employed to discount for mortality before and after retirement, the computation of a deferred life annuity may be shown synoptically as follows: (1) at age 65 the value of a life annuity *due* to pay $1.00 per year based on the 1937 Standard Annuity Table and 2% interest is $12.51. The discounted or present value of $100 due 20 years hence at 2% is $67.30 (see Table VI), or $.6730 per $1.00. The cost at age 45 of a life annuity to pay $100 with first payment commencing at age 65 is therefore, $100 × 12.51 × .6730 = $841.92. So far we have taken account of interest prior to retirement and of interest and mortality after retirement; (2) to take care of the mortality before retirement we have assumed that at age 65 there will be payable a pension benefit of $100 a year for life to each of 75 employees, the survivors of the original group of

100 employees aged 45. There may be credited then to the pension fund, 20 years in advance of retirement when the employees are age 45, the amount of $63,144 which will be adequate to pay a life annuity of $100 to the 75 survivors at age 65. In equation form, properly carried out and showing mortality and interest previous to retirement and thereafter, it appears:

$$100 \times .75 \times \$.6730 \times \$12.51 \times \$100 = \$63,144.$$

Or, the number of original entrants at age 45; times the probability of survival to 65; times the present value of $1.00 at 45 due 20 years hence at 2%; times the value of a life annuity due of $1.00 at 65; times the amount of life annuity payable, equals the estimated value of the twenty-year deferred life annuities of $100 for the survivors of the group of the 100 original employees. The estimated value of twenty-year deferred life annuities of $200 for 100 employees now age 45 would of course be $126,288 (2 × $63,144). The latter figure is given merely to show that the principles of computation remain the same; the result is affected only by the amount of the pension benefits to be provided.

## C. Withdrawal Rates

An allowance for withdrawals in estimating pension costs relates to the rate of turnover among employees. Thus far we have assumed that less funds will be necessary to provide the pension benefits as a result of assumed mortality rates before and after retirement, and as a result of interest. A further discount is possible on the assumption that among a group of employees taken at any age there will be some who will voluntarily or by discharge have their employment terminated before retirement. This will occur among employees whether they are participants in a pension plan or not, although the pension plan itself may decrease the rate of turnover. The factors that influence turnover are numerous but for our purposes need not be analyzed here. Our interest lies in the fact that, whatever the withdrawal rate may be among employees, it may be possible to take account of it in estimating pension costs.

The actuarial methods of taking account of withdrawals may differ, but the problem is analogous to estimating the effect of mortality. A table of withdrawal rates may be constructed from the experience of a particular employer contemplating a pension plan. If the necessary data are lacking then they may be prepared from the experience in some similar enterprise or industry. After the withdrawal rates have been calculated they may be combined with the mortality rates at each age and the resulting rates applied to the group under consideration, to determine the total number of employees whose service will have been terminated by death and withdrawal prior to retirement.[2]

In our example, we shall assume that 40 employees either will die while in service or withdraw prior to age 65. This leaves only 60 employees at age 65 to receive pensions. If we combine a discount for withdrawals with one for mortality, our equation is reconstructed as follows:

$$100 \times .60 \times \$.6730 \times \$12.51 \times \$100 = \$50,515.$$

A discount taken for *withdrawals* further reduces the estimated costs in our example below the figure of $63,144, which took discounts only for interest and mortality before and after retirement.

## D. Salary Scale

In most pension plans the benefits usually are related to the basic salaries or wages received by the individual employees during the period of employment. At the inception of a plan the actual salaries or wages paid are known, but thereafter there will occur increases which also must be considered. Account may be taken of such salary increases as they occur, or they may be estimated in advance. In the latter case it becomes necessary to construct a table showing the rates of salary increases which will develop during employment.[3] Again, to construct such a table, salary data from the employer for whom the plan is being formulated should be used, or the estimates should be made from the wage and salary experience of some similar enterprise.

The effect of allowing for salary increases in advance will be to raise the estimated pension costs more or less, the amount dependent on the method employed to take account of such increases and the conservatism of the forecasts. For example, let us assume that of our 100 employees each receives at 45 a salary of $1,000 a year. If an annual increase of $25 a year is projected until retirement, the total salary per individual for the twenty years will be $24,750. If the increase is to be $50 a year per employee the total salary will be $29,500. A pension benefit of 1% of total salary will

---

[2] See page 178 for illustrative table of withdrawal rates.
[3] See table, page 178.

provide at 65 a life pension of $247.50, based on a salary increase of $25 annually; of $295 at 65, based on an increase of $50 a year. The estimated pension costs therefore will be influenced by the salary scale that it is assumed will prevail over the period of employment, if the pension benefits are related thereto.

### E.  Methods of Funding

In describing a method by which discount for mortality before and after retirement might be taken into account, the use of the deferred life annuity was illustrated. It was shown that the cost of a life income of $100 a year to commence at 65 for each of 100 employees now aged 45 would be $63,144. The mortality table employed was the 1937 Standard Annuity Table with the assumed rate of interest of 2%, and also with the assumption that no withdrawals would occur. If the pension benefits actually were purchased out of hand, that is, by the payment of a lump sum, the illustration might stand. As a matter of fact it would be unusual to find an employer in a position to make the capital outlay necessary to purchase the pension benefits by payment in a lump sum. As was indicated, if the pension benefit had been $200 a year to each of the 100 employees, with no discount for withdrawals, the immediate capital outlay would have been $126,288.

The necessity of a single capital outlay for the purchase of pension benefits has been obviated by actuarial methods of funding, which allow pension funds to be accumulated in installments. In other words, instead of using a lump sum purchase method, annual contributions may be made by an employer in relatively small amounts, which will be adequate nevertheless to provide the pension benefits promised. There are several such methods of funding which, while they have the common characteristic that each allows for what is essentially an installment purchase of the pension benefits, are dissimilar in major respects. These dissimilarities may produce widely different statements of the initial cost, or financial outlay, that an employer must make to inaugurate a plan. The explanation that follows, therefore, is given to indicate that estimates of initial cost showing wide differences (apart from differences resulting from diverse assumptions as to probable interest earnings, anticipated mortality, and so forth) may be accounted for by the fact that different funding methods were employed.

Of these funding methods the ones which are most commonly used are known as the (1) single-premium deferred life annuity,

(2) level percentage of payroll, and (3) level premium accumulation.

### 1. Single-Premium Deferred Life Annuity Method

Let us return to our group of 100 employees and make several further assumptions. For each employee upon retirement at age 65 there will be assumed an annual pension benefit equal to 1% of the total salary received during employment; a salary that will remain constant at $1,000 a year; no withdrawal, other than that caused by death; a pension that is to be purchased by the yearly acquisition of single-premium deferred life annuities. The mortality table to be used will be again the 1937 Standard Annuity Table with interest at 2%.

The pension benefit to each of the 100 employees who survive to 65, based on the above assumption, will be 1% of his total salary.

TABLE X

CALCULATION OF ANNUAL DEPOSITS REQUIRED UNDER SINGLE-PREMIUM
DEFERRED LIFE ANNUITY METHOD

| Age (1) | Number of Employees Surviving at Each Age (2) | Amount of Pension Accruing Between Each Age (3) | Value at the Age Shown of a Deferred Life Annuity of $1 per Year, First Payment Commencing at Age 65 (4) | Single Premiums to Purchase all Pensions which Accrue During the Year (5) |
|---|---|---|---|---|
| 45....... | 100 | $1,000 | $ 6.32 | $6,320 |
| 46....... | 99 | 990 | 6.53 | 6,465 |
| 47....... | 99 | 990 | 6.66 | 6,593 |
| 48....... | 98 | 980 | 6.88 | 6,742 |
| 49....... | 97 | 970 | 7.02 | 6,809 |
| 50....... | 96 | 960 | 7.26 | 6,970 |
| 51....... | 95 | 950 | 7.49 | 7,116 |
| 52....... | 94 | 940 | 7.73 | 7,266 |
| 53....... | 93 | 930 | 7.99 | 7,431 |
| 54....... | 92 | 920 | 8.26 | 7,599 |
| 55....... | 91 | 910 | 8.42 | 7,662 |
| 56....... | 90 | 900 | 8.69 | 7,821 |
| 57....... | 89 | 890 | 8.97 | 7,983 |
| 58....... | 87 | 870 | · 9.37 | 8,152 |
| 59....... | 86 | 860 | 9.67 | 8,316 |
| 60....... | 84 | 840 | 10.08 | 8,467 |
| 61....... | 83 | 830 | 10.40 | 8,632 |
| 62....... | 81 | 810 | 10.96 | 8,878 |
| 63....... | 79 | 790 | 11.42 | 9,022 |
| 64....... | 77 | 770 | 11.90 | 9,163 |
| TOTAL .... | | | | $153,407 |

of $20,000 (20 × $1,000) or $200 a year. The purchase of benefits will be made each year, as earned, for each of those who survive from year to year. This method of purchase is in contrast to that used above, where $126,288 also bought a benefit of $200 a year commencing at 65, payable for life to each of the survivors of the entire group. Although the payment was made in one sum, and the entire transaction concluded with no further payments contemplated, this also involved the use of a single-premium deferred life annuity, the $126,288 being the single premium. Where the benefit, however, is to be purchased yearly, there is employed a *series* of single-premium deferred life annuities. In the present instance, therefore, we wish to purchase each year a single-premium deferred life annuity which will provide at 65 an amount equal to 1% of the salary earned during the year by each of the surviving employees, so that at 65 each of the survivors will be provided a $200 per year (1% × $1,000 × 20 years) life annuity. The method of calculation of the single-premium deferred life annuity already has been shown and needs no reiteration.

If the premiums in column 5 of Table X were accumulated in a fund at 2%, from the ages at which they were contributed to age 65, the amount of the fund at age 65 would be $187,669. It is this sum which is needed at age 65 to provide a $200 per year pension for each of the 75 survivors; that is, 75 (survivors) × $200 (benefit) × $12.51 (value of a life annuity due to pay $1.00 at 65) equals $187,650. The difference between the two figures $187,669 and $187,650 is due to the carrying throughout of a reduced number of significant figures in making the calculations.

Table X itself reveals several things. First of all, the single premiums paid each year should be sufficient, on the basis of the assumptions made, to provide a benefit of 1% of salary to each surviving employee at age 65. A 1% benefit of $20,000, the total salary received by each employee, equals $200. For the 75 surviving employees the benefit commencing at age 65 is $15,000, which will have been provided by the total of the single premiums or $153,407. Secondly, it should be noted that each single premium (column 5) is a complete purchase at each age, in and of itself, of a benefit commencing at 65 of 1% of the total salaries paid during the year. The entire premium outlay of $153,407, the sum of the series of single premiums, may be contrasted with $126,288,[4] the amount required if the entire benefit of $15,000 commencing at

[4] See page 79.

65 were to have been purchased by a one-sum payment. The method of funding pension benefits, by use of a *series* of single-premium deferred life annuity purchases, is a convenient and practical way for an employer to finance his pension plan. It must be recognized, however, that the outlay is higher than when the purchase is made by the one-sum method, because of a loss of interest earnings resulting from the stretching of payments over a twenty-year period.

## 2. Level Percentage of Payroll Method

In illustrating the level percentage of payroll method, we retain the same assumptions made in showing the single-premium deferred life annuity method. Account is taken of mortality, using the 1937 Standard Annuity Table with interest at 2%. The salary of each employee is $1,000 a year, so the payroll each year will be the number of surviving employees for that year multiplied by $1,000. Thus at age 45 there are 100 employees receiving 100 × $1,000 or a total of $100,000. In order to simplify it will be assumed that deaths will occur immediately prior to attaining the next age. Thus at the age of 46, according to our mortality table, there will be 99 survivors. Each earns $1,000, so the payroll for the second year will be $99,000. This procedure carried out for each succeeding year, until the survivors attain 65, enables us to determine the total payroll for each year. The next step is to accumulate the yearly payroll of the survivors at 2% interest until they attain 65; this amount will be $2,261,913.

In the use of a series of single-premium deferred life annuities to provide the pensions, it will be recalled that the total fund necessary at 65 to provide the benefits was $187,650. We must determine now what percentage applied to the payroll each year will accumulate to $187,650. We know that the total payroll of the survivors of the group accumulated each year at 2% to age 65 equals $2,261,913. Thus 8.296% of the payroll will accumulate to $187,650, since $187,650 ÷ $2,261,913 equals .08296. The actual amount required annually under the level percentage of payroll method is shown in Table XI.

If we accumulate the annual deposits in Table XI (column 3) at 2% interest from the age at which they were made until 65, the accumulated funds will then amount to $187,645. Again, the slight discrepancy from $187,650 is simply due to the fact that a reduced number of significant figures were used in the calculations.

TABLE XI

CALCULATION OF ANNUAL DEPOSITS REQUIRED UNDER THE
LEVEL PERCENTAGE OF PAYROLL METHOD

| Attained Age (1) | Amount of Payroll Each Year (2) | Amount Payable Each Year: 8.296% of Payroll (3) |
|---|---|---|
| 45 | $100,000 | $ 8,296 |
| 46 | 99,000 | 8,213 |
| 47 | 99,000 | 8,213 |
| 48 | 98,000 | 8,130 |
| 49 | 97,000 | 8,047 |
| 50 | 96,000 | 7,964 |
| 51 | 95,000 | 7,881 |
| 52 | 94,000 | 7,798 |
| 53 | 93,000 | 7,715 |
| 54 | 92,000 | 7,632 |
| 55 | 91,000 | 7,549 |
| 56 | 90,000 | 7,466 |
| 57 | 89,000 | 7,383 |
| 58 | 87,000 | 7,218 |
| 59 | 86,000 | 7,135 |
| 60 | 84,000 | 6,969 |
| 61 | 83,000 | 6,886 |
| 62 | 81,000 | 6,720 |
| 63 | 79,000 | 6,554 |
| 64 | 77,000 | 6,388 |
| TOTAL | | $150,157 |

It will be noticed that the outlay of $150,157 to purchase the pension benefits again exceeds the $126,288 which was needed to make a lump-sum purchase of the benefits, at age 45. The explanation, as in the case of using a series of single premiums, is that a loss of interest earnings has occurred by delaying payments until later years.

## 3. Level Premium Accumulation

Both the single-premium and the level percentage of payroll methods take account of or discount for mortality before retirement. The level premium accumulation method takes *no* discounts for mortality prior to retirement. The premise of this method, therefore, is that *all entrants will survive to retirement.* In our example, therefore, provision must be made for retirement benefits to 100 employees at 65. Under the level premium accumulation method we have what is equivalent to an individual deposit account set up for each employee. There is paid to it each year an amount which, at 2% compound interest, will be sufficient to purchase a life annuity of $200 a year at 65 for each of our 100 employees. The accumulated value of the accounts of employees who die before retirement are available to reduce the amounts necessary to be paid to provide the benefits for the surviving employees. Also, of course, upon the death of an employee further deposits for his account are discontinued. The process of calculation is similar to that used for the deferred life annuity, except that a discount for mortality as taken in the deferred life annuity is omitted; but as funds are released by the deaths of employees prior to retirement, credits are taken.

The first step is to find the cost of a life annuity *due* of $1.00 per year, commencing at 65. This amount, as we have seen, according to the 1937 Standard Annuity Table with interest at 2% equals $12.51. If $12.51 pays $1.00 a year for life at 65, then the benefit must be multiplied by this factor. The benefit commencing at 65 is $20,000 ($200 a year to each employee in the entire group of 100 original employees) or 1% of $2,000,000. The cost of the benefit is thus $12.51 × $20,000, or $250,200. Inasmuch as the employees are now age 45, interest will be earned before retirement. Thus the problem is to find the amount payable at the beginning of each year which will accumulate at 2% interest to $250,200 in 20 years. If we refer to any standard interest table we will find that $100 per year, payable in advance, accumulated for 20 years at 2% interest, will equal $2,478.33. Thus the amount required each year for 20 years will be $10,096 ($250,200 ÷ 24.7833).

While we have stated that there is no discount taken for mortality in the level premium accumulation method, when deaths occur, the future deposits will be affected thereby. In other words, the initial annual deposit of $10,096 is required only so long as all of the 100 employees are alive; or per living employee there is required a level deposit of $100.96. As soon as a death occurs the annual deposit of $10,096 is reduced by $100.96. Therefore if we use the same assumptions as previously relative to mortality, only 99 employees will survive to age 46. The second year total deposits consequently would be equal to $9,995 (99 × $100.96), except for one further adjustment. There was initially paid in on behalf of the deceased employee $100.96, which at the end of the first year with interest at 2% will amount to $102.98. We will round this to $103 to simplify the illustration. This $103, which is available because of the death of the employee, will not be needed to provide pensions, and thus it will further reduce the second year deposits for the survivors from $9,995 to $9,892 ($9,995—$103). Similar calculations may be carried out until the twentieth year, which will disclose the expected annual deposits until retirement. They are shown in Table XII.

TABLE XII

CALCULATION OF ANNUAL DEPOSITS REQUIRED UNDER THE
LEVEL PREMIUM ACCUMULATION METHOD

| Attained Age (1) | Number of Survivors at Each Age (2) | Estimated Amount of Outlay Based on $100.96 per Survivor (3) | Accumulation of Premiums for One Employee from Age 45 to the Attained Age (4) | Number of Deaths at Each Age (5) | Amount of Funds Released at Each Age by Deaths (6) | Actual Net Deposits for Each Year (7) |
|---|---|---|---|---|---|---|
| 45........ | 100 | $10,096 | $ 103 | 1 | $ 103 | $10,096 |
| 46........ | 99 | 9,995 | 208 | — | — | 9,892 |
| 47........ | 99 | 9,995 | 315 | 1 | 315 | 9,995 |
| 48........ | 98 | 9,894 | 424 | 1 | 424 | 9,579 |
| 49........ | 97 | 9,793 | 536 | 1 | 536 | 9,369 |
| 50........ | 96 | 9,692 | 650 | 1 | 650 | 9,156 |
| 51........ | 95 | 9,591 | 766 | 1 | 766 | 8,941 |
| 52........ | 94 | 9,490 | 884 | 1 | 884 | 8,724 |
| 53........ | 93 | 9,389 | 1,005 | 1 | 1,005 | 8,505 |
| 54........ | 92 | 9,288 | 1,128 | 1 | 1,128 | 8,283 |
| 55........ | 91 | 9,187 | 1,253 | 1 | 1,253 | 8,059 |
| 56........ | 90 | 9,086 | 1,381 | 1 | 1,381 | 7,833 |
| 57........ | 89 | 8,985 | 1,512 | 2 | 3,024 | 7,604 |
| 58........ | 87 | 8,784 | 1,645 | 1 | 1,645 | 5,760 |
| 59........ | 86 | 8,683 | 1,781 | 2 | 3,562 | 7,038 |
| 60........ | 84 | 8,481 | 1,919 | 1 | 1,919 | 4,919 |
| 61........ | 83 | 8,380 | 2,061 | 2 | 4,122 | 6,461 |
| 62........ | 81 | 8,178 | 2,205 | 2 | 4,410 | 4,056 |
| 63........ | 79 | 7,976 | 2,352 | 2 | 4,704 | 3,566 |
| 64........ | 77 | 7,774 | 2,502 | 2 | 5,004 | 3,070 |
| 65........ | 75 | | | | | −5,004 |
| TOTAL..... | | | | | | $145,902 |

In Table XII the minus figure of $5,004 (column 7), illustrated at age 65, arises because of credits taken for employees who die between the ages of 64 and 65. Since there is no deposit required at 65 this sum, $5,004, is returnable to the employer so far as this illustration is concerned. Once more; if we accumulate the net annual deposits or premiums paid each year, to the year when all

surviving employees attain age 65, the value of the fund will be
$187,657. This is approximately the $187,650, estimated to be
needed to pay $200 for life to each of the 75 survivors who reach
age 65.

## 4. Recapitulation

The yearly outlays, under the various methods of funding a pension plan which we have analyzed, are summarized below:

TABLE XIII[5]

SUMMARY TABLE: FUNDING METHODS

| Age | Single-Premium Deferred Life Annuity | Level Percentage of Payroll | Level Premium Accumulation |
|---|---|---|---|
| 45 | $6,320 | $8,296 | $10,096 |
| 46 | 6,465 | 8,213 | 9,892 |
| 47 | 6,593 | 8,213 | 9,995 |
| 48 | 6,742 | 8,130 | 9,579 |
| 49 | 6,809 | 8,047 | 9,369 |
| 50 | 6,970 | 7,964 | 9,156 |
| 51 | 7,116 | 7,881 | 8,941 |
| 52 | 7,266 | 7,798 | 8,724 |
| 53 | 7,431 | 7,715 | 8,505 |
| 54 | 7,599 | 7,632 | 8,283 |
| 55 | 7,662 | 7,549 | 8,059 |
| 56 | 7,821 | 7,466 | 7,833 |
| 57 | 7,983 | 7,383 | 7,604 |
| 58 | 8,152 | 7,218 | 5,760 |
| 59 | 8,316 | 7,135 | 7,038 |
| 60 | 8,467 | 6,969 | 4,919 |
| 61 | 8,632 | 6,886 | 6,461 |
| 62 | 8,878 | 6,720 | 4,056 |
| 63 | 9,022 | 6,554 | 3,566 |
| 64 | 9,163 | 6,388 | 3,070 |
| 65 | | | — 5,004 |
| TOTAL | $153,407 | $150,157 | $145,902 |
| Annual deposits accumulated at 2% Interest | $187,669 | $187,645 | $187,657 |

[5] To restate the assumptions on which the financial outlays shown in the table are based: (1) the number of male employees entering the plan, 100; (2) all employees enter the pension plan at age 45; (3) level annual salary to each employee, $1000 a year; (4) benefit at retirement at age 65, 1% of total salary, or $200 a year for life; (5) mortality rates based on 1937 Standard Annuity Table; (6) interest at 2%.

The differences in the yearly outlays as revealed by the above tables are accounted for by the method of payment. In each instance the annual deposits accumulated at 2% create a fund at 65 of approximately $187,650, the amount needed to pay 75 surviving employees $200 a year for life.

The analysis which we have made, as summarized in the table, was for the major and fundamental need of showing that differences in initial costs, as presented to an employer, may be misleading unless there is a clear understanding that they may be caused by the use of different methods of funding, as well as by diverse assumptions, in making a valuation. *It should be understood that all estimates or valuations of pension costs would present an employer with the same initial costs, if the same methods of funding were employed, and if the assumptions as to mortality, rates of interest, withdrawal rates, salary scales, benefits under the plan, and expense of operating the plan were identical.* Thus, while wide differences in *initial* pension costs, which have been shown in the above illustrations, may be accounted for as a result of the use of different methods of funding, *further* differences might result if, in addition, diverse assumptions were made as to probable interest earnings, anticipated mortality, and so forth.

It may be properly asked at this point which method of funding is preferable. It probably is impossible to provide a categorical answer to the question. The employer's circumstances, general economic conditions, as well as the types of benefits an employer wishes to provide under his pension plan, may determine the method of funding to be adopted. More particularly, however, if an employer selects an insured type of pension plan he will find that his choice will be normally between the single-premium deferred life annuity or the level accumulation methods of funding. If an employer utilizes a self-administered plan, then there may be employed any of the funding methods described, although the level percentage of payroll method is associated with self-administration. In later chapters[6] the several funding methods are discussed again in relation to the types of pension plans with which they are associated.

## II. PAST SERVICE FUNDING

The foregoing description of funding, and the several methods which may be employed, were related to the provision of pension benefits for a group of employees entering a pension plan at 45 and retiring at 65. In practice no such situation is likely to be en-

---

[6] See Chapters VI, VII, and VIII.

countered. Employee groups will differ widely both as to age, sex, and years of service with a particular employer. If a benefit for future service only were provided, such as in our example, it might be inadequate to retire older employees. A 1% benefit of annual salary for future service, in the example given, served to provide a total benefit of 1% of total earnings or $200 a year at retirement. Obviously a higher percentage of salary must be granted for future service (except where Social Security benefits are available for the lower salary brackets), or some other formula must be selected to produce an adequate pension. In lieu of raising the percentage of salary benefit for future service, a credit frequently is granted for past service.

If we assume that all of our 100 employees have had 20 years of past service, a credit of .5% for each year of such service would entitle each employee to an additional benefit of 10% of his annual salary as of the effective date of the plan. The future service benefit of 1% of his annual salary plus the past service credits equals 30%. While even this, in the absence of Social Security coverage, would not produce an adequate pension benefit, the illustration is useful for the purpose of discussing methods of funding past service.

All that has been said in connection with methods of funding pension plans, although discussed in reference to future service of employees, is largely applicable to the financing of past service. The cost at age 45 of the past service benefit may be financed like the future service benefit by a series of single-premium deferred life annuity purchases, by the level percentage of payroll, or the level premium accumulation method. In any case, past service benefits normally must be purchased by the time they become payable. In cases where retirement of certain employees is to be immediate, that is, of those who are already at the selected retirement age, use may be made of immediate life annuities to provide the benefits.

## III. COSTS

### A. In Operation

Upon the installation of a pension plan there become operative the factors whose effect, dependent on the valuation methods employed, have been anticipated. Interest is earned, deaths occur, withdrawals take place, salaries are increased or decreased, new employees enter the plan, and so forth. If the interest earned is higher than had been anticipated the costs are reduced. If the costs have been discounted for mortality, and it is lower than expected, costs will increase. As withdrawals of employees occur, funds may be released which may be applied to reduce the costs (subject to vesting or withdrawal benefits included in the pension plan) unless the costs were already discounted for withdrawals. It is obvious that there may be some deviation in actual experience from what was anticipated in the valuation. As a consequence there are apt to be some increases or decreases in the yearly outlays for the pension benefits independent of the method of funding.

To further bring out the point that the yearly outlays may fluctuate regardless of method of funding, we may refer to our example in which the single-premium deferred life annuity method is used, with future mortality taken into account. A withdrawal from employment of one or more employees before the group reaches age 46 could lower the single-premium outlay required at age 46. There could be released, as a result of the withdrawal, the amount of premium paid in behalf of the withdrawn employee plus accumulated interest. This could be applied to reduce the total premium outlay at age 46. The costs under the level percentage of payroll and level premium accumulation methods might be altered for the same reason.

## B. Initial

The brief explanation of different procedures in making pension valuations has indicated the possible wide range of estimates of initial cost which may result simply from using different methods of funding.[7] The fact is, however, that only after a plan has been in operation for a considerable time, and only then, can the accuracy of an actuarial estimate be determined. It is not to be concluded, however, from this statement that actuarial valuations, or estimates of cost, lack reality. A conservative actuarial valuation of pension costs is more likely to overstate than to understate them. Overstatement of costs can result in no injury but in fact may be beneficial to an employer in a high tax period, although it might deter him from undertaking a pension plan. If understatement of costs has occurred in the estimates, however, serious difficulties may

[7] For an illustration of the different initial cost estimates which arise from differing assumptions as to interest rates, mortality, withdrawal rates, salary scale, and so forth, using, however, the *same* method of funding, level percentage of payroll, see Myers, Robert J., "Some Considerations in Pension Fund Valuations," *Transactions of the Actuarial Society of America*, Vol. 46, Part I, pp. 51-58.

be in store for the pension fund unless a correction or revision of estimated costs is made. Such an underestimate may arise, for example, because of a misappraisal of long-term interest rates; or because the mortality among the older age employees may be less than had been expected. In either of these events impairment of the pension funds may develop. It must be said, however, that, in lieu of actuarial valuation, there would have to be substituted merely guesswork. In the past such guesswork has proved a poor substitute for actuarial methods.

### C. Payroll as a Measure

Usually pension costs are described in terms of a percentage of the payroll of the employees participating in the plan. While some other measure could be used, such as to describe them in terms of cost per share of stock, or as a percentage of the cost of production, the description of cost in terms of percentage of payroll is customary. If we again revert to our illustration, using the table on page 88, the relation of the outlays to payroll is apparent. Under the single-premium deferred life annuity method, the *initial* cost as a percentage of the payroll of $100,000 for the 100 employees is 6.32%; under the level percentage of payroll, 8.30%; under the level premium accumulation, 10.10%.

In these percentages we have apparently different costs. To reiterate, the fact is that in actual operation the pension costs will be the same if the terms of the pension plans are the same (excluding what expense may be), allowing for an actual differential in interest earnings because of the method of funding. For example, if the level percentage of payroll method has discounted for mortality and withdrawals from employment, then under the level premium accumulation method the premiums will be reduced as these events of death and withdrawal occur. Moreover, the cash accumulated for the accounts of deceased employees may be used to reduce further the future annual premiums. Likewise, the premiums under the single-premium deferred life annuity will decline when withdrawals occur, although, as in the case of the level percentage of payroll method, it has anticipated future mortality.

In commercial estimates of pension costs a similar wide variation, which we have indicated as possible theoretical differences, will be found to prevail. The employer may, therefore, be startled to find that an estimate of initial cost by the level premium accumulation method is almost twice that of the single-premium deferred life or of the level percentage of payroll method. In short, an initial cost estimate by the level premium accumulation method may be 18% of the payroll of the group covered, and by the single-premium method, 9%.[8]

Finally, in noting the percentage of payroll differences which may result from using different methods of funding, it must not be overlooked that differences in estimates of initial costs also may be accounted for by the assumption of different rates of mortality and interest, *even when the method of funding is the same.* In addition, there are other factors, such as the amount of retirement benefits and the provision for withdrawal benefits, that may narrow or widen the percentage of payroll spread. Again, the amount of expense that is allowed or charged will be an influencing element.

The most that can be said as a closing generalization is that, when an employer obtains an actuarial valuation of his initial pension costs wherein the three funding methods described are separately employed, it may be possible that he will be presented with statements of initial costs with differences ranging from 8% to 20% of the payroll of the employee-group covered under his plan.

---

[8] It will be noted that the initial cost has been stated as a percentage "of the payroll of the group covered." In our illustration the 100 employees were considered as the entire personnel. However, because of the use of eligibility rules (see Chapter IX), only part of the personnel may be eligible or members of the pension plan upon its establishment, or, for that matter, after it has been in operation. The initial cost, therefore, as a percentage of the *total* payroll, may be reduced. Expressed as a percentage of *total* payroll the initial costs, as given above, might be reduced possibly 30% to 80% depending on the eligibility rules.

# CHAPTER V

## Social Security Pension Benefits

••••••••••••••••••••••••••••••••••••••••••••••••••••••••••••••••••••••••••••••••

THE SOCIAL SECURITY ACT, PASSED IN 1935, PROVIDED FOR GRANTS IN aid to the States for old-age assistance, unemployment insurance, aid to the blind, maternal and child welfare, dependent children, and public health work. Most important for pension planning purposes was the provision for a system of federal old-age benefits (Title II). A Social Security board was created and provision was made for the levying of payroll taxes to finance unemployment insurance and federal old-age benefits. The provision in the act for unemployment insurance and federal old-age benefits marked the entrance of the Federal government into the field of social insurance. In 1939 the act was amended, with particular reference to federal old-age benefits (Title II). The amendment provided for their administration under the Bureau of Old-Age and Survivors Insurance. The benefits were broadened to provide—in addition to old-age benefits for workers—a survivors' benefit to widows, widows and children, children, or parents of deceased workers covered under the act. A trust fund, known as the Federal Old-Age and Survivors Insurance Trust Fund, in which are accumulated the funds necessary to pay the benefits, was set up in the Treasury. Finally, the imposition of payroll taxes and provision for their collection was provided for under what is designated as the Federal Insurance Contributions Act (Internal Revenue Code, Chapter 9, Sub-chapter A).

It is with the old-age benefits, provided to workers who are covered under Title II of the Social Security Act, that we are concerned. Private pension plans are presently designed in relation to whether an employee group is covered by Social Security (old age and survivors' insurance) or not. While not many groups are excluded from coverage, in total numbers they are an important segment of the working population.[1] The principal groups excluded are agricultural laborers, domestic servants, and employees covered by the Railroad Retirement Act; also, employees of the Federal, State, and local governments, of nonprofit organizations engaged exclusively in religious, charitable, educational, or scientific activities, casual laborers of certain types, and the self-employed.

If an employee group is not covered by Social Security benefits the scale of pension benefits provided under private pension plans will normally be relatively larger in amount than for covered groups. Again, if employees are to contribute to a pension plan, their contributions may be larger where no deductions are made from their wages or salaries for Social Security taxes.

## I. KINDS OF BENEFITS—INSURED STATUS

In general the benefits of Social Security are *primary, supplementary*, and *survivors'* benefits. A worker, however, must achieve an insured status before he may qualify for primary benefits, or before his dependents or survivors may be permitted to establish eligibility for supplementary or survivors' benefits.

### A. Insured Worker

*Currently Insured.* A worker is said to be "currently insured" if he has received under covered employment not less than $50 for each of not less than 6 of the 12 calendar quarters immediately preceding the quarter in which he died.[2]

*Fully Insured.* A "fully insured" worker is one who has had not less than one quarter of coverage for each two of the quarters elapsed after 1936 or after the quarter in which he attained age twenty-one, whichever quarter is later, and up to but excluding the quarter in which he has attained the age of sixty-five, or died, whichever first occurs, and in no case less than six quarters of coverage; or has had at least forty quarters of coverage.

---

[1] Not covered by Old-Age and Survivors Insurance, estimated 1944 total—21.4 million; made-up as follows in millions:

| | |
|---|---|
| Railroad | 1.4 |
| Federal government | 2.7 |
| State and local governments | 2.9 |
| Agriculture | 8.1 |
| Nonagricultural self-employed | 4.5 |
| Domestic service, nonprofit, etc. | 1.8 |

See *Social Security Bulletin*, Vol. 8, No. 4, April, 1945, p. 38.

[2] For claims filed after December 31, 1946, it is to be $50.00 paid *in* a quarter; and includes 6 of the last 12, *including the quarter* in which the worker died.

*Quarters of Coverage.* A "quarter of coverage" is (1) any calendar quarter in which a worker is paid at least $50 in *taxable* wages; or (2) any quarter after the first quarter of coverage in the same calendar year in which a worker receives $3,000 in taxable wages, if alive at the end of such quarter.

## B. Kinds of Benefits

*Primary Benefit.* A primary benefit is one to which a fully insured worker becomes eligible at age 65, and is also the amount on which all benefits payable to dependents or survivors of the fully insured worker are based.

*Supplementary Benefits.* A supplementary benefit is a monthly income benefit to which the wife or child of a living primary beneficiary (the worker) *may* become entitled.

*Survivors' Benefits.* The survivors of an insured worker who may become entitled to benefits (subject to their meeting certain conditions) are (1) his widow, with a child under 18 of the deceased worker in her care; (2) his child or children; (3) his widow, if she is age 65 or over, regardless of whether or not she has a child in her care, and (4) a dependent parent, or dependent parents. The survivors' benefits (3) and (4), are conditioned on the worker having been fully insured; whereas the benefits under (1) and (2) are payable if the worker was either currently or fully insured at his death. The amount of the survivor's benefits will depend on the *taxable* wages which had been received by the deceased worker.

Inasmuch as we are concerned with pension or retirement benefits, only an elaboration of the method of computing a worker's primary benefits will be undertaken, with a brief reference to supplementary benefits which may become payable to the wife of a worker during the latter's lifetime.

## II. PRIMARY BENEFITS

The method of computing a worker's primary benefit is simple, and will be shown. As we have stated, a worker, to qualify for benefits at 65, must have been in covered employment for at least 6 calendar quarters, although once he has to his credit 40 quarters of coverage (not necessarily consecutive) he remains qualified for life. However, he must have been paid at least $50.00 in a calendar quarter in order that it be counted as covered. In addition, the worker must no longer work after the payment of benefits commences. He is regarded as "working" if he earns more than $14.99

a month, but not if he is employed at a job which has been excluded from covered employment, such as agricultural labor or domestic service.

The general formula for calculating primary benefits involves two steps: (1) a determination of the average monthly wage received from the time the law became effective (January 1, 1937) to the quarter in which the worker qualifies for benefits, whether at 65 or later, (2) application of a specific formula to the average wage to determine the amount of the monthly old age or retirement benefit.

## A. Determination of Average Wage

To arrive at his average monthly wage a worker adds up all taxable wages received from January 1, 1937 to the quarter in which he qualifies. He divides this amount by the number of months in the period from January 1, 1937 to the quarter in which he qualifies. There are two exceptions. A worker who was age 65 before 1939 cannot add the wages received between his sixty-fifth birthday and January 1, 1939; nor, in dividing his total wages by months, is he required to include the months after he had reached 65 and before January 1, 1939. This exclusion comes from the fact that the original law did not count wages earned after age 65; although there is no limit today, as a result of the 1939 amendment. The second exception to the general rules applies to the young worker who reached his twenty-second birthday after January 1, 1937. He may add up all wages received to the time he qualifies or makes claim for benefits, but in dividing by months, to arrive at his average monthly wage, he may leave out any quarter before he became 22 in which he received less than $50.00.

## B. Determination of Monthly Benefit

After the average monthly wage is computed the monthly benefit may be calculated. The steps are as follows: (a) take 40% of the first $50.00 of the average monthly wage; (b) then take 10% of the balance of the average wage, but no more than $200 of such balance; (c) add the results of (a) and (b) together; (d) finally, take 1% of the sum arrived at in step (c) for each year in which $200 or more has been paid, and add this to the sum obtained under step (c). The result is the monthly retirement benefit. In case the average monthly wage proves to be less than $50 a month, then 40% of the lesser amount is taken; to this amount is added 1% of it for each year in which wages paid were $200 or more.

We may illustrate the calculation of the benefit by taking two workers who have fully qualified for a pension benefit at 65. One will be assumed to have averaged $100 a month, and the other $250 a month. The period of coverage will be taken as 10 years for each worker.

*WORKER A*

| | |
|---|---|
| Average Monthly Earnings.......................................... | $100.00 |
| (a) 40% of the first $50.00.................................. | $20.00 |
| (b) 10% of the remaining $50.00............................ | 5.00 |
| | |
| (c) .................................................... | $25.00 |
| (d) Add 10% (1% × 10 years) of $25.00 (c).................. | 2.50 |
| | |
| Total Monthly (Primary) Benefit at 65......................... | $27.50 |

*WORKER B*

| | |
|---|---|
| Average Monthly Earnings.......................................... | $250.00 |
| (a) 40% of the first $50.00.................................. | $20.00 |
| (b) 10% of (no more than) $200............................ | 20.00 |
| | |
| (c) .................................................... | $40.00 |
| (d) Add 10% (1% × 10 years) of $40.00 (c).................. | 4.00 |
| | |
| Total Monthly (Primary) Benefit at 65......................... | $44.00 |

## C.  Supplementary Benefit to Wife

The wife of a worker entitled to primary benefits also may receive a benefit at age 65, subject to certain conditions. She must be living with, or be supported by, her husband at the time of the filing of a claim; and she must not be entitled, on her own account as a covered worker, to a benefit equal to or greater than her benefits as a wife. A wife's benefit at 65, if she meets these conditions, will be equal to one-half of the primary benefit payable to her husband. For example, in the case of worker *A*, the wife's benefit would equal $13.75 (½ of $27.50). The joint income receivable by the husband and wife would therefore equal $41.25 a month. For worker *B*, the wife's benefit would be $22.00 or a joint income to the husband and wife of $66.00 a month would be received. In Table XIV-A there is shown the primary or retirement benefits to a worker at 65, based on a certain average monthly wage, and years of coverage. Table XIV-B shows the joint income receivable by a worker and his wife, both age 65, likewise based on the primary benefits of the husband. The exact amount of a worker's primary benefit, and thus the benefit for a husband and wife, cannot be computed until the final returns are in; that is to say, until the total *taxable* wages earned and the quarters of coverage are known.

### D. Minimum Income

The minimum income that a worker may receive, who has qualified at 65 for a primary benefit, is $10.00 a month. For a worker and his wife the minimum income at 65 is $15.00 a month.

### E. Maximum Income

The maximum income to a worker is basically limited by the fact that for 1940 and thereafter, no more than $3,000 a year, or $250.00 a month of earnings, may be included in total wages as a basis for arriving at the average monthly wage. The largest monthly income a worker may receive, with sufficient years of coverage, is a maximum of about $60.00. For a worker and his wife the maximum possible income is one and one-half times the worker's primary benefit; and in any case not more than $85.00 a month, the legal maximum (Table XIV-B).

## III. SOCIAL SECURITY AS A BASIS FOR PENSION PLANNING

The formula for computing a worker's pension or retirement benefits plainly evidences the fact that it is weighted in favor of the lower paid workers. As the average wage rises the retirement benefit as a percentage of wages decreases rapidly. For example, an employee whose average monthly wage is $100.00 qualifies with 40 years of coverage for a monthly income of $35.00, or 35% of his average wage. With the same years of coverage an employee with an average wage of $250.00 receives $56.00, or approximately 22% of his average wage. Employees earning $4,000, $5,000, or $10,000 annually, if we reduce these figures to average monthly earnings, will receive benefits, based on forty years of coverage, of approximately 17%, 13%, and 7% respectively.

The benefits under Social Security for lower paid employees ($1,200 to $1,500), despite the fact that they represent a higher percentage of average wages, cannot be said to be anything more than enough to meet subsistence needs, even with the addition of the supplementary benefit that may become payable to a worker's wife. Essentially the purpose of the act was to provide no more than subsistence at retirement, and to that extent it may serve this general purpose.

## TABLE XIV-A

### SOCIAL SECURITY BENEFITS TO WORKER AT 65

| Years of Coverage | Average Monthly Wage of Worker | | | | | | | |
|---|---|---|---|---|---|---|---|---|
| | $50 | $100 | $125 | $150 | $175 | $200 | $225 | $250 |
| 5 | $21.00 | $26.25 | $28.88 | $31.50 | $34.13 | $36.75 | $39.38 | $42.00 |
| 6 | 21.20 | 26.50 | 29.15 | 31.80 | 34.45 | 37.10 | 39.75 | 42.40 |
| 7 | 21.40 | 26.75 | 29.43 | 32.10 | 34.78 | 37.45 | 40.13 | 42.80 |
| 8 | 21.60 | 27.00 | 29.70 | 32.40 | 35.10 | 37.80 | 40.50 | 43.20 |
| 9 | 21.80 | 27.25 | 29.98 | 32.70 | 35.43 | 38.15 | 40.88 | 43.60 |
| 10 | 22.00 | 27.50 | 30.25 | 33.00 | 35.75 | 38.50 | 41.25 | 44.00 |
| 11 | 22.20 | 27.75 | 30.53 | 33.30 | 36.08 | 38.85 | 41.63 | 44.40 |
| 12 | 22.40 | 28.00 | 30.80 | 33.60 | 36.40 | 39.20 | 42.00 | 44.80 |
| 13 | 22.60 | 28.25 | 31.08 | 33.90 | 36.73 | 39.55 | 42.38 | 45.20 |
| 14 | 22.80 | 28.50 | 31.35 | 34.20 | 37.05 | 39.90 | 42.75 | 45.60 |
| 15 | 23.00 | 28.75 | 31.63 | 34.50 | 37.38 | 40.25 | 43.13 | 46.00 |
| 16 | 23.20 | 29.00 | 31.90 | 34.80 | 37.70 | 40.60 | 43.50 | 46.40 |
| 17 | 23.40 | 29.25 | 32.18 | 35.10 | 38.03 | 40.95 | 43.88 | 46.80 |
| 18 | 23.60 | 29.50 | 32.45 | 35.40 | 38.35 | 41.30 | 44.25 | 47.20 |
| 19 | 23.80 | 29.75 | 32.73 | 35.70 | 38.68 | 41.65 | 44.63 | 47.60 |
| 20 | 24.00 | 30.00 | 33.00 | 36.00 | 39.00 | 42.00 | 45.00 | 48.00 |
| 21 | 24.20 | 30.25 | 33.28 | 36.30 | 39.33 | 42.35 | 45.38 | 48.40 |
| 22 | 24.40 | 30.50 | 33.55 | 36.60 | 39.65 | 42.70 | 45.75 | 48.80 |
| 23 | 24.60 | 30.75 | 33.83 | 36.90 | 39.98 | 43.05 | 46.13 | 49.20 |
| 24 | 24.80 | 31.00 | 34.10 | 37.20 | 40.30 | 43.40 | 46.50 | 49.60 |
| 25 | 25.00 | 31.25 | 34.38 | 37.50 | 40.63 | 43.75 | 46.88 | 50.00 |
| 26 | 25.20 | 31.50 | 34.65 | 37.80 | 40.95 | 44.10 | 47.25 | 50.40 |
| 27 | 25.40 | 31.75 | 34.93 | 38.10 | 41.28 | 44.45 | 47.63 | 50.80 |
| 28 | 25.60 | 32.00 | 35.20 | 38.40 | 41.60 | 44.80 | 48.00 | 51.20 |
| 29 | 25.80 | 32.25 | 35.48 | 38.70 | 41.93 | 45.15 | 48.38 | 51.60 |
| 30 | 26.00 | 32.50 | 35.75 | 39.00 | 42.25 | 45.50 | 48.75 | 52.00 |
| 31 | 26.20 | 32.75 | 36.03 | 39.30 | 42.58 | 45.85 | 49.13 | 52.40 |
| 32 | 26.40 | 33.00 | 36.30 | 39.60 | 42.90 | 46.20 | 49.50 | 52.80 |
| 33 | 26.60 | 33.25 | 36.58 | 39.90 | 43.23 | 46.55 | 49.88 | 53.20 |
| 34 | 26.80 | 33.50 | 36.85 | 40.20 | 43.55 | 46.90 | 50.25 | 53.60 |
| 35 | 27.00 | 33.75 | 37.13 | 40.50 | 43.88 | 47.25 | 50.63 | 54.00 |
| 36 | 27.20 | 34.00 | 37.40 | 40.80 | 44.20 | 47.60 | 51.00 | 54.40 |
| 37 | 27.40 | 34.25 | 37.68 | 41.10 | 44.53 | 47.95 | 51.38 | 54.80 |
| 38 | 27.60 | 34.50 | 37.95 | 41.40 | 44.85 | 48.30 | 51.75 | 55.20 |
| 39 | 27.80 | 34.75 | 38.23 | 41.70 | 45.18 | 48.65 | 52.13 | 55.60 |
| 40 | 28.00 | 35.00 | 38.50 | 42.00 | 45.50 | 49.00 | 52.50 | 56.00 |
| 41 | 28.20 | 35.25 | 38.78 | 42.30 | 45.83 | 49.35 | 52.88 | 56.40 |
| 42 | 28.40 | 35.50 | 39.05 | 42.60 | 46.15 | 49.70 | 53.25 | 56.80 |
| 43 | 28.60 | 35.75 | 39.33 | 42.90 | 46.48 | 50.05 | 53.63 | 57.20 |
| 44 | 28.80 | 36.00 | 39.60 | 43.20 | 46.80 | 50.40 | 54.00 | 57.60 |
| 45 | 29.00 | 36.25 | 39.88 | 43.50 | 47.13 | 50.75 | 54.38 | 58.00 |

## TABLE XIV–B

### Social Security Benefits to Worker and Wife at 65

| Years of Coverage | Average Monthly Wage of Worker | | | | | | | |
|---|---|---|---|---|---|---|---|---|
| | $50 | $100 | $125 | $150 | $175 | $200 | $225 | $250 |
| 5 | $31.50 | $39.37 | $43.32 | $47.25 | $51.19 | $55.12 | $59.07 | $63.00 |
| 6 | 31.80 | 39.75 | 43.72 | 47.70 | 51.67 | 55.65 | 59.62 | 63.60 |
| 7 | 32.10 | 40.12 | 44.14 | 48.15 | 52.17 | 56.17 | 60.19 | 64.20 |
| 8 | 32.40 | 40.50 | 44.55 | 48.60 | 52.65 | 56.70 | 60.75 | 64.80 |
| 9 | 32.70 | 40.87 | 44.97 | 49.05 | 53.14 | 57.22 | 61.32 | 65.40 |
| 10 | 33.00 | 41.25 | 45.37 | 49.50 | 53.62 | 57.75 | 61.87 | 66.00 |
| 11 | 33.30 | 41.62 | 45.79 | 49.95 | 54.12 | 58.27 | 62.44 | 66.60 |
| 12 | 33.60 | 42.00 | 46.20 | 50.40 | 54.60 | 58.80 | 63.00 | 67.20 |
| 13 | 33.90 | 42.37 | 46.62 | 50.85 | 55.09 | 59.32 | 63.57 | 67.80 |
| 14 | 34.20 | 42.75 | 47.02 | 51.30 | 55.57 | 59.85 | 64.12 | 68.40 |
| 15 | 34.50 | 43.12 | 47.44 | 51.75 | 56.07 | 60.37 | 64.69 | 69.00 |
| 16 | 34.80 | 43.50 | 47.85 | 52.20 | 56.55 | 60.90 | 65.25 | 69.60 |
| 17 | 35.10 | 43.87 | 48.27 | 52.65 | 57.04 | 61.42 | 65.82 | 70.20 |
| 18 | 35.40 | 44.25 | 48.67 | 53.10 | 57.52 | 61.95 | 66.37 | 70.80 |
| 19 | 35.70 | 44.62 | 49.09 | 53.55 | 58.02 | 62.47 | 66.94 | 71.40 |
| 20 | 36.00 | 45.00 | 49.50 | 54.00 | 58.50 | 63.00 | 67.50 | 72.00 |
| 21 | 36.30 | 45.37 | 50.02 | 54.45 | 58.99 | 63.52 | 68.07 | 72.60 |
| 22 | 36.60 | 45.75 | 50.32 | 54.90 | 59.47 | 64.05 | 68.62 | 73.20 |
| 23 | 36.90 | 46.12 | 50.74 | 55.35 | 59.97 | 64.57 | 69.19 | 73.80 |
| 24 | 37.20 | 46.50 | 51.15 | 55.80 | 60.45 | 65.10 | 69.75 | 74.40 |
| 25 | 37.50 | 46.87 | 51.57 | 56.25 | 60.94 | 65.62 | 70.32 | 75.00 |
| 26 | 37.80 | 47.25 | 51.97 | 56.70 | 61.42 | 66.15 | 70.87 | 75.60 |
| 27 | 38.10 | 47.62 | 52.39 | 57.15 | 61.92 | 66.67 | 71.44 | 76.20 |
| 28 | 38.40 | 48.00 | 52.80 | 57.60 | 62.40 | 67.20 | 72.00 | 76.80 |
| 29 | 38.70 | 48.37 | 53.22 | 58.05 | 62.89 | 67.72 | 72.57 | 77.40 |
| 30 | 39.00 | 48.75 | 53.62 | 58.50 | 63.37 | 68.25 | 73.12 | 78.00 |
| 31 | 39.30 | 49.12 | 54.04 | 58.95 | 63.87 | 68.77 | 73.69 | 78.60 |
| 32 | 39.60 | 49.50 | 54.45 | 59.40 | 64.35 | 69.30 | 74.25 | 79.20 |
| 33 | 39.90 | 49.87 | 54.87 | 59.85 | 64.84 | 69.82 | 74.82 | 79.80 |
| 34 | 40.20 | 50.25 | 55.27 | 60.30 | 65.32 | 70.35 | 75.37 | 80.40 |
| 35 | 40.50 | 50.62 | 55.69 | 60.75 | 65.82 | 70.87 | 75.94 | 81.00 |
| 36 | 40.80 | 51.00 | 56.10 | 61.20 | 66.30 | 71.40 | 76.50 | 81.60 |
| 37 | 41.10 | 51.37 | 56.52 | 61.65 | 66.79 | 71.92 | 77.07 | 82.20 |
| 38 | 41.40 | 51.75 | 56.92 | 62.10 | 67.27 | 72.45 | 77.62 | 82.80 |
| 39 | 41.70 | 52.12 | 57.34 | 62.55 | 67.77 | 72.97 | 78.19 | 83.40 |
| 40 | 42.00 | 52.50 | 57.75 | 63.00 | 68.25 | 73.50 | 78.75 | 84.00 |
| 41 | 42.30 | 52.87 | 58.17 | 63.45 | 68.74 | 74.02 | 79.32 | 84.60 |
| 42 | 42.60 | 53.25 | 58.57 | 63.90 | 69.22 | 74.55 | 79.87 | 85.00 |
| 43 | 42.90 | 53.62 | 58.99 | 64.35 | 69.72 | 75.07 | 80.44 | 85.00 |
| 44 | 43.20 | 54.00 | 59.40 | 64.80 | 70.20 | 75.60 | 81.00 | 85.00 |
| 45 | 43.50 | 54.37 | 59.82 | 65.25 | 70.69 | 76.12 | 81.57 | 85.00 |

It may be noted, however, in examining the foregoing tables of Social Security benefits, that the monthly benefits shown therein assume a regularity of employment which may be optimistic, relative to certain classes of workers. Interruption of employment obviously would lead to lesser benefits. The reductions might be small as a consequence, but any reduction from the possible maximum would be important to the lower-paid workers. It is this group which is most likely to have employment interrupted. In regard to those who earn $3,000 or more, who are most likely to achieve the maximum benefit, the subsistence benefit could be vital; but in contrast to the probable standards of living which they have been maintaining it is grossly inadequate.

The inadequacy of the Social Security benefits for the higher paid employees, or the managerial group, has led, in pension planning, to an emphasis on the supplementing of Social Security benefits for this group. This emphasis is normal and proper. It cannot be said, however, that an employer's pension problem necessarily will be solved by a plan which makes provision only for those earning certain amounts; for example, those who earn over $3,000 a year. A fundamental principle in pension planning is that the retirement benefit must be adequate to retire the employee; and, if possible, in an amount on which he will retire willingly. An employee approaching retirement, who is then earning $1,800 or $2,400 a year or, in terms of his average monthly wage, $150 to $200 a month, and who has forty years of coverage, will be entitled to primary Social Security benefits of respectively $42.00 or $49.00 a month. An employee in either of these salary or wage brackets will need persuasion to retire, unless he has some private income to supplement his Social Security benefit. Therefore, to achieve the major objective of a pension plan, which is the retirement of superannuated inefficient employees, Social Security benefits must be regarded as a point of departure for formulating a private pension plan. The benefits provided by the latter of course will be related or adjusted to those provided by Social Security; but a soundly designed plan will look to whether the benefits of the private plan, when added to the probable Social Security benefits, are in fact adequate to effect retirements.

# CHAPTER VI

## The Group Annuity Plan

**·····································································**

THE GROUP ANNUITY IS AN INSURED PENSION PLAN. WHEN A pension plan is said to be *insured* there is meant as a minimum that, as contributions are made under the plan by the employer, or the employer and the employees as the case may be, the funds are invested by a life insurance company, and the pension benefits purchased thereby are guaranteed. There is implied also, of course, a guarantee as to principal and a definite rate of interest. If a plan, however, is described as insured, and is identified further as a group annuity, considerably more functions are attributable to the life insurance company than the investment of the pension funds. The typical group annuity is designed by the actuaries of a life insurance company, usually is sold to and installed for an employer by its field representatives, is administered by the insurance company, and, as stated, the pension funds are invested by it. In the light of this, it might be expected that a company selling group annuity plans would develop a more or less standardized plan, which is largely the case. While it is true that several types of group annuities are issued or sold by a life insurance company, and that the types may be offered in different forms, thus affording a choice to an employer of a group annuity plan most suitable to his situation, nevertheless taking everything into account they will be standardized. Further, what we have said as to standardization of the group annuity is true not only of those issued by a particular life insurance company, but of those issued by different companies. For example, two employers having group annuities of the same type and form, although utilizing the services of different insurance companies, usually will be found to have pension plans with essentially the same characteristics, even though the amounts of pension benefits provided under each may differ. The fact that the group annuity is standardized will facilitate an analysis of its features. Such an analysis is generally applicable to the plans currently offered by one or another of the commercial life insurance companies engaged in the sale of group annuities.

## I. METHOD OF FUNDING

In our treatment of pension costs there was shown the method of computation of a single-premium deferred life annuity, as well as its use in funding the pension benefits for a group of 100 lives. It is the single-premium deferred life annuity[1] which is currently used by the major life insurance companies to fund the pension benefits under their group annuity plans. There is a discount taken, therefore, only for interest and anticipated mortality among an employee group. In the case of salary increases that may call for an increase in the pension benefits, or of withdrawals from employment which may reduce the pension outlays, these events are taken account of as they occur.

There are several characteristics of the single-premium deferred life annuity that are important to note. First of all, in terms of $1.00 of deferred life annuity income (or pension benefit) purchased from year to year, the amount of single-premium outlay required each year to make the purchase increases each year. Whereas at age 45 there is required approximately $6.32 to secure $1.00 for life at 65, at age 64, to obtain $1.00 of income commencing at 65, there is required $11.90, according to the Standard Annuity Table with interest at 2%.

As a consequence, to the extent that pension benefits are purchased year by year for the same lives by the single-premium deferred life annuity method, we have a constantly rising premium to retirement. In passing, the fact that in a group annuity plan the single-premium deferred life annuities are related to individual lives partially explains its descriptive name; thus a group annuity may be considered as a collection, or *group*, of annuities on the individual lives of employees covered under a pension plan.

The second characteristic of the single-premium deferred life annuity is that, in the event of the death of an employee on the life of whom benefits, or income, have been purchased, there are no death benefits. This is true whether death takes place during the period of deferment before income commences, for instance from ages 45 to 65, or at any time from age 65 onward after income has

---

[1] It is possible to fund a group annuity plan through the use of an annual, or level premium deferred life annuity. This method, however, seldom is employed both for administrative reasons and because it may involve a lifetime guarantee of the level premium deferred life annuity rates.

commenced.[2] Finally, the single-premium deferred life annuity has no cash value, except under certain circumstances that will be brought out later.

## II. TYPES OF GROUP ANNUITIES

### A. Definite-Benefit Type

An employer contemplating the use of a group annuity will be faced with one decision almost immediately. He must decide whether or not the pension benefits at retirement are to bear some definite relation to the employees' compensation received prior to retirement. Practical considerations will influence the final conclusion, but if the employer wishes a group annuity which will provide pension benefits at retirement to his employees in a definite ratio to their compensation, he will be offered what is interchangeably known as a *fixed-benefit, definite-benefit*, or *unit-purchase* type of group annuity. We shall refer to it hereafter as the definite-benefit type.

The definite-benefit type of group annuity presupposes that, through its use, an adequate retirement benefit for the employee will have been provided, one having a calculable relation to his years of service with the employer and to his compensation prior to retirement. A simple illustration of the definite-benefit approach may be seen in the formula used in our calculation of pension costs. The benefit, it will be recalled, was 1% of a yearly salary of $1,000 for each year in the plan from age 45 until retirement at 65. The total salary expected was $20,000, therefore the definite benefit was a $200 life annuity at 65. Under a definite-benefit group annuity, where the pension benefit is in definite relation to the compensation received, the employee knows, in fact can calculate, at least his minimum pension, subject to salary changes. Salary increases normally increase his pension benefits, but each time a salary increase is received the additional benefits also could be calculated.

While for the employee there exists a *constant* in the definite-benefit group annuity, in that his pension is fixed in relation to

---

[2] It should be noted that a group annuity plan, which uses single-premium deferred life annuities to provide the pension benefits, may allow an employee, upon his retirement, or shortly prior thereto, to elect one of several annuity options which may provide a death benefit. Also, if the plan is contributory, an employee's contributions will usually provide a death benefit prior to retirement, inasmuch as they are normally refunded to the employee's beneficiary or estate upon his death.

compensation and service, the variable will be the employer's cost. For example, while the latter knows his initial costs for the original group of employees covered under the plan, the average age of the group may rise or the distribution as to sex be altered; or, the group annuity rates may be increased by the insurance company. As the average age of an employee group rises, normally the single-premium costs increase; annuity rates for females are higher than for males of the same age, and group annuity rates are guaranteed by the insurance companies for a limited time only. Again, while salary increases may be projected where an employer has a definite salary scale, this also brings into play a further element that may vary the employer's cost. In spite of all this, because of withdrawals from employment and deaths, and the retirement of employees, while an employer's initial costs may rise for a time, they ultimately will tend to flatten out, and may decline even below the initial costs. Thus, notwithstanding the fact that the single-premium costs rise in relation to the purchase of pension benefits from year to year for an individual employee life, the yearly costs for an employee group may become stabilized or even decline, for the reasons stated.

### B.  Money-Purchase Type

An employer may prefer to have a group annuity plan wherein his costs are definitely fixed. While this could be brought about by his contributing yearly a flat amount toward the purchase of pension benefits for each employee, it is usually arranged by the employer's contributing a percentage of the employee's annual compensation. For example, instead of providing, as in the case of our 100 lives, a retirement benefit of 1% of yearly compensation, the employer might contribute 10% of salary, or $100 a year for each employee, toward the purchase of retirement benefits.

As for the employee, the use of this *money-purchase* principle (group annuity) makes for uncertainty as to what he may receive at retirement, for each year the single premium will rise, and the $100 cited will buy less retirement benefits for him. Probable salary increases make for further uncertainty, for the employee cannot know in advance at what ages he will receive salary increases. Further, if the group annuity rates should be increased by the insurance carrier, this action would decrease the amount of benefits purchasable by the employer's contributions. The broad distinction therefore between the definite-benefit and the money-purchase type of group annuity is that in the former the annuity or pension benefit is definite, with the employer's contribution the variable; in the latter the employer's contribution is definite, with the pension benefit the variable.

Through the purchase of past service benefits by an employer for his employees, or by the use of an adjusted percentage of contribution in relation to the sex, salary, age, and service of an employee, there may be given to a money-purchase group annuity something of the character of the definite-benefit type. However, the application of the bare money-purchase principle will result in the consequences for the employees mentioned in the preceding paragraph.

## III. EMPLOYEE CONTRIBUTIONS

Since the group annuity was first introduced as a scheme for providing pension benefits, it has largely made use of employee contributions. In the last few years there has been a tendency toward non-contributory or employer-pay-all plans, but in the main the majority of newly established group annuity plans continue to be contributory.

The contribution schemes employed will differ, dependent on whether the group annuity employed is of the definite-benefit or money-purchase type. Also the amount of employee contributions called for may vary, dependent on circumstances, particularly whether the plan is to supplement Social Security benefits or not.

### A. Contributory—Definite-Benefit

The contributions made by employees are usually for the yearly annuity benefits purchased as credits for *future* service. If annuity benefits are to be purchased for past service, rendered prior to entrance into the plan or its establishment, the employer normally pays the entire cost.

As we have indicated, the definite-benefit type of group annuity specifies the retirement income as a percentage of compensation. By compensation there is usually meant basic compensation, or the average earnings in a given time such as a year, with overtime, bonuses, and extra compensation excluded. It is also possible, however, to provide that the retirement benefit shall be one percentage of earnings under a certain amount, and a different percentage for anything over. For example, a 1% benefit for each year of future service might be granted on the first $3,000 of earnings, and 1½% on the excess.   When this is done, one amount of contribution from the employee usually is obtained on the first $3,000 of earnings, and a higher contribution on earnings in excess of $3,000.

It is also customary in a definite-benefit group annuity plan to relate in some fixed ratio an employee's contributions to the future service annuity purchased for him.   In terms of $1.00 a year future service annuity credit purchased, typical ratios used are 2, 2½ or 3. If the benefit purchased, for example, is $1.00 of future annuity and toward its purchase an employee contributes $2.00, the ratio is 2 to 1.   This ratio of employee contributions to the future service annuity purchased for him is known as $r$.   If the employer makes the entire contributions there exists no $r$ or ratio.   It should be noted that the ratio of the employee's contributions is to the annuity benefit purchased, and *not* to the employer's contributions. Any cost for the yearly future service annuity purchased, which is in excess of the employee's contributions, is met by the employer. The employer's cost will vary with such factors as normal retirement age, form of the annuity, amount of the pension credit, sex and age of the employee, and annuity rates in effect at the time of purchase.

The amount of the employees' contribution usually will be affected by the question of whether or not the employees are covered under Social Security.   If they are not, then larger contributions and larger pension benefits will be provided for.   The following tables illustrate a simple contribution method.   In the one case the plan is designed to supplement Social Security benefits; in the other it is not.   Both assume the use of a definite-benefit type of group annuity.

PLAN TO SUPPLEMENT PRIMARY SOCIAL SECURITY BENEFITS

| (1) | Employee's Contribution as a Percentage of Earnings | | Pension Benefit or Yearly Annuity Credit Purchased for an Employee as a Percentage of his Annual Earnings | |
|---|---|---|---|---|
| (1) Value of $r$ | (2) $3,000 or Under | (3) On Any Excess Over $3,000 | (4) $3,000 or Under | (5) On Any Excess Over $3,000 |
| 2 | 2% | 3% | 1% | 1½% |

By applying the above method, if the annual earnings of an employee are $3,000, he will contribute $60 a year (column 2).   There will be purchased for him an annuity credit of $30 (column 4). If the employee's annual earnings are $5,000, then he will contribute an additional $60 (column 3), for which he will receive an additional annuity credit of $30 (column 5). The value of $r$ in other words, or the ratio of the employee's contribution to the annuity benefit purchased for him, is 2 to 1. It should be pointed out again that the cost of the annuity credit, to the extent that it exceeds the employee's contribution, is met by the employer. Of two otherwise identical group annuity plans the employer's cost is less in the one in which $r$ is more, for then, of course, the employees contribute more toward meeting the total cost.

PLAN WITHOUT PRIMARY SOCIAL SECURITY BENEFITS

| (1) | (2) | (3) |
|-----|-----|-----|
| | | Pension Benefit, or Yearly Annuity |
| Value of r | Employee's Contribution as a | Credit Purchased for Employee as a |
| | Percentage of Earnings | Percentage of Annual Earnings |
| 2 | 4% | 2% |

The value of $r$ is shown again as 2; the annuity credit is 2% of earnings and the contribution is 4% of earnings.

Neither as to the annuity credits nor the contributions, however, is there a distinction made between earnings under or over $3,000, inasmuch as the plan is devised for an employee group without benefit of Social Security.

## B.  Earnings Classes—Definite-Benefit

The contributions from the employees and the annuity credits granted to them may be related to their exact earnings, or earnings classes may be established. In the latter case employees may be classified yearly in salary or compensation brackets, and then whatever contribution formula has been selected may be applied. The following table illustrates the method, with the value of $r$, or the ratio of an employee's contribution to his annuity credits, being again 2. It may be seen, for example, that an employee, earning from $1,050 to $1,349.99 who contributes $2.00 a month, or $24.00 a year, obtains an annuity credit for the year of 1% of compensation, or $12.00. So long as he remains in this earnings bracket his contribution continues to be the same each year, as does the annuity credit. The mean earnings figure, it should be noted, is used to compute the contributions and benefits; that is, the employee earning between $1,050.00 and $1,349.99 is assumed to have earned $1,200.00 for the year.

| Earnings Class | Annual Earnings | Employee's Monthly Contributions | Yearly Annuity Purchased for Each Year of Future Service Participation |
|---|---|---|---|
| 1................. | Under $1,050.00 | $1.50 | $ 9.00 |
| 2................. | $1,050 to 1,349.99 | 2.00 | 12.00 |
| 3................. | 1,350 to 1,649.99 | 2.50 | 15.00 |
| 4................. | 1,650 to 1,949.99 | 3.00 | 18.00 |
| 5................. | 1,950 to 2,249.99 | 3.50 | 21.00 |
| 6................. | 2,250 to 2,549.99 | 4.00 | 24.00 |
| 7................. | 2,550 to 2,849.99 | 4.50 | 27.00 |
| 8................. | 2,850 to 3,149.99 | 5.00 | 30.00 |
| 9................. | 3,150 to 3,449.99 | 5.50 | 33.00 |
| 10.....:......... | 3,450 to 3,749.99 | 6.00 | 36.00 |
|  | etc. | etc. | etc. |

If exact earnings were used as a basis for obtaining contributions and giving annuity credits, any change in the earnings would immediately change the contribution and annuity credits. To avoid constant adjustments, and to reduce administration expense, it is usually provided in group annuity plans that when an employee enters the plan he is classified according to an earnings bracket, and at intervals of a year or six months he is reclassified if there has been any change.

### C.  Contributory—Money-Purchase

In the case of a definite-benefit type of group annuity it was stated that contributions which are obtained from the employee are usually in a specified or fixed ratio to the annuity credits purchased for his benefit; and that the employer's contributions are in an amount necessary to take care of the annuity costs, over and above what the employee pays. Under money-purchase plans the contributions both of the employer and the employees are specified, each contributing yearly a stipulated percentage of the employee's compensation; and it is the contributions of the employer *and* the employees which are set up in some fixed relation or ratio to one another. Thus the employer may contribute on the basis of 1, 2 or 3, to that of the employee. For example, if the employee's contribution is 1% of compensation, the employer may contribute 2%. The sum of the joint contributions of the employer and employee are used then to purchase future service annuity credits. The amounts of annuity or pension benefits purchased thereby will vary, for they will be affected by such factors as normal retirement age, form of the group annuity, actual amounts contributed, sex, age, and the annuity rates in effect at the time of purchase.

The percentage of contributions is usually differentiated in the money-purchase as in the definite-benefit type, if the plan is to supplement Social Security, as between earnings of $3,000 or under, and those in excess of $3,000. For example, using a 2 to 1 ratio, the employee might contribute 2% and the employer 4% on the first $3,000 of earnings. On earnings over $3,000 the employee might contribute 3% and the employer 6%. If a plan were to be established where no Social Security benefits were involved, and the ratio were held at 2 to 1, the employee might contribute 4% and the employer 8% of compensation. It is usually required in any case that the ratio be at least 1 to 1; that is, as a minimum, the employer is expected to match the employee's contributions.

### D.  Earnings Classes—Money-Purchase

Earnings classes also may be used in money-purchase plans as a basis for contributions in lieu of exact earnings. The table below illustrates this procedure with the use of a 2 to 1 ratio; the employee contributing 2% of earnings, the employer 4%. It will be observed that the relation shown here, in contrast to the table for the definite-benefit type, is *between the employee and employer contributions*, without reference to the amount of annuity purchased. The mean earnings for the year again are used in computing the amount of the employee's contribution. Thus the contribution of an employee earning from $1,050.00 to $1,349.99 is 2% of $1,200, $2.00 a month, or $24.00 a year. The employer's contribution is twice that of the employee's, $4.00 a month, or $48.00 a year. We have already indicated the factors that will influence the actual amount of annuity credits which may be purchasable by the joint contributions.

| Earnings Class | Annual Earnings | Employee's Monthly Contribution | Employer's Monthly Contribution |
|---|---|---|---|
| 1................ | Under $1,050.00 | $1.50 | $ 3.00 |
| 2................ | $1,050 to 1,349.99 | 2.00 | 4.00 |
| 3................ | 1,350 to 1,649.99 | 2.50 | 5.00 |
| 4................ | 1,650 to 1,949.99 | 3.00 | 6.00 |
| 5................ | 1,950 to 2,249.99 | 3.50 | 7.00 |
| 6................ | 2,250 to 2,549.99 | 4.00 | 8.00 |
| 7................ | 2,550 to 2,849.99 | 4.50 | 9.00 |
| 8................ | 2,850 to 3,149.99 | 5.00 | 10.00 |
| 9................ | 3,150 to 3,449.99 | 5.50 | 11.00 |
| 10................ | 3,450 to 3,749.99 | 6.00 | 12.00 |
|  | etc. | etc. | etc. |

## IV. GROUP ANNUITY FORMS

Insurance companies issuing group annuities offer not only the several types discussed above, but also either the definite-benefit or money-purchase type in various "regular forms." The regular form which is selected will have a bearing on the benefits provided as well as on the costs of the group annuity plan. Typical forms are (1) No Death Benefit—Life, (2) With Interest—Life, (3) No Interest—Modified Cash Refund, and (4) With Interest—Modified Cash Refund. Each of these forms in a definite-benefit plan provides a different type of benefit; each consequently has a different initial cost outlay. In the case of money-purchase plans, the use of one or another of these forms will similarly provide a different type of benefit, and the form selected will influence the *amount* of retirement annuity purchasable by the joint contributions of employer and employee.

TABLE XV

TYPICAL RETIREMENT, WITHDRAWAL, AND DEATH BENEFITS
OF GROUP ANNUITY REGULAR FORMS

| Regular Form | Living Benefits | | | |
| | Upon Retirement | | Upon Withdrawal from Employment | |
| | To Employee | To Employer | To Employee | To Employer |
| --- | --- | --- | --- | --- |
| No Death Benefit—Life..... | Life Income | Nothing | Nothing | Refund[a] Credit |
| No Interest—Modified Cash Refund.................. | Life Income | Nothing | Cash[b] Refund | Refund[c] Credit |
| With Interest—Life......... | Life Income | Nothing | Cash[d] Refund | Refund[e] Credit |
| With Interest—Modified Cash Refund.................. | Life Income | Nothing | Cash[d] Refund (see note) | Refund[e] Credit (see note) |

[a] If the employee is in *good health* at time of withdrawal either or both of the following: (1) if the employer's contributions have been for future service benefits only, then he will receive a refund credit of 96% of such contributions, plus credited interest; (2) if the employer also has made contributions for past service annuities, he will also receive a refund credit. of 96% of such contributions plus credited interest, or 100% of such past service contribution, whichever is greater.

[b] The sum of the employee's contributions, without interest thereon.

[c] If the employer's contributions have been for future service benefits only, then he will receive 96% of such contributions plus credited interest, but minus 4% of employee's contributions if the employee withdraws before a stipulated time has elapsed; if past service annuity credits have been purchased then a refund as in (a-2) above. Credits to employer will be granted, however, only if employee terminates services while in good health.

[d] The sum of the employee's contributions, plus credited interest thereon.

[e] If the employer's contributions have been for future service benefits only, then he will receive 96% of such contributions plus credited interest, but minus 4% of employee's contributions plus credited

The explanation of these various forms will be developed best by showing in tabular form the typical benefits they provide at (1) retirement, (2) withdrawal or termination of employment, and (3) death, before or after retirement. Their relative costs per $1.00 of benefit commencing at age 65 are illustrated in Table XV.

It will be apparent from the table and footnotes thereto that the phrases *with interest* or *no interest* indicate that the group annuity plan is contributory. Also implied in these phrases is the fact that, in the case of *with interest*, the employee's contributions are returned with interest in the event of death or withdrawal; and in the case of *no interest* the contributions alone are returned.

It also should be noted that in all instances in which an employee terminates employment, he must be in good health in order that the employer receive a refund credit. This condition is necessary inasmuch as the single-premium deferred life annuity, which is

TABLE XV (*Cont.*)

TYPICAL RETIREMENT, WITHDRAWAL, AND DEATH BENEFITS
OF GROUP ANNUITY REGULAR FORMS

| | Death Benefits | | | |
| --- | --- | --- | --- | --- |
| | Before Retirement | | After Retirement | |
| Regular Form | To Employee's Beneficiary | To Employer | To Employee's Beneficiary | To Employer |
| No Death-Benefit—Life..... | Nothing | Nothing | Nothing[h] | Nothing |
| No Interest—Modified Cash Refund................. | Cash[b] Refund | Nothing | Cash[f] Refund | Nothing |
| With Interest—Life......... | Cash[d] Refund | Nothing | Nothing[h] | Nothing |
| With Interest—Modified Cash Refund................. | Cash[d] Refund | Nothing | Cash[g] Refund | Nothing |

interest; if past service annuities have been purchased then also a refund as in (a–2) above. Credits to employer will be granted, however, only if employee terminates services while in good health.

[f] There will be paid to the employee's beneficiary the amount of his contributions without interest, less the sum of the annuity payments which were made to him prior to his death.

[g] There will be paid to the employee's beneficiary the amount of his contributions plus credited interest to his retirement date, less the sum of the annuity payments which were made to him prior to his death.

[h] Unless an option is available, and selected by an employee, which may provide a death benefit.

*Note:* An employee, upon withdrawal from employment, in lieu of a cash refund, normally may leave his own contributions with the insurance company and obtain a paid-up deferred life annuity to commence at normal retirement date in an amount purchased by his own contributions; also, if the employer's contributions are vested in the employee, and the employee leaves his own contributions with the insurance company, their joint contributions may be applied to the purchase of a paid-up deferred life annuity to commence at the employee's normal retirement date.

used to fund group annuity plans, discounts for mortality. If a "good health" clause were not a condition for an employer's credit, there would be selection against the insurance company. If the employees who withdrew were in poor health, and a credit for premiums on their lives were allowed to an employer, the insurance company would find itself ultimately incurring losses. The remaining employees after the withdrawal of the impaired lives would have a better chance on the average to survive to retirement and live longer thereafter than was assumed at the time the annuity rates were set for the original group. The table further brings out the apparently contradictory fact that, while the single-premium deferred life annuity is the method used to fund the group annuity, a death benefit may be provided. This death benefit, however, only relates to the *employee's* contributions before retirement, and, when payable after retirement, is in the form of a modified refund. The employer's contributions have been applied to the purchase of single-premium deferred life annuities, discounted for expected deaths.

Finally to be noted in Table XV is that, while a cash refund is obtainable by an employee in the event of his withdrawal from employment, group annuity contracts usually provide that an employee also can leave the sum of his contributions with the insurance company. If he does so, there will be made available to him a so-called paid-up deferred life annuity to commence at the normal retirement date laid down in the plan. Again, if the employer's contributions are vested in the employee upon withdrawal, then the employee will be entitled to receive a paid-up deferred life annuity purchased by the sum of his contributions and the employer's, to commence at the normal retirement age set forth in the plan. This annuity likewise will be payable if the employee survives to such date. If an employee dies, however, prior to attainment of normal retirement age, usually there will be refunded, as a death benefit, the sum of his own contributions.

## V. REGULAR FORM INITIAL COSTS

### A. Definite-Benefit Type

Inasmuch as the types of benefits provided by the various regular forms differ, it is natural to expect a difference in the initial costs of each. Table XVI brings out this fact, showing premium rates for retirement commencing at age 65 with the use of a ratio of 2, the employee contributing yearly 2% of compensation for each \$1.00 of future service annuity purchased for his account. The premiums shown are *gross rates*, based on the Standard Annuity Table with interest at 2%.

### TABLE XVI

#### NORMAL RETIREMENT AT AGE 65

Male Employees

(1) $r = 2$.

(2) Each column indicates the *single-premium cost*, at the ages shown, to purchase \$1.00 future service annuity income commencing at age 65.[a]

| Age Nearest Birthday at Start of Year | No Death Benefit— Life | No Interest— Modified Cash Refund | With Interest— Life | With Interest— Modified Cash Refund |
|---|---|---|---|---|
| 45 | \$ 6.69 | \$ 7.15 | \$ 7.23 | \$ 7.30 |
| 46 | 6.87 | 7.32 | 7.40 | 7.47 |
| 47 | 7.06 | 7.51 | 7.58 | 7.64 |
| 48 | 7.25 | 7.70 | 7.76 | 7.83 |
| 49 | 7.46 | 7.90 | 7.95 | 8.02 |
| 50 | 7.68 | 8.11 | 8.16 | 8.22 |
| 51 | 7.91 | 8.34 | 8.37 | 8.43 |
| 52 | 8.15 | 8.57 | 8.59 | 8.66 |
| 53 | 8.41 | 8.82 | 8.83 | 8.90 |
| 54 | 8.68 | 9.08 | 9.08 | 9.15 |
| 55 | 8.97 | 9.35 | 9.35 | 9.41 |
| 56 | 9.28 | 9.64 | 9.64 | 9.70 |
| 57 | 9.62 | 9.95 | 9.94 | 10.00 |
| 58 | 9.97 | 10.29 | 10.26 | 10.33 |
| 59 | 10.35 | 10.64 | 10.61 | 10.67 |
| 60 | 10.76 | 11.02 | 10.99 | 11.05 |
| 61 | 11.21 | 11.43 | 11.39 | 11.45 |
| 62 | 11.69 | 11.88 | 11.83 | 11.89 |
| 63 | 12.21 | 12.36 | 12.31 | 12.36 |
| 64 | 12.79 | 12.88 | 12.82 | 12.88 |

[a] The annuity income commencing at age 65 will be paid monthly; the premium cost per \$1.00 of annuity income is on the basis that premiums will be paid monthly.

We stated that $r$ as used in Table XVI would be 2. In the premium rates shown, with the exception of the No Death-Benefit —Life form, the employer's cost thus will be the premium shown at the respective ages, minus \$2. For example, at age 45 under the second column, the employer would contribute \$5.15, and the employee \$2.00; likewise in the third and fourth columns, at age 45 the employer's cost would be the amounts shown less \$2. The same subtraction should be made at each age for each form except in the case of the No Death-Benefit—Life form. This latter form is used mostly for employer-pay-all plans and in cases where past service benefits are purchased; no contributions from the employees are required.

Where employees are asked to contribute to a plan, dissatisfaction may arise if no interest is to be paid on their contributions upon withdrawal from the plan, or if no refunds of at least their own contributions, less the annuity payments received, are to be allowed if they should die after retirement. In the light of this, it is clear that the *with interest—modified cash refund* form is most attractive to the employees; and the employer may be better advised to select this form even though it be necessary to use a higher value of *r*, if he is unwilling to absorb the additional cost himself. In fact, certain insurance carriers will not issue a group annuity where no interest is payable on the employees' contributions. One carrier goes so far as to issue only the *with interest—modified cash refund* group annuity as its regular form for the funding of future service annuity benefits.

### B. Money-Purchase Type

The combined contributions of the employer and employee, as previously explained, are used under a money-purchase type to purchase annuity benefits. Table XVII indicates the *amounts* of annuity purchasable at certain ages in relation to the different regular forms, with the ratio of the employer—employee contribution being 2 to 1, and the sum of the joint contributions being made to equal $10.00. The employer is contributing $6⅔ and the employee $3⅓. It is to be understood that the amount of annuity shown at the respective ages is that which is purchasable by $10.00; and the amount of annuity has been determined from use of the Standard Annuity Table with interest at 2%.

### C. Summary

The distinction between the money-purchase and the definite-benefit plans may now be further clarified by references to the tables we have set forth.

If we refer to our earnings classes on page 110 we see that an employee in the annual earnings class of $1,050 to $1,349.99 contributes $2.00 monthly or $24.00 a year. He receives an annuity credit for the year of $12.00. The cost of the annuity credit is met from the employee's contribution of $24.00, plus whatever the employer may have to contribute. If we assume the employee is aged 45, and that his earnings remain constant to the normal retirement age of 65, the employee will receive annuity credits of $12.00 × 20 (years) or a total of $240.00. Thus $240.00 is the

## TABLE XVII

### NORMAL RETIREMENT AT AGE 65

#### Male Employees

(1) The sum of the employer and employee contributions = $10.00, payable monthly.
(2) Each column indicates the *amount of annuity* purchasable by the joint contributions of $10.00 at the ages shown; income to commence at age 65, payable monthly.

| Age Nearest Birthday at Start of Year | No Death-Benefit Life | No Interest— Modified Cash Refund | With Interest— Life | With Interest— Modified Cash Refund |
|---|---|---|---|---|
| 45.............. | $1.49 | $1.38 | $1.36 | $1.34 |
| 46.............. | 1.46 | 1.34 | 1.33 | 1.31 |
| 47.............. | 1.42 | 1.31 | 1.29 | 1.27 |
| 48.............. | 1.38 | 1.27 | 1.26 | 1.24 |
| 49.............. | 1.34 | 1.24 | 1.23 | 1.21 |
| 50.............. | 1.30 | 1.20 | 1.20 | 1.18 |
| 51.............. | 1.26 | 1.17 | 1.17 | 1.15 |
| 52.............. | 1.23 | 1.14 | 1.14 | 1.12 |
| 53.............. | 1.19 | 1.11 | 1.11 | 1.09 |
| 54.............. | 1.15 | 1.07 | 1.07 | 1.06 |
| 55.............. | 1.11 | 1.04 | 1.04 | 1.03 |
| 56.............. | 1.08 | 1.01 | 1.01 | 1.00 |
| 57.............. | 1.04 | .98 | .98 | .97 |
| 58.............. | 1.00 | .94 | .95 | .94 |
| 59.............. | .97 | .91 | .92 | .91 |
| 60.............. | .93 | .88 | .89 | .88 |
| 61.............. | .89 | .85 | .87 | .85 |
| 62.............. | .86 | .82 | .84 | .82 |
| 63.............. | .82 | .79 | .81 | .79 |
| 64.............. | .78 | .76 | .78 | .76 |

definite-benefit or retirement annuity which will be payable to him commencing at age 65. While the employee's contribution is fixed, and the benefit purchased definite, the employer's share of the yearly cost of the annuity credit increases each year as the employee becomes one year older. For example, let us refer to Table XVI on page 115 and assume the *with interest—modified cash refund* is the regular form of group annuity employed. The total cost of an annuity credit of $12.00 at age 45 to commence at 65 is $12.00 × 7.30 or $87.60. Of this, the employee pays $24.00 and the employer $63.60. At age 55 for the same employee, and assuming there has been no change in premium rates, the total cost of the yearly $12.00 annuity credit has risen to $9.41 × $12.00 or $112.92. Of this the employee still pays $24.00, the employer, however, contributes $88.92. And so on until the employee is retired.

In the case of an employee age 45 under a money-purchase plan, whose mean yearly earnings are $1,200 a year, the retirement benefits which will be purchased for him may be developed similarly through reference to the earnings class table on page 110 and to Table XVII on page 117, which shows the amount of benefits purchasable by the joint contributions of the employer and employee. The ratio between the employer-employee contributions, it will be recalled, was 2 to 1; that is, the employer contributes 4% of compensation and the employee 2%. An employee earning $1,200 a year, therefore, contributes $24.00 a year, and the employer $48.00. The sum of these is $72.00 which is applied to buy annuity credits. At age 45, Table XVII discloses that $10.00 will purchase $1.34 of annuity credit commencing at age 65 under a *with interest—modified cash refund* form; thus $72.00 buys 7.2 × $1.34 or $9.65 for our employee. If we now assume the employee's earnings remain constant at $1,200, and no change in the schedule of premium rates, at age 55 the joint contributions of $72.00 will purchase 7.2 × 1.03 or $7.42 of annuity benefit commencing at 65. The amount of annuity credit of $7.42 purchased at 55 may be contrasted with the annuity credit of $9.65 purchased at age 45; in both instances the joint contributions of employer and employee of $72.00 have been used to make the purchase. The annuity credits purchased at each age from 45 to 64 by the joint contributions may be calculated similarly as above and totaled, and thus they would equal a "definite benefit" despite the declining amount of annuity purchased at each succeeding age. This fact would appear to make the money-purchase plan identical with a definite-benefit type. This resemblance is due, however, to the assumption of no variables in the above illustration. Actually, the compensation of the generality of employees under a pension plan would change in their period of service prior to retirement. Even where an employer had a salary scale, and increases in salary could be projected, such increases could not easily be anticipated and related to the ages of the employees, a factor in calculating the amount of benefits purchasable by the joint contributions. The possibility of change in annuity premium rates also introduces an additional uncertainty; for, in the past at least, there have been several rate increases which would have operated to reduce the amount of benefits purchasable by the joint contributions under a money-purchase plan. Such rate changes, moreover, have not fallen equally on males and females, for the annuity rates for females have tended toward an adjustment relatively higher than the rates for males of the same age.

In contrast, in the case of definite-benefit plans the retirement benefit is a definite percentage of compensation.  This percentage holds regardless of salary changes.  While salary shifts would lead to changes in the *amount* of the retirement benefit, the latter would still remain in a fixed relation to compensation.  The factors of rising single premiums as employees grow older or possible upward revisions of annuity rates, both of which result in higher single-premium costs per dollar of annuity credit, would be absorbed usually by increased contributions from the employer, without reducing the amount of an employee's retirement benefit under a definite-benefit plan.

## VI.  OPTIONS AT RETIREMENT

The usual group annuity, issued in any of the regular forms we have discussed, provides that an employee may, subject to certain conditions, elect an optional form of annuity at retirement differing from that provided in the regular form.  The typical optional forms of retirement annuity are (1) cash refund, (2) contingent annuitant, (3) non-refund or life income, and (4) increased benefit option.  The availability of these options to an employee depends on the regular form of group annuity initially selected to provide the pension benefits.

*Cash Refund Option.*  This option provides that an employee may elect to receive a smaller amount of retirement income than is provided for at retirement in the regular form.  The insurance company agrees to pay, upon the employee's death after retirement, a death benefit equal to the difference, if any, between what he would have received if he had died immediately before retirement, and the actual amounts which he has received under the cash refund option up to the time of his death.

The cash refund option usually may be utilized under the *with interest-life* form.  As our chart shows, where the *with interest-life* form is the regular form of annuity there is no death benefit payable after retirement.  If an employee elects the cash refund option he must do it at a specified time prior to retirement, otherwise satisfactory evidence of the good health of an employee at retirement is required by the insurance company before this option will be granted.  This latter stipulation is necessary to protect the insurance company.  If this requirement were omitted, the employees in poor health facing retirement might all tend to select the cash refund option to the disadvantage of the insurance company; or, in other words, the insurance company might incur a risk and possible loss not contemplated in the annuity rates originally set for the regular form.

*Contingent Annuitant Option.* An employee reaching normal retirement age may only be concerned with himself, or he may have a wife or someone else dependent upon him. In order to provide for such a dependent after his own death he may feel that the cash refund option will not serve his purpose; for as stated this option affords a death benefit only if the employee dies prior to receiving what is guaranteed to him thereunder. The contingent annuitant option will be effective only if an employee attains retirement age, but it will guarantee an income not only so long as the employee lives, but for the lifetime of a surviving dependent. The income payable under this option, which commences at normal retirement age, will be in a reduced amount as compared with what an employee would receive if he were the sole annuitant. The reduced income will be payable with the stipulation that either all, two-thirds, or one-half of the reduced income shall continue for the life of the surviving dependent, who is known as the contingent annuitant. It should be noted that the contingent annuitant option may be available at an earlier retirement date than the normal one, upon giving evidence of good health satisfactory to the insurance company at the time of such early retirement.

The actual amount of the income payable under the contingent annuity option will depend on the age and sex of both the employee and the contingent annuitant, and on the proportion of the reduced retirement income which is to be continued to the contingent annuitant; that is all, two-thirds, or one-half. As with the cash refund option it must be selected at a specified time prior to the employee's normal retirement date. If selected at retirement, or shortly prior thereto, evidence of good health of the employee must be furnished satisfactory to the insurance company before it will be granted. This requirement is necessary to protect the company, for the reasons cited relative to selection of the cash refund option.

*Non-refund or Life Income Option.* In contrast to the cash refund or contingent annuitant options, the non-refund or life income option maximizes the retirement income but provides nothing in the event of the employee's death after retirement. With no dependents, or no heirs in whom he may have an interest, the employee under this option receives the maximum life income possible at retirement. It is offered usually when the regular form of group annuity is the modified cash refund form with or without interest.

*Increased Benefit Option.* A group annuity plan may provide for normal retirement at age 60. If the plan is to supplement Social Security benefits which do not become payable until the employee is at age 65, an employee who retires at 60 will have to wait five years before the Social Security benefits commence. In order to obtain a uniform retirement income an employee may elect to receive an increased retirement income from 60 to 65 and a reduced amount thereafter when Social Security benefits begin. The practical effect of this option is to provide a uniform retirement income from 60 onward, through adjusting the group annuity retirement benefits in relation to Social Security benefits.

This option is usually available when the normal retirement date is prior to age 65; it also may be available when normal retirement is at 65, but earlier retirement is permitted under the plan, such as at age 60. By reason of its function, it is sometimes called the Social Security adjustment option. Evidence of good health may be required to obtain this option.

## VII.  FULL CASH REFUND GROUP ANNUITY

The regular forms of group annuity, as discussed above, are the typical ones that are made available to an employer. Moreover, of these the *no death benefit—life* form is the one normally used for providing past service credits, and the *with interest—modified cash refund* for future service.

A form which is seldom employed is that known as the *full cash refund* group annuity. It may be utilized where it is desired to provide a death benefit prior to normal retirement from the *employer's* contributions. The modified cash refund form, it will be recalled, refunds only the *employee's* contributions if death occurs, with or without interest, as the case may be. The employer's contributions thereunder are used to purchase single-premium deferred life annuities with no death benefit therefrom either before or after retirement. The full cash refund group annuity, in the case of an employee's death before retirement, allows provision for a refund to his beneficiaries of the employer's contributions made for the employee's account. After retirement there is operative a cash refund option (unless some alternative option is selected), under which there is payable as a death benefit an amount equal at least to the difference between the amount of the full death benefit at the time of retirement, and the amounts of annuity income which have been paid to the employee up to the time of his death.

The provision for a death benefit in the full cash refund group annuity means that basically no discount for mortality is taken for deaths prior to retirement, and thus the single-premium deferred life annuity, which we have explained as the method used to fund group annuities, is not applicable to this form. What is involved therefore is the retention of the method of single payments (but with no discount for mortality prior to normal retirement), which will, when accumulated at interest to normal retirement, provide the annuity income called for under the pension plan. The result is that a considerably higher premium is necessary each year to purchase $1.00 of annuity income to commence at normal retirement age and to guarantee a death benefit. Table XVIII shows the yearly cost of a single-premium deferred annuity[3] at the respective ages to provide $1.00 future annuity under a *full cash refund—with interest* form, using a definite-benefit type of group annuity. This may be compared with the rates shown in Table XVI, on p. 115.

In Table XVIII the cost, as shown at the respective ages, is for $1.00 of annuity commencing at the normal retirement age of 65. If the value of $r$ is again 2 to 1, the employee will contribute $2.00; thus the employer's cost will be the amounts as shown at the respective ages, less $2.00.

A substantial difference in the above rates may be noted in comparison with those of the *no death benefit—life* form in Table XVI. At age 45, in the latter, to purchase $1.00 of future annuity credit payable at 65 requires an outlay of $6.69, whereas under the full cash refund at the same age the outlay is $14.14. The explanation of the differential, of course, is that the full cash refund form provides larger benefits to the employees than the *no death benefit—life* form, or than any other of the regular forms for which rates are shown in Table XVI.

---

[3] There is a distinction between a single-premium *deferred life annuity,* and a single-premium *deferred annuity.* The former involves life contingencies both prior to and after annuity income commences. There is no death benefit. The single premium deferred annuity is similar to a *Retirement Annuity* contract (see p. 62), when the latter is purchased by a single premium rather than by level premiums. Under a single-premium deferred annuity, if death occurs prior to retirement, the death benefit is equal to at least the premium contributions, with or without interest, as the case may be. Of course, when annuity income commences there will be no death benefit if the income is payable as a life annuity.

## TABLE XVIII

### FUTURE SERVICE ANNUITY PREMIUM RATES

Regular Form: With Interest—Full Cash Refund
Type: Definite-Benefit Plan
Normal Retirement Age 65
Rates for Male Employees

| Age Nearest Birthday at Start of Year | Single-Premium Cost of $1.00 of Deferred Annuity* |
|---|---|
| 45 | $14.14 |
| 46 | 14.39 |
| 47 | 14.63 |
| 48 | 14.89 |
| 49 | 15.14 |
| 50 | 15.39 |
| 51 | 15.65 |
| 52 | 15.90 |
| 53 | 16.16 |
| 54 | 16.42 |
| 55 | 16.67 |
| 56 | 16.93 |
| 57 | 17.19 |
| 58 | 17.45 |
| 59 | 17.71 |
| 60 | 17.97 |
| 61 | 18.23 |
| 62 | 18.49 |
| 63 | 18.74 |
| 64 | 19.00 |

*The annuity income commencing at age 65 will be paid monthly; the premium cost per $1.00 of annuity income is on the basis that premiums will be paid monthly.

## VIII.  PAST SERVICE

### A.  General

The discussion of pension benefits thus far has been largely in terms of benefits for future service of an employee after he has become a member of the pension plan, with occasional references to benefits for past service.  Under most group annuity plans, in addition to the pension benefit granted for each year of future service an employee will render his employer, there is usually provided a benefit for service rendered prior to the establishment of the plan. Where the pension benefits are related to years of service, there is a practical need for past service credits, as they are termed; certain employees will be at or near the normal retirement age provided in the plan, so that there will be insufficient time for them to accumulate credits for future service to provide for an adequate pension.

In general, past service benefits are purchased only for those workers who are in the employ of the company at the time the plan is established, and who are eligible to become members. Where past service benefits are purchased, the regular form used is the *no death benefit—life* form with the employer meeting the entire cost. This holds whether the group annuity is of the definite-benefit or money-purchase type.

### B. Formula for Past Service Benefits

The usual group annuity formula for providing past service benefits is to relate them to the years of past service and the compensation received. Sometimes the maximum service for which credit will be granted may be limited, such as to 20 years or less. Past service credits may be limited by providing that no service before a certain age will be considered. Also, occasionally, no more than a certain amount of annual compensation may be considered. Compensation may be defined as the earnings at the effective date of the plan, the average earnings for a certain number of years prior to the date of the plan, or the average earnings of an employee in an earnings classification.

It is customary to provide a past service credit in a lesser amount than that provided for future service. For example, if the future service credit is 1% of current earnings, the past service credit may be ½ of 1% of earnings; if 2% is used for future service, then 1% may be allowed for past service.

### C. Employer's Mode of Purchase

The employees for whom past service benefits usually are purchased are those who are (1) at retirement age when the plan is established, or (2) those who are entitled under the plan to past service credits at the time of establishment but who have one or more years of future service prior to normal retirement. In both instances the costs of past service credits are met by the employer.

*Employees at Retirement Age.* For those employees who are to be retired when the group annuity plan is established, the pension benefit becomes payable immediately. The amount of retirement income will depend on the formula used to compute past service credits, but the cost of the benefit must be advanced to the insurance company before pension benefits will be paid to the retired employees.   In this instance, therefore, the employer deposits a lump sum to cover the costs.   The amount will depend on such factors as the age and sex of the retired employees, the amount of the benefits, and the group annuity rates in effect at the time of purchase. , Upon receipt by the insurance company the funds are applied to purchase life annuities for the accounts of the retired employees, and the income to them commences immediately.

*Employees Not at Retirement Age.*   For those employees who have not arrived at the normal retirement age the past service credits are computed individually, and then totaled to determine the cost of the annuities to provide the past service benefits. While an employer *might* pay for these by a lump sum, the usual course is to amortize the cost over a number of years by annual payments to the insurance company.   The period of time over which the employer may meet the cost of past service benefits is normally not longer than twenty years, and usually less.   A major determining factor as to how many years over which past service benefits may be purchased will be the composition of the employee group eligible to the plan.   For example, a high percentage of older age employees who have only a short time to go before retirement may require an acceleration in the rate of payments.

The procedure on the part of the insurance company upon receipt of the funds is to apply them to the purchase of single-premium deferred life annuities for the accounts of employees entitled to past service annuity credits.   The usual course is to make an outright purchase of past service annuities for those employees nearest to retirement age, to the greatest possible extent permitted by the amount of the employer's installment contribution.   As additional contributions for past service are made by the employer, they are applied toward buying past service annuities for another group of employees in relation to their proximity to retirement age, and so on until finally all past service annuities are paid for.   This is what is sometimes termed the age-order method of purchase.

Another method sometimes used is the following: an employer's lump sum cost of past service annuities is computed and he then makes installment payments of ¼ or ⅓ of this amount to cover the past service benefit for *each* employee entitled to such.   The practical significance for an employee as between this method and the age-order procedure lies in the possibility that the pension plan might be terminated; or that he might withdraw from employment where some or all of the past service annuities were vested.   If the termination of the plan should occur under the age-order method, only the older employees might have had their past service credits fully purchased. In the event of withdrawal from employment, a younger employee might find (despite a vesting provision entitling him to receive some or all of the employer's contribution for past service) that because of the use of the age-order method, he would not receive any past service annuities.

The process of funding the past service annuities over a period of years generally will lead to a higher cost to an employer than if purchases were made in a lump sum. This is true partly because an interest charge must be made by the insurance company to offset an interest loss sustained by their not having received the funds for past service credits in a lump sum at the inception of the plan, and partly because the nearer to retirement are the employees for whom past service purchases are made, the greater the probability of their living to receive annuity incomes. On the other hand, the withdrawal or deaths of employees, for whom past service annuity credits may not have been purchased outright, may modify the costs. While as previously stated discounts for withdrawals are not taken under group annuity plans, where the purchase of past service annuities is deferred, some employees will withdraw from employment or die before past service annuities have been purchased for their accounts. To this extent the employer might be relieved of the expense of buying past service annuity benefits.

The periods selected by an employer for the purchase of past service annuities are usually either of 10, 15, or 20 years. In the last case, under the current rate structures of group annuities, an annual payment equal to approximately 6% of the lump-sum cost will be adequate to complete the purchases necessary to provide the past service benefits as employees reach retirement. For tax reasons, however, in recent years the actual time to complete the purchase of past service benefits is apt to run about 11 years. An employer could effect purchase over a shorter period, but he is limited to an annual income tax deduction of *10% of the actual lump-sum costs of past service.* When the purchase of past service benefits, therefore, is made in relation to tax deductibility, because of interest charges, and because of such installment purchases of past service benefits, the actual time to complete them will be slightly more than 11 years.

Finally, it should be noted that an employer purchasing past service annuity credits under a group annuity plan does not obligate himself to make such purchases. He merely advises his employees that it is his intention to do so, circumstances permitting. Also he may make an annual contribution one year, and skip the next. If the employer thereafter finds it financially feasible, he can make up the omitted year or years by increasing his usual annual contributions for past service benefits.

## IX. EXPENSE

The premium rates we have shown for definite-benefit group annuity plans as well as the amount of annuity purchasable by joint contribution under the money-purchase plan, are commercial rates. In other words, they are the gross premium rates,[4] including a charge for expense, that would have to be paid by an employer who currently established a group annuity plan. The expense or *loading* as it is technically known, is an amount added to the net premium rates. The calculation of loading is a technical matter that we shall not explore, but it is obvious that the insurance company must collect something to cover the costs of operating its group annuity business, in addition to the net premiums necessary to provide the pension benefits.

The loading charges added to the net premium under group annuity plans are about 8%. From this must be met administrative costs, acquisition costs, and costs for providing a reserve against unexpected losses in interest earnings and/or mortality. The administrative costs consist of general overhead cost, the clerical and statistical work necessary to establishment of the plan, and the costs of servicing the plan. The acquisition costs, or new business costs, include the commissions that must be paid to brokers who have sold the group annuity plan, or the salaries of its own representatives who may have done the selling. Finally, the assumptions as to interest earnings or mortality may turn out adversely. There may be less interest earned than anticipated, or the mortality of an employee group may be less than anticipated both prior to and after retirement. The loading charge to a small degree attempts to provide for these contingencies.

---

[4] Three of the principal insurance companies now writing group annuities quote different gross rates. All of them use the 1937 Standard Annuity Table; one company, however, uses the table rated down one year with interest at 2% (in effect everyone is actually treated as one year younger), which raises the initial or gross rates slightly; the two others use the Standard Annuity Table, as in our illustration, but with interest rates of 2¼% and 2½% respectively, which brings the gross rates lower than those we have employed.

## X. GENERAL UNDERWRITING PROCEDURES

*Preliminary.* The preparation of a group annuity plan requires that there be made available the census data on the employer's personnel. The data usually consist of four items: (1) date of birth, (2) date of employment, (3) sex, and (4) salary or earnings of each employee. All of these are necessary to make an accurate computation of the initial annual costs of an employer's pension plan.

*Preparation of the Plan.* Before any use can be made of the above census data certain major decisions, even though tentative, must be made on the following:

1. The employees who shall be eligible to the plan.
2. The normal retirement age.
3. Whether a contributory or non-contributory plan.
4. Whether a definite-benefit or money-purchase plan.
5. The formula for determining annuity credits or pension benefits.
6. The formula for determining employee contributions, if any.
7. The regular form of group annuity to be employed.

The employer's pension adviser or the insurance company's group annuity representative will normally make tentative decisions on these points after consultation with the employer, and after a survey of the latter's employment situation, type of business, and financial strength or resources. A plan then will be prepared and, for reasons of cost considerations, usually an alternative plan as well. Whatever may be the final plan which is offered to an employer, or that he may adopt, it must conform to the underwriting rules of the insurance company. The most important of these rules will be enumerated.

## XI. UNDERWRITING RULES

*Eligible Employee Groups.* For an employee group to be eligible to obtain group annuity coverage it must have a common or single employer, although closely associated employee groups, such as those of subsidiary companies with a parent company, are acceptable.

A further rule is that the eligible employee group must consist at least of 100 employees (although some companies will consider groups of 50 employees or over), and a certain minimum annual premium income from the group is required.

If the plan is contributory, at least 50 employees or 75% of the eligible employees, whichever is greater, must elect to participate a short time after its effective date, to make it operative. If the plan is non-contributory, an employer-pay-all plan, then all eligible employees must be allowed to participate. After the plan is in operation, in the event the employee group covered decreases below the number cited above, the insurance company usually reserves the right to refuse to accept further premium payments.

*Past Service Benefits.* The employer is required to pay the cost of past service annuity credits. Past service annuity credits usually may be purchased only under a plan which provides for future service annuities. Any formula may be used for the purchase of past service benefits so far as the insurance company is concerned, provided it does not discriminate or permit an employer to select individual lives, or amounts of earnings. In other words, the employer cannot make exceptions to the general formula in purchasing past service annuities.

*Employee Contributions.* No contributions normally will be accepted from employees, in excess of those called for under the group annuity plan, toward the purchase of additional annuity benefits. In the event of termination of employment, no further contributions are accepted from an employee; the employee may not add to the withdrawal benefits he may be entitled to under the plan, by continuing contributions after severance of employment.

*Good Health Provision.* No medical examination or evidence of good health is required of employees eligible to a group annuity plan. Evidence of good health of an employee may be required by the insurance company, however, where the employee wishes certain options at retirement not offered under the regular form; or where an employee withdraws from employment and the question of a credit to the employer, or a surrender value for the latter's contribution, is involved.

*Annuity Forfeiture.* No provision may normally be written into a group annuity contract which permits a reduction or forfeiture of an employee's annuity income after retirement, if such employee should engage in activities or an occupation prejudicial to the employer.

*Minimum Retirement Income.* A pension formula, used under a group annuity plan to determine the benefits, might in some cases produce a lesser income at retirement than is desired. A provision may be included in the group annuity contract under which at the employee's retirement the employer may purchase additional annuities to bring the retirement income up to some stipulated minimum. These additional annuities usually may be purchased only at the employees' normal retirement dates.

*Maximum Retirement Income.* The major insurance companies limit the amount of annuity income that may become payable to any eligible employee in a plan. This limitation is brought about by either of the following methods. An annuity maximum is established in relation to (1) the number of eligible employees in the group covered, or (2) the size of the group *and* an average of the earnings of the fifty highest paid eligible employees.

The major underlying reason for these underwriting restrictions lies in the fact that without them, a lack of balance might develop in the amounts of annuity income payable as between the lower and the higher paid employees, with possible costly results. For example, a few high paid employees who were receiving excessively large amounts of annuity income in proportion to the average, might prove to be the longer-lived of the group. The consequences of such a situation would be either losses to the insurance company or higher annuity rates for the employer. A further need for such a limitation may be found in the fact that there is some evidence that mortality among the higher paid employees is less than among the lower paid, or at least, among the industrial grade employees.

## XII. ADMINISTRATIVE ASPECTS

*Group Contract.* A group annuity plan after its formulation is embodied finally in a master contract between the employer and an insurance company, known as a group annuity contract. A group contract is a document containing twenty to twenty-five pages. It covers, in *articles* or *parts,* the rights and obligations of the employer and employees, as well as those of the insurance company. We will summarize briefly these articles or parts in the order in which they are found in a typical group annuity contract.

*Article I: Definitions.* The meaning of all the terms used throughout the contract is carefully set forth. Among the principal terms defined are: future service annuity, past service annuity, retirement annuity, normal retirement dates, optional retirement dates, contingent annuitant, service of employees, and compensation.

*Article II:* Herein will be stated definitively the eligibility rules for an employee to become a member of the plan; the effective dates for individual coverage, the normal retirement date, and the employees' contributions, if any. There will be stated too the future service benefits and the past service credits, if any. Also the maximum amount of annuity to any one employee, which is obtainable through the use of the above schedule, will be stated.

*Article III:* A statement is made as to the method of computing the amounts and the time for payment of the cost of future service benefits. A full description of the cost of past service, and its method of payment, also appears. The length of the *grace* period for payment of the considerations or premiums is given; as is the status of the contract in case of suspension of future service premiums, or discontinuance of the contract.

*Article IV:* Matters that largely affect the employee are dealt with. The mode of payment of the retirement income, the amount of the retirement income at normal retirement date, or on the optional retirement date, are stated. The conditions for the election of a contingent annuitant, if available to the employee, are stipulated. The employee's benefits in case of death or termination of employment and also the considerations for an employer's refund credit, as well as its amount, if an employee withdraws, are set forth.

*Article V:* The general provisions of the group contract are set forth. These pertain to issuance of certificates of participation to the employee, the right to name a beneficiary, a prohibition against borrowing or assignment of the employee's interest, and the information to be furnished by either or both employer and employee, as the insurance company may request, in regard to ages, condition of health, or evidence of survival of employees. The right to participate in dividends, or the right that rate credits will be granted, is mentioned. The mortality table used and the interest assumption in connection therewith are described. Finally, provision is made for the modification of the contract as between the employer and the insurance company, but with due protection to the employees that any modifications shall not affect employee rights which have previously accrued. The period, usually one year, after which the contract is incontestable, is set forth. Finally, there is an agreement that the employer's application to the company for the group contract, a copy of which is attached, and the contract itself constitute the entire contract between the insurance company and the employer. The employee, it should be noted, is not a party to a group annuity contract but the beneficiary thereunder.

*Article VI:* The final article, or part, or pages of a group annuity contract, will consist of tables from which may be computed . (1) the cost of future and past service annuities for an individual employee; (2) the amount of annuity provided at normal retirement either by the employer or the employer-employee contributions; (3) the percentages of normal retirement income which will be paid to an employee who elects an earlier retirement. Usually an employee may retire, with the consent of the employer, at an earlier retirement date than the normal retirement date. Finally, if the option of electing a contingent annuitant is to be provided, a table will appear showing the amount of reduced income to the employee payable during his lifetime, and the percentage of such income payable to the contingent annuitant in the event of the employee's death.

*Guarantee of Rates.* The usual group annuity contract guarantees the premium rates in effect at the time of issuance for five years. The insurance company reserves the right to change, thereafter, on any contract anniversary date, its premium rates or the terms of the contract without, however, affecting any retirement annuities purchased for employees prior to such rate changes or alteration in the terms of the contract.

*Dividends or Rate Credits.* In the event the insurance company find its earnings warrant it, an employer may receive dividends or rate credits, which will reduce future premium costs. If the insurance company which underwrites the group annuity contract is a *mutual* company, then any refund is described as a dividend. If the insurance company is a *stock* company then any premium refund is described as a rate credit. The over-all earnings of the insurance company as well as its experience with a particular group annuity plan, will determine whether dividends or rate credits will be payable.

## XIII.  SELECTION OF GROUP ANNUITY COMPANY

The issuance of group annuity contracts until recent years has been confined to a small number of life insurance companies. The period of time in which they have been engaged in the business on any scale has been relatively short as compared to other phases of their business; not much beyond fifteen years. There is available very little published information of the group annuity experience of these companies as compared with the available data on their insurance operations. Mainly for these reasons, therefore, the most that can be offered are generalizations. It should be said also that even with the published data on their experience, in as complete a form as could reasonably be expected, it might be difficult to be specific. For example, we have seen that group annuities may be of different types, and are issued in various forms. These are available, subject to underwriting limitations, both to small and to large employers. To obtain comparability between companies, therefore, it would be necessary to institute an independent investigation. The purpose of the investigation would be mainly to determine the relative costs of plans among different carriers. This would constitute a research project of considerable scope, and would involve statistical difficulties. As a minimum, to obtain comparability, the plans (1) would have to have been issued approximately at the same time to similar sized organizations, (2) the mortality tables, interest assumptions, and loading charges would have to be the same, (3) the employees covered in the plan under study would have to be approximately the same in number, sex, and age distribution, (4) the premium income to the insurance carriers and the benefits paid out would have to be approximately the same, (5) the types of plans and their regular forms would have to be the same, and (6) to the extent that the respective employers had bought past service benefits, the methods of purchase would likewise have to have been similar. If a study of this kind could be made, and from it a conclusion could be reached as to which would have been the preferable insurance carrier for an employer in the past, it might serve as a guide in the selection of a company for those contemplating establishment of a new plan.

An employer selecting a group annuity company, who approaches the matter with customary business acumen, will be concerned usually with four things: (1) the financial strength of the company, (2) the terms of the group annuity contract, (3) the service rendered by the company, and (4) the comparative costs of a plan in one insurance carrier as against another.

*Financial Strength.* In the short history of group annuities the bulk of the business has been issued by seven major companies. There can be no question of the financial strength or resources of these companies. Their assets since entering the group annuity field have ranged from about two hundred million dollars for the smallest to five or six billions for the largest. The financial strength of insurance carriers who underwrite group annuity plans, with the entrance of new and smaller companies into the field in recent years, however, is one that cannot be entirely ignored. The deposits under a large group annuity contract may ultimately amount to millions of dollars. The experience of the last decade with declining interest rates and with the increase in longevity of annuitants has not made the group annuity business a profitable one for those companies holding the bulk of it. To the extent that they have sustained losses, however, their financial strength and resources have been entirely adequate to absorb them.

*Terms of the Group Annuity Contract.* In our summary of a group annuity contract, there was given what may be expected to be found in a typical contract. It should be pointed out, nevertheless, that a wise buyer will study several specimens of the different group annuity contracts to determine whether they have all the terms, privileges, and options that are to be reasonably expected and that are necessary to his situation.

*Service.* Under a group annuity plan the relationships are between an employer and an insurance carrier. It is doubtful if any distinction can be made between the major group annuity companies as to the services rendered. They are equally well equipped. The services which are rendered by a company, usually through its group annuity field representatives, are mainly as follows: (1) preparation of initial cost figures, and calculations of such adjustments as may be necessary from time to time; (2) payment of death, withdrawal, and annuity benefits; (3) preparation of figures and reports for the Treasury Department; (4) preparation of booklets or other literature which explain or describe the plan to the employees; (5) keeping of records of the individual employees, and other records necessary to efficient operation of the plan; (6) making annual reports to the employer of paid-up annuities credited to the account of individual employees; (7) explaining to the employees, through personal interviews when necessary, their rights and privileges under the plan; (8) obtaining the employee applications for entrance into the plan; and (9) generally keeping the employer posted as to the status of his plan through annual or interim reports. It should be noted that these services usually will be rendered by the group annuity representatives of the insurance company, even though the adoption of the plan may have been brought about through an insurance broker or pension consultant.

*Comparative Costs.* We have already indicated the fact that the available data are insufficient to appraise cost differentials, if any, which may have prevailed in the past as between insurance carriers issuing like group annuity plans. If these were known, we stated, they might serve as a guide for an employer establishing a new plan. This conclusion is based on the reasoning that past performance could be treated as an index of what to expect in the future. This would be true to a limited degree, but an insurance company that had in the past produced the lowest relative costs to its group annuity policyholders might for reasons of policy or necessity fail to provide equally low costs in the future. Also, the limited experience with group annuities of the issuing companies, in any case, has not been extensive enough to validate predictions as to relative future costs of one carrier as against another.

Notwithstanding what has been said, the employer seeking a group annuity plan is well advised to secure at least several group annuity proposals from different companies. While this involves an investment of time, possibly not available, or presupposes a degree of technical background to evaluate the claims that inevitably will be presented by group annuity company representatives, he at least will obtain information on the other three items discussed above. If neither the time nor knowledge is available to evaluate the proposals, then he may find a solution by placing his pension problem in the hands of a pension consultant.

# CHAPTER VII

## Individual Annuity Policy Plan

........................................................................

THE INDIVIDUAL ANNUITY POLICY PLAN[1] LIKE THE GROUP ANNUITY is an insured pension plan. The fact that a life insurance company is an interested party in both types makes for a common denominator, in that in either case there is a guarantee of the pension benefits, or of principal and interest, in return for the premiums paid; however, they otherwise differ in a number of major aspects. The explanation of the individual annuity plan which follows will develop its characteristics, and consequently its differences from the group annuity plan.

The individual annuity plan comes into existence more or less in the following manner. An employer with the aid of his advisers tentatively decides at what age his employees shall be retired; the amount of the pension benefits; the group of employees who shall be eligible under the plan, and when they shall be eligible; whether death benefits shall be provided; when, as well as to what extent, death benefits shall be made available to the employees; the basis of the employees' contributions, if any, and other details. All the terms of the pension plan are worked out without any reference necessarily to the insurance company which may be finally selected to invest the pension funds; although the plan must be so formulated that it will meet the Federal law and the Treasury regulations governing pension plans. An insurance company is then selected, which will issue individual annuity policies of a type that will provide the benefits in accordance with the terms of the pension plan. It may be necessary to secure individual annuity policies from more than one insurance company to fully underwrite the plan, either because the underwriting rules of one company may differ from another, or because one company may issue a type of contract desired for the plan not offered by the other. It is true that, when a pension plan of an employer contemplates the

---

[1] Also referred to as the *individual annuity plan.*

136

use of individual annuity policies, consideration will be given to what the market affords. The character of the individual annuity policies which may be purchased from insurance companies, in other words, will determine the final design of the plan. In general, however, an employer using individual annuity policies to finance his plan will utilize such types of contracts as may best effectuate the terms of his plan, provided there is no resulting discrimination as between employees.

## I. METHOD OF FUNDING

The typical method of funding an individual annuity pension plan is by the use of individual annuity contracts which normally involve the use of the level accumulation[2] or level premium method. This method presumes that of a group of employees under a pension plan all will survive to normal retirement age; thus no discount is taken for deaths that may occur. Also no discount is taken for withdrawals from employment by employees, nor are any future salary changes anticipated in the premium. In the event of the deaths or the withdrawals of employees the total premiums for all employees may be reduced as these events take place, and the accumulated value of the individual annuity contracts may be disposed of in accordance with the terms of the pension plan. If salary increases occur, which require increases in the employees pension benefits, then the increased benefits are purchased for the employees at the time of the increases.

In contrast to the single-premium deferred life annuity method of funding, which in relation to an individual employee involves a rising premium each year until actual retirement, the level premium method maintains a constant or level premium on an employee's life until retirement.

A further difference is that, whereas the single-premium deferred life annuity method of funding provides no death benefits (or cash values, except under a group annuity plan where the employee withdraws in good health), the level premium accumulation method provides for a death benefit, as well as a cash value in the event of an employee's withdrawal. The cash value is available upon withdrawal, independent of the condition of the employee's health.

There are six types of individual annuity policies which are apt to be employed, either singly or in combination, to finance an in-

---

[2] See Chapter IV on Pension Costs.

dividual annuity pension plan. The types are (1) retirement annuity, (2) retirement income, (3) level premium deferred life annuity, (4) single-premium deferred life annuity, (5) immediate life annuity, and (6) cash refund life annuity.[3]

Of these, major use is made only of the retirement income policy, with the circumstances determining whether any or all of the others are to be utilized. Furthermore, it is only the retirement annuity and the retirement income policies that involve the level premium accumulation method. We have given a general description of certain characteristics of the retirement annuity and the retirement income policies,[4] but at the expense of some repetition it seems advisable again to examine them.

## A.  Retirement Annuity Policy

A review of the discussion of the retirement annuity contract in Chapter III, and of Chapter IV where the level premium accumulation method of funding is illustrated, should provide the reader with an understanding of the general nature of the retirement annuity and the method of premium computation thereunder. In discussing the latter in Chapter IV we dealt with a group of 100 lives, and traced for comparative purposes the operation of level premium accumulation funding in contrast to the single-premium deferred life annuity method, and that of level percentage of payroll. That discussion may have given the impression that the computation of the level premium on a retirement annuity policy takes into consideration the death or survival of other lives prior to the time retirement takes place. Such is not the case, and this fact clearly distinguishes it from the single-premium deferred life annuity and the typical level percentage of payroll methods.

The calculation of the level premium of a retirement annuity, purchased at any age, involves first a determination of the amount of cash, or capital sum, required at a selected retirement age to produce a given income under a particular type of annuity. It therefore takes account only of deaths which will occur *after* retirement. When this capital sum has been determined it is accumulated at a given interest rate through the use of level annual premiums. Prior to the retirement of employees, therefore, the employer, who uses individual retirement annuity policies to

---

[3] A chart showing the usual benefits provided by these contracts appears on pages 154-156.

[4] See Chapter III.

finance his pension plan, essentially has a number of pure investment accounts, which will be represented by the individual retirement annuity policies on the lives of his employees.

We shall illustrate further the nature of the retirement annuity contract by the use of a commercial level premium rate in relation to an employee aged 45, who is to receive at age 65 a nominal pension benefit of $10.00 a month, or $120.00 a year. The usual retirement annuity contract (also the retirement income contract) is issued in units which will pay $10.00 a month at retirement for life, 10 years certain.[5] The capital sum necessary to be accumulated at 65 therefore must be in an amount sufficient to pay $10.00 a month on a life annuity, 10 years certain. One insurance company requires cash to have been accumulated by age 65 of $1,587.00, if $10.00 a month for life, 10 years certain, is the benefit. Its gross level premium (which includes a charge for expenses), payable from 45 to 64, amounts to $68 a year. Until the employee reaches retirement at age 65, the yearly level premiums of $68 (less the loading or expense charge included therein) will simply accumulate at interest in the retirement annuity contract as in a bank account;[6] in the interim it is these premium deposits which provide a cash value in the event an employee withdraws from employment, or a death benefit[7] if he dies before reaching retirement.

## B.  Retirement Income Policy

We have stated that the retirement annuity policy is an *investment* contract prior to the retirement of an employee and that, upon retirement when income commences, it becomes an *annuity* contract. The retirement income policy likewise has the same dual aspects, but in addition it has a third element which consists of an insurance feature.[8] Most employers, when they encounter the retirement income policy, believe that they are dealing with a typical insurance policy rather than an annuity contract which will pension their employees. This belief arises from their identifying

---

[5] Some insurance companies will issue these contracts on a unit basis, to pay $2.50 or $5.00 a month, 10 years certain, at retirement.

[6] If a contract is canceled in the early years there is a surrender charge.

[7] The death benefit usually is equal at least to the amount of premiums paid on the contract, or to the cash value of the contract if it is larger in amount than the sum of the premiums.

[8] Technically, there also is a minor insurance element in the retirement annuity to make provision for refunds of premiums as a death benefit. Common usage, however, makes reference to a retirement annuity, as a contract *without* an insurance feature.

the retirement income policy with the general run of life insurance policies with which they are familiar, such as whole life (straight life), twenty payment life, or twenty year endowment.  The consequences have been that some employers, considering individual annuity pension plans, have thought that they were being presented with a scheme for providing insurance benefits for their employees, rather than pension benefits.  Other employers, who have not held this view, have been inclined to the belief that the inclusion of an insurance feature in the retirement income policy, in contrast to the retirement annuity policy which has no such feature, would substantially increase the financial outlays for their pension plan.  Neither of these viewpoints is entirely correct, as indicated by Table XIX and the related discussion.

It is true there is no necessary connection theoretically between pensions for superannuated employees at retirement and death benefits prior thereto; but as a practical matter there is an increasing tendency to provide death benefits in newly established pension plans.  Social Security provides for death benefits to dependents in the event the worker fails to survive to retirement.  Group Life[9] insurance to provide death benefits is commonly utilized in connection with group annuity or self-administered pension plans. The use of an insurance feature, as contained in the retirement income policy, is thus simply a method of approximating the functions of group life insurance; or of substituting for it, by including in one contract a provision for both a retirement and an insurance benefit.

### C.  Comparative Premium Outlays

In Table XIX are shown the comparative outlays required by one mutual life insurance company issuing both retirement annuity and retirement income contracts.  The age selected is 45, with a level premium payable in each case from ages 45 to 64.  The premium outlays are illustrated with the expected dividends[10] deducted.[11]  At age 65 under either contract the value at maturity

---

[9] See Chapter X for a discussion of Group Life insurance.

[10] Future dividends, illustrated as payable by life insurance companies on insurance or annuity contracts are carefully qualified; they are to be considered as neither estimates nor guarantees.  Future dividends must be regarded, therefore, simply as illustrations of what *will* be payable if the dividend scale, in effect at the time of illustration, is maintained.

[11] Stock life insurance companies usually issue a non-participating contract in which there is no provision for dividends.  Non-participating contracts usually will have a lower *initial* premium than participating contracts issued by mutual life

will amount to $1,587.00, which, in relation to the guaranteed annuity rate, will be adequate to pay $10.00 a month for life, 10 years certain. The death benefit under the retirement annuity is the amount of the premiums paid, or the cash value, whichever is larger; the death benefit under the retirement income contract is the face amount of the insurance or the cash value, whichever is larger.

TABLE XIX

COMPARATIVE PREMIUM OUTLAYS OF RETIREMENT
ANNUITY AND RETIREMENT INCOME CONTRACTS
Purchased at Age 45

| | Retirement Annuity | | Retirement Income | |
| | Gross Level Premium—$68.49 | | Gross Level Premium—$74.01 | |
| | Male | | Male | |
| Year | Premium Outlays | Death Benefit | Premium Outlays | Death Benefit |
|---|---|---|---|---|
| 1 | $68.49 | $ 68.49 | $74.01 | $1,000.00 |
| 2 | 67.91 | 136.98 | 74.01 | 1,000.00 |
| 3 | 67.63 | 204.03 | 68.26 | 1,000.00 |
| 4 | 67.31 | 271.34 | 67.98 | 1,000.00 |
| 5 | 66.99 | 338.13 | 67.69 | 1,000.00 |
| 6 | 66.65 | 404.78 | 67.39 | 1,000.00 |
| 7 | 66.31 | 471.09 | 67.08 | 1,000.00 |
| 8 | 65.96 | 537.05 | 66.75 | 1,000.00 |
| 9 | 65.60 | 602.65 | 66.42 | 1,000.00 |
| 10 | 65.23 | 674.00 | 66.07 | 1,000.00 |
| 11 | 64.85 | 756.00 | 65.71 | 1,000.00 |
| 12 | 64.46 | 839.00 | 65.33 | 1,000.00 |
| 13 | 64.05 | 925.00 | 64.94 | 1,000.00 |
| 14 | 63.63 | 1,012.00 | 64.53 | 1,000.00 |
| 15 | 63.20 | 1,102.00 | 64.09 | 1,072.00 |
| 16 | 62.76 | 1,195.00 | 63.64 | 1,169.00 |
| 17 | 62.31 | 1,288.00 | 63.17 | 1,269.00 |
| 18 | 61.86 | 1,386.00 | 62.68 | 1,372.00 |
| 19 | 61.38 | 1,485.00 | 62.19 | 1,478.00 |
| 20 | 60.90 | 1,587.00 | 61.77 | 1,587.00 |

In the over-all picture a retirement income contract, with a larger death benefit in the earlier years than is provided by a retirement annuity, will not call for a much greater premium out-

insurance companies. For a discussion of non-participating versus mutual life insurance see: Huebner, S. S., *Life Insurance*, D. Appleton-Century Co., Inc., New York, N. Y., 1935, pp. 466-472.

lay.[12] The actual percentage difference, or spread, between the premium outlays required on a retirement income contract and those on a retirement annuity will vary with the different insurance companies issuing both contracts. The probable percentage spread will be from 3% to 9%; that is, the premium outlays for a retirement income contract will not exceed those of a retirement annuity by more than these percentages, assuming that the dividends, illustrated as expected to be paid on both contracts, are realized.

## II. TYPES OF INDIVIDUAL ANNUITY PLANS

In analyzing group annuity plans it was pointed out that they may be established on the principle of either definite-benefit or money-purchase plans. Individual annuity plans likewise may be set up on either principle; but the level premium accumulation method of funding under individual annuity plans (as against the use of the single-premium deferred life annuity method of group annuities) gives rise to several differentiating characteristics.

### A. Definite-Benefit

In illustration of the use of the definite-benefit principle under an individual annuity plan we may return to the formula used in the computation of pension costs. We there provided for a male aged 45 a benefit at 65 equal to 1% of his salary for each year of participation in the plan until retirement. The total salary expected was in the amount of $20,000 and the benefit, therefore, was $200 a year, life annuity due at 65. The typical level premium contracts pay the retirement benefits monthly as a life annuity, 10 years certain, so we shall depart slightly from this earlier illustration where the benefit was assumed to be paid yearly, and for life only. An annual pension of $200 a year may be reduced to a monthly income of $16.66. The cost for a male life age 45 to obtain $16.66 at age 65, 10 years certain, may be shown by the use of the retirement annuity premium rate of $68.49 employed above. The premium cost thus would be $114.10 ($68.49 × 1.666 units), if we ignore any dividends that may reduce the premium.

The level premium of $114.10 is the yearly cost until retirement, and thus by its use there are eliminated any variables which may

---

[12] It should be noted that the illustration relates to *premium outlays* and assumes persistency of both contracts to maturity, except as death may lead to their termination.

thereafter affect the employer's cost so far as providing the monthly benefit of $16.66 for the individual life, age 45. Dividends may reduce the initial cost of $114.10 to a lesser figure, but the cost cannot be higher. The employer under the level premium method, therefore, knows his initial as well as his maximum costs, so far as they relate to the original benefits purchased for all employees who enter the plan upon its establishment. Any premium rate changes made by the insurance companies thereafter cannot affect the costs of the original benefits purchased for this group. If salary increases occur then, of course, additional benefits must be bought at the employee's attained age and at the prevailing rates. In respect to an individual employee, however, if we assume the pension benefit which is purchased for him on a level premium basis is to be his maximum, there can be no increases in such premium thereafter, either because of the increasing age of the employee or because of a general rise in premium rates for new employees who may enter the plan.

### B.  Money-Purchase

If an employer decides to make use of the money-purchase principle under an individual annuity plan, the level premium funding method also will bring about somewhat distinctive characteristics. For example, we will assume that an employer appropriates a sum equal to 10% of an employee's salary, the latter being $1,000 a year, toward the purchase of pension benefits. There then will be available $100 a year with which to buy the pension benefits. Using a level premium of $68.49 for age 45, which purchases $10.00 a month, 10 years certain, commencing at age 65, the employer's contribution of $100 will purchase about $15 a month, or an annual benefit of about $180. Because the benefit has been purchased on a level premium basis, neither the fact that the employee grows older nor any future change in premium rates will affect either the employee's original retirement benefit,[13] or its premium cost.

While use of the money-purchase principle under the level premium individual annuity plan brings about the immediate purchase of a *specific* benefit, thus eliminating the effects of increasing age and possible premium rate changes, it should be noted that this is a direct consequence of using the level premium method of purchase. It does not obviate the fact that the money-purchase

---

[13] Salary decreases, unless excluded, could of course lead to a reduction of the benefit inasmuch as the employee's contribution is related to compensation.

principle is employed. The benefit still remains indefinite in the sense that it is in no prearranged ratio to salary, or salary and service.

## III.  EMPLOYEE CONTRIBUTIONS

### A.  Definite-Benefit

The system of employee contributions used in individual annuity definite-benefit plans is superficially analogous to that used under group annuities. The terminology employed in explaining group annuity employee contributions, for reasons which are discussed below, is not used with reference to employee contributions under the individual annuity plan. There seems to be common agreement that, under whatever type of plan is selected by an employer for pensioning his employees, if the definite-benefit principle is employed, the range of contributions should be between 2% and 5% of salary. If there is no Social Security coverage then employees may be called upon to contribute as high as 6%.

A typical contribution scheme under individual annuity plans is to require a 3% contribution from those earning $3,000 or under, and 5% from those earning in excess, where the retirement benefit is 1% of compensation for each year of service. Another is to require a contribution of 2% of the first $3,000 of salary and 3% of the excess, when the pension benefit is 1% of the first $3,000 of salary and 1½% of the excess. There are innumerable variants and combinations which may be and are used. The main objective in all cases is to reduce the employer's cost, at the same time holding the employee's contributions at a reasonable level.

The resemblance between group annuity plans, which use a fixed ratio such as 2 to 1, that is, a 2% contribution for $1.00 of annuity benefit, and individual annuity plans, requiring a 2% contribution where the retirement benefit is 1% of yearly compensation, would seem to result from the fact that they involve the same principle. For example, an employee, under a group annuity, aged 45 and earning $1,200, where the ratio is 2 to 1, contributes $24.00 a year, and receives for that year an annuity credit of $12.00 payable at age 65. With no salary change to retirement age of 65, he would have annuity credits or a pension of $240 a year ($12 × 20 years). An employee, under an individual annuity plan, of the same age and in the same salary bracket, where 2% was the contribution and the retirement benefit at age 65 was 1%

for each year of service, would also contribute $24.00, for which he would receive at retirement $240 a year ($12 × 20 years). The annuity income or pension at retirement under both plans is the same, and also in each case the employee has contributed $24.00 a year or a total of $480. Under the level premium accumulation method of the retirement annuity contract, however, there is no unit of annuity credit of $1.00 purchased yearly for the employee, such as occurs in the group annuity plan. The retirement annuity contract, as we have pointed out, merely accumulates cash, pending the time of retirement, when the accumulated funds are applied to provide the annuity income. As a consequence it may be seen that, despite the fact that the example we have used called for employee contributions in the same amount, and at retirement provided an identical benefit, there is an essential difference.

This may be brought out more clearly if we assume the establishment both of a group annuity plan and an individual annuity plan, which are to be terminated at the end of their first year in operation. To avoid complications, introduced by a consideration of surrender charges, as found in both group annuity and retirement annuity contracts, we shall return again to the example used in showing pension costs.

In our pension cost computation, at age 45, the first year single-premium deferred life annuity cost for 100 employees to provide a benefit of 1% of salary was $6,320.00, or $63.20 per employee. Under the level premium method, at age 45, the cost was $10,096.00, or $100.96 per employee. If at the end of the first year no further payments should be made the situation would be as follows: the employee under the single-premium deferred life annuity funding method (group annuity) would have a fully paid-up deferred life annuity which, if he survives to age 65, would pay him $10.00 a year (1% of a $1,000 salary). The employee under the level premium accumulation method (retirement annuity) on the other hand would be entitled to a cash value of $100.96. If this cash value were left to accumulate to age 65 at 2%, the rate of interest assumed, the annuity income at 65 would amount to approximately $13.50; this relatively larger amount is explainable because of the higher initial level premium outlay. Now from a contribution standpoint, if we assume each employee had contributed 2% of his salary of $1,000, or $20.00, the ratio of contribution to benefits purchased under the group annuity is 2 to 1; or $20.00 for the 1% deferred life annuity benefit of $10.00. Under the level premium accumulation, however, there simply is created a cash value of $100.96, toward which the employee has contributed $20.00; the annuity income of $13.50 is in such definitive amount only after the cash value has accumulated at 2% interest to 65, and the annuity income actually has been purchased.

A further technical point of difference between employee contributions under group annuity and individual annuity plans may be noted. In the former, the fact that employees contribute makes for a difference in the premium rate charged per $1.00 of annuity purchased; and there will be a further premium difference, depending upon the rate of interest which is to be credited on the employee contributions. This is not the case with retirement annuity or retirement income contracts. Premium rates are quoted in relation to the monthly income desired at retirement; thus $68.49 at age 45 provides for a unit of retirement annuity of $10.00 a month, 10 years certain, at age 65. Any employee's contributions, of course, will reduce the employer's cost as under a group annuity plan; but neither the amount of the employee's contributions, nor the question of whether or not they are returnable with interest or without, are items of information which the insurance company needs to know in order to quote premium rates. Stated differently, if $10.00 a month is to be the pension benefit at 65, it is purchased by the payment of the premium rate required at the then age of the employee for the type of annuity desired at retirement. The premium *rate* will be the same, whether or not the employees are contributing under the individual annuity pension plan.

## B. Money-Purchase

Contributions under a money-purchase individual annuity plan may be made on the same basis as in a group annuity. The employer and employee, that is, may match each other's contributions, or the employer may contribute on the basis of 1½ or 2% of an employee's salary for each 1% the employee contributes. Flat amounts may be used rather than a percentage of salary, if desired. The effects of money-purchase in individual annuity plans will differ from those in a group annuity, as outlined above. The money-purchase principle, however, is used rarely in individual annuity plans, and in recent years its use is rare in group annuity plans. Because of the difference in the method of funding, however, the money-purchase principle, employed under the individual annuity plan with its use of level premiums, is more likely to provide a definite or specific retirement benefit, bought with the employer-employee contributions (or where the employer only contributes), than when it is used in a group annuity. While fluctuations in salary could affect the ultimate benefits purchased in either case, if the contributions are related to salary, the effects of increasing age or premium rate changes, which may affect the amount of benefits purchasable by the joint contributions under the single-premium deferred life annuity funding of the group annuity, are partially obviated through the use of the guaranteed level premiums of retirement annuity or retirement income contracts.

## IV. EARNINGS CLASSES

Whereas the establishment of earnings classes is typical of group annuity plans, as relates both to the employee's contributions and the yearly annuity credits purchased for his benefit, it is otherwise with individual annuity plans. While earnings classes may be employed under the latter, the following method is usual. If the plan is a definite-benefit one, it is provided that the pension benefits shall be payable on the basis of units of not less than $5.00 or $10.00 a month at retirement, with fractional benefits allowed only when the units are in excess of these amounts, such as $7.50 or $12.50 a month. To affect the pension benefit the salary or wage increase must be in an amount which, after application of the benefit formula, e.g. 1% or 1½% of compensation, will add at least either $5.00 or $10.00 to the retirement benefit. If the money-purchase principle is utilized, the percentage of contributions must be related to salary or wages, so that the actual contributions (also if flat amounts) will be adequate to purchase a minimum benefit of $5.00 or $10.00 a month at the inception of the plan. In the case of increased contributions, which occur because of salary increases, it is necessary to provide that these similarly must be in an amount sufficient to increase the retirement benefit at least $5.00 or $10.00 before they may be utilized.

The reason for retirement benefits being computed in terms of not less than $5.00 or $10.00 a month under individual annuity plans lies basically in the fact that insurance companies issue retirement annuity and retirement income contracts only in units which provide these amounts at retirement.

The justification for the insurance companies following this procedure is that it holds down their administrative costs, and consequently ultimate costs to the buyers of individual contracts. From the point of view of the administration of a pension plan this procedure minimizes frequent adjustments in the benefits which would be necessary if small increases in benefits were required to be taken account of. In terms of the employee's interest, so long as cumulative increases in compensation are considered, which when taken together make for an increase of either $5.00 or $10.00 a month in the benefit, this procedure is satisfactory. It nevertheless must be observed that the use of earnings classes, or exact earnings, in an individual annuity plan, as a basis for computation of increased benefits brought about by salary increases, will provide pension increases less frequently (particularly at the older ages) than under a group annuity plan. For example, in a definite-benefit group annuity plan, whereas an increased benefit may be purchased, even when it is no more than fifty cents a month, the increased benefits, as purchased under the individual annuity plan, occur only when they will amount to $5.00 or $10.00 a month at retirement. Conversely, however, in the event of decreases in salary, any downward adjustment of the pension benefits would be less frequent in an individual annuity plan.

## V. FORMS OF RETIREMENT CONTRACTS

The typical retirement annuity or retirement income contract, as we have noted, is issued in a form which will provide either $5.00 or $10.00 a month, 10 years certain, at the normal retirement age as established under an individual annuity policy pension plan. While the language of group annuities, that is *regular forms,* is not applicable in a discussion of the individual annuity plan, there are several variants from the typical contract which make payments at retirement on a 10 year certain basis.

*Life Annuity Form.* It is possible to obtain retirement income contracts which will pay pension benefits on a life annuity basis (without refund) in the event of death after retirement. The premium rates for such contracts will be less than when a life annuity, 10 years certain period, is guaranteed.

*Life Annuity—5 years certain.* A retirement income contract which makes payment of the benefits on a life annuity, 5 year certain basis, also may be used in lieu of the form providing simply for a life annuity without refund, or for a life annuity, 10 years certain. It also will call for a different premium rate.

The comparative premium rates for these forms are shown below. In each instance the retirement age is 65, the premium rate is for a male life, aged 45, and the benefit is $10.00 a month.   Each form provides life insurance in addition to the pension benefit; the insurance coverage, however, differs with each form.   The gross premium shown is a level premium payable until retirement (unless death or withdrawal takes place), but it may be reduced by dividends.

RETIREMENT INCOME CONTRACT

Male Life  Age 45

Gross Premium Rates to Obtain $10.00 a Month Life Income
Commencing at Age 65

| Life Annuity 10 Years Certain | Life Annuity 5 Years Certain | Life Annuity |
|:---:|:---:|:---:|
| Insurance—$1,000 $74 | Insurance—$928.00 $69 | Insurance—$904.00 $67 |

## VI.  OPTIONS AT RETIREMENT

Individual annuity policies, whether retirement annuity or retirement income contracts, offer a number of options when retirement takes place, in lieu of the basic option.   For example, if retirement income policies providing for a life annuity, 10 years certain option, have been used to finance a pension plan, an employee may select an alternative option, subject to the terms of the pension plan.   He may make his election of an option at the actual date of retirement, and no evidence of good health is required.   The following are the principal alternative options usually found in retirement annuity or retirement income contracts as issued by the major life insurance companies.

*Interest.*   The accumulated cash value at retirement, such as the $1,587.00 above, may be left on deposit with the insurance company.   The employee will receive interest monthly on this amount at the rate guaranteed in the retirement contract, with the principal sum ultimately to be payable to him, or to his beneficiaries or estate.

*Principal and Interest.*   The cash value, instead of being left on deposit as a source of interest alone, may be drawn upon in monthly installments consisting of principal and interest over a period of years until consumed.   This option may be useful if retirement occurs before 65, for then the payments may be adjusted in relation to Social Security benefits which commence at 65.

*Cash Refund Annuity.*   An employee may elect that the cash value available at retirement be paid to him under a cash refund

annuity.  This option means that, if he should die before having
received payments which totaled the purchase price, or $1,587.00,
payments would be continued to his heirs or estate until they had
equaled the purchase price of $1,587.00.

*Life Annuity.*  A life annuity without any refund provision, or
years certain period, is usually available.

*Joint and Survivor Annuity.*  This option, like the contingent
annuitant option of the group annuity, has as its purpose to guarantee to the employee and some other life (usually a wife) an income so long as either may live.  It provides a reduced annuity
income, with the survivor usually receiving either all, one-half, or
two-thirds of the reduced income.  It sometimes is offered with a
10 or 20 year certain period provision, so that if both of the joint
annuitants should die shortly after commencing to receive annuity
income, payments for the certain period would be continued to a
third party or the estate of the last survivor.

## VII.  EMPLOYER'S MODE OF PURCHASE

The benefits which are purchased under an individual annuity
plan may be both for past and future service as in a group annuity.
The latter, however, uses one regular form for past service (*no
death-benefit—life* form) and another for future service.  Also
past service credits either are purchased in a lump sum or over
a period of possibly 10 to 20 years.  The individual annuity plan,
in contrast, customarily merges the costs of past and future services into a level premium which covers both.  For example, we
may take the case of a male age 45 who under an individual annuity
plan will receive at 65 a benefit equal to 1% of his salary for each
year of future service, and ½% for each year of past service.  If
his salary is $1,200 a year his benefit for future service will be
$240.00 (1% × $1,200 × 20 years); his benefit for past service, if
he has had service of 20 years, will be $120 (½ × $1,200 × 20
years).  The sum of the future and past service benefits is $360, or
$30.00 a month commencing at age 65.  The level premium at age
45, used above, under a retirement income contract is $74.01 for
$10.00 a month at 65, 10 years certain.  The cost of $30.00 a month
is therefore $74.01 × 3 (units) or $222.03.  This $222.03 is payable
as a level premium (less possible dividends) until the employee
retires.  Actually, one-third of this level premium, that is $74.01,
represents the cost of past service, but it is merged with the pre-

mium cost for future service benefits to make a total level premium of $222.03.

The form of the retirement contract, therefore, when it provides benefits on a 10 year certain basis, normally will be exactly the same both for past and future service benefits. As a consequence, the elective options at retirement described above are equally available in relation to the cash maturity value at retirement, created from the purchase both of the past and future service benefits.

Other types of annuity contracts may be employed to fund an individual annuity plan. Of these types several have a practical use only in relation to certain employees; others may function to fund an entire plan, or they may be used for past service benefits in conjunction with retirement annuity or retirement income contracts which provide for future service benefits. Their application will be briefly discussed.

## VIII.  EMPLOYEES AT RETIREMENT AGE

*Single-Premium Annuity.*  For employees at the retirement age, when an individual annuity plan is established, there may be purchased either (a) immediate life annuities or (b) cash refund life annuities, under either of which income commences immediately. A cash refund annuity may be selected if an employee is in poor health, and if it seems desirable and possible to assure some death benefit. The purchase of benefits for employees at retirement, whether in the form of immediate life or cash refund annuities, is by lump sum payments, although an alternative scheme is available.

*Immediate Income—Post-payment.*  The alternative scheme, mentioned above, for the payment of premiums for benefits to employees at retirement age, involves the following procedure. If an employee age 65, in the plan, is to be retired immediately, an annuity income to him commences at once. The premium cost, however, instead of being met in a lump sum, is paid over a period of ten years. If the employee dies during the premium-paying period of ten years no further premiums are payable.

## IX.  EMPLOYEES NOT AT RETIREMENT AGE

*Level Premium Deferred Life Annuity.*  As to those employees who have two or more years of service prior to retirement, the purchase both of past and future service benefits may be made with a level premium deferred life annuity contract in lieu of retirement annuity or retirement income contracts. A level premium deferred life annuity differs from a single-premium deferred life annuity in that it is paid for by level annual premiums. It may not be possible to use this type of contract in a pension plan in the case of a large employee group because of the unwillingness of insurance carriers to underwrite it. When this type is used, however, it involves separate contracts on the lives of the employees. There are no death benefits either prior to or after retirement. It naturally carries a lower premium than that of the retirement annuity or retirement income contract, because of the lesser benefits that are provided. For example, in the case of an employee at age 45, a retirement income or a retirement annuity contract to provide $10.00 a month, 10 years certain at age 65, calls for a gross premium rate of $74 and $68 respectively, while the cost of $10.00 a month, payable at 65 under a level premium deferred life annuity, will approximate only $55. This comparison again illustrates the statement in the chapter on pension costs that the type of benefit is an important determinant of the cost of a pension plan.

*Single-Premium Deferred Life Annuity.* An individual single-premium deferred life annuity policy makes use of the same principle as that employed in the single-premium deferred life annuities of group annuity plans. Where this policy is used to fund an individual annuity plan, however, separate contracts are issued to cover the employees and they are not subject to the governing provisions of a master contract as is the case in a group annuity plan. This fact makes for some inflexibility in respect to the employer's interests, for normally an employee who terminates employment will take the individual single-premium deferred life annuity contract with him. This is in contrast to a group annuity where it is possible for the employer to receive a credit for the single premiums paid for each employee who withdraws in good health. If the terms of the individual annuity pension plan provide for full vesting of the employer's contributions, however, this fact may not be important. As a practical matter, if individual single-premium deferred life annuity contracts were to be used, they normally would be employed to provide the past service benefits, in combination with retirement annuities or retirement income contracts to cover future service benefits.

If full vesting of the employee's contributions is not contemplated in the pension plan, then a modified or partial vesting may be effected in this way. The single-premium deferred life annuities purchased for past service may be fully vested, with no vesting for future service benefits purchased by the retirement annuity or retirement income contracts.

## X.  DIVIDENDS

### A.  Source

We have noted that individual annuity policies may be obtained as participating or non-participating contracts. Mutual life insurance companies issue most of their contracts in a participating form; whereas stock life insurance companies issue non-participating contracts. On a participating contract there normally is paid an annual dividend to the policyholder, which may be used to reduce his future premium outlays. A stock company, while it makes no provision for dividends to its policyholders, usually compensates for this by issuing its contracts at lower gross premium rates than those quoted by mutual companies.

A life insurance company, like any other financial enterprise, may suffer losses or enjoy gains in its operations. In the course of its yearly operations, to the extent gains occur, there may arise a divisible surplus. This surplus is an over-all gain after all proper charges have been made against that year's income. A holder of a participating contract who receives a dividend is obtaining a share of the divisible surplus. There are three major sources from any or all of which a life insurance company may make gains, or accrue a divisible surplus; and out of which there may be paid a dividend to the owner of a participating contract. The source of gains may be from (1) interest, (2) mortality, or (3) loading charges.

*Gains from Interest.* In the computation of life insurance premiums it is assumed some rate of interest will be earned. For example, an insurance company may have calculated its reserves and premium rates on the assumption that it will earn at least 2½%. If the actual earnings in a given year turn out to be 3½% the excess interest earnings for that year, or some portion thereof, may become a part of the divisible surplus.

*Gains from Mortality.* Gains from mortality may occur either under insurance or under annuity contracts. Mortality gains under insurance contracts will arise if there are a lesser number of deaths than were expected; under annuity contracts (that is an-

# INDIVIDUAL ANNUITY POLICY PLAN

## TABLE XX

### Typical Retirement, Withdrawal, and Death Benefits of Individual Annuity Contracts

| | Living Benefits | | | |
| --- | --- | --- | --- | --- |
| | Upon Retirement | | Upon Withdrawal from Employment | |
| Type of Individual Annuity Contract | To Employee | To Employer | To Employee | To Employer |
| Retirement Income......... | Life Income | Nothing | Cash Value[a] | Cash Value[b] |
| Retirement Annuity......... | Life Income | Nothing | Cash Value[a] | Cash Value[b] |
| Level Premium Deferred Life Annuity................. | Life Income | Nothing | Paid-up[c] Deferred Life Annuity | Nothing[d] |
| Single-Premium Deferred Life Annuity................ | Life Income | Nothing | Paid-up[c] Deferred Life Annuity | Nothing[d] |
| Immediate Life Annuity..... | Life Income | Nothing | ——[e] | ——[e] |
| Cash Refund Life Annuity... | Life Income | Nothing | ——[e] | ——[e] |

[a] The employee's share in the cash value will depend on the terms of the pension plan. In lieu of a cash value, the employee may possibly receive either (1) an income as may be provided by his share of the cash value, (2) a paid-up deferred annuity (which will possess a cash value), (3) the entire contract, or a fraction thereof, on which he may continue premium payments.

[b] The employer's share in the cash value will depend on the terms of the pension plan; in any case such cash value cannot revert directly to the employer, and must be used for the benefit of the employees covered by the pension plan.

[c] Usually no cash value is available; it is possible certain insurance companies may allow a cash value on surrender of the paid-up deferred life annuity, if the employee proves good health. In such cases the employee's share in the cash value would depend on the terms of the pension plan.

[d] See Note c; for the employer's share in the cash value and disposition thereof, see Note b.

[e] This contract is utilized for employees at retirement age, who are to be retired immediately.

[f] Either the insurance proceeds, that is, the face amount of the contract, will be payable, or the cash value of the contract, whichever is larger; the share that the employee's beneficiary will receive, however, will depend on the terms of the pension plan.

nuity contracts where life contingencies are involved) gains will arise if there are a greater number of deaths than were expected. We shall illustrate.

(Under Insurance Contracts.) If we refer to the extract of the American Experience Table of Mortality on page 51 of Chapter III, it will be noted that the number of survivors at age 45 of an original group of 100,000 lives starting at age 10 is 74,173. It is expected that there will die in the course of the ensuing year 828 lives, and thus only 73,345 of the group will be living at age 46.

TABLE XX (*Cont.*)

TYPICAL RETIREMENT, WITHDRAWAL, AND DEATH BENEFITS
OF INDIVIDUAL ANNUITY CONTRACTS

| Type of Individual Annuity Contract | Death Benefits | | | |
| --- | --- | --- | --- | --- |
| | Before Retirement | | After Retirement | |
| | To Employee's Beneficiary | To Employer | To Employee's Beneficiary | To Employer |
| Retirement Income......... | Insurance Proceeds[f] or Cash Value | Insurance Proceeds[g] or Cash Value | 10 Years[j] Certain | Nothing |
| Retirement Annuity......... | Cash Value[h] or Premiums Paid | Cash Value[i] or Premiums Paid | 10 Years[j] Certain | Nothing |
| Level Premium Deferred Life Annuity................. | Nothing | Nothing | Nothing | Nothing |
| Single-Premium Deferred Life Annuity................. | Nothing | Nothing | Nothing | Nothing |
| Immediate Life Annuity..... | ———[e] | ———[e] | Nothing | Nothing |
| Cash Refund Life Annuity... | ———[e] | ———[e] | Refund[k] | Nothing |

[g] Either the insurance proceeds, that is, the face amount of the contract, will be payable, or the cash value of the contract, whichever is larger. The employer's share will depend on the terms of the pension plan; but in any case the insurance proceeds or cash value cannot revert directly to him, and must be used for the benefit of employees covered by the pension plan.

[h] The death benefit will be the amount of the premiums paid, or the cash value, if the latter is larger; for the share the employee's beneficiary will receive see Note f.

[i] See Note h for the death benefit; for employer's share and disposition thereof, see Note g.

[j] Upon the death of the retired employee before having received income payments for 10 years, there will be continued to his estate or beneficiary further payments, which, when added to those made prior to the retired employee's death, will complete 10 years of income payments. In lieu of a life annuity, 10 years certain, an employee may receive either (1) a life annuity, with 5, 15, or 20 years certain payments, (2) a life annuity, (3) a cash refund life annuity, (4) a joint and survivor life annuity.

[k] Upon the death of the retired employee before having received income payments equal in amount to the premium cost of the annuity, there will be payable to his estate or beneficiary an amount equal to the difference between the sum of the annuity payments made prior to the retired employee's death, and the premium cost of the annuity.

Assuming that each of the 74,173 living at age 45 are insured for $1,000, the expected death claims will be $828,000 ($1,000 × 828). If actually 728 die, the insurance company will be obligated to pay only $728,000 in death claims, or $100,000 less than had been expected. The determination of mortality savings constitutes a technical process, and the actual gain therefore will be dependent on a number of factors, such as the form of insurance on the lives of the group insured. Non-technically, however, we may assume that the 74,173 lives aged 45 insured themselves for one year for $1,000 each. Further, they contributed as premiums $828,000 (without reference to interest that may be earned thereon, or expenses) to meet the 828 expected death claims. If there occurred only 728 deaths, there would be a mortality saving of $100,000.

The gains of a life insurance company in the course of a year's operations, resulting from a lesser mortality than had been expected under the mortality table employed, thus may make a further contribution to its divisible surplus.

(Under Annuity Contracts.) In relation to an annuity contract, the possibility of mortality gains arising from having a greater number of deaths than had been expected has already been indicated in Chapter III. We there showed the computation of an immediate life annuity, using both the American Experience and the Combined Annuity Mortality Tables. If we refer to the computation on page 52 based on the American Experience Table it will be noted that the insurance company is obligated to make annuity payments of $1,000 to each of three survivors who are alive at age 95, or a total of $3,000. If we now assume that the last survivor had died at age 94, the insurance company would have been relieved of the obligation to make these final payments of $3,000 to the three individuals who had been expected to survive to age 95. The reserves maintained to provide these payments, therefore, might become a part of a divisible surplus. Similar gains might arise from other types of annuities issued by the insurance company.

*Gains from Loading.* The premiums quoted by life insurance companies for insurance contracts or annuities contain a loading charge for the expense of acquiring business and of general operations, as elsewhere observed; and there may be included in the loading a margin for the contingencies of unexpected investment losses, or of lesser interest earnings than had been assumed probable. It may turn out, however, that expenses for a given year are lower than had been anticipated; or that any margins that had been included in its premiums for adverse experiences are not needed. In either or both events a further addition to divisible surplus might be made from this source.

## B.  Distribution

The brief description of the sources of dividends has made no reference to the methods used by insurance companies in allocating them to various classes of policyholders. It is enough to mention here that there are several procedures or technical methods that may be used, which among other things aim to preserve equity among different age groups and the holders of different types of policies.[14] Our main purpose has been to show the major sources from which an insurance company may make gains in its operations, and, out of any divisible surplus created thereby, how a company may make a dividend distribution to its policyholders.

A secondary purpose, implicit in the explanation, is to show that, while these sources may give rise to gains, they may likewise be productive of losses, or at least of no gains. In consequence, whereas the major life insurance companies have a history of relatively stable dividends on most of their level premium policies, such as the retirement annuity and retirement income contracts, their operations comparatively do not result necessarily in equivalent dividends to policyholders. Stated more specifically, of two life insurance companies issuing individual annuity contracts more or less identical in their terms, and at similar gross premium rates, the dividends received by the respective policyholders may be significantly different in amount. An illustration of dividend differences, as they may affect the premium outlays of a purchaser of a retirement income contract, appears later in the chapter.

## XI. EXPENSE

The items of expense, of which account must be taken in the loading charges for individual annuity contracts, are similar to those discussed in connection with group annuity contracts.[15] The actual expense charges, however, will range from 6% of the net premium to approximately 20%. The lower expense figure is applicable to individual contracts purchased by single premiums; the higher to those purchased on a level premium basis.

It may be noted that a comparison of the loading charges of the level premium individual annuity contract with the single-premium deferred life annuities of a group annuity contract shows the latter to have a lower expense charge. It should not be inferred from this fact that a pension plan underwritten by group annuity contracts, particularly one offering benefits similar to those provided by re-

---

[14] For a technical discussion of methods of allocating dividends, see: Knight, Charles K., *Advanced Life Insurance*, Chapman & Hall, Limited, London, 1926. Also LeVita, M. H., *An Arithmetic of Life Insurance*, Life Office Management Association, New York, N. Y., 1936.

[15] See Chapter VI, p. 127.

tirement income or retirement annuity policies, such as the full cash refund type of group annuity,[16] will necessarily be cheaper in the long run.   It is true that the commission rates are usually higher on level premium retirement income and retirement annuity policies than on group annuity contracts, for reasons that fundamentally relate to differences in the nature of the benefits provided under each, as well as to the respective methods of the issuing companies in obtaining, underwriting, and servicing pension business.[17] A further factor in accounting for the differences in initial expense charges or loading of the premiums is that the rates of the individual annuity contracts are guaranteed; thus the margin, included in the loading for the contingencies of unexpected investment losses, changes in interest rates, and unanticipated longevity among annuitants, probably will be larger.   Group annuity rates may be raised yearly, after the fifth year, to take account of any losses which may have occurred from these events.   Important in this connection is the dividend on retirement income and retirement annuity contracts.   It will normally be larger per $1.00 of premium paid than that under a group annuity contract, if for no other reason than the refund of relatively higher, and unused, loading charges included in the individual annuity gross premiums.

The expense of operating a pension plan, considered apart from the net financial outlays which must be made to provide the retirement benefits, is a consideration in the selection of a pension plan; but there are other considerations equally important, if not more so, some of which have been set forth.   A discussion of the various factors to which consideration must be given in the selection of a pension plan—group annuity, individual annuity, or self-administered—appears in a later chapter.[18]

## XII.   GENERAL UNDERWRITING PROCEDURES

*Preliminary.*   The personnel data, necessary to be obtained from an employer before a computation of his initial annual costs may be made, will include that required under a group annuity plan, namely: (1) date of birth, (2) date of employment, (3) sex, and (4) salary or earnings of each employee.   In addition, however, assuming that the individual annuity policies which are used to

---

[16] See pp. 121-123.
[17] See pp. 128-134.
[18] See Chapter XI, "Choice of Plan."

underwrite the pension plan are retirement income contracts, it usually is necessary to obtain information on (5) the occupation, (6) the race, and possibly (7) the marital status of each employee. The reasons for obtaining these latter items are discussed below in connection with underwriting rules.

*Preparation of the Plan.* Before a plan can be prepared, based on the above census data, it will be necessary to come to a conclusion on the items set forth in the discussion of group annuities,[19] with several exceptions. Inasmuch as employee contributions will not affect the premium rates where retirement annuity or retirement income contracts are to be utilized, it is not essential to determine in advance whether the plan shall be contributory or noncontributory, nor to determine the basis of employee contributions, in formulating the plan. In other words, employee contributions under level premium retirement income or retirement annuity contracts do not affect the premium rate structure, as they do under group annuity plans. Notwithstanding this fact, employee contributions, as they may be finally arranged under an individual annuity plan, will reduce the employer's share of the cost.

As with group annuity plans, those insurance companies willing to underwrite pension plans through issuance of individual annuity contracts have underwriting rules which must be complied with before they will accept the business. It is difficult to generalize in this connection. First, there are a substantially greater number of companies willing to underwrite an individual annuity pension plan (particularly where the contract to be used for underwriting is the retirement income policy) than there are companies engaged in the group annuity business. Secondly, the underwriting rules of insurance companies issuing individual annuity contracts may differ widely, both generally and in their particulars. Finally, these underwriting rules are in a state of flux, or of development, which further limits the validity of other than the most restricted generalizations.

## XIII. UNDERWRITING RULES

### A. General

*Eligible Employee Group.* The usual requirement for the underwriting of a pension plan with individual annuity contracts is

---

[19] See page 128.

that there exists a common employer, although, as in the case of group annuity plans, employee groups of allied companies, or of subsidiaries with a parent company, are acceptable.

*Good Health Requirements.*  If a pension plan is to be underwritten by contracts which contain an insurance feature, a medical examination is required of each employee at the time of his entrance into the plan; although a waiver of medical examination is offered by some insurance companies to employees below certain ages, and in some cases where the insurance feature is not in excess of a given amount.

*Past Service Benefits.*  Past or future service benefits may be purchased separately and from different insurance companies.  It is customary, however, to use the same type of individual annuity policy, when the plan is underwritten in one insurance company, to cover both past and future service.

*Minimum Units of Purchase.*  Individual annuity contracts usually will be issued in units of not less than five or ten dollars a month at normal retirement for an employee.

*Maximum Income.*  The maximum amount of annuity income which will be issued to any one employee is a matter of the underwriting rules of a particular insurance company.  Generally, this maximum is specified under the terms of the pension plan itself, and will usually present no practical underwriting problem.  The underwriting limitations of group annuity plans as to the maximum annuity income on the lives of particular individuals, or the limitation which prevents an employer from selecting certain individuals to receive higher benefits than are provided for by the general pension formula, are not applicable to individual annuity pension plans.

## B.  Particular

*Acceptable Employee Groups.*  All employee groups are not equally acceptable to different insurance companies.  If retirement income contracts are desired, and the group has a high proportion of unskilled or semiskilled employees, or if the occupations are extra-hazardous, or if the group is heavily non-Caucasian, certain insurance companies may refuse to underwrite the pension plan.  If the plan contemplates the use of other than retirement income contracts, such as retirement annuity contracts to underwrite the plan, it may be acceptable to a few insurance companies, but not to most of them; likewise is this true if the plan contemplates the use of individual level premium deferred life annuity contracts to fund the pension benefits.

*Turnover Experience.* If the turnover experience of a particular employer's personnel is high, some insurance companies may decline to underwrite a plan on an individual annuity policy basis, unless the plan covers only employees who have had at least five years of service, and/or who are beyond a certain minimum age at the time of their entrance into the plan.

*Retirement Income—Retirement Annuity Contract Ratio.* If the pension plan is to be funded by retirement income contracts, an insurance company, willing to underwrite it on this basis, may require that a certain proportion of the employees prove insurable and thus qualify for this contract. The usual ratio is either 4 or 5 to 1; that is, either 1 out of 4 or 1 out of 5 will be accepted even if uninsurable, and issued a retirement annuity contract (without insurance) provided the others qualify for the retirement income contract.

## XIV.  ADMINISTRATIVE ASPECTS

A pension plan financed exclusively by individual annuity contracts may be set up in either of two ways. The employer may purchase these contracts directly from an insurance company for the benefit of employees in a pension plan, or he may create a trust. In the latter case the contracts are purchased by the trustees for the employees' benefit. It is the exception rather than the rule when an employer makes direct purchase from an insurance company.[20] Therefore the discussion will be confined largely to individual annuity pension plans which make use of a trust. It should be mentioned, however, that the method of direct purchase has been seldom used for reasons which mainly relate to the Federal law and to Treasury Department regulations. If the employer retains the ownership of the individual annuity contracts he may not take as an income tax deduction his contributions made toward their purchase; if the employees are given ownership, the employer's contributions will be taxable income to them in the year of the employer's contributions. There are also administrative aspects, as noted elsewhere,[21] that may make the use of a trust desirable; even in those instances where tax reductions for the employer or tax avoidance for the employees are not a major consideration.

[20] But see *Group Permanent Retirement Income Plan*, pp. 231-232. Also certain non-profit corporations, tax-exempt, sometimes make direct purchase.
[21] See Chapter IX, *Basic Provisions of Pension Plans.*

## XV.  PRELIMINARY PROCEDURES

*Creation of a Pension Plan.*  A corporation which desires to establish a pension plan, assuming it can do so under its charter and by-laws, and in consonance with the law of the State in which it is incorporated, must observe certain formalities.  The plan must be authorized by its board of directors, and as a practical matter, it is generally submitted for approval to its stockholders.  The resolutions of the board of directors usually will authorize the establishment of a pension plan in general terms, and further authorize certain executive officers to complete the arrangements for carrying it out.  In the case of an individual annuity plan the officers, usually the president and the secretary of the corporation, are empowered to enter into a trust agreement with a trustee or trustees for the purpose of effectuating the pension plan.  The trustee or trustees are nominated by the board of directors, subject to removal or replacement.

*Formulation of the Plan.*  The terms of a pension plan usually are formulated by a pension committee or certain executive officers, normally after conference with pension specialists or consultants. When the details of the plan have been agreed upon, and acceptable initial pension costs or financial outlays, necessary to place it in operation, have been calculated, a formal plan is drafted, and a trust agreement also.  In some instances the *plan* is contained in one document and the trust in another.  Frequently, however, the *plan* and the provision for a trust are incorporated in one instrument.  In either case, the final document is executed by the president and secretary for the corporation, and by the trustee or trustees on behalf of the trust, the latter being charged with the administration of the pension plan.

## XVI.  THE TRUST INSTRUMENT

On the assumption that the pension plan and the provision for a trust are to be included in one document, denominated as the pension trust agreement, the main provisions may be outlined. The contents are set forth in *articles* and *sections* and the length of such a document may be twenty-five or thirty pages of typewritten matter.

*Preamble.*  The usual preamble of the trust agreement states that an agreement of trust has been entered into by the corporation, under the laws of the state of domicile, and a trustee or trustees are named in the preamble. The preamble further states that a pension plan has been properly authorized by the board of directors of the corporation, and that there has been created the A. B. C. pension plan, or the A. B. C. pension trust, for the benefit of the employees, which plan the trustees agree to administer in accordance with the terms of the agreement.

*Article I.* The corporation agrees to make the contributions necessary to provide pension benefits for the individual employees; it, however, reserves the right to suspend contributions, and therefore makes no commitment or guarantee that it will continue its contributions. If employees are to contribute, the basis of their contributions is set forth. The term or duration of the trust is given, usually an indefinite one, but with a proviso so worded as to take cognizance of any State law or rule against trusts in perpetuity.

*Article II.* The rules or conditions which must be met for an employee to become eligible to the plan are set forth, as well as the time when he may enter the plan after having become eligible. Provision is made for the establishment of an individual trust account for each employee participating in the plan, to which are credited the employer's contributions sufficient to meet the premium on each individual annuity contract as may be applied for on the employee's life. A specific statement appears directing the trustees to invest the employer's contributions for each employee's account in individual life, retirement income, endowment, or annuity policies to provide such retirement benefits as an employee may be entitled to under the terms of the pension plan. Settlement of disputes as to an employee's eligibility to the plan, so far as questions of fact are involved, are authorized to be determined finally by the trustees.

*Article III.* The normal retirement ages for the participating employees are stated. A provision is made for an earlier or later retirement than the normal age, probably with the consent of the corporation, on an adjusted retirement income basis.

*Article IV.* A pension formula for the calculation of retirement income benefits for the employees is set forth, which may include credits for future service, past service, or for both. Directions to the trustees are given for handling increases or decreases in the pension benefit in the event of salary changes. A definition is given of what shall constitute absence from employment, and of duration sufficient to warrant the elimination of an employee from the plan. Also, if an employee remains in employment after normal retirement age, it is generally provided that no further contributions by the employer shall be made for his account. Amendment of the plan is provided for, as it relates to the provision for the employees' retirement benefits; however, a stipulation is made that such amendments shall not affect the benefits created by contributions from employees' accounts prior to the adoption of the amendment. The trustees are authorized to make the applications for life insurance, retirement endowment, or annuity policies on the lives of the participating employees, with all rights in such policies to be vested in the trustees, who may exercise such rights without question, subject to the terms of the pension plan. The trustees are authorized further to charge the premiums for the policies thus acquired by them to the accounts of the respective employees; furthermore, the trustees are directed to hold such policies for the employees in trust, to the extent of their respective interests in the same.

*Article V.* Inasmuch as certain employees may die or terminate employment before attaining normal retirement age, there is outlined the benefits which will be payable to an employee if he should die, resign, or be discharged. Mention may appear of benefits which will be payable in the use of total and permanent disability. In the case of an employee who dies after having reached the normal retirement age, a description is given of any death benefits which will be payable.

*Article VI.* Provision may be made for the creation of a *suspense account,* into which all money initially coming into the hands of the trustees is to be placed. The use of the funds in the suspense account is limited to the payment of the premiums on the lives of the participating employees, to the payment of any expenses incurred by the trustees for administering the trust, and to any other specific purposes of the trust. The trustees are allowed to invest such funds in the suspense account as are not immediately necessary for the payment of premiums in such manner as may be authorized under the trust agreement. In the event of the termination of the trust it is provided that the funds in the suspense account shall be divided among the remaining participants in the plan, in the proportion that the value of an employee's account bears to the total value of all the accounts.

*Article VII.* It is stipulated that any death or withdrawal benefits payable under the plan may be distributed to an employee's beneficiary, or to himself, with a view to the purpose of the trust, and to the needs of the distributee. It is usually provided, however, that the distribution of any death or withdrawal benefits shall be made over a specified period, not to exceed a certain number of years. The employee is given the right to nominate a beneficiary as to any death benefits which may become payable.

*Article VIII.* It is stipulated that no employee shall have the right to assign, anticipate, or hypothecate any policies on his life, or any other part of his account; also that the policies on his life or the amounts credited to his account shall not be subject to seizure by legal process.

*Article IX.* The administration of the trust in respect to the duties, the rights, and the powers of the trustees is detailed as follows: the right of the trustees to resign on proper notice; the right of the corporation to remove or replace any trustee; the specific investments which the trustees may utilize, in addition to life insurance, endowment, and retirement or annuity policies; the trustees' rights to contract, buy, and sell property or securities, and the right to borrow for the purpose of maintenance of the plan; exemption of the trustees from liability except for fraud, bad faith, or negligence; and the right of the trustees to hold title to the policy contracts, and to receive the benefits and distribute the latter, subject to the terms of the plan.

Provision is made for trustees' meetings, the keeping of minutes, voting, and the selection of a custodian for the policies or funds; the hiring of accountants, attorneys, brokers, and other counsel; the right of the trustees to charge certain expenses to the trust; an accounting yearly to the corporation; and the compensation of the trustees, if any.

Other protective provisions are included to relieve the corporation, the officers, and directors from liability, if for any reason the benefits from the policies on the lives of the employees should not be paid in accordance with these terms. The trustees are authorized to secure indemnity from any employee's account, if they should become liable to meet estate or inheritance taxes on his behalf. Insurance companies which may issue individual annuity policies to trustees for the account of employees are relieved of the necessity of ascertaining that such policies are issued for the proper persons, and they may rely on the application of the trustees as being in accordance with the terms of the trust. Insurance companies are discharged from any liability for any change in the individual annuity contracts or for beneficiary changes which may be made, and they are free to assume that the trustees in any of their requests are acting within their authority.

*Article X.* It is provided that the trust may be terminated if: the corporation notifies the trustees of its intention to discontinue its contributions; the corporation dissolves voluntarily or involuntarily; or a receiver or trustee in bankruptcy is appointed. In the event of termination, the trustees may continue the plan until all funds have been expended for further premium payments on the policies, or, at any time prior or subsequent thereto, the trustees may terminate the trust and liquidate. Upon liquidation each employee is granted the right to any money, property, or policies held for his account, and a proportionate share of funds in the suspense account. The manner of distribution is left to the trustees, such as the specified period of time in which distribution shall be made. The trust is deemed to be in liquidation until a complete distribution of its assets has been completed.

*Article XI.* The trust is described as irrevocable, although it may be amended, revised, modified, or altered at any time, so long as the rights or benefits previously accrued to the employees are not affected. The assets of the trust may be used only for the exclusive benefit of the employees, and may not revert to the corporation, except as they may result from overpayments due to inaccuracy in actuarial computations. The trustees may formulate rules and regulations for the administration of the trust, if they are not inconsistent with the purposes and provisions of the trust agreement.

*Article XII.* The corporation is specifically relieved of any obligation or liability to continue to make contributions to the pension plan. It also reserves the right to terminate the employment of any employee in the pension plan. In other words, participation in the pension plan in no way gives rise to a contract of employment.

*Article XIII.* The law of the State which shall govern the regulation and construction of the provisions of the trust is set forth, irrespective of the situs of the trustees or the beneficiaries. If any provision of the trust is held to be invalid it is provided that this fact shall not affect the remaining provisions, and, except for the invalid provisions, the trust shall be enforced. If distribution to any participant or beneficiary is prevented by any rule of law it is stipulated that such share or interest shall revert in equal parts to the remaining participants if the plan so provides, or in any case to the suspense account. Authority may be granted to one of the trustees (if more than one is designated) to sign all documents or papers as the authorized trustee. The effective date of the pension plan is set forth, and the number of executed copies of the trust in existence is indicated. A paragraph causing the trust to be executed, and the date thereof, closes the trust agreement, to which the signatures of the president and secretary of the corporation are affixed, as well as the signature of the designated trustee or trustees. Finally, the document is imprinted with the corporate seal.

## XVII. SELECTION OF INDIVIDUAL ANNUITY COMPANY

The approach in selecting an insurance company to underwrite an individual annuity plan may be, and should be, different from that in selecting a company to underwrite a group annuity plan. As regards the latter, it was seen that the standardization of group annuity plans, the usage of similar gross premium rates, the probable equivalency of service rendered, and the lack of published experience of group annuity costs, limited the analysis to general observations.

As for insurance companies underwriting individual annuity plans, it should be noted first of all that there are probably well over a hundred who will underwrite a plan through the issue of individual annuity contracts, as against about twenty who are engaged in the issue of group annuity plans. Most of the former will underwrite with retirement income contracts, and some will underwrite with retirement annuity policies. A few will issue level premium deferred life annuities or single-premium deferred life annuities as individual contracts, to finance the pension benefits. Most of them, furthermore, will make available immediate life annuities or cash refund annuities, for employees who are at retirement age. In other words, the larger number of companies engaged in the issuance of individual annuity contracts makes for a broader market in terms of the buyer's interest, but for the same reason requires greater selectivity. Secondly, there is available published information as to the retirement income contract, which is used to underwrite the majority of individual annuity plans, indicating the past and probable future cost of this contract. Thirdly, there exist some significant differences in the terms or provisions of retirement income contracts as issued by different companies; that is, there is not complete standardization or uniformity. Fourthly, an employer who establishes an individual annuity plan may find it desirable or necessary to utilize the services of more than one insurance company. Finally, the service aspects under individual annuity plans are normally provided for somewhat differently than they are under group annuity plans.

## A. Factors in Selection

*Financial Strength.* The history of life insurance companies in America has been distinguished by the absence of any significant failures.[22] Where failures have occurred the losses to policyholders have been small. It is unnecessary therefore to make an extended analysis on this score. It nevertheless must be noted that even a small individual annuity pension plan may mount to an accumulated investment for the employees, of $100,000 in a period of ten years. The employer, consequently, must take cognizance of the caliber of the insurance company underwriting his plan. There are sources for obtaining this information other than from the company itself, if it seems advisable to inquire into the financial resources or character of the company.[23]

*The Contract.* Individual annuity contracts, issued as immediate life annuities or cash refund life annuities purchased by single premiums, will be more or less standardized in their provisions. This likewise is apt to be true of individual level premium deferred life annuity and single-premium deferred life annuity contracts. As to the latter, however, if they are purchased in their pure form, that is without death benefits prior to or after retirement, the practice among the companies issuing them may differ in regard to the allowance of a cash value if an employee withdraws from employment. Also, whereas the usual basis for providing the retirement income is a life annuity, it may be found that an option, such as a joint and survivor annuity, may be included in a contract by one company and excluded by another.

Of individual annuity contracts, the retirement income, as well as the retirement annuity, usually will show the greatest variation in their terms as issued by different insurance companies. The major differences will relate to: (1) the mortality table and the guaranteed interest rate used in the computation of premiums in the

---

[22] See Huebner, S. S. & McCahan, David, *Life Insurance as Investment,* D. Appleton-Century Co., Inc., New York, N. Y., 1933.
[23] See *Best's Life Insurance Reports,* Alfred M. Best Co., Inc., New York, N. Y.

case of a retirement income contract, and the interest rate only, in that of a retirement annuity; (2) when a cash value accrues; (3) the surrender charges which are applicable if an early termination of the contract should occur; (4) whether it is participating or non-participating as a paid-up annuity, and whether it is participating as to surplus earnings prior to retirement, and as to annuity payments which commence at retirement; (5) the income options which will be available to a beneficiary upon the death of an employee, and the rate of interest guaranteed under such options; (6) the options available to an employee at retirement, in lieu of the basic option, e.g. 10 years certain; and (7) the mortality table and the guaranteed interest rate used to compute the annuity income payable at normal retirement. A specimen contract either of a retirement income or a retirement annuity, which may be obtained from any insurance company issuing such contracts, will usually provide information on these points.

*Service.* We pointed out in connection with group annuity plans that service is usually rendered by a group annuity representative from the office of the insurance company underwriting the plan. This is not the customary situation with individual annuity plans. As a rule this type of plan is handled from its inception, in consultation with the employer, by an agent of a particular insurance company, an insurance broker, or in more recent years by pension specialists or consultants. The placement of individual annuity contracts is handled by the agent or broker, and frequently the pension consultant; the installation of the plan and its supervision are also part of their functions.

For service of an individual annuity plan, therefore, an agent, broker, or pension consultant must be looked to by an employer. The major services will consist of: (1) designing of the pension plan, (2) obtaining of applications from the eligible employees for participation in the plan, (3) supervising of the medical examination of employees, if any, (4) cooperating in the drafting of any trust agreement with the attorney who draws the same, (5) cooperating with the attorney in obtaining approval of the plan by the proper government authorities, such as the Treasury Department, (6) preparing or cooperating in the preparation for the employer of the annual report concerning the status of the pension plan, which must be submitted annually by the employer to the Treasury, (7) handling of death claims and withdrawal benefits, (8) consulting and advising with an employee, particularly where his individual annuity contract has an insurance feature, as to the proper distribution methods of any policy proceeds if the pension plan makes such proceeds available to his heirs upon his death, (9) informing the employer of changes in Treasury regulations or of the law which may affect the taxable status of his plan, or which may affect the participating employees, (10) checking each year his list of employees to establish whether there are any employees newly eligible to the plan, and of (11) informing the employer of any changes in the insurance market which might enable the employer to obtain contracts on *new* employees either more advantageous in their terms, or lower in cost, thus possibly making available to an employer a company whose practices would provide a flexibility necessary to operate his plan on a basis more satisfactory to his employment situation.

*Comparative Costs.*   The cost of immediate life and cash refund life annuities will be affected by the mortality table used, the rate of interest guaranteed, and the amount of the loading charge.   If these annuities are to be purchased in a non-participating form, as they are normally issued, a simple rate quotation, to obtain a given income on a monthly or yearly basis at a particular age, is all that is necessary for a cost comparison.   If they are to be purchased in a participating form, the same elements mentioned immediately above will affect the cost, but the possibility of receiving dividends must be appraised.

Single-premium deferred life annuities are normally issued in a non-participating form when purchased as individual contracts. Individual level premium deferred life annuity contracts may be obtained in a participating form, but published experience as to dividends that may be expected is lacking.   In either case the gross premium rate will reflect the mortality table used, the rate of interest guaranteed, and the loading charge.

The retirement income contract and the retirement annuity are issued in participating form, although stock life companies may issue them on a non-participating basis.   In the latter case, a comparison of the premium rates will reflect immediately any premium cost differential as between two stock life companies.

In the case of participating contracts it is necessary to consider the dividends actually paid in the past, or illustrated as payable in the future, to arrive at comparative premium outlays.   In other words, while the initial or gross premium for each unit may differ as quoted by two companies, the actual outlay will be affected by the amount of the dividend. The comparative future outlays for a unit of retirement income contract purchased at age 45 for a male life, to pay $10.00 a month, 10 years certain, at 65 is shown below for four different companies. The insurance benefit in each case is $1,000. The gross premium is the first year outlay; thereafter dividends have been applied to reduce the gross premium. The projected premium outlays are shown for a period of ten years, as the respective companies indicate will be necessary, based on the maintenance of their 1946 dividend scales.

| Year | Company A | Company B | Company C | Company D |
|---|---|---|---|---|
| 1 | $73.97 | $72.30 | $74.27 | $80.10 |
| 2 | 65.18 | 66.64 | 67.97 | 73.16 |
| 3 | 64.92 | 66.56 | 67.98 | 72.72 |
| 4 | 64.66 | 66.47 | 68.00 | 72.27 |
| 5 | 64.40 | 66.31 | 67.99 | 71.80 |
| 6 | 64.14 | 66.14 | 67.96 | 71.33 |
| 7 | 63.86 | 65.87 | 67.93 | 70.84 |
| 8 | 63.59 | 65.63 | 67.89 | 70.33 |
| 9 | 63.31 | 65.37 | 67.82 | 69.82 |
| 10 | 63.02 | 65.10 | 67.75 | 69.28 |

The significance of the differences in outlays may be more fully appreciated when these premium costs are applied to actual benefits provided by a pension plan. For example, a small plan might provide at least $2,000 a month at the normal retirement age for the employees covered at its inception. If all the employees of the group were age 45, the premium cost of $10.00 a month, as shown above, would be multiplied by 200 ($10.00 × 200 = $2,000). In company A, therefore, the tenth year annual outlay would be $12,604 ($63.02 × 200), and in company D, $13,856 ($69.28 × 200); or a difference of approximately 10%. It is true that other factors than cost warrant consideration, but, all things being equal, an annual difference of 10% or even of 5% yearly in premium outlays as between insurance companies becomes significant in relation to the costs of a pension plan.

### B. Probability of Dividends—Reliability of Comparison

The merit of giving consideration to dividends on retirement income contracts and applying them to reduce the gross premiums, for the purpose of showing actual net outlay, is sometimes attacked on the grounds that, inasmuch as dividends are not guaranteed, they cannot be relied upon. The employer who accepts this view may be better advised to purchase non-participating retirement income contracts, in which case he generally will be quoted a lower gross premium rate than any shown for the four companies above. It should be pointed out, however, that the retirement income contract, as issued by most insurance companies, which may be used by an employer to cover the employees under his pension plan, is exactly the same contract which may be purchased by an individual who is not a member of a pension plan. For this reason the general experience of an insurance company with all its retirement contracts, whether issued to individuals who have purchased them for personal retirement or to an employee under a pension plan, is reflected in the apportionment of dividends to such contracts. The opposite situation generally prevails in relation to group annuity contracts, constituting one of the main reasons why cost comparison between group annuity contracts is rendered difficult if not impossible.

The fact that all retirement income contracts are treated alike for dividend purposes by most companies, whether they are owned by individuals or by employers directly or indirectly for the benefit of their employees, offers a means of comparison between them, if published information of their past and probable dividend history is available. This is the case, and several sources may be referred to for this information.[24]

There remains the question, of course, as to whether dividends on retirement income contracts, as issued by mutual insurance companies, may be reasonably anticipated in the future. While the answer might be better given in relation to specific companies, and qualifications consequently made, the normal expectation would be that any mutual company would pay a dividend on its retirement income contracts. First of all, the present annuity rates of these contracts apparently are computed on conservative assumptions as to interest and mortality; secondly, a refund of some of the loading charges as well as some gains from mortality savings may be expected, even though contributions to the dividend from excess interest earnings may be nonexistent. The likelihood of dividends on retirement annuity contracts may be more open to questions, however, where the guaranteed rate of interest during the accumulation period of the contract is in excess of $2\frac{1}{2}\%$.

In judging the reliability of dividend comparisons between different mutual companies issuing retirement income contracts, one

---

[24] See Flitcraft *Compend*, Flitcraft, Inc., Oak Park, Ill. Also *Unique Digest*, National Underwriter Co., Cincinnati, O.

must take cognizance of a multitude of factors germane to their respective methods of underwriting their business.  In the main, these factors will relate to their investment policy and skill, their medical standards in the selection of risks, their general underwriting policies, whether conservative or liberal, and their acquisition costs, or what they must pay for their business in the way of sales promotion, advertising, and commissions.  *It is certain that no two companies will be identical in all of these respects.*  Generally speaking, the amount of the dividends paid over a period of time by an insurance company on its respective contracts will reflect its efficiency, and will affect the costs to an owner of such contracts. The fact that there exist considerable differences in costs of regular insurance, e.g. ordinary life, as between different insurance companies is indisputable, and may be shown by dividend comparisons extending back thirty to forty years.[25]  While the low-cost companies issuing ordinary life and other insurance contracts have occasionally shifted position—that is for a decade perhaps one might be slightly lower than another—their relative low-cost position has been maintained.  By extension, it would seem reasonable to expect that these same companies in connection with their issuance of retirement income contracts (except as they may have excessively liberalized their underwriting practices where these contracts are issued for pension plans) will maintain a similarly comparative low cost to those who purchase retirement income contracts, whether for personal use or to underwrite individual annuity pension plans.

---

[25] *Extract from letter to a correspondent*—". . . In a recent actual result study we showed a 10 year actual history for policies issued in 1904, 1914, 1924, and 1934 and the composite record for policies issued in 1920, 1921, 1922, etc. to 1934.  This study covers 41 companies and indicates the trend in costs of life insurance for a 40 year period.  Depending upon year of issue and the 10 years following, the costs may vary from around $5 a thousand to as much as $12."—Flitcraft *Courant*, Flitcraft, Inc., Oak Park, Ill., Nov., 1945.

# CHAPTER VIII

## Self-administered Plan

A SELF-ADMINISTERED PENSION PLAN[1] IS ONE UNDER WHICH AN employer deposits with an outside agency, in trust, the necessary money to actuarially fund the pension benefits for his employees in accordance with the terms of a contractual plan, such outside agency not being an insurance company. It will be noted that, because the funds are placed in trust with an outside agency, and because the benefits for employees are funded actuarially and on a contractual basis,[2] a self-administered plan is distinguished sharply from a company-administered plan such as was discussed in Chapter II. It is only since the Federal law was amended in 1942 that it has become possible to define self-administered plans in the above terms. Prior to that date, pension plans described as self-administered were an admixture. For example, the money to finance the pension benefits may have been trusteed but the plan may not have been properly funded; or, the balance-sheet reserve method of accumulating funds may have been employed. Again, a plan may have used an outside agency and the pension funds may have been trusteed and actuarially sound, yet withal there may have been absent a contractual agreement that an employee who had met the conditions necessary to obtain a pension actually would receive it at retirement, or, if he should, that he would continue to receive it. In short, prior to 1942, most so-called self-administered plans were a composite of characteristics, encountered in what we designated as company-administered plans.

The nonuse of an insurance company's services in the investment

---

[1] Also actuarially referred to as a self-insured plan.

[2] By contractual there is meant only that, if an employee qualifies for a pension under the terms of a plan, he normally will be entitled to receive it. Forfeiture of a pension may take place only for exceptional reasons, such as the accepting of employment with a competitor after retirement. It should be understood also that an employer in establishing a pension plan makes no guarantee as to its continuance. If it is discontinued, however, employees, in employment at such time and eligible to benefits under the plan, will have a contractual right to a proportional benefit.

and administration of pension funds is a major distinguishing characteristic of self-administered plans. It should be mentioned, however, that in general there is nothing to prevent the managers or the trustee of a self-administered plan from utilizing particular contracts, or the facilities of life insurance companies under certain circumstances if they find it desirable. The circumstances or situations where this might be done are treated later in the chapter.

The preliminary formulation of a self-administered plan is somewhat similar to that described in connection with group annuity and individual annuity plans.[3] The personnel data which must be obtained, however, is more extensive than is required for the preparation of insured plans. With this information obtained, costs are calculated in relation to the terms of the plan, such as eligibility rules, normal retirement dates, pension benefits, and so forth. The formulation of the terms of the plan itself usually involves conferences of the employer and pension consultants, and/or an independent actuary.[4] The latter must prepare an actuarial estimate of costs, regardless of who may have formulated the preliminary details of the plan. When final agreement on the terms of the plan is reached, and the employer accepts as feasible the actuarial estimates of the financial outlays necessary to support it, a trust agreement is drafted by legal counsel; the funds necessary to place the plan in operation are deposited with a trustee or trustees, usually a bank or trust company which may invest the funds as permitted by the trust agreement; announcement is made to the employees; and the plan, usually after Treasury Department approval has been obtained, is placed in operation.

## I. METHOD OF FUNDING

Under self-administered plans it is possible to use any or all of the funding methods previously discussed.[5] The single-premium deferred life annuity principle, level premium deferred life annuity, level accumulation, or level percentage of payroll may be used. In practice usually one, but probably no more than two of these funding methods will be employed. If the plan provides for past service, the purchase of the benefits might be accomplished through the use of the single-premium deferred life annuity or the level per-

---

[3] See pp. 128 and 158-159.

[4] An "independent" actuary is so denominated for the reason that he is not attached to the staff of any insurance company. Sometimes he is known as a consulting actuary.

[5] See Chapter IV; also footnote, p. 104.

centage of payroll method. Future service benefits might be funded by the level premium accumulation or level percentage of payroll method. The majority of self-administered plans, however, tend to confine themselves to the level percentage of payroll method.

In illustrating the level percentage of payroll method in Chapter IV, the yearly outlays took account of anticipated deaths only. This was done in the interests of simplicity. Normally, however, when the level percentage of payroll method is used to calculate costs, there will be a discount taken for withdrawals from employment, and assumptions will be made as to the salary scale which will prevail for employees from the time they are eligible to the plan until their retirement. Thus the level percentage of payroll method, as typically employed in relation to a normal retirement age for employees covered by the pension plan, discounts for (1) mortality, (2) interest earnings, (3) withdrawals from employment prior to normal retirement, and (4) probable salary increases. In addition it may take account of retirements, as they occur at various ages, and of terminations by disability. It will be noted that this method anticipates all the major events which may be expected to occur in the operation of a pension fund, and which may be valued or accounted for; consequently, under a self-administered plan employing the level percentage of payroll method, there results an *estimate* of pension costs. It should be noted, therefore, that this method is in contrast to the funding methods used under group annuity or individual annuity plans. The former takes account only of the factors of mortality and interest earnings; the latter, simply of interest earnings.[6] In relation to pensioners, of course, all three types of plans take into account interest earnings and mortality subsequent to retirement.

## A. Experience Table

Prior to making an estimate of pension costs by level percentage of payroll, it is desirable, although not always practical, that an actuary investigate the experience of an employer with his personnel. The investigation may seek to determine some or all of the following: (1) rates of mortality, (a) among active employees, and (b) among retired employees, (2) rates of disability and of termination thereof by death or recovery, (3) rates of withdrawal

---

[6] If the retirement income contract is used under an individual annuity plan, then, of course, mortality is taken account of in connection with the insurance feature.

from employment, (4) rates of retirement, and (5) the wage and salary scale. When a new plan is established the usual absence of complete employee records and experience of a large enough group of employees, who have been exposed for sufficient time to the risks on which rates are sought, may limit the investigation. The actuary therefore must draw on the experience of employers in similar enterprises to evaluate withdrawal or other rates or to project salary scales. He may adopt rates for mortality and disability from standard tables.

Whether an investigation provides adequate statistical data from which the respective rates mentioned above may be computed, or whether it is a composite of other employers' experiences plus the use of standard mortality or disability tables, the rates when computed are incorporated in an *experience* table. Without detailing the methods by which the rates are computed, the following table illustrates the hypothetical experience rates in relation to a group of active male employees who enter employment at age 30, and all of whom will retire at 65; it ignores, however, the rates of mortality among pensioners which, as stated above, would normally be accounted for through the use of a standard mortality or annuity table.

It should be noted in reference to experience tables that no two tables will be alike, where the respective rates, such as shown in the accompanying table, are determined from the statistics or employee data of different employers. For example, smaller enterprises may tend to show lower withdrawal rates or, stated differently, less turnover than larger ones. Also the nature of an enterprise, its geographical location, its wage scales, and numerous other factors similarly will produce withdrawal rates quite different from another enterprise which may be engaged in the same type of business.

In relation to disability rates there may be disparities between a business which involves hazardous occupations, and one in which such hazards are absent. Again, an employer's policy in handling disability cases may lead to a weighting or modification of apparent disability rates. For example, if disability benefits are generous, or there is any reason to expect that disability retirements will be handled administratively on a liberal basis, in other words that disability retirements will be allowed even though the reason be occupational disability or a hardship case, then the expected disability rates may be increased, as the judgment of the actuary may dictate.

EXPERIENCE TABLE

Termination Rates and Salary Scale[7]

| Age | Mortality Rates | Withdrawal Rates | Disability Rates | Total Termination Rates | Salary Scale |
|---|---|---|---|---|---|
| 30...... | .00207 | .25 | .0016 | .25367 | 1000 |
| 31...... | .00221 | .17 | .0016 | .17381 | 1064 |
| 32...... | .00238 | .13 | .0017 | .13408 | 1126 |
| 33...... | .00256 | .09 | .0018 | .09436 | 1186 |
| 34...... | .00276 | .07 | .0018 | .07456 | 1244 |
| 35...... | .00298 | .05 | .0019 | .05488 | 1300 |
| 36...... | .00322 | .04 | .0020 | .04522 | 1354 |
| 37...... | .00347 | .04 | .0021 | .04557 | 1406 |
| 38...... | .00374 | .03 | .0022 | .03594 | 1456 |
| 39...... | .00404 | .03 | .0023 | .03634 | 1504 |
| 40...... | .00436 | .03 | .0024 | .03676 | 1550 |
| 41...... | .00470 | .02 | .0025 | .02720 | 1594 |
| 42...... | .00507 | .02 | .0026 | .02767 | 1636 |
| 43...... | .00547 | .02 | .0028 | .02827 | 1676 |
| 44...... | .00590 | .02 | .0030 | .02890 | 1714 |
| 45...... | .00636 | .02 | .0031 | .02946 | 1750 |
| 46...... | .00686 | .01 | .0034 | .02026 | 1784 |
| 47...... | .00740 | .01 | .0037 | .02110 | 1816 |
| 48...... | .00798 | .01 | .0040 | .02198 | 1846 |
| 49...... | .00861 | .01 | .0044 | .02301 | 1874 |
| 50...... | .00929 | .01 | .0048 | .02409 | 1900 |
| 51...... | .01002 | | .0052 | .01522 | 1924 |
| 52...... | .01081 | | .0057 | .01651 | 1946 |
| 53...... | .01165 | | .0061 | .01775 | 1966 |
| 54...... | .01257 | | .0068 | .01937 | 1984 |
| 55...... | .01355 | | .0076 | .02115 | 2000 |
| 56...... | .01461 | | .0086 | .02321 | 2014 |
| 57...... | .01576 | | .0098 | .02556 | 2026 |
| 58...... | .01699 | | .0113 | .02829 | 2036 |
| 59...... | .01832 | | .0131 | .03142 | 2044 |
| 60...... | .01975 | | .0152 | .03495 | 2050 |
| 61...... | .02130 | | .0179 | .03920 | 2054 |
| 62...... | .02296 | | .0211 | .04406 | 2056 |
| 63...... | .02475 | | .0253 | .05005 | 2056 |
| 64...... | .02668 | | .0300 | .05668 | 2056 |

## B.  The Salary Scale

In general, employees' salaries or wages are presumed to increase in relation to age, although modified somewhat by length of service, with an acceleration occurring at the younger ages, a slowing down

---

[7] It should be understood that these rates are illustrative. They are not to be considered in any sense as rates which would be employed in a valuation.

at the middle ages (for certain grades of employees there are no increases after they attain middle age), and a tapering off at the upper ages. In the final period of employment possibly no increases will be assumed to occur. The column *salary scale* brings out an estimated salary progression.

The determination of a salary scale, as in the cases of withdrawal and other rates, calls for an investigation of the facts: an examination of the actual wages and salaries an employer pays, the rates of increase among the various grades of employees, the probable maximums, and all the similar factors that will assist in the construction of the scale. After the data on wages and salaries have been collated, the construction of the scale may be made in several ways, one of which will be discussed.

## 1. Rate of Salary Increase

The benefits under self-administered plans are usually computed or expressed as a percentage of *average* salary earned over the period of service, or as a percentage of the *final average* salary earned in the last five or ten years of service; in both instances a credit is given to an employee for each year of completed service, possibly subject to some maximum or minimum. Both the benefit and the contributions to provide the benefit, therefore, are related to salary. Consequently, an increase in the salary of a specific employee normally calls for an increase in his retirement benefit; likewise there will be an increase in the contribution to provide the benefit unless the salary increase has been anticipated in the method of funding. If the probable salaries that will be received over the period of service, or the final average salary, can be more or less anticipated or predicted, it then becomes possible to compute the costs resulting from salary increases; thus at the time of the actual salary increases no change in the rate of contributions is necessary inasmuch as the increases were anticipated or accounted for in making the estimates of pension costs.

In Chapter IV we assumed the average annual rate of salary for a group of 100 employees to be $1,000 a year for each surviving employee from the time of entrance into the plan at age 45, until normal retirement at age 65. We thus not only assumed a level salary for each individual, but the same salary. Obviously, in practice neither salaries nor wages will be level over the period of employment to retirement, nor will they be the same for different employees. In the construction of a salary scale it is expected that the average salaries for a group of employees at one age will be in a definite relationship to the average salaries of the surviving employees at the next succeeding age. For example, by reference to the salary scale on page 178, the average salary for employees entering a plan at age 30 is shown to be $1,000. This is not the actual salary of any particular employee, of course, but it is the *average* annual rate of salary of all employees entering at age 30, earned between ages 30 and 31. The salary at age 31 of $1,064 is the average annual rate of salary earned between ages 31 and 32 by those who survived to age 31. Mathematically, the salary figure given at age 30 could be stated as 1.000, and at age 31 as 1.064, the *.064* being considered as the expected rate of increase for the employees who enter at age 30 and survive in service to age 31; and so on for each succeeding age. It is important to emphasize that the salary scale merely sets forth relative *average* salaries, but not actual salaries. For while actual salaries are utilized in making final cost calculations, it is the ratio of increase that will be applied to actual salaries and be utilized to estimate the total salaries that employees of various ages and of duration of service may be expected to receive in future years.

With experience rates computed and a salary scale constructed, as shown in the experience table, the actuary's next step is to construct a *service* table. This is similar to a mortality table but it is termed service table because its purpose is to disclose the number of employees who continue in service to the time of retirement. As we have already seen, the probability of an employee remaining or surviving to retirement age is affected by rates of mortality, withdrawal, and disability. Service tables therefore will reflect the effects of these rates as applied to employees in various age groups and in respect to duration of service, and will indicate the number of employees who may be expected to remain in employment until retirement age. In the service table which follows the experience rates, as set forth in the experience table, are incorporated, so that they may be more conveniently observed as they are applied to a hypothetical personnel.

It will be noted from the service table that at each age the various rates of withdrawal, mortality, and disability may be combined and applied to the survivors remaining in service at the attained age. At age 30, for example, the combined rates account for a decrease in numbers in service prior to attaining age 31 of 2,537 employees. While we have shown separate disability rates it may be noted that, unless disability benefits are to be provided, termi-

| | (Termination Rates) | | | Service Table | | | | |
|---|---|---|---|---|---|---|---|---|
| Age | Mortality Rates | Withdrawal Rates | Disability Rates | Number Surviving in Service | Number Dying in Service | Number Withdrawing from Service | Number Disabled | Total Number Terminating Service |
| 30 | .00207 | .25 | .0016 | 10,000 | 21 | 2,500 | 16 | 2,537 |
| 31 | .00221 | .17 | .0016 | 7,463 | 16 | 1,269 | 12 | 1,297 |
| 32 | .00238 | .13 | .0017 | 6,166 | 15 | 802 | 10 | 827 |
| 33 | .00256 | .09 | .0018 | 5,339 | 14 | 480 | 10 | 504 |
| 34 | .00276 | .07 | .0018 | 4,835 | 13 | 338 | 9 | 360 |
| 35 | .00298 | .05 | .0019 | 4,475 | 13 | 224 | 9 | 246 |
| 36 | .00322 | .04 | .0020 | 4,229 | 14 | 169 | 8 | 191 |
| 37 | .00347 | .04 | .0021 | 4,038 | 14 | 162 | 8 | 184 |
| 38 | .00374 | .03 | .0022 | 3,854 | 14 | 116 | 9 | 139 |
| 39 | .00404 | .03 | .0023 | 3,715 | 15 | 111 | 9 | 135 |
| 40 | .00436 | .03 | .0024 | 3,580 | 16 | 107 | 9 | 132 |
| 41 | .00470 | .02 | .0025 | 3,448 | 16 | 69 | 9 | 94 |
| 42 | .00507 | .02 | .0026 | 3,354 | 17 | 67 | 9 | 93 |
| 43 | .00547 | .02 | .0028 | 3,261 | 18 | 65 | 9 | 92 |
| 44 | .00590 | .02 | .0030 | 3,169 | 19 | 63 | 10 | 92 |
| 45 | .00636 | .02 | .0031 | 3,077 | 20 | 61 | 10 | 91 |
| 46 | .00686 | .01 | .0034 | 2,986 | 20 | 30 | 10 | 60 |
| 47 | .00740 | .01 | .0037 | 2,926 | 22 | 29 | 11 | 62 |
| 48 | .00798 | .01 | .0040 | 2,864 | 23 | 29 | 11 | 63 |
| 49 | .00861 | .01 | .0044 | 2,801 | 24 | 28 | 12 | 64 |
| 50 | .00929 | .01 | .0048 | 2,737 | 26 | 27 | 13 | 66 |
| 51 | .01002 | | .0052 | 2,671 | 27 | | 14 | 41 |
| 52 | .01081 | | .0057 | 2,630 | 28 | | 15 | 43 |
| 53 | .01165 | | .0061 | 2,587 | 30 | | 16 | 46 |
| 54 | .01257 | | .0068 | 2,541 | 32 | | 17 | 49 |
| 55 | .01355 | | .0076 | 2,492 | 34 | | 19 | 53 |
| 56 | .01461 | | .0086 | 2,439 | 36 | | 21 | 57 |
| 57 | .01576 | | .0098 | 2,382 | 38 | | 23 | 61 |
| 58 | .01699 | | .0113 | 2,321 | 40 | | 26 | 66 |
| 59 | .01832 | | .0131 | 2,255 | 41 | | 30 | 71 |
| 60 | .01975 | | .0152 | 2,184 | 43 | | 33 | 76 |
| 61 | .02130 | | .0179 | 2,108 | 45 | | 38 | 83 |
| 62 | .02296 | | .0211 | 2,025 | 46 | | 43 | 89 |
| 63 | .02475 | | .0253 | 1,936 | 48 | | 49 | 97 |
| 64 | .02668 | | .0300 | 1,839 | 49 | | 55 | 104 |
| 65 | | | | 1,735 | | | | |

nation of employment for this reason may be included with the withdrawal rates. In such case the service table would show decrements in employment as a result only of mortality and withdrawal rates, the latter including the disability terminations.

The object of the table, it should be clear, is to forecast the relative number of employees who will remain in employment until retirement. In addition to this information, however, there remains a further vital question to decide, which relates to the rate of interest to be used in the calculations.

### C.  Rate of Interest

It will be assumed that some rate of interest will be earned on funds which are to be accumulated to provide pension benefits. The decision as to what rate of interest will be assumed, strictly is not the responsibility of the actuary but of the employer. The actuary indirectly, however, will be a party to the decision for, in assuming a rate of interest, attention must be given to the probable size of the annual contributions to create and maintain the pension funds. In other words, a small fund normally cannot be presumed to yield as high a return as a medium sized one, where safety and diversification are considerations, as they must be in the case of pension funds. Again, however, a medium sized fund, say of several million dollars, may earn a somewhat higher return than one of ten or twenty millions; with funds of this size or larger, satisfactory investments may lead to relatively lower interest returns. In any case the actuary must have a rough idea of the probable annual contributions which must be invested. In addition, he may have to indicate to what extent and when disbursements for pension benefits will be paid out, so that the investment portfolio may be adjusted accordingly. Nevertheless, the decision as to the expected interest earnings more properly falls on the employer, for it is he who assumes directly or indirectly the risks that the pension funds will be maintained at an adequate level to provide the pension benefits upon the retirement of his employees. Normally, the rate assumed to be earned will be similar to or slightly higher than that guaranteed by life insurance companies. With agreement upon the assumed rate of interest, the actuary possesses the additional factor which enables him to proceed to make his valuation.

### D.  The Valuation

The method of determining costs under the level percentage of payroll method has been described in Chapter IV in the discussion of comparative pension costs. There, however, we dealt with a closed group, having only one age of entry, specifically age 45. In an actual valuation of pension costs, however, employees will be entering the plan at various ages, with different amounts of benefit to be provided in relation to their salary and service, and with differing probabilities of survival. The principle of determining costs, however, remains the same as previously discussed except that now additional discounts are to be taken for termination of employment by withdrawals and/or disability.

The determination of the cost of the pension benefits by reference to the several tables may take the following steps: (1) calculation of the salaries each group of employees remaining on the payroll at each age may be expected to receive, by application of the salary scale to the number of survivors at each age; (2) determination of the amount of retirement benefits that will be payable in relation to such salaries by reference to the pension formula of the plan; (3) application of annuity factors to the retirement benefits thus determined, in order to find their value as of the date of retirement; and (4) calculation of the percentage of payroll for each employee at each age, which at an assumed rate of interest will create at retirement an annuity fund (as determined in step 3) adequate to provide the pension benefits. These percentages, as arrived at from service tables, are then applied to the actual salaries being received by employees at each age, and in relation to the duration of their service, to determine the aggregate initial cost. With the aggregate cost established, the percentage of payroll necessary to be contributed yearly is obtained by dividing the aggregate cost by the total annual payroll.

This brief description of valuation by the level percentage of payroll methods, while broadly indicating the procedure followed, has been simplified. A detailed description would have involved consideration of actuarial techniques and processes that are complex and beyond the scope of this work.[8] It may be noted also that a valuation for level percentage of payroll funding which takes account of the various factors mentioned involves considerable labor, although various methods to shorten the work have been evolved. Also the description of the valuation process has been in relation to a non-contributory self-administered plan. If employee contributions are to be obtained, which are to be used toward providing the basic pension benefits[9] as set forth in the plan, a further valuation of employees' contributions would be required.

---

[8] See Bibliography: Technical Literature.

[9] Employee contributions are applied under some self-administered plans to purchase pension benefits *in addition* to the basic pension benefits provided by the employer.

Finally, while a valuation along the lines discussed is necessary upon the establishment of a self-administered plan, it is also essential that, periodically, perhaps each year or every five years,[10] a new valuation be made. The purpose is to determine whether the original assumptions as to rates of mortality, rate of interest, and so forth are being realized in the operation of the fund, and whether the accumulated pension funds plus expected future contributions will be adequate to provide the benefits. At such valuation dates, if the assumptions as to rates of mortality, withdrawals, or interest earnings have proved to be too optimistic or too conservative, adjustments may be made.

### E.  Disability Costs

If total and permanent disability benefits are included in a self-administered plan there must be a valuation of the cost. There are different actuarial methods employed for the purpose. In any case, the rates of disability must be ascertained or estimated, and possibly the rates of termination of disability due to death or recovery. Based on this information and on the amount of disability payments, and when they become payable under the terms of the plan, cost computations can be made. Two methods will be briefly indicated; but consideration of typical disability benefits provided under self-administered plans will be found in Chapter XII.

*Group Term Method.* In calculating disability costs there may be used what is known as the *group term* method. By this method the disability costs are met on a year to year basis, in similar manner to group (term) life.[11] In other words, a yearly contribution is made, in the sense of a renewable term insurance premium, which will be adequate to take care of disability claims as they occur. Stated differently, disability benefits are handled on a pay-as-you-go or current cost basis; therefore no reserves are accumulated. The assumption of this method, as with group (term) life, is that the amounts contributed yearly will of themselves be adequate to provide the benefits.

*Level Percentage of Payroll Method.* The costs of disability also may be financed on a level percentage of payroll basis. This procedure is largely similar to the method described above which was employed to determine the costs of the retirement benefits, but

---

[10] Aside from the valuations that periodically will be necessary as a practical matter, the time of the valuation will be influenced by the requirements of the Treasury Department for periodic reports.

[11] See pp. 214-215.

under which, of course, reserves were accumulated. However, inasmuch as it is disability costs that are being valued, the rate of disability applied to the personnel at each age, as shown in the service table, will be the starting point of the valuation of such costs. The actual costs of disability as finally computed will depend on the terms of the plan. The costs consequently will be influenced by such factors as the amount of the benefit, service, and/or age requirements before the benefit becomes payable. Also, as with the costs of retirement benefits, the cost of disability benefits will be influenced by the rate of interest assumed to be earned, and by the mortality table employed; that is, whether the latter is a table based on disabled lives, and whether it takes account of termination of disability by recovery.

## F. Expense

### 1. Factors

The major expense items of self-administered plans which are measurable involve the following: (1) fees for actuarial service in establishing the plan, and such fees as may be charged at successive valuation dates; (2) legal fees for drafting the trust agreement and securing Treasury approval of the plan, and for such advice as may be needed from time to time thereafter; (3) medical fees incurred in awarding disability benefits and possibly in relation to the allowance of certain annuity options at or prior to retirement; (4) management fees of a corporate trustee responsible for investment of the pension funds; and (5) expenses connected with the maintenance of records of each individual employee covered by the pension plan. A further expense, less susceptible of being measured or accounted for than the above, is that attributable to the time executives of the corporation spend in consultation with trustees on investment and administration of the pension fund. While it is true that a corporate trustee such as a bank may be responsible for investment and management of the pension funds, certain corporate executives generally are delegated to consult or act as a pension committee. The duties of the pension committee, among others, call for periodic consultations with the trustees principally in connection with investment of the pension funds.

### 2. Incidence

Among the expenses which may be more or less definitely measured or accounted for, not all are regularly recurring, or at least to the degree that they occur upon the establishment of a plan. Such expenses include legal fees which upon the inception of a plan constitute a relatively larger item of expense than they do thereafter. This is similarly true of initial actuarial charges; for while under a carefully managed self-administered fund there are annual or periodic valuations the actuarial fees for such valuations will tend to average less than the initial charges.

### 3. Fixed Charges

The measurable expenses after the plan has been established will be accounted for mainly by (1) cost of maintenance of records, (2) actuarial fees, and (3) trustees' fees.

*Record Maintenance.* The cost of keeping records will tend to differ as between plans, particularly where a corporation, rather than a trustee, maintains the records of the individual employees covered under a plan. For some corporations use special cards for purposes of the pension plan while others use stock cards to keep the records of their personnel. Also, the necessary details of handling such records will be influenced by the terms of the plan itself; such as whether the plan is contributory, whether it provides withdrawal benefits, and whether a trustee or a corporation is to make payment of the benefits provided by the plan. For these and other reasons the costs of such record-keeping obviously will vary as between plans. In the absence of current published experiences, or statistical surveys of such costs, no satisfactory generalizations are possible.

*Actuarial Service.* The charges for actuarial services necessary for periodical valuations of a self-administered fund will depend on the volume of work required in the valuation. This in turn is mainly dependent on the terms of the plan, the size of the fund, and the number of employees. Also such fees will be influenced by intangible factors that customarily influence the charges for professional services. If the charges for actuarial services are reduced to an annual expense, after the establishment of a plan, it is doubtful that such services for a small fund are obtainable for less than $500 a year; these charges range upward in relation to the size of the fund, and they possibly may reach $5,000.

*Trustees' Fees.* The fees or charges of corporate trustees who are equipped to manage and invest pension funds may be ascertained from the trustee normally in advance of the creation of the fund. To some extent there may be bargaining as to such charges, but generally a uniform schedule is quoted by any given bank, with an allowance for an adjustment of the charges up or down as experience with a particular fund progresses. While the fees may be based on the amount of principal in the pension fund, or on the annual contributions and disbursements from the fund, the former method is more common. In relation to fees based on the amount of principal, two schedules are set forth below representing the probable charges of several large although different New York City banks.[12]

## SCHEDULE A

*Annual Fees:*
    ¼ of 1% of the first $1,000,000 of principal
    ⅒ of 1% of all principal amounts in excess

## SCHEDULE B

*Annual Fees:*
    ¼ of 1% of the first $2,000,000 of principal
    ⅛ of 1% of the next $3,000,000
    ⅒ of 1% of all over $5,000,000

For smaller funds, such as where the initial amounts of principal are $100,000 to $200,000, the percentage rate would naturally be higher; probably ranging from ½ of 1% to ¾ of 1% of such initial amounts, graduating downward as the amount increases, until it reaches the lower percentage rates for the larger amounts set forth in the above schedule.

These fees, it should be noted, do not include any charge for pension payments to the pensioners by the trustee, in the event the trust agreement provides that such disbursements shall be handled by the trustee. Charges for this service are a matter for separate agreement between the corporation and the trustee.

## II. EMPLOYEE BENEFITS AND CONTRIBUTIONS

*Benefits.* The statement on page 175, that self-administered funds may use any method of funding there mentioned, or may use them in combination, means of course that provision may be made for any type of benefit that is desired. Insurance or death benefits may be carried in the fund itself, and disability benefits provided

---

[12] "Pension Trusts—Types, Service and Publicity," *Trusts & Estates Magazine*, March, 1943.

as noted above; withdrawal benefits of the employer's contributions may be provided in whole or part. Also there may be offered such annuity options as a life annuity, 10 years certain, a joint and survivor annuity, or others, in lieu of a straight life annuity at retirement. Thus there may be offered under self-administered pension funds such benefits as an employer may wish to provide, and such as he feels he can afford or finance. Accordingly for reasons of cost, policy, or the employer's circumstances there may be provided simply a retirement or pension benefit. The risk of providing an insurance benefit, in addition, usually is not assumed in self-administered funds; if assumed, the benefit is restricted as a rule to provide a nominal death benefit.

*Employee Contributions.* The usual self-administered plan is non-contributory, the employer making all contributions necessary to provide the benefits. If employees are to contribute, however, then any contribution scheme that is practical and non-discriminatory as between employees may be employed. Contributions of employees usually are refunded with interest, as under insured plans, in the event of death or withdrawal.

## III.  SELF-ADMINISTRATION AND INSURANCE COMPANIES

Earlier reference was made to the fact that the trustees of a self-administered fund may make use of the facilities of life insurance companies. They may do this through a contractual arrangement usually entered into either at the time of the establishment of the plan, or at the time the employees are retired. The first method consists of a formal arrangement with the insurance company, and results in what may be described as *modified self-administration;* the second, as *terminal reinsurance.* In a general sense either method constitutes a modification of straight self-administration of pension funds, but they are sufficiently different to justify the distinction made. The following descriptions will develop their respective differences.

### A.  Modified Self-Administration

Under a modified self-administered plan the funds to provide pension benefits are accumulated jointly by an insurance company and a corporate trustee prior to the retirement dates of employees. The larger proportion of the fund, however, normally will be self-administered until retirements occur; and as to this portion of the fund any method of funding selected by the actuary and/or the employer, consistent with the terms of the plan, may be adopted.

On the one hand a plan of this type seeks to provide through an insurance company an insurance benefit for employee participants in the pension fund, and at the time of their retirement to have the insurance company make payment of the pension benefits. On the other hand this plan aims to retain self-administration of the major share of the fund, thereby allowing discounts to be taken for withdrawals and direct provision to be made for disability, if desired.

To illustrate the procedure let us assume that an employee, age 45, becomes eligible to the pension plan. His monthly earnings are $100 a month, which we assume will remain unchanged to his normal retirement at age 65. The retirement benefit under the plan is to be 30% of his monthly earnings. He will receive at 65, therefore, $100 × 30%, or $30.00 a month. The insurance benefit, to be provided under the terms of the plan, is 100 times the monthly retirement benefit, or $1,000 insurance for each $10.00 of monthly retirement income. The amount of insurance to be purchased consequently is $3,000. The trustee of the fund applies to the insurance company for $3,000 insurance on the ordinary life plan. The contract contains the usual standard provisions, one of which guarantees the right to use the accumulated cash value at certain ages, such as 65, for annuity income at guaranteed annuity rates. In addition, however, the insurance company guarantees to the trustee that, when the employee attains age 65, the trustee may convert or exchange the ordinary life contract for an annuity upon deposit of the necessary funds. The amount of cash the trustee will be called upon to pay to the insurance company will vary with the individual case. In our present example, which illustrates the provision, it would be that amount which, when added to the cash value of the ordinary life policy, will pay $30.00 a month of life annuity income, usually on a 10 year, or 100 months, certain basis.

It will be noted that a modified self-administered plan has certain of the characteristics of an individual annuity plan. An insurance benefit is provided, and the pension benefits are paid by the insurance company. It differs, however, in that, prior to retirement, the accumulation of the funds to provide the benefits, except as the accrued cash values of the ordinary life policies are used for the purpose, are self-administered. There are also technical differences. For example, there may be a larger element of insurance, or amount at risk, in connection with an insurable employee covered under a modified self-administered plan than there is under an individual annuity plan where use is made of retirement income contracts. However, in respect to employees who prove uninsurable, both plans are alike; for, under modified self-administered and individual annuity plans, uninsurable employees are issued retirement annuity contracts by the insurance company, without an insurance feature, in which are accumulated the entire funds to provide the pension benefits. There is no modified self-administration of the funds in relation to such uninsurable employees; the insurance company alone handles their accounts.

### B. Terminal Reinsurance

It is frequently provided in the trust agreements of self-administered funds that the trustee shall be authorized, or that the employer shall have the right to direct the trustee, to invest accumulated pension funds in annuity contracts of insurance companies upon the retirement of employees. Where a self-administered fund actually follows such a procedure this constitutes what we have termed *terminal reinsurance*.

The purpose of terminal reinsurance may be at least twofold. From an administrative aspect it may be simpler and as economical to have the insurance company send out the pension checks as to have the corporation or trustee do so. More important, however, may be the fact that the number of actual pensioners is small, or the amounts of pension income payable to one retired member are considerably higher than the average of payments to others. A spread or transfer of the risks for either of the latter reasons may prove desirable.

Several major points of difference between a modified self-administered plan and a self-administered fund, where terminal reinsurance is used, may be noted. In the case of a self-administered fund, where terminal reinsurance is authorized or employed, life insurance benefits are not an integral part of the pension plan; group life insurance, however, may be carried by the corporation as a separate contract, to provide death benefits. A more significant difference is that annuities, purchased as a consequence of terminal reinsurance, are purchased on a *present market* basis. By this is meant that the purchase of such annuities is subject to their being available, and they are bought at the current rates quoted by insurance companies. In contrast, under modified self-administered plans the insurance company guarantees, upon the issuance of the ordinary life contract, the right to acquire annuities at an employee's retirement, and guarantees as well the annuity rates, or options, which may be exercised at some future time.

## IV.  COMBINATION OF SELF-ADMINISTERED AND INSURED PLANS

In certain situations it may be desirable, or the employer may prefer, to use both self-administered and insured types of pension plans in combination.This is entirely feasible, provided the benefits under the respective combination are non-discriminatory as between employees. Several combinations are possible, and they have been utilized to a limited extent by employers.

The division of pension coverage under combination plans may be differentiated in several ways, such as on the basis of compensation, or on that of past and future service benefits.  When a combination plan is adopted on the basis of compensation all wage-earning employees may be covered under a self-administered plan, and salaried employees by individual annuity contracts.  Again the division of coverage may be based on a distinction between *amounts* of compensation.  Self-administration might be utilized for employees earning annually $3,000 or less, and individual or group annuities for those earning in excess of $3,000.

If the division of coverage is made in relation to past and future service benefits, a self-administered plan might be employed to cover past service and an individual annuity or group annuity plan for future service.  Again a group annuity might be employed for purchase of past service benefits, and self-administration for future service.

Finally, all three types of plans may be used in combination. For example, under some plans a minimum or service pension to *all* employees may be provided upon retirement.  Certain employees may be entitled to additional pension benefits based on compensation and future service.  Self-administration may then be used to provide the service pension; employees earning over $3,000 and up to $6,000 a year may be covered by a group annuity, and those employees earning in excess of the latter figure, by individual annuity contracts.

A further discussion of the applicability and utility of a combination self-administered and insured plan will be found in Chapter XI.

# V. ADMINISTRATION

## A. General

Self-administered pension plans, as they have been defined, make use of a trustee or trustees under an agreement or declaration of trust to invest and manage the pension funds. The benefit provisions of a self-administered plan and the details of its administration are provided for in a *plan*, with the duties and powers of the trustees as to investment and management of the pension funds described in a trust agreement. Thus the legal arrangements are similar to those of individual annuity plans, where the latter employ a trust. There are certain major differences of course in the provisions of a self-administered plan and trust agreement, which are mainly a consequence of the method of funding and the nonuse of insurance companies for the investment of the pension funds. It will be sufficient to note here several items characteristically encountered in the terms of a self-administered plan and its complementary trust agreement.[13]

## B. Plan

Generally under self-administered pension funds the terms of the plan are stated in a separate written instrument, which is variously denominated as the *pension* or *retirement plan*, or as the *rules and regulations* of the pension plan. However it may be designated, there will appear a description of eligibility rules, benefits, retirement ages, and so forth. There will be provision for the creation of a trust, and for a retirement or pension committee. It is the composition, and particularly the duties, of the pension committee which require discussion.

### 1. Pension Committee

*Membership.* The members of the pension committee, retirement committee, or retirement board as it is alternately described, are appointed by the board of directors of the corporation which creates the pension plan and they are subject to the control of the latter. The committee is normally comprised of three to five members, generally officers of the corporation. Usually, however, they are not trustees of the pension plan. This is in contrast to the usual procedure of individual annuity plans, or at least for small

---

[13] The details of the self-administered plan provisions, such as methods of providing benefits, types of benefit, and so forth are treated in Chapters IX and XII.

funds of this type, where it is common practice to nominate individual trustees who function both in a trust capacity and as a pension committee.

*Duties.* The pension committee either of a self-administered or an individual annuity plan is required to administer the plan in accordance with its terms and may formulate rules and regulations not inconsistent therewith. The functions of the committee under a self-administered plan, however, extend to matters not associated with or necessary for an individual annuity plan. The committee is charged with the responsibility of having the pension fund periodically valued by an actuary; with the fixing or changing of the rate of expected interest earnings as circumstances warrant; and with the adoption of service and mortality tables for the periodic valuations after consultation with the actuary. Finally, the committee may be required to act in consultation with the trustee as to investment of the pension funds. In this connection the pension committee either may have the authority to direct the investments, or may act jointly with the trustee. In either case the authority of the pension committee or the trustee is further limited by the terms of the trust agreement.

## C. The Trust Agreement

The responsibility of the trustee of a self-administered fund (and/or of the pension committee) is simply to invest the pension funds contributed by the corporation subject to such restrictions as are set forth in the trust agreement.

*General.* The trustee may be authorized to invest the pension funds generally in stocks, bonds, or other securities, and real or personal property at the sole discretion of the trustee.

*Restrictions.* It is sometimes provided that the trustee shall be limited to securities which are legal investments for trust funds or for life insurance companies. A further limitation may be that at no time more than 10% of the funds shall be invested in the securities of any one issuer, except in those issued by Federal, State or Municipal authorities. Finally, any investment in securities of the corporation establishing and operating the pension plan may be prohibited.

# CHAPTER IX

# Basic Provisions of Pension Plans

·····································································

THE BASIC PROVISIONS OR TERMS OF PENSION PLANS ARE THOSE IN which are found a description of (1) eligibility rules for membership in the plan, (2) eligibility rules for the receipt of the pension benefit, (3) normal retirement ages, (4) optional retirement ages, (5) retirement benefits, (6) employer and employee contributions, (7) termination of service benefits prior to retirement (vesting), (8) disability benefits, (9) optional modes of settlement of benefits, and (10) provision for termination or modification of the plan. These provisions contain what may be stated as the *who, what,* and *when* of pension plans. The remaining provisions largely have to do with the *how,* and fall into an administrative category; that is, they pertain to the mechanics or the machinery for implementing the basic provisions or terms of the plan. Whether the type of pension plan is a group annuity, an individual annuity, a self-administered, or a combination plan, the basic provisions as outlined will be more or less common to all. It is possible, consequently, with some exceptions, to detail and discuss them as they may be typically encountered, or as they may be normally included in a plan, without necessary reference to a particular type. Also it should be understood that the analysis deals with pension plans which provide a definite benefit at retirement, unless qualified with reference to money-purchase plans.

## I. ELIGIBILITY RULES FOR MEMBERSHIP

### A. Eligible Employee Groups

A pension plan may be established to which are made eligible either (1) all employees, (2) wage earners, (3) salaried employees, (4) salaried employees earning over certain amounts such as $3,000 annually, or (5) all employees earning in excess of certain amounts such as $3,000 annually.

The employee groups most commonly made eligible for pension coverage are either all employees or those on a salary basis. It is rarely that a pension plan is established solely for wage earners, although a recent plan, established for workers in the garment industry, supported by joint contributions from employers and workers in the industry, is a possible example. Plans covering only salaried employees earning over $3,000, or all employees earning over $3,000, constitute numerically a small proportion of existing plans, although they are found in important industries and sizable organizations. In such plans, where the earnings of employees are used as a qualifying test, they should be integrated with Social Security benefits if tax advantages are to be obtained. The technical aspects, and the practical significance of *integration*, are treated briefly later in the chapter.

The particular circumstances of an enterprise, discussed in Chapter XI, may influence the decision as to what employee groups shall be eligible for pension coverage. The mere designation, however, of a certain class of employees as one which may qualify for pension coverage does not mean that all employees of a qualified class necessarily will become members. This is because of other eligibility rules which are found in most pension plans.

## B. Other Eligibility Rules

Typical eligibility rules for membership include an age requirement. While an employee may be of a class qualified to become a member of the pension plan, he usually must be either over a certain minimum or under a certain maximum age to be eligible to the plan. More often than not both requirements may prevail; that is, the employee must have attained a certain minimum age but he must not exceed a given maximum age. In addition, whether or not an age requirement is included as an eligibility test, usually there is a stipulation that the employee must have completed a certain number of years of service prior to admission to the pension plan.

*Age.* The usual minimum age provision is that an employee must have attained 25, 30, or 35, with a prevailing tendency to select age 30 as the minimum. The rule is usually applicable to employees in the service of the employer upon establishment of the plan as well as to future employees. A maximum age, when used in conjunction with a minimum, may be 55, 60, or 65, with a tendency to exclude as ineligible employees age 60 or over.

Although some pension plans may provide neither a minimum nor maximum age as a test of eligibility for membership, in the absence of the former, a maximum age usually is encountered. The use of a maximum age only is more common to insured plans, self-administered ones using a hiring limitation, discussed below, in lieu of a maximum age. In any case, the maximum ages selected, beyond which an employee will be ineligible, tend to be between 60 and 65.

*Service.* It is usual to couple with a minimum age requirement a further condition for eligibility; an employee must have completed a certain number of years of service. The service requirements for eligibility to membership in pension plans may range from 1 to 5 years, with a prevailing tendency to use a five year service period. An employee therefore may be eligible as to age, but until he completes the service or waiting period he may not become a member of the plan.

*Hiring Limitation.* Another eligibility rule, more apt to be encountered in self-administered plans than in insured types, although feasible in the latter, is what is known as a hiring limitation. In lieu of a definite statement as to a maximum eligibility age it may be provided that an employee may become a member of the pension plan only if he was under a certain age at the time of his employment. The hiring age, frequently specified as a test of eligibility, is either 45 or 50.

In the formulation of eligibility rules it is important to consider an employer's circumstances, and for tax reasons, to relate the rules to the Federal law and Treasury regulations; particularly as the latter may prohibit discrimination in favor of highly paid and supervisory employees. In consequence, the eligibility rules of a pension plan, as established by one employer, may not be practical, or technically suitable, for another.

In general, the practical considerations which lead to a minimum and/or a maximum age, as well as a service requirement, directly or indirectly relate to an employer's costs or financial outlays. It is felt that employees at the younger ages, below thirty perhaps, where personnel turnover is normally higher than at older ages, are disinterested in a pension plan which may benefit them possibly thirty or forty years hence. If, as a consequence of this attitude, turnover among the younger employees will be unaffected by including them in the plan, the possible expense to an employer of their inclusion may be avoided by a minimum age requirement.

A second reason for a minimum age arises where a plan is contributory.  The young employee who is included as a participant in a pension plan may prefer to use the amount of his contributions to maintain or raise his living standards, and consequently he may respond negatively to participation.  Where death and withdrawal benefits are available under a pension plan, however, this negative attitude of younger employees may be changed to one of positive interest.

The introduction of a maximum age as an eligibility rule for membership in pension plans is directly related to cost, or the financial outlays.  It is usually the older employees who will persist in employment until the retirement age is reached.  The direct cost or the financial outlays, made necessary by including in a plan the older employees with only short periods of service before retirement, may be substantial.  An employer, by excluding certain of the older employees, thus may find it possible to finance a pension plan for the remainder of his employees.

A service requirement recognizes the fact that among new employees the withdrawal or turnover rates are apt to be high in the first few years.  Inasmuch as it is the permanent employees in whom an employer will have the greater interest, it is frequently believed that the expense of covering short-service employees under the pension plan is needless.  In addition, the adoption of a service period, such as three or five years, may be influenced by the attitude of insurance companies in the case of individual annuity plans; particularly when there is no minimum age.  Employee groups which show initial, or persistent, high turnover are generally unattractive to the majority of the large insurance companies underwriting such plans.

## II.  ELIGIBILITY RULES FOR RECEIPT OF THE PENSION BENEFITS

An employee may qualify as a member of a pension plan, but in addition must satisfy certain conditions to obtain the full pension benefits.  These conditions, or eligibility rules, in most plans require that an employee must have attained a specified normal retirement age, and/or have rendered a certain number of years of service to obtain the full pension allowance.

The conditions, or eligibility rules, for receipt of the pension benefits may differ, particularly as between insured and many self-administered plans.  For example, a self-administered plan may be of a kind for which all employees are eligible, but the rules and regulations thereof will specify that an employee must render either 15, 20, or 25 years of service and attain the normal retirement age to obtain the full pension benefits. Again, it may be stipulated simply that if a given number of years of service are rendered, retirement on a full allowance will be permitted without reference to attainment of a normal retirement age. Under insured plans, in contrast, the attainment of a normal retirement age is almost universally specified as a condition for receipt of the full pension benefit, but rarely is there an *explicit* stipulation of the number of years of service which must be rendered. The number of years of service required of an employee will be dependent on the age at which he became eligible to membership in the plan, measured in relation to the stipulated normal retirement age.

## III. NORMAL RETIREMENT AGE

The normal retirement age, selected in most newly established plans, is age 65. Sometimes provision is made that females shall retire at 60. In the occasional plan, where males are retired at 60, females may retire at 55.

A major force which has influenced the selection of 65 as a retirement age is the fact that a worker's Social Security benefits do not commence until age 65. However, employers are better advised to establish a normal retirement age which bears some relation to the age when superannuation occurs among employees in their respective enterprises, for other factors than age may have a bearing. For example, the personnel of a bank or an insurance company may have a longer efficient working lifetime than employees of companies engaged in coal mining. In the latter case a normal retirement age of 55 or 60 may better serve the employer's purposes.

A second important consideration leading to the general use of 65 as a normal retirement age relates to cost. An earlier normal retirement age, such as 55 or 60, usually increases an employer's cost or financial outlays, because of the shorter funding period prior to retirement and the higher outlay for annuities at these earlier normal retirement ages. Initial costs particularly will be sharply higher, principally because, in relation to the past service credits customarily provided for older-aged employees, there will be relatively shorter periods in which to fund the costs of the benefits. An alternative scheme for an employer whose situation requires an early retirement age, such as 60, would be to exclude from the formal pension plan those aged 50 or over.   Those excluded may be provided for on an informal, or year-to-year basis, the employer meeting the cost of such retirement benefits as may be payable to the excluded employees from current operating income.

## IV.  OPTIONAL RETIREMENT AGES

*Early Retirement.*   It is customary to provide that an employee, with the consent of his employer, may retire earlier than the normal retirement age as stated in the pension plan.   For example, if the normal retirement age is 65, and an employee retires at 60, the benefit usually will be a proportion, or the actuarial equivalent, of what he would have received if he had remained to normal retirement age.   As a rule this right to earlier retirement is conditional upon an employee having had either 10 years of service with the employer, or 10 years of membership in the pension plan.   A provision of this type may be mutually advantageous to employer and employee.   For example, an employee who is partially but not totally and physically disabled, or who is no longer efficient occupationally, may desire to quit.   Again where permanent lay-offs are contemplated, to the extent that older employees may be affected, the privilege of early retirement may cushion the situation for both the employee and the employer.

On the other hand, while a provision for earlier retirement makes for flexibility, it likewise may have certain negative aspects.   From the employee's viewpoint the annuity income payable upon earlier retirement will be drastically reduced.   The reasons are several. For example, if we assume that the employee's normal retirement age is 65, and that he actually is retired at age 55, ten years of future contributions for his account will have been discontinued. Also the amount already accumulated for the employee's benefit will purchase a lesser annuity income at the earlier retirement age, because of the possibility that annuity payments will be made for a longer period.   From the employer's point of view earlier retirements may lead to selection against the pension funds.   For example, if earlier retirement is allowed for reason of poor health, pension payments will be made to an employee who might not have survived to normal retirement age.   Finally, where the right to earlier retirement based on years of service rendered, such as twenty years, is contractual, definite pressure or selection may occur against the pension funds.   Employees who have satisfied the service requirements, but who are still relatively young and employable, may quit their jobs, obtain their pension, and accept other employment.

*Later Retirement.* Later retirement than the normal may also be possible by mutual agreement between the employer and employee. An employee for example who is to retire at 65 may wish to continue to work, or the employer may desire his services. In such cases any further contributions to the pension plan on behalf of such employee, either by the employer or employee, cease. Pension payments may be made to the employee just as though he had retired. Occasionally there is stipulated, when later than normal retirement is permitted, that actual retirement must take place no more than five, or at the most, ten years after normal retirement age. It is thought unwise to retain "retired" employees among the personnel too long after normal retirement age, from the point of view of the morale of the younger members of the work force. The latter may regard the retention of these "retired" employees as a block to promotion to higher and better paid jobs or positions.

## V.  RETIREMENT BENEFITS

The actual retirement benefits that an employee will receive at retirement will depend on, among other things, whether the pension plan is of a money-purchase or a definite-benefit character. If a money-purchase plan is used, the benefits cannot be forecast as accurately as they can in the case of a definite-benefit plan. In the latter, however, though the pension benefit may be definite in relation to either or both of an employee's compensation and service, the actual retirement benefit that an employee will receive will be somewhat dependent on the operational effects of the pension formula.

### A.  Pension Formulas Generally

Almost a first consideration in designing a pension plan is to decide what benefits should be provided upon retirement. Accepted almost as an axiom is the fact that the pension benefit must be adequate to *effect* retirement. While the question—*what is adequate?*—may be conducive to differences of opinion, there is agreement that if the amount of the retirement benefit does not bear some reasonable relation to the annual or average compensation received in the period of service, or received in the years more or less immediately prior to retirement, the plan will fail of its purpose.

The major purpose of a plan, of course, is to enable an employer to effect the retirement of superannuated employees; but in addition, the employees should be satisfied or willing to retire. That they will be satisfied is unlikely if the retirement benefit is drastically out of line with the compensation they have received, or is grossly inadequate to sustain decent living standards.

In general, pension plans, under which the pension formula will produce a scale of retirement benefits for the personnel generally of either 40% or 50% of the average compensation received in the five or ten years prior to retirement, are regarded as adequate. If the employee group is without Social Security benefits, however, it may be necessary in a given plan to increase the benefits for lower-paid employees ($1,200-$1,500) to 60%, or even 70%, if their retirements are to be satisfactorily effected.

## B. Specific Pension Formulas

The most frequently used formulas provide pension benefits either as (1) a percentage credit of the average annual earnings, or of the average final earnings of the last five or ten years of service, for each year of service rendered, or (2) a flat percentage of the annual earnings of a particular year, as, for instance, the current annual compensation of an employee at the time he becomes eligible to the plan.

*Earnings Percentage—Service.* A pension formula which provides the pension benefits as a percentage of the average annual earnings for each year of participation in the pension plan, or for each year of service rendered prior to retirement, or as an average of final earnings for each year of service, are the most commonly employed. If credits for past service are granted, the actual compensation that was paid to an employee, at the time he became eligible, or upon the establishment of the plan, or an average of the annual earnings for a few years prior thereto, are normally used as a basis for computing past service benefits.

Where employees are covered by Social Security, and where the pension plan is one which is intended to cover all employees, the past service credits provided may be ½%, ¾%, or 1% of current compensation (or, as stated above, of the average of an employee's earnings for a few years prior to his becoming eligible), multiplied by some or all of the years of past service. Future service benefits may then be computed, or granted, as either 1% or 1½% of the average annual or average of the final earnings.

For reasons which relate to the level of an employee's wage or salary, or because of lack of past service credits, or because an employee may have insufficient time to earn future service credits, it is frequently necessary, where the above formulas are utilized, to provide for minimum pension benefits. For example, assume that an employee age 45 with no past service credits who is to retire at 65 is eligible to a plan. If the future service credit is 1% of annual earnings, times service, on a level salary basis he would be limited to a maximum of 20%; to take care of such cases a minimum pension of 25% or 30% may be provided.

One further aspect of this formula may be noted. While at the inception of the plan an employee's future service benefit may be as above, that is, an expected 20% of the annual compensation received when the plan is established (1% × 20 years), the benefit as a percentage of the final yearly earnings may be less. In the above case, if the employee received an annual compensation of $1,200.00 upon establishment of the plan, assuming no change in compensation until retirement, then based on a 1% benefit for each year of future service he would receive a pension of $240.00 or 20%. However, if at age 55 he was raised to $1,800, which similarly remained unchanged until retirement, the benefit as a percentage of his final compensation would shift. For the first 10 years the employee received $12,000 ($1,200 × 10), and for the second ten years, $18,-000 ($1,800 × 10). His retirement benefit then would be 1% of his average annual earnings, or $300 ($30,000 total compensation divided by 20 years equals $1,500 average earnings; 1% of $1,500 equals $15.00, times 20 years equals $300). As a percentage of the average of final compensation of $1,800.00, however, the retirement benefit would be approximately 17% ($300 ÷ $1,800 = 16.67%).

The average of final earnings in the last five or ten years of service (or use of the final salary) is sometimes employed as a base in computing the retirement benefit by the earnings percentage-service formula. For example, if we know or assume that an employee, age 45, will receive an average annual compensation of $1,800 during the last five or ten years in service, there may be provided a benefit of 1% of such average earnings for each year of service. Thus, with twenty years of service, his retirement benefit would be $360.00 (1% × $1,800.00 [average of the final earnings] × 20 years). It may be noted that this terminal approach, as it might be called, produces generally higher benefits than those produced when the average earnings over the entire period of service are used as a base; except possibly for the wage-earning employees.

*Flat Percentage.* An alternative formula to the above is that which provides that the pension benefit shall be a flat percentage of the compensation of a particular year, or of the average of annual earnings for several years, without regard to years of service. Thus, there might be provided a retirement benefit for employees of either 30%, 40%, or 50% of the current annual compensation at the time of entrance into the plan. Using again the above example, assume that the pension benefit is a flat 20% of the current annual earnings. Based on $1,200 annual earnings an employee, age 45, would receive $240.00 a year at retirement. If the flat percentages were applicable to salary increases, and the employee at age 55 is raised to $1,800 which he receives until retirement, the pension benefit would amount to $360.00.

The use of a flat percentage formula, where increases in salary are treated as above, holds the retirement benefit percentage-wise in the same relation to wage or salary increases as it bore to an employee's original compensation. The use of this formula, therefore, will result in a benefit at retirement which is based on final salary, unless some limitations are introduced. A limitation might be that no increase in retirement benefits will be granted on salary increases granted in the last 5 or 10 years prior to retirement.

Theoretically, the pension formula selected to compute or provide the benefits is tied in with the problem of securing a benefit, sufficient in amount to encourage employees to retire, and at a reasonable cost to the employer; consequently, any formula which achieves these ends should be acceptable. There are several other considerations, however, which will be discussed.

Many employers like a formula which recognizes or "rewards" service; consequently the computation of retirement benefits as a percentage of the average annual earnings, or as an average of the final earnings for each year of service rendered, is preferred. An earnings percentage-service formula is generally satisfactory if a provision also is made for minimum pensions, either for those employees who lack past service or who are among the lower paid. The usual application of this formula, however, normally provides lower pensions in relation to final earnings (except possibly where an average of the final earnings is used as a base) than a flat percentage formula.

It should be noted also that, if pension benefits are computed as a flat percentage of compensation, or if they are based on an average of the final earnings times years of service, while the pension may be higher, so likewise may be the costs. Moreover, the use of an average of final earnings (also final salary) as a base for computing pension benefits has been criticized [1] as possibly leading to funding, or financial difficulties. Pension plans which base the retirement benefits on an average of the final earnings usually make use of a salary scale; but salary increases cannot be estimated with complete accuracy. Moreover, under a pension plan where an average of final earnings is used as a base, the higher paid employees may be given flat salary increases a few years prior to retirement, simply to increase the pension benefits. Also cyclical upswings in business, bringing rapid changes in the price level (war periods), may drastically raise the scale of compensation of all employees; thus they may render unstable a fund that when created was based on normal assumptions as to the scale of wages or salaries expected to prevail.[2]

### C. Integration Formulas

Regardless of the pension formula which may be used to compute the amount of the retirement benefits, the plan must operate without resulting discrimination in favor of the highly paid or supervisory employees, to obtain Treasury approval. In general, plans, which are well designed and are set up for the purpose of covering all employees or all salaried employees, will provide retirement benefits which will be technically non-discriminatory as between participating employees. Nor are such plans limited to the amount of retirement benefits which may be provided, except indirectly by several Treasury regulations.[3] The pension benefit, of course, must bear some reasonable relation to an employee's compensation, and the compensation to which the pension benefit is related must itself have been "reasonable."

A pension plan, however, which provides that only those employees earning over a certain amount, such as $3,000 a year, shall be eligible to membership or to pension benefits is limited automatically in terms of the amount of benefits which may be

---

[1] Latimer, M. W., "Industrial Pension Systems," Industrial Relations Counselors, New York, N. Y., 1932, pp. 348-357.

[2] See Chapter XI for further discussion.

[3] See Treasury Mimeograph 5717 (July 13, 1944); also 30% rule, I.T. 3674 (July 11, 1944); also Prentice-Hall *Pension and Profit Sharing Service*.

provided.   In a special mimeograph[4] issued by the Treasury Department, among other things, it was provided as follows:

A salary classification plan is integrated with Social Security if no employee can receive a greater annuity in proportion to pay (including the Social Security Annuity) than any lower paid employee, assuming identical periods of service. The comparison is made with the employees excluded entirely from the plan as well as with lower paid employees within the plan.

A pension plan, in other words, which makes use of a "salary classification" [5] scheme, in order to be approved by the Treasury Department, must meet the general test of integration as stated above.   Without detailing the specific formulas, tables, or illustrative material given in the mimeograph as aids to and tests of integration, the practical result is a limitation on the amount of retirement benefits which can be provided to employees under a "salary classification" plan.   This may be seen from the following illustration.

Take the case of an employee age 45 earning $6,000 a year, with provision for normal retirement at age 65.   The first $3,000 of the employee's earnings are covered by Social Security, *and therefore should be excluded in calculating benefits.*   On the balance of $3,000 an employee could receive approximately 30% or $900 a year.   The employee's Social Security benefits on the first $3,000 of earnings would provide approximately $600 a year.[6]   The sum of the two benefits, $900 plus $600, or $1,500, would be the approximate pension or retirement income the employee could expect to receive.   In relation to his earnings of $6,000, expressed as a percentage, the benefit would be 25%.

In general, a salary classification plan which excludes employees earning less than $3,000 a year will provide benefits ranging from about 25% to 35% of the compensation in excess of $3,000.   Thus

---

[4] "Integration of Pension Plans of Employees with the Retirement Benefits of the Social Security Act."    Mimeograph No. 5539, July 8, 1943.  In Prentice-Hall *Pension and Profit Sharing Service,* paragraph 9256.

[5] It should be noted that a plan which includes all salaried employees is technically not a "salary classification plan."   The latter is one which excludes those earning less than $1,000, $2,000, $3,000, and so forth.

[6] It will be observed that the Social Security benefit on the first $3,000 of earnings is shown as approximately 20%, or $600; whereas on earnings in excess of $3,000 the possible retirement benefit is 30%, or $900.  This differential or apparent lack of integration with Social Security is permissible under the pension regulations of the Treasury Department—". . . the total Social Security Act benefits of an employee, in view of the supplementary benefits provided by such law, may be considered as 150 percent of the primary insurance benefit provided thereby." (Regulations 111, Section 29.165-3).

the "automatic" pension formulas that are enforced by use of a salary classification will usually be found to provide lower over-all retirement benefits than plans which do not require *integration*.

## VI.  EMPLOYER AND EMPLOYEE CONTRIBUTIONS

### A.  Employer Contributions

The amount of the employer's contributions under a pension plan, made initially upon its establishment or after it is in operation, will be influenced by various factors previously discussed, particularly in Chapter IV.   It is sufficient to note here, therefore, that the basis of an employer's contributions, both in relation to the plan as a whole and to the participating employees, will be defined in the plan.   If a plan is of a contributory definite-benefit type it normally provides that the employer shall contribute the amounts, over and above the employee contributions, necessary to provide the definite benefit.   If a plan is non-contributory the employer will make the entire contribution.   If a contributory money-purchase plan is used the employer's contributions will be stated as in some fixed relation to those of the employees.

### B.  Employee Contributions

The typical employee contribution schemes provide that the contribution shall be a percentage of some or all of the annual compensation, as discussed in the chapters on group annuity and individual annuity policy plans.   It was mentioned also that the amounts of contribution required will vary, being dependent on whether the employees are covered by Social Security, and on whether the plan is of a money-purchase or a definite-benefit type. If it is of the latter type contributions will range from 2% to 5% of compensation, with the employees earning less than $2,000 sometimes being exempted from making contributions.   If all contribute, the lower percentage will generally be applicable to earnings under $3,000, and the higher to those earning in excess.

In some pension plans it is provided that the employee contributions shall be graded in accordance with the *age at entry*.   The methods to achieve this may vary, but the underlying purpose is to proportion or equalize contributions from employees in relation to the total cost of purchasing their respective benefits.

For example, assume that two male employees *A* and *B*, ages 45 and 55 respectively, each have annual earnings of $3,000 or $250 a month, which remain unchanged to retirement. The benefit to be provided is 1% of annual earnings for each year of future service; and the employees are to contribute 3% of their compensation. $A$'s monthly benefit will be 1% of $250 × 20 years, or $50.00 a month. $B$'s monthly benefit will be $25.00 a month (1% of $250 × 10 years), or one-half of $A$'s. The total gross cost of $A$'s benefit, using an annual retirement annuity gross level premium of $68.49 (the unit cost at age 45 of $10.00 monthly retirement benefit at 65), will be $6,849.00. The total cost of $B$'s benefit (unit cost = $161.03) will be $4,025.75.

It will be noted that the total outlay for $A$'s benefit dollar-wise is greater than for $B$'s, principally because, in relation to the pension formula, $A$'s longer service earns a larger benefit. $A$'s own contribution is $1,800.00, or, as a percentage of the total cost of his benefits, 26.3%; $B$ contributes $900.00, or, as a percentage of the cost of his benefits, only 22.4%. If $A$'s contribution as a percentage of the total cost of his benefit were the same as $B$'s, that is 22.4%, he would have contributed about $300 less. If the ages of $A$ and $B$ were 35 and 55, based on the same assumptions and using retirement annuity gross level premiums, $A$ would pay approximately 30.4% of the total cost, and $B$ only 22.4%.

In the light of the above, contribution rates from employees may be adjusted in relation to their ages at entry into the pension plan in an attempt to equalize their contributions. However, plans which attempt this are in the minority, for several possible reasons which may be mentioned. The regulation of contributions normally causes an increase in administrative costs; it may call for burdensome or even prohibitive contributions from older employees; finally, unless the contributions from younger employees are to be increased as they pass through successive older ages, the older employees upon establishment of the plan may regard the contribution scheme as discriminatory.

Finally, a contribution scheme may be mentioned, which is occasionally employed under individual annuity plans, where the contract contains an insurance feature. The contribution required from an employee will be that amount which is allocable to the cost of the life insurance feature, as distinguished from the contribution required to purchase the annuity income. This contribution scheme, while apparently equitable, may call for rather large and burdensome contributions for insurance from those in the older age group. Also in the case of employees who are substandard or impaired risks, if insurance is obtainable, it normally will be *rated up;* that is, there will be extra premiums for the insurance coverage. The negative aspects of this contribution scheme may be somewhat modified if employees over 55 are excluded from insurance coverage, or if extra-premium costs are met by the employer.

## VII. TERMINATION OF SERVICE BENEFITS PRIOR TO RETIREMENT: VESTING

By *vesting* is meant the right or interest that a participating employee acquires in the employer's contributions to a pension plan, when termination of his employment occurs prior to normal retirement age. It will be noted that no reference to employee contributions has been made in this definition of vesting. The reason is that, where a pension plan is contributory, employee contributions in most of the modern plans are always returnable directly, or indirectly, with or without interest, upon death, or upon severance of employment for other reasons prior to retirement.

Whether the employer's contribution should or should not be vested in the employee upon severance of employment fundamentally involves the question of whether an employer's contributions are deferred wages. Without further discussing this controversial subject,[7] the practice of vesting in newly established plans, at least of the insured type, has become common. The method of vesting, that is the amount of the employer's contribution which shall be made available, when this amount shall be payable, and in what manner, will vary from plan to plan. Certain of the methods, most commonly utilized in relation to vesting upon severance from employment, or in the case of death, will be described.

### A. Severance Benefits

#### 1. Immediate Vesting

A small number of pension plans, usually those which cover only salaried employees, or employees of the white-collar class, or those where a high minimum age and a long service period are required as conditions of eligibility, may be found to provide for immediate vesting.

#### 2. Deferred Vesting

Plans which defer vesting the employer's contributions grant the employee an equity in such contributions in several ways:

[7] See Chapter I.

*Service.* The sole criterion may be that an employee who has 5, 10, 15 or 20 years of service, may, upon termination of employment, receive all of the employer's contribution. Again, vesting may be graduated, with the provision that an employee who has 5, 10, 15 or 20 years of service upon termination of employment will be entitled respectively to 25%, 50%, 75%, and 100% of the employer's contribution.

*Age.* Age alone may be the test, with the provision that for an employee who attains age 45, 50, or 55 the employer's contributions shall be completely vested.

*Service and Age.* A double requirement may be provided, namely that an employee must have had 10 or 15 years of service, and also must have attained age 40 or 45.

*Membership.* Sometimes membership in the plan may be utilized as a requirement for vesting. Thus an employee with 5 or 10 years of membership in the plan may be completely vested; or an employee may be granted ⅓ at the end of 5 years of membership, ⅔ after 10 years, and 100% after 15 years of membership in the plan. In addition, there may be coupled with membership a requirement that an employee must have completed a certain number of years of service.

*Years Prior to Retirement.* The sole test may be that an employee must be within 5 or 10 years of normal retirement, in which case complete vesting will be allowed upon severance.

*Disability.* Occasionally, under pension plans which make no *direct* provision for disability, there may be a provision that the entire value of the employer's contributions shall be vested in the employee regardless of his age, service, membership, or other conditions which may normally restrict the amount or time of vesting. Again, a limitation may be imposed granting full vesting only if disability occurs after a certain age, such as 55.

## B. Death Benefits

Death benefits are a subject of vesting largely under individual annuity pension plans, which employ retirement annuity and/or retirement income contracts. Neither group annuity nor self-administered plans customarily carry a death benefit as an integral benefit of the plan, but they may use some form of group life insurance for this purpose.

Under an individual annuity plan, using retirement annuity and/or retirement income contracts, there may be a provision that, for employees without insurance on their lives (uninsurables), the death benefit will consist of the entire premiums paid on the individual contract or the cash value, whichever may be larger, without qualifying conditions. In the case of insurable lives, either the full death benefit may be payable or the benefit may be limited to 25% for each 5 years of service, or membership in the plan, up to 100%. Age at death, as a rule, is not a condition for vesting death benefits. In the event that the full benefit is not payable, the balance of any proceeds of the insurance reverts to the trustees, to be used for future premium payments.

What shall be vested, or when vesting shall occur, involves technical as well as practical considerations. On the *what* side from a technical aspect, where the method of funding takes a discount for anticipated deaths such as is involved in using single-premium deferred life annuities and normally in using the level percentage of payroll principle, there will be no death benefit from the employer's contribution to be vested. Likewise, if there has been a complete discount for withdrawals from employment, there can be no specific provision for a benefit to be vested in employees who sever employment.

On the practical side, in relation to how and when employer's contributions should be made available to an employee on severance (in the absence of a discount for withdrawal), several possible methods were indicated above in the discussion of severance benefits.[8] If we set aside the controversial questions raised or involved in immediate vesting, it is agreed that deferred vesting should not commence too soon or be postponed too long. Early deferred vesting, partial or complete, is discouraged (as is immediate vesting) on the grounds that it may be the cause of an employee terminating his employment in order to obtain the vested benefits. This may be arguable in regard to younger employees, where the vested amounts would not be large; and as for older employees, terminations are normally low in any case. It has been observed that an employee who quits to obtain vested benefits may be well rid of. Under insured plans, however, where employees upon severance are allowed to take vested paid up annuities, the handling by an insurance company of the small amounts involved may prove administratively expensive. Directly or indirectly this might in time affect an employer's cost.

If partial or complete vesting, however, is postponed too long

---

[8] Also see Chapter XII.

employees may not develop a feeling of security which, among other things, a pension plan should engender. This is particularly true in relation to the older employees. For this group, whose members usually have had 10 or 15 years of service and whose turnover is normally low, a provision for early vesting of the employer's contributions upon severance of employment should not increase an employer's costs to any important degree.

As a generalization, subject to an employer's circumstances, the most simple provision for vesting of severance benefits is one that is based either on service or on membership in a plan. A graduated vesting of ⅓ at the end of five years of membership in a plan, ⅔ after 10 years, and 100% at the end of 15 years, with immediate vesting for employees 55 or over, should prove generally satisfactory, if a minimum eligibility age of 25 or 30 is used. A service requirement might be added as a further condition for vesting, or it might be used in lieu of membership in a plan, if for practical reasons this seemed desirable.

Finally, in relation to those plans which provide a death benefit prior to retirement, while it is possible to defer or gradually vest the death benefits, experience indicates that to make payable to an employee's beneficiary the full death benefits is the more desirable procedure. The indirect benefit to the employer or employees which results from graduating the payment of death benefits (with the retention of some amount by the trustees for future premium deposits) is unlikely to be financially important in the maintenance of a pension plan. In any case the effect on the morale of employees, in not making death benefits payable to an employee's beneficiaries, may be unhealthy. A plan whose terms provide for a retention of some or all of the death benefits by the trustees has a certain speculative flavor, in the sense that the employees may feel that their lives are insured for the benefit of the plan, rather than for their dependents.

## VIII. DISABILITY BENEFITS

By disability we refer here to total and physical permanent disability. As we have noted, total and permanent disability benefits are not directly provided under insured plans. Under individual annuity pension plans, however, which make use of retirement income or retirement annuity contracts, it is possible to make some *indirect* provision for disability. Under these contracts, as we have observed, a cash value accrues, which can be turned over or paid out in installments to the totally disabled employee. This procedure is hardly a systematized scheme for taking care of disability, but it partially serves the purpose; for the cash values increase as employees grow older, when the incidence of disability similarly rises.

Direct provision for disability frequently is made under self-administered plans.[9] It is commonly provided, however, that 10 or 15 years of service, plus attainment of a particular age, are necessary before disability benefits will be granted. The benefit itself may be of a limited amount, and for a limited time. It normally will not approximate the value of the retirement benefit, although if disability occurs near the age of normal retirement the disability payments may be equal to the amount of the retirement benefit.

Whether an employer should assume the cost or risks of providing total and permanent disability benefits in a self-administered plan is controversial.[10] The decision will depend on the nature of the enterprise, the occupational hazards, the amount of disability benefit contemplated, over how long a time the benefit shall be paid, the conditions to be met before it is payable, the composition of the employer's personnel, an employer's past experience, and other considerations. It may be that the disability payments from Workmen's Compensation will be partially adequate for an employer's purposes, although this will prove of small value in the case of the total disability of employees in the salaried or executive class, and in that of non-occupational disabilities. In any case it is generally agreed that a careful study must be made before provisions for disability benefits are included in a self-administered pension plan.

## IX. OPTIONAL MODES OF SETTLEMENT

The phrase *optional mode of settlement* is a technical term, taken from insurance phraseology, used to describe the various methods under which a settlement of the benefits provided under a pension plan may be made with the employee or his beneficiary.

While previous reference[11] has been made to these "options," they must be considered as important and valuable features, made available under most pension plans, whether of the insured or self-administered type. An example of such options is the privilege

---

[9] See Chapter XII.
[10] See Chapter XI.
[11] See Chapters VI and VII.

of naming a contingent annuitant, or, in lieu of a straight life annuity, of selecting a cash refund type.

## X.  TERMINATION OR MODIFICATION OF THE PENSION PLAN

A corporation which establishes a funded pension plan hopes to maintain the plan, and to gain for its employees and itself the expected advantages.  A corporation nevertheless cannot guarantee, without jeopardizing its existence in the future, that a pension plan once established will be maintained in the face of all possible future developments.  It is thus standard practice to incorporate in a plan a provision to the effect that the corporation may alter, modify, or terminate the plan if in the future it is deemed necessary.

The interests of the participants are safeguarded, however, as to the benefits purchased for them prior to the alteration or the modification of the original plan, by a stipulation that such benefits shall not be affected.  If a plan should be terminated the participating employees are entitled to receive at least the benefits which have been purchased for them prior to termination, although in such form as may be provided by the terms of the plan.

# CHAPTER X

## Group Life

.............................................................................

G ROUP LIFE INSURANCE IS A FORM OF INSURANCE ISSUED TO groups of employees with the same or a common employer. While group life insurance has only an indirect connection with pension plans, its frequent use by employers, to provide moderate death benefits for employees covered either by a group annuity or a self-administered pension plan, calls for a brief discussion.

Until recent years the type of insurance employed under group life involved the use of what is known technically as *one-year* renewable term[1] insurance, the nature of which is explained below. It was formerly understood, therefore, that an employer who had group life coverage possessed group insurance issued on a one-year renewable term basis. With the introduction of other types of life insurance as a mode of coverage under group life plans, it has become necessary to employ a distinguishing terminology. Group life, therefore, while retaining its generic connotation as a form of life insurance coverage for a group of employees with a common employer, may be (1) group temporary, (2) group paid-up, or (3) group permanent.

## I. GROUP TEMPORARY

Group life insurance which makes exclusive use of one-year renewable term insurance may be identified as group term, although sometimes referred to as *group temporary*. Renewable term in-

---

[1] *Term* insurance, in general, is a type of life insurance which provides simply a death benefit if death occurs during the period or *term* the insurance is in effect. A disability clause normally may be obtained in conjunction with term insurance, providing for a waiver of the premiums in the event of total and permanent disability and, sometimes, in addition, for disability income payments. Usually a contractual right is granted to convert the term insurance to some form of permanent life insurance, which may be exercised prior to or at the expiration of the term period. Also the right may be given to renew the insurance at the expiration date for a further period. Where the latter privilege is granted it commonly is referred to as *renewable term* insurance.

surance, as employed under Group Temporary, is issued for a term of one year, and usually may be renewed at the end of each year at the option of the owner or policyholder upon payment of the required premiums.

The nature of one-year renewable term insurance may be indicated by the use of a simple illustration. We may assume that a group of 100 individuals wishes to insure its members for $1,000 each, the insurance to be payable in the event of their respective deaths in the ensuing year. We may assume further that in the course of that year there will occur one death among the group; although who will die is unknown. The amount of the death claim will be $1,000 payable to the estate or the beneficiary of the individual who has died. What will each of the 100 individuals have to contribute as his share of the cost of meeting the death claim? Or, in other words, what will be the "premium" for each member of the group? Of course, the premium cost will be $10.00 per individual; $1,000 (death claim) ÷ 100 (number in the group). Inasmuch as the total premium of $1,000, the amount necessary to meet the death claim, will be paid at the beginning of the year, there will be some interest earned on the premium. If we assume further that the premium fund of $1,000 will be at interest for the entire year, that is that the death claim will be paid at the end of the completed year, the cost per individual may be reduced slightly below $10.00. If the interest to be earned is 3½%, for example, the individual premium cost would be $1,000.00 discounted at 3½% for one year, divided by 100; or, $966.20 ÷ 100 equals $9.66, the premium cost per individual. If, however, someone is made responsible for the investment of the premium fund and the payment of the death claim who makes a charge for these services, some amount (loading charges) would be added to the net premium of $9.66 to cover expenses. Broadly, this illustration indicates the process used by insurance companies in arriving at the premiums for lives covered by group temporary.[2]

The fact that the risk of death assumed under group temporary is on a year-to-year basis means, as a practical matter: (1) that the amount at risk on each individual life is $1,000 throughout a given year, and (2) that in each succeeding year the premium cost

---

[2] This illustration of premium construction has been purposefully simplified, but it should be noted that the premiums charged for group temporary take account of several valuable privileges not mentioned above; e.g., the right of conversion on termination of employment to permanent forms of insurance, and the extension of the coverage in the event of total and permanent disability.

per $1,000 of coverage will increase in relation to the preceding
year, inasmuch as the probability of death will be greater.

*Premium Costs.*　The gross premium costs of group life coverage
for an individual aged 45, covered until age 64, are shown in the accompanying table.　These rates are based on the American Men
(Ultimate) Table of Mortality,[3] with interest at $3\frac{1}{2}\%$.　The major
insurance companies writing group temporary currently employ
this mortality table for the computation of premiums.　The rates
shown are applicable to groups of employees who are standard risks
(no extra hazards), and they allow the privilege of conversion to
permanent forms of coverage and the extension of coverage in the
event of total and permanent disability.

GROUP TEMPORARY

Annual Gross Premium Rates

Age 45-64

$1,000 Insurance

| Age | Premiums |
|---|---|
| 45 | $10.02 |
| 46 | 10.62 |
| 47 | 11.30 |
| 48 | 12.04 |
| 49 | 12.88 |
| 50 | 13.78 |
| 51 | 14.78 |
| 52 | 15.89 |
| 53 | 17.09 |
| 54 | 18.43 |
| 55 | 19.87 |
| 56 | 21.47 |
| 57 | 23.20 |
| 58 | 25.08 |
| 59 | 27.12 |
| 60 | 29.39 |
| 61 | 31.82 |
| 62 | 34.45 |
| 63 | 37.33 |
| 64 | 40.44 |

*Average Premium Cost.*　Whereas in the case of an *individual*
covered by group temporary the premium rises yearly, it should be
noted that in the case of a *group* of lives such a rise usually does not
occur.　The fundamental reason is that the composition of an employee group normally will shift from year to year as a result of
withdrawals from employment, deaths, retirement, and consequent

---

[3] See Appendix B for table.

replacements with new and younger employees. The average age therefore may not alter from year to year. It is expected under group temporary coverage that the average age will tend to remain more or less the same; thus for the group as a whole the average premium cost may remain more or less level. For example, if an insured employee group initially had an average age of 45, in a succeeding year, with the composition of the group remaining unchanged, the average age might be expected to be above 45. However, because of replacements of personnel, usually at younger ages, there may be maintained the original average age of 45; thus the average premium cost for the second year may be more or less the same as that for the first year. But, however, if the average age rises, and/or claim experience is adverse, there may occur some premium increases in the succeeding years.[4]

## A. Underwriting Rules

*Insurable Groups.* Generally, the employees of an individual, partnership, or corporation are acceptable for group temporary coverage. Other groups, such as governmental employees or members of associations will be covered, dependent on the law of the jurisdiction in the former case and on the underwriting rules of a particular insurance company in the latter. Parent corporations with subsidiaries may obtain a single group temporary contract to cover all of its employees, subject usually to the condition that the employees reside in the possessions or the jurisdictions of the United States.

*Eligible Groups.* Employee groups which are considered insurable must meet certain other requirements. There must be at least fifty[5] employees eligible for coverage. If the employer is to pay all the premiums, then all employees, or all of those of a certain class, must be insured. If the employees contribute to the cost, then at least fifty employees must be insured, or 75% of those who are eligible, whichever is the larger number. Normally only full-time employees are eligible for group temporary insurance.

*Coverage Plan.* Employees are covered by group temporary

[4] Offsets to premium increases that may be caused by an increase in the average age may arise from dividend sources: expenses tend to decline with the duration of the group contract; also, if contingency reserves are set up the interest thereon may decrease future outlays. For further discussion see: "Does Group Life Insurance Cost Show a Tendency to Increase with the Age of the Contract?", *Papers and Transactions,* Vol. 30, Actuarial Society of America, New York, N. Y., 1929, pp. 167-171.

[5] Some insurance companies accept 25 employees if the state law of the employer's domicile permits.

either in (1) level amounts, or in relation to (2) salary or wages, (3) occupations, or (4) length of service. When employees are covered by level amounts each employee receives the same unit of coverage, such as $1,000. Salary or compensation, however, is the usual basis for coverage, particularly when the employees are to contribute. For example, employees earning less than $100 a month may be covered in the amount of $1,000; those earning $100 but less than $200, in the amount of $1,500; those earning $300 or more, $2,500. If compensation is not stable, as in the case of wage-earners, then an occupational classification, with the issuance of flat amount of insurance to employees of a given class, may be used as a basis. For example, executives may be allowed $2,500; foremen and salesmen, $2,000; and all other employees $1,000. A length-of-service plan may provide a minimum of $1,000, with increases of $100 in coverage for each future year of service up to some stipulated maximum. This method, however, leads to a relatively large volume of insurance being placed on the lives of the older employees with a corresponding increase in the premium costs. Thus from the point of view of cost it may be less desirable than the other coverage plans. The method, however, carries with it the reward-for-service idea and is frequently used in connection with a non-contributory or employer-pay-all plan.

*Minimum Coverage.* While certain group-writing companies may require no minimum amount of coverage, others may require at least $50,000. In the case of individual employees, it is normally required that there be at least $500 on each life.

*Maximum Coverage.* The maximum amount of insurance that will be issued to any one employee is determined by (1) the total amount of insurance for the group as issued at the inception of the coverage, and (2) the amounts of insurance on the lives of the fifty employees insured for the highest amount, in accordance with the table which follows.

An illustration of the maximum amount of insurance obtainable by an individual employee under the accompanying schedule may be seen in the following example. Of a group of 100 employees we may assume that 70 are to be insured for $1,000 each, and 20 for $2,000. The total coverage of these 90 employees would amount to $70,000 plus $40,000 or $110,000. We will assume that the remaining ten employees wish to have $4,000 each, or a total of $40,-000. The entire coverage would be $110,000 plus $40,000, or $150,-000. The schedule shows that, when the total coverage is between

MAXIMUM COVERAGE

| Total Insurance in Group When Actually Issued | | Maximum Amount, if at Least 50 Employees Are Insured for at Least | | | Maximum Amount if There Are Not 50 Employees Insured for at Least $1,000 |
|---|---|---|---|---|---|
| | | $5,000 | $2,000 | $1,000 | |
| Under $ | 100,000 | | | $ 2,500 | $ 1,500 |
| $  100,000 to $ | 200,000 | | $ 4,000 | 3,000 | 2,000 |
| 200,000 to | 350,000 | | 5,000 | 3,000 | 3,000 |
| 350,000 to | 500,000 | $ 7,000 | 5,000 | 4,000 | 4,000 |
| 500,000 to | 700,000 | 10,000 | 5,000 | 5,000 | 5,000 |
| 700,000 to | 900,000 | 10,000 | 6,000 | 6,000 | 6,000 |
| 900,000 to | 1,100,000 | 10,000 | 7,000 | 7,000 | 7,000 |
| 1,100,000 to | 1,300,000 | 10,000 | 8,000 | 8,000 | 8,000 |
| 1,300,000 to | 1,500,000 | 10,000 | 9,000 | 9,000 | 9,000 |
| 1,500,000 to | 6,000,000 | 10,000 | 10,000 | 10,000 | 10,000 |
| 6,000,000 to | 7,000,000 | 11,000 | 11,000 | 11,000 | 11,000 |
| 7,000,000 to | 8,000,000 | 12,000 | 12,000 | 12,000 | 12,000 |
| 8,000,000 to | 9,000,000 | 13,000 | 13,000 | 13,000 | 13,000 |
| 9,000,000 to | 10,000,000 | 14,000 | 14,000 | 14,000 | 14,000 |
| 10,000,000 to | 11,000,000 | 15,000 | 15,000 | 15,000 | 15,000 |
| 11,000,000 to | 12,000,000 | 16,000 | 16,000 | 16,000 | 16,000 |
| 12,000,000 to | 13,000,000 | 17,000 | 17,000 | 17,000 | 17,000 |
| 13,000,000 to | 14,000,000 | 18,000 | 18,000 | 18,000 | 18,000 |
| 14,000,000 to | 15,000,000 | 19,000 | 19,000 | 19,000 | 19,000 |
| 15,000,000 and over | | 20,000 | 20,000 | 20,000 | 20,000 |

$100,000 and $200,000, the maximum allowed on any one life is $3,000; thus each of the 10 employees would be limited to $3,000.

*Individual Selection.* Group life is issued only on a basis which precludes an employer from selecting the individual employees to be covered. In a non-contributory plan all employees of a given class are automatically covered as soon as they are eligible. An employee will be insured for that amount to which the class in which he belongs entitles him. For example, under a contributory plan, if he is entitled to $2,000, he may not take $1,000 or $3,000; of course, if an employee chooses to do so, he can refuse to apply for insurance and can remain outside the plan.

*Medical Examination.* No medical examination is required for group temporary coverage if an employee is newly eligible to a plan. A medical examination may be required under certain circumstances, such as, if he should fail to apply for coverage within a specified time after having become eligible, or if he should desire to reenter a plan after having dropped out.

*Employee Contributions.* No employee usually is allowed to contribute more than 60 cents a month, or $7.20 yearly per $1,000 on his life, toward the cost of group temporary coverage. Exceptions to this occur when the group coverage calls for an extra premium, such as when the employees are in an extra-hazardous industry, but the employee contributions may not then exceed 80 cents a month per employee, or $9.60 a year per $1,000.

## B. Administrative Aspects

*Group Contract.* Under group life as under a group annuity the contractual relation is between the employer and the insurance company. The employee is issued a certificate, which shows that he is a participant in the plan. The group temporary contract is a short document, consisting of not more than 6 to 9 printed pages and setting forth various stipulations and provisions, the most important of which will be enumerated.

*Eligibility Rules.* A statement is made as to when employees will become eligible for coverage; frequently three months after employment.

*Contributions from Employees.* The maximum amount which employees may contribute is indicated, if the plan is a contributory one.

*Amount of Insurance.* The basis for coverage, such as a salary classification, is set forth, with a statement as to the amount of insurance to which an employee in a particular classification is entitled. A provision for decreases or increases in coverage, as an employee's classification may change, also appears.

*Termination of Individual Coverage.* It is provided that coverage under the group contract ceases as follows: upon the termination of the contract; upon the cessation of premium contributions by an individual employee; upon the shift of an employee from the classification under which he was covered under the group contract; or by an employee severing his employment.

*Conversion Privileges.* It is usually provided that an employee, upon termination of employment, may convert all or part of his group temporary coverage within thirty-one days after leaving his employment, without evidence of insurability, to some permanent form of coverage offered by the insurance company. Such permanent form will be issued at the employee's attained age, based on the then quoted premium rates of the insurance company for the particular permanent contract which is desired in exchange for the group coverage. A further conversion right may be offered, in the event that the entire group contract is discontinued, to anyone who has been insured for five years prior to the termination of the coverage. An employee may then convert a portion of his insurance to a permanent plan offered by the insurance company, without evidence of insurability. This privilege is subject to the same stipulations as those which are made when an employee terminates employment, and it may not apply under certain circumstances, such as, if a new group contract is to replace that which has been terminated.

*Premiums.* Premium rates per $1,000 of coverage appear in the contract, and these are quoted usually on a monthly basis. A statement of the mortality table to be used and the guaranteed interest rate normally is set forth. The usual mortality table is the American Men (Ultimate) Mortality Table, with interest at 3½%.

*Facility of Payment.* Group temporary contracts, except as they are limited by State laws, generally provide that payment up to $250.00 of the insurance proceeds may be made to persons who have incurred expense in connection with the last illness or burial of an employee; the balance of the proceeds are made available to the employee's estate or beneficiary.

*Options of Settlement.* An employee usually is given the right that the insurance proceeds be paid to his beneficiaries under an installment option disbursing principal and interest; sometimes under an annuity option. In either case the exact method of distribution may be subject to the approval of the insurance company.

*Dividends or Rate Credits.* If the group temporary is issued by a mutual company, agreement is made that surplus earnings, if any, will be distributed in the form of dividends. If a stock company, rate credits will be granted. In either case the *experience* will determine the amount of dividends or rate credits, and thus will depend on (1) the amount of premium income received from the case, (2) the actual death claim experience of the employee group, and (3) the length of time the policy has been in force. In other words, each group contract stands on its own in relation to premium refunds, whether dividends or rate credits.

*Rate Guarantees.* Premiums are payable on a year-to-year basis; the gross premium rates may be modified or altered by the insurance company on any anniversary or renewal date of the group life coverage.

*Employee Certificates.* A certificate is issued to employees which in no way modifies the terms of the group contract, but administratively is useful to provide the employee with certain information. The face of the certificate usually sets forth (1) the name of the employee, (2) the amount of his insurance coverage, and (3) the name of the beneficiary. The certificate further describes the provisions for limited death coverage in the case of total and permanent disability of an employee (if the master contract so provides), the optional settlements available to him, and possibly the guaranteed rate of interest thereon; finally, the employee's right to nominate or change beneficiaries, and his conversion rights upon termination of employment, are described.

## C. Wholesale Insurance

The limitation of group temporary insurance to groups of at least 50 lives excludes many smaller employee groups who might wish this form of coverage. A modified form of group temporary cover-

WHOLESALE INSURANCE

Annual Gross Premium Rates

$1,000 Insurance

| Age | Premiums |
|-----|----------|
| 45 | $12.55 |
| 46 | 13.18 |
| 47 | 13.90 |
| 48 | 14.68 |
| 49 | 15.56 |
| 50 | 16.51 |
| 51 | 17.56 |
| 52 | 18.73 |
| 53 | 19.99 |
| 54 | 21.40 |
| 55 | 22.92 |
| 56 | 24.60 |
| 57 | 26.43 |
| 58 | 28.40 |
| 59 | 30.55 |
| 60 | 32.94 |
| 61 | 35.50 |
| 62 | 38.27 |
| 63 | 41.30 |
| 64 | 44.57 |

age, however, is available for groups of less than fifty, which likewise makes use of one-year renewable term insurance. It may be identified by various names, but normally is called *wholesale* insurance. The underwriting rules are similar to those which are applicable to group temporary, with certain exceptions which will be enumerated.

*Size of Group.* The group to be covered must consist of at least 10 lives, but of less than 50.

*Premiums.* The premiums, as in the case of group temporary, will vary from year to year in accordance with the attained ages of the employees insured. The premiums also will be higher than those for group temporary at the same ages. Typical rates for ages 45 to 64 are shown in the table on page 222.

*Minimum Amount.* The minimum amount issued on one life may be either $500 or $1,000, dependent on the rules of the insurance company who is the underwriter.

*Maximum Amount.* The maximum amount of insurance issued on one life usually is limited to $5,000. Further limitations of the amount on any one life also are provided. Assuming that different amounts of coverage are desired by the employees of a group, the amount available to an employee in the highest class may be limited to 2½ times the average amount of insurance on all the lives covered, subject to the maximum; or in accordance with a schedule such as the following:

| *Lives Insured* | *Limits* |
|---|---|
| 10-19 | 2½ times the lowest class |
| 20-29 | 3   times the lowest class |
| 30-39 | 3½ times the lowest class |
| 40-49 | 4   times the lowest class |

For example, in the case of a group with 30-39 employees, if the lowest class were issued $1,000 each, the highest amount of coverage available to any one employee would be $3,500.

*Medical Examinations.* Usually, wholesale insurance may be obtained without medical examination, if all employees apply for their coverage within 31 days after they become eligible. Exceptions are made when there is known or suspected to be an impaired risk in the employee group; when the insurance applied for is in excess of a certain amount; when an employee is over a given age; or as they may be required under the rules of a particular insurance company or the laws of a certain state.

*Contract.* While the issuance of wholesale insurance is subject to a request from an employer, and to his agreement to make premium deductions from employees' wages or salaries if the plan is contributory, the contractual relationship is between an insurance company and each employee. An individual policy is issued for each employee who is insured. In other words, there is no master contract involved, such as is issued to the employer under a group life or a group annuity plan.

*Conversion Rights.* An employee who terminates his employment while the wholesale insurance is in force may within thirty-one days convert his term insurance without medical examination to any of the permanent forms offered by the insurance company. A permanent form will be issued to an employee at a rate based upon his attained age, and in accordance with the current premium rates for the form of contract desired.

*Dividends or Rate Credits.* Premium refunds in the form of dividends or rate credits will be payable, dependent on the experience of the company with the employee group covered.

Several other forms of group life insurance are available to employees, which are underwritten similarly to group temporary, but under which there are employed insurance contracts that contain a so-called investment, or cash value element. These forms constitute a relatively recent development in the field of group coverage, and they have had a short history as compared with group temporary. The latter, since its initial use approximately thirty years ago, has had a tremendous growth. It is estimated there are some 26 billions of dollars of group temporary coverage presently outstanding. The principle of one-year renewable term insurance, therefore, as a means of providing protection for employee groups, has received wide acceptance.

The absence of an investment element or a cash value in group temporary, especially as it affects employees who face termination of their employment while covered thereunder, has led to some employee dissatisfaction, particularly when the latter contribute to the cost of the insurance. For example, an employee who is covered by group temporary may shift or terminate employment. His insurance then ceases, unless he converts to a permanent form of coverage. While it is true that he may convert without medical examination, he must pay a premium rate as of his attained age. This rate may be prohibitive in the case of an older employee. Even with a younger employee it may be burdensome, particularly if new employment be difficult to obtain. Also, an employee may have come to regard his group temporary coverage as a permanent part of the insurance protection he has built up for his family's needs; consequently, he may not have added to his personal life insurance as much as he might in the absence of group coverage. Thus this employee reasons that, in the absence of group temporary, he might have purchased additional personal life insurance at a lower premium rate than he must pay to effect conversion to a permanent form of insurance at his attained age upon the termination of his employment. While this type of thinking may appear irrational, inasmuch as group temporary for most employees constitutes low-cost coverage, it is nevertheless encountered.

A means of ameliorating some of the "impermanency" of group temporary, and a method of providing a benefit by way of a cash value or permanent insurance when a worker terminates his employment, are offered under certain newer forms of group life. They are known as *group paid-up* and *group permanent*. Their essential natures and differences will be described.

## II.  GROUP PAID-UP

We have seen that group temporary is one-year renewable term insurance, and that each year the premium cost per $1,000 increases. Another form of insurance, to which we have had no occasion to refer previously, is that which is purchasable with a single payment, known as *single-premium* life insurance. Under this form, an individual who wishes to be covered by insurance for the rest of his life without further payment of premiums may advance the cost in one sum. For example, at age 45, according to the American Experience Table of Mortality with interest at 3%, an individual could obtain $1,000 of insurance for a gross single-premium cost of approximately $578. In the event of his death, no matter when it occurred thereafter, the insurance company would pay $1,000. This form provides permanent life insurance coverage, and, inasmuch as a first premium payment is the sole one required to obtain a death benefit, it is described as *paid-up* life insurance. Under paid-up life insurance there exists a cash value, which is available upon the surrender or termination of the insurance, or against which loans may be made.

Group paid-up makes use of the single-premium life, or the paid-up life insurance principle, in relation to employee groups covered thereby. It, however, partially retains the use of one-year renewable term insurance which, used in conjunction with paid-up life insurance, makes group paid-up a modified form of group temporary. Its operation may be best developed through an illustration. We shall assume that an employee, age 45, is to receive $1,000 coverage on the group paid-up form. We shall assume also that the employee will contribute $1.20 a month toward the cost of the insurance, or $14.40 a year, which amount will be used to purchase paid-up life insurance. At age 45, $14.40 will buy approximately $25.00 of paid-up life insurance. It is necessary for the employer, therefore, to purchase only $975 of one-year renewable term in order that the employee be provided a total of $1,000 in death benefits. The process is shown in the following table. It assumes that each year from age 45 to 64 an employee contributes $14.40 which is used to buy paid-up life insurance, and that the balance of $1,000 coverage is provided by one-year renewable term purchased by the employer.

It will be noted from the accompanying table that each year the employee's contribution is used to purchase paid-up life insurance. Each yearly contribution of $14.40, in other words, is a single payment, which purchases the amount of paid-up insurance for the respective years that is shown in column 4. If an employee terminates employment he may take with him the sum of the yearly amounts of paid-up insurance which have been purchased by his contributions (column 5). For example, an employee who quits at age 50, having completed five years of service under the plan, would have paid-up insurance equal to the sum of the amounts purchased for ages 45 to 50, or $145.58 (column 5). The $145.58 is permanent life insurance with no future premiums due thereon. In lieu of this paid-up insurance the employee may obtain an amount equal to at least his own contributions, or the cash value of the paid-up insurance if it is larger in amount than the sum of his own contributions. The further privilege usually is granted to the employee to convert to a permanent form without medical examination the difference between the face amount of his insurance, e.g. $1,000, and the paid-up insurance. Thus, if $145.58 were the amount of the paid-up insurance, the employee could convert $854.42 at his attained age to some permanent form. Here again we have the same conversion right that we encountered in group temporary.

The employer's contributions, as in group temporary, are utilized

GROUP PAID-UP

$1,000 Insurance

| Age | Employer's Contribution (1) | Insurance Purchased by Employer (One-Year Renewable Term) (2) | Employee's Contribution (3) | Yearly Insurance Purchased by Employee's Contribution (Paid-up Life) (4) | Accumulated Insurance Year to Year Bought by Employee's Contributions (5) |
|---|---|---|---|---|---|
| 45......... | $ 9.77 | $974.66 | $14.40 | $25.34 | $ 25.34 |
| 46......... | 10.09 | 949.75 | 14.40 | 24.91 | 50.25 |
| 47......... | 10.46 | 925.27 | 14.40 | 24.48 | 74.73 |
| 48......... | 10.85 | 901.22 | 14.40 | 24.05 | 98.78 |
| 49......... | 11.30 | 877.60 | 14.40 | 23.62 | 122.40 |
| 50......... | 11.77 | 854.42 | 14.40 | 23.18 | 145.58 |
| 51......... | 12.29 | 831.52 | 14.40 | 22.90 | 168.48 |
| 52......... | 12.86 | 809.06 | 14.40 | 22.46 | 190.94 |
| 53......... | 13.45 | 786.88 | 14.40 | 22.18 | 213.12 |
| 54......... | 14.10 | 765.14 | 14.40 | 21.74 | 234.86 |
| 55......... | 14.78 | 743.68 | 14.40 | 21.46 | 256.32 |
| 56......... | 15.51 | 722.51 | 14.40 | 21.17 | 277.49 |
| 57......... | 16.28 | 701.77 | 14.40 | 20.74 | 298.23 |
| 58......... | 17.09 | 681.32 | 14.40 | 20.45 | 318.68 |
| 59......... | 17.93 | 661.16 | 14.40 | 20.16 | 338.84 |
| 60......... | 18.85 | 641.29 | 14.40 | 19.87 | 358.71 |
| 61......... | 19.78 | 621.71 | 14.40 | 19.58 | 378.29 |
| 62......... | 20.75 | 602.41 | 14.40 | 19.30 | 397.59 |
| 63......... | 21.77 | 583.26 | 14.40 | 19.15 | 416.74 |
| 64......... | 22.82 | 564.40 | 14.40 | 18.86 | 435.60 |

for the purchase of one-year renewable term insurance (column 2); but in a yearly amount, as represented by the difference between $1,000 and the amount of accumulated paid-up life insurance shown in column 5.

## A. Underwriting Rules

The underwriting rules of group temporary are generally applicable to group paid-up. It should be mentioned, however, that an employee cannot obtain the cash value of his paid-up insurance, or make loans against the same while he remains in employment; employment must be terminated before either right is available. Also, while our illustration shows the plan as contributory, it may be established on a non-contributory or employer-pay-all basis.

## III. GROUP PERMANENT

The forms of insurance used under group permanent, where the purpose is to provide group life coverage, may be any of the usual permanent forms of insurance purchasable by an individual such as whole life paid-up at 90, life paid-up at 65, or ordinary life. These forms of life insurance coverage are equivalent in their nature to single-premium life insurance discussed above. However, instead of the purchase being made by a single payment, level annual premiums—which are the mathematical equivalents of single premiums—are made. In the event an employee terminates his employment he may be granted at least a cash value, or an amount of paid-up insurance, upon the cessation of premium payments. The amount of cash value or paid-up insurance granted to an employee will be dependent on the terms of the group permanent plan, as well as on the length of time for which the level annual premiums have been paid on his life. As relates to the paid-up insurance which may be acquired upon cessation of premium payments, it has the same status as paid-up insurance obtained by the payment of a single premium; that is, permanent life insurance with no further premiums due thereon. For example: at age 45 we saw in the case of group paid-up that $14.40 purchased $25.34 of paid-up insurance. If any of the above-mentioned forms of permanent insurance were terminated at age 45, and if they possessed a cash value of $14.40, then approximately $25.34 of paid-up insurance could be obtained; assuming, of course, that in all instances the mortality table and the guaranteed interest rate were the same.

The use of level premium contracts, such as ordinary life, or whole life paid-up at 90 under group permanent, represents a complete transition from group temporary and an abandonment of the principle of one-year renewable term insurance. There is provided therefore under group permanent a unit of coverage, such as $1,000, on a premium outlay basis which, while initially higher at any given age than a one-year renewable term premium, remains constant or level. The contracts used will contain cash values, paid-up insurance values, income options, and other features. In fact, the contracts will be similar in most respects to those which may be purchased by individuals from insurance companies.

A group permanent life insurance coverage plan may be established either on a contributory or non-contributory basis. We may show its operation in relation to an employee who is covered in the amount of $1,000 from ages 45 to 64. The contributions of the employee may be arranged similarly to the method shown for group paid-up; in this illustration, however, we shall assume that the employee contributes one-half of the premium cost, and that upon termination of employment he receives the then available paid-up life insurance. In passing, the decision as to the amount of contributions which will be required from employees under group life coverages is a practical one, as it is in the case of employee contributions under pension plans. Aside from the fact that the contribution scheme must be administratively and otherwise satisfactory to the employer and to the issuing insurance company, the determination of what amount the employees shall contribute is tied in with what they "will" contribute. This in turn is dependent upon circumstances, and upon what the employees believe they will obtain in return for their contributions. Under permanent forms of group life coverage it may be that, because an employee takes with him on termination of employment at least his own contributions, or the cash value of the contract on his life, or an amount of paid-up insurance, he will be willing to contribute dollar-wise a larger amount than he would in the case of group temporary.

One of the effects of the elimination of one-year renewable term insurance in group permanent, it will be noted, is to maintain the employer's contribution in relation to an individual life at the same amount for the life of the contract. Again, as in group paid-up, there are created paid-up insurance values and cash values which may be turned over to the employee upon severance of employment. Finally, under a group permanent plan an employee terminating employment may be permitted to take with him the face amount of the insurance, that is the entire contract on his life, and to continue premium payments thereon. The premium that he will pay thereafter will be the same as was charged originally for his age upon his entrance into the plan. For example, our employee who enters the plan at age 45 and leaves his employer at the age of 50, taking his contract, would continue payment of the original premium of $36.50.

## A. Underwriting Rules

The underwriting rules of group permanent are in the course of development, and may differ as between insurance companies. In

GROUP PERMANENT

$1,000 INSURANCE

Whole Life Paid-Up at 90

Gross Premium Rate at Age 45 = $36.50

| Year | Employer's Contribution | Employee's Contribution | Paid-Up Life |
|------|-------------------------|-------------------------|--------------|
| 1 | $18.25 | $18.25 | $ 38 |
| 2 | 18.25 | 18.25 | 76 |
| 3 | 18.25 | 18.25 | 113 |
| 4 | 18.25 | 18.25 | 149 |
| 5 | 18.25 | 18.25 | 184 |
| 6 | 18.25 | 18.25 | 219 |
| 7 | 18.25 | 18.25 | 253 |
| 8 | 18.25 | 18.25 | 286 |
| 9 | 18.25 | 18.25 | 318 |
| 10 | 18.25 | 18.25 | 349 |
| 11 | 18.25 | 18.25 | 379 |
| 12 | 18.25 | 18.25 | 408 |
| 13 | 18.25 | 18.25 | 437 |
| 14 | 18.25 | 18.25 | 465 |
| 15 | 18.25 | 18.25 | 491 |
| 16 | 18.25 | 18.25 | 517 |
| 17 | 18.25 | 18.25 | 542 |
| 18 | 18.25 | 18.25 | 566 |
| 19 | 18.25 | 18.25 | 589 |
| 20 | 18.25 | 18.25 | 611 |

general, as with group paid-up, they are similar to those of group temporary. It should be pointed out also that group temporary may be issued in connection with group permanent for employees who may not be eligible for the latter. For example, if a minimum age is provided before an employee is eligible to group permanent, it is possible to cover him with group temporary until such time as he qualifies for the permanent insurance.

Until an employee terminates employment he has no right to the cash value or paid-up values of the permanent insurance on his life; but when termination occurs, as stated above, it may be provided that an employee can take his contract with him and continue premium payments thereon. No medical examination is required in order that he may exercise this privilege; also, inasmuch as there is no one-year renewable term element to be converted at the attained age upon the termination of employment, an employee thereafter pays the original premium as charged at the time of his entrance into the group permanent plan.

The analysis of the several types of group life coverage that are available to an employer has been made for a dual purpose. First, to indicate that an employer, contemplating or already possessed of a self-administered or group annuity plan, has a choice of several types of group life coverage, if he desires to provide supplementary death benefits through the medium of life insurance. Secondly, however, while in the description we confined the discussion to its use as group life coverage, group permanent has a further application in relation to providing pension benefits. When employed to provide retirement benefits it may be distinguished as a *group permanent retirement income plan;* or in the interests of brevity, a *group retirement income plan.*

## B. Group Permanent Retirement Income Plan

The objective of group permanent, as used for pension purposes, is not only to provide retirement benefits, but also to make provision for insurance or a death benefit. In consequence, the contractual benefits that are provided for employees under a group permanent retirement income plan are similar to those offered by individual retirement annuity and retirement income contracts, which have been discussed. The analysis in Chapters III and VII of the retirement income and retirement annuity contracts is generally applicable to the features of a group permanent retirement income plan, and the discussion consequently may be shortened. A group retirement income plan is distinguishable from the usual individual annuity pension plan, however, in two major aspects: (1) the method of underwriting; and (2) administration.

### 1. Method of Underwriting

A group retirement income plan may be utilized normally only where the number of employees to be covered totals at least fifty. Also, it may be required that the insurance coverage be not less than some minimum such as $250,000. Assuming that an employee group meets the tests as to number and insurance coverage requirements, the employees may be admitted to the plan without medical examination or other evidence of insurability. An exception to this general rule occurs when an employee is eligible for an amount of insurance coverage, collateral to his pension benefits, which exceeds certain limits. These limits are automatic. The largest amount of coverage which will be available to any one employee without medical examination is determined by the total coverage issued to all employees, and the average amount of insurance provided for the fifty lives who are to receive the largest amounts. As a practical matter probably 90% of the employees will be admitted to the plan without evidence of insurability.

If the plan is contributory the usual group coverage rule is applicable, namely that 75% of the eligible employees must apply for admission before the plan becomes effective. Also the employer is usually required to contribute at least 25% of the cost of the insurance benefits provided thereunder.

### 2. Administration

While a trust may be used, and must be in certain states whose laws require it, a group retirement income plan customarily employs a master contract, such as was described in connection with group annuity plans. Administratively, therefore, it becomes unnecessary to issue individual retirement income or retirement annuity contracts on the lives of the employees who enter the plan. In the event an employee terminates his employment, an individual contract may be issued to him. This contract may be continued if the terms of the group retirement contract so provide.

A master contract will contain all the provisions of the pension plan as they relate to eligibility, retirement and death benefits, employee contributions, if any, an employee's right to a cash value, paid-up insurance, or continuation of coverage, if he should terminate employment, and other matters. In short, many of the provisions found in a trust agreement under the usual individual annuity pension plan are contained in a master contract. A master contract also will contain provisions and tables as found in individual retirement income or retirement annuity contracts, such as guaranteed cash values, guarantees as to premiums and annuity rates, options at retirement, and similar contractual agreements.

In conclusion, we may note some other points of difference from the usual individual annuity plan which makes use of separate retirement annuity or retirement income contracts. Under group permanent retirement income plans, service is generally rendered by group representatives of an underwriting insurance company. Finally, while dividends are payable annually, they will be based on an insurance company's experience with a particular plan.

# CHAPTER XI

# Choice of Plan

AN EMPLOYER IN SELECTING A PLAN FROM AMONG THE TYPES described in this work usually will have to examine the underlying considerations, which, although they are not always germane to his decision, may need an appraisal. An initial question, or one that probably will arise at some point in his investigation of pension plans, will be whether to self-administer or to insure his plan. If his decision is to insure, a further question may arise as to whether to adopt an individual or a group annuity plan. Finally, there may be involved a choice of a combination of plans, such as the simultaneous utilization either of a self-administered and an insured plan, or of the several types of insured plans.

The major underlying considerations that will influence the choice of a plan are those which relate to risk factors, types of benefit offered or made available by the various plans, and administrative expense. In turn, the significance of these considerations for a particular employer must be evaluated in relation to his circumstances. The analysis which follows, therefore, initially treats in a general way of these underlying considerations. This, in turn, is followed by a discussion of their relation to the particular circumstances of an employer that limit the choice of plan, possibly make for alternatives, or impose no limitations.

## I. RISKS

*Generally.* Risks may be dealt with either by transfer, avoidance, assumption, or by the use of a combination of these methods. Transfer, or a pooling of risks, is exemplified in all forms of commercial insurance. Avoidance may take the form of not undertaking a particular project or certain elements of it, or it may consist in a minimization of risks such as occurs in market surveys prior to sales campaigns. Assumption of risk means that, upon the occurrence of the adverse event or the negative circumstance

233

which constitutes the risk, any loss occasioned thereby falls either on the individuals, the business enterprise, or the financial fund that assumed it.

*Risks in Operation of Pension Funds.* The major risks involved in the operation of a pension fund are those relating to withdrawals, salary increases, mortality, disability, investments, and interest earnings. All of these risks may be assumed in the operation of a self-administered pension fund, but some may be avoided as a matter of choice; most of them may be transferred to an insurance company, but several may not. Of these respective risks not all are equally measurable or calculable. There exists a fundamental disagreement among independent and insurance company actuaries, and other students of pension planning, in respect to the way of handling some or all of such risks in the best interests of employer and employees. At one extreme the advocates of insured plans contend that only in an exceptional situation will self-administration be successful, and that all risks incident to the operation of a fund which an insurance company is willing to assume should be transferred to it. The opposite view is that most employers may use a self-administered plan to greater advantage. All risks it is asserted may be assumed safely by the fund, and indirectly, if not directly, by the employer; moreover, the pension fund may be operated at a lesser expense. Some independent actuaries may, in regard to small funds or certain risks such as withdrawals, take a relatively more conservative view than others as to how they should be handled; but in general the above statement broadly summarizes the attitude of proponents of self-administration.

## A. Withdrawals

Insurance companies that underwrite pension plans, either in the form of the typical group annuity or through individual annuity contracts, do not discount for withdrawals from employment prior to retirement.[1] Aside from the increased technical and administrative complexities which a discount for withdrawals under insured plans presents, the position of an insurance company implies that the rates of withdrawals cannot be forecast accurately, and that a discount for them is a risk to be avoided. In other words, if the rates of withdrawal cannot be satisfactorily computed, then proper charges cannot be made, or contributions obtained, which

---

[1] See footnote, page 235.

will adequately take account of withdrawals. The preferable course of action therefore is to ignore the probability of terminations of employment by withdrawals, but to grant the right to an employer to take credits for the premiums paid on behalf of withdrawing employees, to be used to reduce future financial outlays.

The point of view of many independent actuaries is that, while it may be true that completely accurate withdrawal rates cannot be formulated, it is unrealistic to assume that there will be no withdrawals. They contend that if there is no vesting, or if vesting is dependent on 15 to 20 years of service, or similar years of membership in a pension plan, an employer's initial deposits to the pension fund may be reduced by making use of withdrawal rates. Such a reduction may enable an employer more easily to inaugurate a pension plan. They further contend that if the rates are conservative, with no withdrawals assumed after age 55, for example, and with periodical valuations to check the accuracy of withdrawal assumptions, the risk of any impairment of the pension funds caused by withdrawal assumptions is nominal.

At all events, the consequence of the differing attitudes on the wisdom of discounting for withdrawals is that an employer who finds it necessary or wise to reduce his initial deposits to the pension fund through the use of withdrawal rates must perforce select self-administration.[2]

## B. Salary Increases

What has been stated relative to the differing attitudes on withdrawal rates is equally true of the use of salary scales. Under insured plans salary increases are not anticipated, that is, they are not taken account of in initial cost calculations, but are dealt with as they occur. It is contended that over a period of years the normal swings in the business cycle, the demands of organized labor, and wars and inflation may drastically affect wages and

---

[2] An apparent exception to this may be found in a form of group annuity pension plan known as *deposit administration*. Under this form an insurance company will allow an employer to make pension deposits in annual minimum and maximum amounts. When an employee retires, the necessary funds to provide his pension benefits are applied by the insurance company to the purchase of an immediate annuity. For employees who terminate employment prior to normal retirement, unless otherwise provided in the plan, no annuities are purchased. A deposit administration group annuity is available only for large employee groups, e.g. 1,000 in number, and its use is not generally encouraged by the insurance companies. While the deposit administration type of group annuity thus operationally takes account of withdrawals, the process is indirect and is not technically comparable to the methods used for withdrawal discounts under self-administration.

salaries; therefore, long-term assumptions as to wage or salary scales may be invalidated. If estimates as to salary changes cannot be made with any accuracy, as in the case of withdrawals, they constitute a further risk to be avoided. Independent actuaries may and do take the opposite position; while again admitting possible inexactitude, they contend that periodical valuations of the pension funds will minimize any risk that may be involved as a result of actual wages or salaries deviating from the assumptions.

The use of salary scales, it should be noted, in contrast to the use of withdrawal rates, will normally increase an employer's initial deposits somewhat as against their nonuse.

### C. Mortality

Either self-administered types or insured types of pension plans may be based on the same mortality tables. The tendency of insurance companies is to use relatively more conservative tables; in justification there are advanced several major reasons. They cite the historical evidence which shows a constant tendency toward less mortality prior to the usual retirement ages, as well as an increasing longevity among annuitants.

The mortality tables utilized by self-administered funds, it is argued, do not need to be as conservative as insurance company tables; for the latter are devised, or used, in relation both to employee groups covered under pension plans and to individuals who purchase annuities. It is the purchases of this latter group that color or adversely affect insurance company experience with annuities; stated differently, it is the healthier or longer-lived individuals who tend to purchase annuities from insurance companies. Insurance company experience with individual annuity buyers therefore cannot be generalized and applied to employees under pension plans, where the coverage is of a group nature and without individual selection.

A more fundamental cleavage between the proponents of insured plans and those of self-administered plans occurs not so much over which mortality table may be the better in discounting for mortality as in the applicability of the table. The advocates of insured plans contend that a self-administered fund must be exceptionally large in order that the mortality experience among employees may be in accordance with the rates shown by the mortality table employed.   In other words, referring to the coin-tossing illustration used earlier, the law of averages cannot be expected to apply unless the number of employees is large.   In addition, it is argued that the mortality expectations in relation to pensioners are less reliable; for even in the case of relatively large self-administered funds the number of pensioners will be small as compared to the active lives in the work force.   Excessive longevity among certain of the pensioners therefore may embarrass the pension fund, or may lead to a reduction of all retirement benefits.

The advocates of self-administration consider that these difficulties are exaggerated.   First of all they point out that the mortality among employees prior to retirement is a minor factor in terminations of employment, for the latter are largely accounted for by withdrawals.   Thus any unfavorable deviations in mortality experience from the expected, prior to retirement, will be offset largely by withdrawal experience where conservative assumptions are made as to the latter.   In regard to pensioners it is held that the average amounts of annuity income payable to the average pensioners are not large enough to represent a major hazard.   At such times as individual pensioners are to receive annuity incomes considerably above the average, any risk to the pension funds which might be occasioned thereby may be handled by transferring it to insurance companies through the purchase of annuities.

### D.  Disability

Total and permanent disability benefits were available under insured pension plans on a limited basis until approximately the early 1930's; since that time they no longer have been offered. Self-administered plans, as noted elsewhere, may and do provide disability benefits.

Advocates of insured plans contend that the past experience of insurance companies with total and permanent disability benefits was unfortunate and costly; that this experience constitutes evidence that disability benefits cannot be underwritten and offered satisfactorily in connection with pension plans.

The opposing view admits that the insurance companies' experience with total and permanent disability, offered in connection with *personal* insurance or annuity policies, was unsatisfactory, but it does not believe that this experience justifies the conclusion that disability benefits cannot be offered to employees covered by a pension plan.[3]  It is held that the experience with disability was unfortunate because of adverse selection against the company, over-insurance, and the lack of administrative controls; but under self-administration at least, these conditions may be precluded by the terms of the plan and employer control.   Under self-administered pension plans of reasonable size, therefore, the independent actuarial view is that disability benefits may be properly and safely offered if the amounts are limited and are payable only for total and permanent disability after a reasonable period of service, and if the disability benefits are allowed only if certified as such by one or more physicians.

## E.  Investments

The investments of life insurance companies are limited in general to first mortgages and fixed interest-bearing securities of the highest grade, legally authorized as a medium for investment by State laws.   Their portfolios are widely diversified.   Employers' funds under insured pension plans are merged with all other reserves, which insurance companies maintain to meet their obligations to policyholders.   From an investment aspect therefore an employer's premium deposits under pension plans are pooled with the premiums of all other policyholders without segregation. Gains or losses which may occur through investments consequently are spread among the entire body of policyholders.

Self-administered funds, subject to any limitations contained in a trust agreement, may be invested in such securities, fixed-interest-bearing or otherwise, real or personal property, as the trustees

[3] In this connection one prominent insurance company actuary, connected with the design and development of group annuity plans, stated in 1934 that his own company's financial experience with total and permanent disability under its group annuity plans had been on the whole satisfactory. He gave as reasons for its discontinuance that strict insurance requirements in allowing disability claims were not entirely satisfactory to employers. The employers, in other words, may have wished to retire employees on a disability basis, who were no longer efficient, but not always were such employees totally and permanently disabled in a medical sense from the point of view of the insurance company. Finally, he stated that, inasmuch as his company had discontinued issuance of total and permanent disability generally, such issuance was also discontinued under group annuity contracts in the interest of a consistent company policy. Hohaus, R. A., The Record, Vol. 23, American Institute of Actuaries, Nov., 1934.

It might be argued in offset to this statement that as of 1934 group annuity experience had not been of sufficient duration, and the contracts outstanding with disability benefits had not been sufficiently large in number, to provide a basis for any final conclusions. In any case, the comment of the insurance company actuary is significant, if for no other reason than that it tends to disassociate disability experience under pension plans from experience with disability under personal insurance and annuity contracts.

may select. Securities issued by an employer operating a pension fund may be a medium for such investment if desired, subject to disclosure to the Treasury Department. Any gains or losses incurred by a fund will of course fall on the fund itself. The funds of a self-administered pension plan, it is argued by advocates of insured plans, usually will be too small in amount to enable proper diversification for safety, or at least, when invested, they will result in a portfolio of securities that can only in a minor way approach the investment diversity of insurance portfolios. Also, it is contended that this fact plus the discretion afforded to trustees of self-administered funds may lead to a lack of employee confidence in the security of their benefits.

The view of self-administration advocates is that, if a fund is small, security may be obtained by investing it in United States Government bonds. If a fund is large, diversification is possible; in addition, the absence of legal restrictions on investments by which insurance companies are surrounded will redound to the advantage of a self-administered fund. For example, the investment of part of a pension fund in high-grade common stocks may prove advantageous, a privilege generally denied to life insurance companies. Furthermore, a feeling of security by employees may be obtained by restricting the investment of a substantial portion of a pension fund to the type of securities legal for personal trust funds or for life insurance companies.

## F. Interest

There exists less controversy than on other points as to whether self-administered funds or insurance companies will provide a larger interest return. However, it is emphasized by advocates of insured plans that an insurance company guarantees the interest rate, whereas there is no guarantee of the rate by trustees under self-administration, and rarely, if ever, by an employer.

The point of view of self-administration advocates is that the investment market is open mutually to skilled investment managers both of self-administered and insurance company funds; and that a guarantee of 2% or 2½%, as offered by the insurance companies, is of minor significance. Moreover, any excess interest earnings of self-administered funds are fully retained and may be used to reduce an employer's contributions. Under insured plans, while any excess interest earnings over the guaranteed rate might be paid to an employer through dividends or rate credits, nevertheless the declaration or disbursement of such excess earnings is at the discretion of the management of an insurance company.

## II. OTHER CONSIDERATIONS

### A. Rate Guarantees

The preceding discussion at several points, either directly or by implication, stated the conflicting views on the value of insurance company guarantees. But essentially it contrasted the differing attitudes as to the security or ultimate solvency of a pension fund as operated either under an insured or self-administered plan. The proponents of insured plans occasionally make a further point with the statement that under insured plans there is a guarantee of the premium rates by the insurance company, and that there is no substitute for or equivalency of such a guarantee possible in self-administered funds.

The advocates of self-administered pension plans state that the guarantee of premium rates by insurance companies is of limited value for most employers. In relation to group annuities they point out that rates are guaranteed only for five years, and thereafter they may be increased yearly if the insurance company deems it advisable. They further state that in the past decade insurance companies have raised group annuity rates five times, or about 50%, and in the process have recouped any losses which may have been sustained under their original premium rate guarantees. As for individual annuity contracts, the premium rates likewise have been increased substantially; and aside from the value of the premium rate guarantee given for the original employees covered by an individual annuity plan, such rate guarantees are of no more value than those provided under group annuity plans.

In return, the contenders for insured plans admit that annuity rates have been increased substantially in the past decade, largely as a consequence of a decline in the rate of interest,[4] and of im-

---

[4] In relation to the effect of a decline in interest earnings on self-administered pension funds, the following comment jointly made by several English consulting actuaries is pertinent:

"In recent years the grave disadvantages of having to reduce the valuation rate of interest have been very apparent. Funds which were established ten or fifteen years ago under the Local Government and Other Officers Superannuation Act, 1922, on the basis of interest at 4%, the annual charge being fixed accordingly, are now being valued at 3¼% or 3½%, and even after credit has been taken for any excess interest which may be yielded by the existing investments over this rate, the valuations are disclosing substantial deficiencies."

provement in mortality.  A self-administered fund, therefore, established in the early 1930's, would have had to receive substantial increased contributions from the employer in the succeeding decade in order to have remained solvent or properly funded.  The value of a premium rate guarantee cannot be ruled out because there occurred rate increases subsequent to the establishment of an insured plan; for, if a group annuity or individual annuity plan had been *discontinued*, the benefits purchased for employees up to that time would have been guaranteed and could not have been affected by subsequent rate increases.

## B.  Flexibility

An argument sometimes advanced for self-administration is that a self-administered pension plan is more flexible than an insured plan.  While by flexibility reference may be to the fact that any method of funding, or of discounts for withdrawals, or of anticipation of salary increases is possible in self-administration, greater stress frequently is placed on the fact that an employer operating a self-administered plan is not obliged to make fixed annual deposits.  For example, if in a poor year profit-wise an employer wishes to reduce or omit his annual deposits, he may do so under self-administration, and he may increase or restore them in succeeding years.  The implication is that such flexibility is not possible under group annuity or individual annuity plans.

The general answer provided by proponents of insured plans is that this so-called flexibility is double-edged, or has boomerang aspects.  An employer who establishes a pension plan has certain objectives such as reduced labor turnover, increased efficiency, improved morale, and retirement of superannuated employees.  If an employer adopts a pension plan under which contributions may be reduced or omitted easily, it is entirely probable that the privilege will be exercised, and the attainment of the above beneficial objectives consequently may be defeated.  Again, from an industrial relations viewpoint, the very existence of a right to omit or reduce contributions with facility may impair employee confidence in the pension plan.  The rank and file of employees, who are normally dubious about an employer's motives for introducing employee benefit plans, may regard this so-called flexibility simply

---

Brown, C. H. L., and Taylor, J. A. G., "Some Observations on the Rate of Interest as Affecting Pension Funds," *Journal of the Institute of Actuaries*, Vol. LXIX, Part III, No. 326, 1938, pp. 274-286.

as an escape clause, devised for the employer's benefit but not in the employees' interests. If an employer establishes a pension plan, therefore, the assumption should be that he can and will make the necessary contributions to maintain it, as he certainly will maintain his fire, compensation, or other forms of insurance. If a pension plan is necessary in the first instance, its need usually will be continuous; therefore the cost should be considered a fixed charge, and wages or salaries might be better adjusted downward before the pension plan is impaired. If the time should come when the full contributions to maintain the plan cannot be made, then the better policy would be to modify the benefits or terminate the plan.

Finally, it is pointed out that under insured plans there is also the possibility that the "privilege" of suspending or omitting contributions may be obtained. A deposit administration group annuity offers to employers the right to make annual contributions between certain minimums and maximums; and under the typical form of group annuity, suspension of a contract is possible with the right to reinstate. Individual annuity plans also may be obtained if desired, in which a so-called stop-and-go privilege is granted; an employer thereunder may suspend payments up to and including five years. He thereafter may reinstate his plan either by back payments or on a current basis.

## III. EXPENSE

The major expenses connected with the operation of a pension fund whether for a self-administered or an insured plan have been discussed. Those who hold for self-administration, regardless of the merits of insured plans as alleged by their advocates, believe that in general a self-administered fund will prove less expensive to operate. In support of this position the proponents point out that, under a self-administered plan, (1) there are no commissions to be paid by the employer, nor is he subject to any of the insurance company's general overhead; (2) there are no promotional or advertising expenses, such as are incurred by insurance companies in obtaining pension business, which must be shared; (3) the employer knows exactly what accounts for his expenses, and they are subject to his control; and (4) the expense charge, or premium loading, of insurance companies is excessive particularly in relation to a large pension fund.

In return, the proponents of insured plans state that over the probable lifetime of a pension fund commissions constitute a small percentage of total expense charges; also, the service rendered in consideration thereof both to the employer and to his employees under insured plans normally exceeds that offered under self-administered plans. Stated differently, if an insured and a self-administered plan should provide exactly the same benefits, and the service rendered in each case were equivalent, then relatively the service charges under self-administered funds would approximate the commission payments; for the latter in the final analysis are essentially service charges. So far as the general overhead of an insurance company is concerned, the magnitude of its operation, considered either in relation to its underwriting and administration of pension plans or to its operations generally, should prove to be a positive advantage in inducing an employer to insure his plan. General overhead costs constitute an expense which is spread or charged against all funds held by an insurance company for its policyholders.

The employer's share of expense therefore will be thinned or minimized because of this wide base of which his pension funds are a part. In contrast, each self-administered fund is a separate entity standing on its own feet.

The promotional and advertising expenses incurred in obtaining insured pension business, it is argued, are nominal. They may be treated as a part of the general overhead, or possibly they may be allocated as an acquisition cost of pension business; but whatever the basis for allocation of such expenses they cannot be considered as of major importance. Furthermore, it is added, a considerable portion of insured pension business is obtained for the insurance company by agents or brokers operating on a commission basis; thus little or no advertising or promotion expense on the part of the insurance company is involved.

While it is true an employer may know exactly what accounts for his expenses under a self-administered plan, it is held that this knowledge is more theoretical than practical. It is stated, for example, that accounting for expenses under self-administered plans is usually inadequate, inasmuch as proper charges for the time of highly paid executives devoted to investments are not or cannot be made. Again, the costs of record-keeping under self-administered pension plans frequently are inaccurately accounted for or are not allocated to the expense of operating the pension plan. These conditions or facts thus minimize the validity of the statement that expenses are subject to an employer's control. But even the admission that they may be subject to an employer's control, in itself is no evidence that the expenses of operating a self-administered fund will be less than the expenses of an insured plan, where the respective benefits provided and the service rendered are comparable.

Finally, it is pointed out that rarely are a self-administered plan and an insured plan truly comparable in their general terms, method of funding, or in equivalency of the benefit; thus expense comparisons are meaningless. But assuming self-administered and insured plans were comparable in all the above and other respects, it is contended (1) that the initial expense charge as contained in the premium is intentionally conservative, and does not necessarily reflect an employer's ultimate expense; for under insured plans where the actual expense proves to be less than was anticipated the employer may receive a refund of loading charges either through dividend payments or by rate credits; (2) that a comparison of the initial expense charges as made by an insurance company with the initial costs of a self-administered plan would usually favor the latter, where normally there is shown only the cost of benefits with no advance allowance (loading) for expense; and (3) that the expense charge under an insured plan at least is known in advance, a definite amount, whereas in the case of a self-administered plan (except for initial expense) the best information on expenses that may be obtained is an estimate.

## IV. TYPES OF BENEFIT

The discussion thus far has been limited to setting forth the respective attitudes of the proponents of self-administered plans and the advocates of insured plans. It may be noted that the controversial aspects have related mainly to the risk factors and the relative expense of operation, rather than to the types of benefit which are offered by each vehicle. In general both types may offer comparable types of benefits to employees,[5] with the exception of disability benefits.[6]

As between group annuity and individual annuity pension plans there also exists a division of opinion as to which an employer would prefer to adopt. This division of opinion narrows basically to a consideration of (1) the types of benefits which each plan offers, (2)

---

[5] An individual annuity plan normally would provide a larger insurance benefit than a self-administered fund, where the risk of providing an insurance benefit is assumed by the latter.

[6] See later discussion on this point, page 251.

the respective availability of each plan to an employer, and (3) the cost comparisons.

As to the relative benefits, it will be recalled that an individual annuity plan usually offers a retirement benefit on a ten year certain basis, provides for a death benefit, and offers withdrawal values on various bases; a typical (non-contributory) group annuity plan offers a withdrawal value as a paid-up deferred life annuity and a retirement benefit in the form of a straight life annuity.

In regard to availability, the individual and group annuity plans are not readily comparable, for the choice will depend somewhat on an employer's size and/or the composition of his personnel.[7]

The relative costs of group annuity and individual annuity plans cannot be compared apart from the types of benefits offered by the respective plans. If we assume that either plan is equally available to an employer, the adoption of an individual annuity plan by its very nature will provide greater employee benefits than a typical group annuity. The former likewise will carry higher costs, principally because the benefits provided are larger.[8] It is clear that under a pension plan which offers a death benefit, for example, the contribution or premium rate must include some charge for the benefit. While the actual cost to the employer of providing a death benefit through the use of an individual annuity plan may be modified relatively by competition between companies which underwrite only individual annuity plans, a group annuity plan which carries no death benefit usually will provide a somewhat lesser cost.

A cost comparison between an individual annuity and a group annuity plan could be made fruitfully therefore only with a proper allowance for differences in benefits. As a practical matter such a comparison is difficult, if not impossible. Comparisons sometimes made in advocacy of either plan, which revolve about such matters as relative expense charges, commissions, surrender penalties, dividends, and so forth, may be largely ignored. Such comparisons usually are futile because of the major differences in benefits provided by the two plans. Technically they are not comparable, e.g. in the methods of funding, and in the respective methods and rules for underwriting; also the types of service required under each plan, as well as the method of rendering it, will differ. It is the employer's

---

[7] See pp. 247-249.

[8] The cost differential, it should be pointed out, is not measurable by the differences in *initial* cost. This is accounted for mainly by reason of a group annuity using single premiums to fund the plan, and the individual annuity employing level premiums.

circumstances, as discussed below, which should be the determining factor in the choice of a group annuity or an individual annuity plan; likewise his decision as to whether to self-administer or to insure the plan.

## V.  EMPLOYER'S CIRCUMSTANCES

It is essential, or at least desirable, that an employer understand the fundamental and technical differences between the various types of pension plans described in this work prior to selecting a plan; but it is not possible to generalize therefrom *the* plan that will be universally applicable or desirable for all employers or all employee groups. Such considerations as risk factors, types of benefit, expense charges, methods of funding, ability to discount for withdrawals, flexibility, and so forth, must be evaluated in relation to an employer's circumstances. The principal circumstances are the size of his personnel, its composition, and the employer's financial strength or resources.

### A.  Size of Personnel

*Small.* A small personnel, for pension purposes, is one that consists of 100 employees or less. In this area an employer is limited largely to an individual annuity plan; this plan may be established if there is only one employee. As has been pointed out, in order that an employer may obtain a group annuity plan, underwritten by any of the major life insurance companies issuing group annuity contracts, he must have at least 50 eligible employees.[9] If the terms of a pension plan provide eligibility rules requiring a minimum age of 30 and five years of service, it is probable that there will be less than 50 eligible employees; thus a group annuity plan normally will be unavailable to an employer with 100 employees. Self-administration, even if the entire 100 employees were participants in the plan, must be excluded; only in an exceptional situation would an employer with a personnel of 100 or less be warranted in assuming the risks and expense of self-administration.[10]

*Intermediate.* A personnel of intermediate size may be described as one which ranges from over 100 employees up to 2,000. In this area controversy over the more preferable type of plan commences, being manifested principally by competition between banks, which

---

[9] In several states banking institutions with a small personnel have been able to utilize a group annuity plan through association with other banks.

[10] See pp. 249-250.

are equipped to manage pension funds as trustees under a self-administered plan, and insurance companies.

As to the probable size of a personnel which would warrant the use or consideration of a self-administered plan, several opinions of detached observers may be mentioned. Murray Latimer stated: "For most establishments with not more than a few thousand employees, reinsurance will quite likely prove advisable unless the maximum pension is considerably limited."[11] In a pension study of the National Industrial Conference Board this observation was made: "It would seem, therefore, that when the number of employees is less than 10,000 serious consideration should be given to the advisability of placing the risk with an insurance company."[12]

It should be noted that, while the size of the total personnel is a central consideration, in addition the terms of the pension plan will influence the number of employees who will be eligible. For example, if all employees were otherwise eligible to the plan, because of age and/or service requirements, probably no more than 40 to 60% of the active personnel would be participants at any given time. Consequently for a personnel in the lower range of the intermediate size of from 100 to 2,000 an insured plan would be indicated, with the choice being between an individual annuity and a group annuity plan. In the upper range, even where the eligibility rules would leave perhaps 1,000 eligible employees, this number likewise seems too small to provide a wide enough base for self-administration. This opinion is tentative, for it must be recognized that experience in the United States with properly managed self-administered funds is of short duration. In any case, where the eligible group to be covered by self-administration is 1,000, or possibly double this number, withdrawal discounts should be conservative. Also provision should be made for terminal reinsurance of the pension benefits, unless under the terms of the plan a low maximum pension is provided.

*Large.* A large personnel, based on the preceding division, extends from 2,000 upward. At the lower range the remarks which were made above with reference to an intermediate sized personnel are equally applicable. However, a personnel numbering 5,000 or more employees is perhaps sufficiently large (unless an all-salaried, or a $3,000 or over, pension plan is contemplated) to warrant a consideration of self-administration from a risk aspect. At this point

---

[11] Latimer, Murray, "Industrial Pension Systems," Industrial Relations Counselors, New York, N. Y., 1932, p. 465.

[12] "Elements of Industrial Pension Plans," National Industrial Conference Board, Inc., New York, N. Y., 1931, p. 34.

the number of eligible employees may provide a base broad enough to justify the assumption that the experience of the fund will be more or less in accordance with the expectations; or at least that the deviations may be satisfactorily corrected at the periodical valuations. Financially, the size of the pension fund should enable proper diversification. Therefore, if we assume that the risks of self-administration in the case of large pension funds have been minimized, the remaining controversy between the advocates of self-administered plans and those of insured plans will be over the expense of administration.

The opposing views on the expense of self-administered and insured plans have been stated, but there exists little published substantive evidence on the expense of operating a self-administered pension plan which may be measured against the expense charges of a comparable insured plan such as the group annuity.[13] Reference is made to the latter because, as between insured or self-administered plans, the controversy centers largely in the use of self-administration or of group annuity; but, in addition, a self-administered plan rarely will be found which is designed to provide types of benefits comparable to those offered under individual annuity plans. As to group annuity contracts, in the past the entire loading or expense charge contained in the premiums has been retained for the most part by the insurance companies. Dividends, through which refunds of expense charges (loading) generally would be made, have been largely nonexistent. This absence of dividends may be explained principally by a decline in interest rates, necessitating the use by the insurance companies of the entire loading charges to offset the resulting losses; or otherwise stated, as a consequence of experience disclosing the original net premium rates (before inclusion of loading charges) were inadequate in the first instance. It does not follow, however, that, because insurance companies in the past have retained the full loading or expense charge on most group annuity contracts, this will be true in the future. If no dividends should be returnable to an employer in the future, and if developments should indicate that the net pre-

---

[13] The following statement from an article written by an officer of a large American corporation having approximately 40,000 employees is of interest:

"It is a debatable question whether the cost of administering a self-insured plan is less than the overhead charged by insurance companies. The overhead expenses of some self-insured plans in England of which we have record are higher than the overhead charged by insurance companies."

Folsom, M. B., "Old Age on the Balance Sheet," *Atlantic Monthly*, Sept., 1929.

miums collected are adequate to cover the cost of the pension benefits, it probably then would be proper to treat the loading charges as representing the true expense of operating a pension fund on a group annuity basis.

Returning to the expense of operating a self-administered fund, until published authoritative experience thereunder is available and until further experience with insured plans develops, particularly with the group annuity, uncertainty as to the relative expense of operation of self-administered and insured plans will prevail. It would seem, however, in the case of the larger pension plans where the personnel approximates roughly 20,000 or more, that a self-administered plan open to all employees should prove at least as economical to operate as an insured plan; and where the personnel approximates 50,000 or more that self-administration should prove to be cheaper.

## B. Composition of Personnel

The composition of an employer's personnel may be a factor in the choice of a plan principally in relation to whether a group annuity or an individual annuity plan is indicated; that is, if we assume that self-administration is to be ruled out, then the remaining choice may be between the insured plans.

Where an employer's personnel consists largely of unskilled or semi-skilled help a group annuity may be the preferable plan. It is among the industrial grade or lower paid employees that turnover normally is higher; consequently, where a plan is to cover all employees (unless a long service period and a high minimum age are made eligibility tests), a group annuity with its lesser surrender charges in the early years may prove more satisfactory. The individual annuity plan is better adapted to stable groups of employees, e.g. white-collar and salaried employees, such as are represented by the staffs of banks, colleges, trade associations, and the clerical, supervisory, and executive groups of business and industry.

## C. Financial Strength

The financial strength or resources of an employer may be a factor in the choice of a plan. We stated above that only in exceptional circumstances should self-administration be considered by employers with a small personnel. One exception might be an employer who, because of relatively large resources or wealth, might be willing to guarantee the pension benefits provided under his plan. A further exception might be an employer with an intermediate sized personnel who would not guarantee the pension benefits as such, but who, having had a long history of stable earnings and large profit margins, could reasonably be expected to appropriate for any deficiencies which might develop in his self-administered fund.

The financial strength of an employer might be a further consideration where his choice lay between a group annuity and an individual annuity plan. If an employer can afford only a retirement benefit—death benefits therefore to be excluded—a group annuity plan is indicated, for the typical group annuity by its terms provides no death benefits.

## VI. USE OF COMBINATION PLANS

In Chapter VIII [14] it was pointed out that self-administration might be used in combination with an insured plan. It will be apparent that insured plans may be used also in combination, to the exclusion of self-administration. In actual pension practice, however, combination plans on any basis have been used only to a minor extent, as shown at least by the survey presented in the final chapter. Numerous reasons probably can be offered in explanation of this fact, such as the unfamiliarity of employers with the possible use of combination plans, the technical complications presented in using more than one type of plan, or administrative difficulties. It is the last reason which normally will preclude the use of a combination plan by most employers, for administratively a combination plan is not feasible for an employer with a small personnel.

Nevertheless, among employers who have an intermediate or large-sized personnel, their choice of plan might be facilitated through the use of a combination plan. Circumstances will determine the wisdom of this procedure, and whether an employer should use a combination of insured plans, or a combination of self-administration and an insured plan. But the latter combination may provide a more satisfactory solution or choice than the "either or" approach of to insure or to self-administer. An employer, making use of a combination of an insured and a self-administered plan, would not only extricate himself from the impasse sometimes created by the claims and counter-claims for either scheme, but, more important, he would diversify. Thus in time experience of both plans within his own organization would be obtained. Based

---

[14] See p. 191.

on this experience he later might shift more reasonably to a self-administered or to an insured basis, or, of course, he might maintain the original combination plan.

A further possible advantage to an employer utilizing both a self-administered and an insured plan would be in relation to the provision for disability benefits. A group annuity contract makes no provision for disability, and an individual annuity plan does so only indirectly. A separate self-administered fund for disability benefits, where the pension benefits are provided through an insured plan, is probably impractical. The separate fund to provide disability benefits normally would be too small to self-administer. Disability benefits for all employees, however, could be provided satisfactorily if a combination self-administered and insured plan were utilized. The self-administered plan would be used to provide disability benefits not only for employees covered thereunder but, also, for those employees included under the insured plan.

# CHAPTER XII

# Pension Survey

·············································································

THE MAJOR PORTION OF THIS WORK HAS BEEN DIRECTED PRImarily to an examination and a description of the means and methods that an employer may utilize to provide pension benefits for his employees on an actuarially sound or funded basis; and secondly to a consideration of collateral or supplementary benefits which, while technically they are appendages or adjuncts to a pension plan, frequently are involved, namely, death, withdrawal, and disability benefits.

We turn now to an examination of what a substantial number of employers has done in the way of pension planning; that is, to an analysis and survey of a fairly large number of plans actually in operation, established by large, small, and medium-sized companies in various fields of business and industry.

The number of plans reported upon in this survey totals 612. These plans were obtained as a result of inquiries directed to several thousands of corporations of various size, with headquarters widely distributed over the United States.

It is not suggested, however, that from a statistical viewpoint this number represents more than a fairly large sample of industrial pension plans in operation. This qualification is made for several reasons; principally because the majority of the requests were sent to the larger enterprises in different industries, and also, to a minor extent, to corporations who were known to have a particular type of pension plan in operation. It nevertheless is believed that the 612 plans include sufficient numbers of the several funded types of pension plans employed by business and industry to indicate the typical characteristics of each type, and, as between types, to show their respective similarities and differences.

As to type, the 612 plans include 313 group annuity, 152 individual annuity, 121 self-administered, and 26 combination and other plans.[1]  In the latter category are 17 plans, which are a combination either of a self-administered and an insured plan, or of the several types of insured plans; the remaining 9, *other* plans, consist of 5 group permanent retirement income and 4 modified self-administered plans.[2]

All the plans included in the survey are of the funded type (pay-as-you-go[3] plans having been excluded).  The terms of these plans have been communicated to the employees, usually in booklet form or the equivalent, and are in effect and operation.  Approximately 90% of the 612 plans received the approval of the Treasury Department.  As to the remainder, based on an analysis of their formal terms, it was concluded that approval would be obtained.[4]

The analysis or survey of the 612 plans which follows largely con-

---

[1] It should not be inferred that this distribution is indicative of the actual distribution, as to type, of plans now in existence in the United States.  Of the probable 7,500 funded industrial pension plans in the country the distribution would appear to be about as follows: individual annuity plans, 4,800; group annuity, 2,000; self-administered, 700.  The estimated number of self-administered plans may include possibly 200 combination and other plans.  Authoritative evidence as to the actual division of pension plans by type must await Treasury Department publication of such figures.  The estimate of 2,000 group annuity plans is reasonably accurate, for the number of group annuity contracts underwritten by the major insurance companies that account for the bulk of such business is available from State insurance reports.  Individual annuity plans are not similarly reported; but confirmation of the estimate is suggested from a check made by the writer.  Six of the larger insurance companies, engaged in the issue of individual annuity contracts for pension plans, were found to have participated in approximately 2,800.  Inasmuch as there are possibly 75 other companies also issuing individual annuity contracts for use under pension plans, to credit each with participating, on the average, in 25 individual annuity plans seems reasonable.  The estimate of the number of self-administered plans is less supportable, but is in accord with other opinion.

[2] See pp. 188–189.

[3] By a *pay-as-you-go* plan is meant one in which no reserves are accumulated, and pension payments are made from operating income or surplus.  As noted in Chapter II, all informal plans operate on a pay-as-you-go basis; also many of the earlier formal company-administered plans operated likewise.  Evidence that the method of pay-as-you-go is still employed by many corporations was uncovered in the survey, but, almost without exception, such corporations made use of an informal pension plan.  An exception was a very large corporation (a utility), which distributes to its employees a booklet describing its pension plan in complete detail, with formal rules and regulations clearly and definitively set forth.  It is stated in the booklet, however, that no accumulation of reserves, or funding, to provide pension benefits is contemplated; and that pension benefits will be payable from operating income.

[4] It should be noted that Treasury Department approval is only for a period of one year, and does not constitute *permanent* approval.  If, however, there are no substantive changes in the plan or in the employee coverage from year to year, or in the Federal law or Treasury Department regulations, as a practical matter, initial approval may be considered permanent.  It nevertheless behooves an employer to make certain that from year to year his plan meets Treasury Department requirements, if an income tax deduction for his contributions to the plan is to be obtained.

stitutes a report on their basic provisions,[5] as contained in the booklets or other materials describing the respective plans. Certain other information presented, however, was obtained either by requesting it of the employer or from collateral sources known to be reliable.

The detailed findings were tabulated, and for convenient reference they are reproduced in table form in this chapter. In the interests of the general reader the discussion has been compressed, and is confined mainly to a consideration of the central tendencies revealed in the tables; i.e., having reference only to the most typically encountered basic provision, either as found in the plans considered in their entirety, or as may be typical of the several major types—group annuity, individual annuity, or self-administered plans.

## I.  GENERAL ANALYSIS OF PLANS

### A.  Business and Industrial Classifications

The complete table showing the types of business or industry represented in this study appears on page 255. The classifications have been expanded, in the interests of detailed information, beyond the more generalized breakdown of manufacturing and non-manufacturing corporations. It may be noted, however, that approximately 60% of the plans are to be found among manufacturing industries. For several reasons this percentage is probably too low in relation to what the actual distribution of plans, as between manufacturing and non-manufacturing enterprises, will prove to be. First, the large majority of all industrial pension plans in existence were adopted during World War II. In this period manufacturers probably were more favorably situated profit-wise to initiate and establish plans than almost any other group of enterprises in business or industry. More important, the present survey has been weighted or influenced by the fact that plans were requested, and a considerable number received, from the 400 largest commercial banks in the country; and that a few plans established by some of the smaller banks also are included.

The number of banks represented in the survey, consequently, is relatively large. Under the classification of banks, insurance companies, investment houses, totaling 107 in the table, 92 are banks. Thus, while bank plans are included with all the other plans for

---

[5] See Chapter IX, "Basic Provisions of Pension Plans."

## TABLE A

### Industrial Classification

| Type of Industry | Total Companies — Companies | Total Companies — Per Cent | Group Annuity — Companies | Group Annuity — Per Cent | Individual Annuity — Companies | Individual Annuity — Per Cent | Self-Administered — Companies | Self-Administered — Per Cent | Combination and Others — Companies | Combination and Others — Per Cent |
|---|---|---|---|---|---|---|---|---|---|---|
| Advertising agencies | 2 | 0.3 | — | — | 2 | 1.3 | — | — | — | — |
| Aircraft, parts, accessories, and equipment | 10 | 1.6 | 5 | 1.6 | 2 | 1.3 | 3 | 2.5 | — | — |
| Amusements | 3 | 0.5 | 1 | 0.3 | — | — | 2 | 1.7 | — | — |
| Automotive vehicles, parts, accessories, and equipment | 21 | 3.4 | 8 | 2.6 | 8 | 5.3 | 5 | 4.1 | 1 | 3.8 |
| Banks, insurance companies, investment houses | 107 | 17.5 | 59 | 18.8 | 22 | 14.5 | 25 | 20.7 | 1 | 3.8 |
| Building materials | 22 | 3.6 | 15 | 4.8 | 3 | 2.0 | 3 | 2.5 | 1 | 3.8 |
| Chemicals, drugs, toilet articles | 41 | 6.7 | 23 | 7.3 | 5 | 3.3 | 10 | 8.3 | 3 | 11.5 |
| Coal; mining and distribution | 3 | 0.5 | 3 | 1.0 | — | — | — | — | — | — |
| Electrical equipment, appliances, and supplies | 27 | 4.4 | 11 | 3.5 | 10 | 6.6 | 3 | 2.5 | 3 | 11.5 |
| Food, beverage, dairy, tobacco products | 50 | 8.2 | 23 | 7.3 | 15 | 9.9 | 12 | 9.9 | 1 | 3.8 |
| Glass products | 4 | 0.7 | 1 | 0.3 | 1 | 0.7 | 2 | 1.7 | — | — |
| Instruments and scientific equipment | 7 | 1.1 | 4 | 1.3 | 1 | 0.7 | 2 | 1.7 | — | — |
| Leather products | 2 | 0.3 | 1 | 0.3 | 1 | 0.7 | — | — | — | — |
| Machinery; accessories and parts | 63 | 10.3 | 27 | 8.6 | 27 | 17.8 | 9 | 7.4 | 2 | 7.7 |
| Metal and metal products (extraction and manufacture) | 51 | 8.3 | 30 | 9.6 | 15 | 9.9 | 4 | 3.3 | 2 | 7.7 |
| Paper and paper products | 12 | 2.0 | 7 | 2.2 | 3 | 2.0 | 2 | 1.7 | — | — |
| Petroleum and petroleum products | 28 | 4.6 | 20 | 6.4 | 1 | 0.7 | 4 | 3.3 | 3 | 11.5 |
| Public utilities | 57 | 9.3 | 39 | 12.5 | — | — | 18 | 14.9 | — | — |
| Publishing and printing | 17 | 2.8 | 8 | 2.6 | 8 | 5.3 | 1 | 0.8 | — | — |
| Rubber and rubber products | 8 | 1.3 | 2 | 0.6 | 3 | 2.0 | 1 | 0.8 | 2 | 7.7 |
| Services | 5 | 0.8 | — | — | 5 | 3.3 | — | — | — | — |
| Shipbuilding | 5 | 0.8 | 2 | 0.6 | — | — | 2 | 1.7 | 1 | 3.8 |
| Trade (wholesale and retail) | 27 | 4.4 | 6 | 1.9 | 7 | 4.6 | 10 | 8.3 | 4 | 15.4 |
| Transportation (railroads excluded) | 8 | 1.3 | 6 | 1.9 | — | — | 1 | 0.8 | 1 | 3.8 |
| Textiles and clothing | 15 | 2.5 | 5 | 1.6 | 7 | 4.6 | — | — | 3 | 11.5 |
| Wood, lumber, and wood products | 5 | 0.8 | 1 | 0.3 | 3 | 2.0 | 1 | 0.8 | — | — |
| Miscellaneous | 12 | 2.0 | 6 | 1.9 | 4 | 2.6 | 1 | 0.8 | 1 | 3.8 |
| TOTALS | 612 | 100.0 | 313 | 100.0 | 152 | 100.0 | 121 | 100.0 | 26 | 100.0 |

general analysis purposes, in addition, a separate tabulation for banks, relative to certain items of information, is given.[6]

## B.  Date of Establishment

Table B shows the date of establishment of all except 9 of the plans.  Approximately 81% of the plans were established during the years 1940-45.  The relatively smaller number of plans established in 1945, in contrast to the preceding year, should not be construed as reflecting the actual experience for 1945; for this survey was initiated in the middle of 1945 while most pension plans are established at the close of the calendar (fiscal) year.  It is true, however, that, with the end of World War II in 1945 and with the subsequent reconversion problems and general economic uncertainty, there was a decline in the number of new plans established.  But, in the light of the rate at which plans had been created in the four prior years, a relative decline probably was to be expected in any event.

It is interesting to observe that, in comparison with the 81% figure given above, during 1940-45, 143, or 94.1%, of the individual annuity plans were established, as compared with 83.5 and 72.5, respectively, for self-administered and group annuity plans.  The oldest group annuity plans, uncovered in the study, were established in 1924; the oldest individual annuity plan, in 1935.  The earlier origin of self-administered plans is evident.  The analysis revealed, however, that the older self-administered plans were company-administered, until amended and revised in recent years.

## C.  Number of Employees

In examining Table C, which groups the plans in relation to the size of personnel or the number of employees, it will be observed that approximately 43% of the plans surveyed were established by corporations either with 1,000 to 4,999 employees (191 plans) or with 5,000 to 9,999 employees (71 plans).  It should be explained, however, that in relation to the probable total of industrial pension plans (7,500), no significance can be attached to this percentage for several reasons.  In this survey a very high proportion of the requests for plans were addressed to corporations national in their operations, and with a relatively large personnel.  It also is well known that the greater proportion of individual annuity plans are to be found among employers with 100 to 200 employees.

---

[6] See pp. 324-325.

## TABLE B

### Date of Establishment
### All Plans

| Year Established | Total Companies | | Group Annuity | | Individual Annuity | | Self-Administered | | Combination and Others | |
|---|---|---|---|---|---|---|---|---|---|---|
| | Companies | Per Cent | Companies | Per Cent | Companies | Per Cent | Companies | Per Cent | Companies | Per Cent |
| 1945[a] | 47 | 7.7 | 18 | 5.8 | 16 | 10.5 | 11 | 9.1 | 2 | 7.7 |
| 1944 | 154 | 25.2 | 57 | 18.2 | 46 | 30.3 | 41 | 33.9 | 10 | 38.5 |
| 1943 | 110 | 18.0 | 40 | 12.8 | 44 | 28.9 | 22 | 18.2 | 4 | 15.4 |
| 1942 | 57 | 9.3 | 24 | 7.7 | 24 | 15.8 | 8 | 6.6 | 1 | 3.8 |
| 1941 | 89 | 14.5 | 68 | 21.7 | 11 | 7.2 | 7 | 5.8 | 3 | 11.5 |
| 1940 | 36 | 5.9 | 20 | 6.4 | 2 | 1.3 | 12 | 9.9 | 2 | 7.7 |
| 1939 | 13 | 2.1 | 9 | 2.9 | 1 | 0.7 | 1 | 0.8 | 2 | 7.7 |
| 1938 | 23 | 3.8 | 19 | 6.1 | 2 | 1.3 | 2 | 1.7 | — | — |
| 1937 | 10 | 1.6 | 10 | 3.2 | — | — | — | — | — | — |
| 1936 | 8 | 1.3 | 8 | 2.6 | — | — | — | — | — | — |
| 1935 | 9 | 1.5 | 7 | 2.2 | 1 | 0.7 | 1 | 0.8 | 1 | 3.8 |
| 1934 | 10 | 1.6 | 8 | 2.6 | — | — | 1 | 0.8 | — | — |
| 1933 | 11 | 1.8 | 11 | 3.5 | — | — | — | — | 1 | 3.8 |
| 1932 | 5 | 0.8 | 4 | 1.3 | — | — | 1 | 0.8 | — | — |
| 1931 | 3 | 0.5 | 2 | 0.6 | — | — | — | — | — | — |
| 1929 | 2 | 0.3 | 2 | 0.6 | — | — | — | — | — | — |
| 1928 | 1 | 0.2 | — | — | — | — | 1 | 0.8 | — | — |
| 1927 | 2 | 0.3 | — | — | — | — | 2 | 1.7 | — | — |
| 1925 | 2 | 0.3 | 2 | 0.6 | — | — | 2 | 1.7 | — | — |
| 1924 | 3 | 0.5 | — | — | — | — | 1 | 0.8 | — | — |
| 1923 | 1 | 0.2 | — | — | — | — | 1 | 0.8 | — | — |
| 1922 | 1 | 0.2 | — | — | — | — | 1 | 0.8 | — | — |
| 1914 | 1 | 0.3 | — | — | — | — | 1 | 0.8 | — | — |
| 1913 | 2 | 0.2 | — | — | — | — | 2 | 1.7 | — | — |
| 1912 | 1 | 0.2 | — | — | — | — | 1 | 0.8 | — | — |
| 1904 | 1 | 0.2 | — | — | — | — | 1 | 0.8 | — | — |
| Others | 1 | — | — | — | — | — | 1 | 0.8 | — | — |
| Information not obtained | 9 | 1.5 | 4 | 1.3 | 5 | 3.3 | — | — | — | — |
| Totals | 612 | 100.0 | 313 | 100.0 | 152 | 100.0 | 121 | 100.0 | 26 | 100.0 |

[a] Includes first half of 1945 only.

## TABLE C
### Number of Persons Employed

| Number of Employees | Total Companies | | Group Annuity | | Individual Annuity | | Self-Administered | | Combination and Others | |
|---|---|---|---|---|---|---|---|---|---|---|
| | Companies | Per Cent | Companies | Per Cent | Companies | Per Cent | Companies | Per Cent | Companies | Per Cent |
| Under 100 | 39 | 6.4 | 5 | 1.6 | 32 | 21.1 | 2 | 1.7 | — | — |
| 100 to 249 | 55 | 9.0 | 27 | 8.6 | 15 | 9.9 | 11 | 9.1 | 2 | 7.7 |
| 250 to 499 | 43 | 7.0 | 28 | 8.9 | 10 | 6.6 | 4 | 3.3 | 1 | 3.8 |
| 500 to 999 | 55 | 9.0 | 28 | 8.9 | 13 | 8.6 | 12 | 9.9 | 2 | 7.7 |
| 1,000 to 4,999 | 191 | 31.2 | 116 | 37.1 | 32 | 21.1 | 36 | 29.8 | 7 | 26.9 |
| 5,000 to 9,999 | 71 | 11.6 | 45 | 14.4 | 7 | 4.6 | 17 | 14.0 | 2 | 7.7 |
| 10,000 to 14,999 | 33 | 5.4 | 13 | 4.2 | 3 | 2.0 | 15 | 12.4 | 2 | 7.7 |
| 15,000 to 19,999 | 14 | 2.3 | 5 | 1.6 | 1 | 0.7 | 5 | 4.1 | 3 | 11.5 |
| 20,000 to 24,999 | 14 | 2.3 | 9 | 2.9 | 2 | 1.3 | 3 | 2.5 | — | — |
| 25,000 to 49,999 | 13 | 2.1 | 5 | 1.6 | 2 | 1.3 | 4 | 3.3 | 2 | 7.7 |
| 50,000 and over | 22 | 3.6 | 7 | 2.2 | 3 | 2.0 | 11 | 9.1 | 1 | 3.8 |
| Information not obtained | 62 | 10.1 | 25 | 8.0 | 32 | 21.1 | 1 | 0.8 | 4 | 15.4 |
| Totals | 612 | 100.0 | 313 | 100.0 | 152 | 100.0 | 121 | 100.0 | 26 | 100.0 |

Confirmation of the greater use of individual annuity plans among the smaller employers, despite the weighting of the survey, is evident. For example, it will be observed that, of the 39 corporations employing under 100 people, 32, or 82%, utilize individual annuity plans.

Again, whereas 21% of all individual annuity plans are found among employers with a personnel of 100 or under, less than 2% of group annuity and self-administered plans, respectively, are among employers of such size. Also, where the larger concentrations of plans appear, that is, among the employee groups ranging in size from 1,000 to 9,999, the 262 plans include 52% of the group annuity, 44% of the self-administered, but less than 26% of the individual annuity plans. It is noticeable that combination plans are utilized almost exclusively by the larger employers. This latter fact is natural and to be expected, for it is only the larger employers that normally find a combination of self-administered and/or insured plans administratively feasible.

In the case of the very large employers, with 50,000 employees and over, self-administered plans outnumber either type of insured plan. This classification contains 22 plans, of which 11, or 50%, are self-administered; 32% are group annuity plans, and 14%, individual annuity plans.

## D. Eligibility Rules for Membership

### 1. Eligible Employee Groups

The analysis that shows the employee groups who may qualify for membership appears in Table D. The plans have been grouped, first, according to whether they are open only to *salaried* employees or to *all* employees; and, secondly, according to whether, within these categories, an earnings test is a further criterion of eligibility.

Of the 612 plans in the survey, 475, or approximately 78%, are open to all employees; 136, or 22%, are limited to salaried employees. Of the 475 plans 413, or 87%, are open to all employees without reference to the amount of earnings; of the 136 plans limited to salaried employees 79, or 58%, are similarly unrestricted.

The most common earnings test imposed for eligibility is $3,000. 77 plans, or about 13% of the 612, use $3,000, with a more frequent use of this earnings test found among the salaried plans. Of the 136 plans open to salaried employees 30% are limited to employees

## TABLE D
### Eligible Employee Groups

| Eligibility Requirements | Total Companies | | Group Annuity | | Individual Annuity | | Self-Administered | | Combination and Others | |
|---|---|---|---|---|---|---|---|---|---|---|
| | Companies | Per Cent | Companies | Per Cent | Companies | Per Cent | Companies | Per Cent | Companies | Per Cent |
| Limited to Salaried Employees.... | 136 | 22.2 | 45 | 14.4 | 72 | 47.4 | 15 | 12.4 | 4 | 15.4 |
| All Salaried Employees......... | 79 | 12.9 | 24 | 7.7 | 43 | 28.3 | 12 | 9.9 | — | — |
| All Salaried Employees Earning a Minimum of.. | 57 | 9.3 | 21 | 6.7 | 29 | 19.1 | 3 | 2.5 | 4 | 15.4 |
| $600................ | 1 | 0.2 | 1 | 0.3 | — | — | | | | |
| $1,000.............. | 1 | 0.2 | — | — | 1 | 0.7 | | | | |
| $1,380.............. | 1 | 0.2 | — | — | 1 | 0.7 | | | | |
| $1,400.............. | 1 | 0.2 | 1 | 0.3 | 1 | 0.7 | | | | |
| $1,800.............. | 4 | 0.7 | 1 | 0.3 | 3 | 2.0 | | | | |
| $2,000.............. | 2 | 0.3 | — | — | 2 | 1.3 | | | | |
| $2,400.............. | 3 | 0.5 | — | — | 3 | 2.0 | | | | |
| $2,700.............. | 1 | 0.2 | 1 | 0.3 | — | — | | | | |
| $2,800.............. | 1 | 0.2 | — | — | 1 | 0.7 | | | | |
| $3,000.............. | 41 | 6.7 | 17 | 5.4 | 17 | 11.2 | 3 | 2.5 | 4 | 15.4 |
| Varies as to sex... | 1 | 0.2 | 1 | 0.3 | — | — | | | | |

## TABLE D (Cont.)

### Eligible Employee Groups

| ELIGIBILITY REQUIREMENTS | TOTAL COMPANIES | | GROUP ANNUITY | | INDIVIDUAL ANNUITY | | SELF-ADMINISTERED | | COMBINATION AND OTHERS | |
|---|---|---|---|---|---|---|---|---|---|---|
| | Companies | Per Cent | Companies | Per Cent | Companies | Per Cent | Companies | Per Cent | Companies | Per Cent |
| NOT LIMITED TO SALARIED EMPLOYEES | 475 | 77.6 | 268 | 85.6 | 80 | 52.6 | 105 | 86.8 | 22 | 84.6 |
| All Employees | 413 | 67.5 | 234 | 74.8 | 65 | 42.8 | 93 | 76.9 | 21 | 80.8 |
| All Employees Earning a Minimum of | 58 | 9.5 | 33 | 10.5 | 14 | 9.2 | 10 | 8.3 | 1 | 3.8 |
| $600 | 4 | 0.7 | 4 | 1.3 | — | — | — | — | — | — |
| $900 | 1 | 0.2 | 1 | 0.3 | — | — | — | — | — | — |
| $1,000 | 2 | 0.3 | 2 | 0.6 | — | — | — | — | — | — |
| $1,040 | 1 | 0.2 | 1 | 0.3 | — | — | — | — | — | — |
| $1,200 | 5 | 0.8 | 1 | 0.3 | 2 | 1.3 | 1 | 0.8 | 1 | 3.8 |
| $1,500 | 2 | 0.3 | 2 | 0.6 | — | — | — | — | — | — |
| $1,800 | 2 | 0.3 | — | — | 1 | 0.7 | 1 | 0.8 | — | — |
| $2,000 | 1 | 0.2 | 1 | 0.3 | — | — | — | — | — | — |
| $2,400 | 1 | 0.2 | — | — | 1 | 0.7 | — | — | — | — |
| $2,500 | 1 | 0.2 | — | — | 1 | 0.7 | — | — | — | — |
| $3,000 | 36 | 5.9 | 20 | 6.4 | 8 | 5.3 | 8 | 6.6 | — | — |
| Varies as to sex | 2 | 0.3 | 1 | 0.3 | 1 | 0.7 | — | — | — | — |
| Others | 4 | 0.7 | 1 | 0.3 | 1 | 0.7 | 2 | 1.7 | — | — |
| INFORMATION NOT OBTAINED | 1 | 0.2 | — | — | — | — | 1 | 0.8 | — | — |
| TOTALS | 612 | 100.0 | 313 | 100.0 | 152 | 100.0 | 121 | 100.0 | 26 | 100.0 |

earning $3,000 and over, whereas only 8% of the plans open to all employees are thus restricted.

Finally, in relation to eligible groups there is a difference between the several types of plans. Approximately 47% of the 152 individual annuity plans are restricted to salaried employees; among group annuity and self-administered plans 15%, or less, are so limited.

## 2. Other Eligibility Rules

It was pointed out in the chapter treating the basic provisions of pension plans that an employee may be a member of a group eligible to participate in a pension plan but that, in addition, most plans, particularly of the insured type, impose additional rules for membership.

Table E sets forth the findings for plans which impose either a service requirement, or a minimum age, or a maximum age, as eligibility rules for membership in the plan.

*Service.* Approximately 80% of all plans have a service requirement for membership of one year or more. Either 1 or 5 years is the waiting period most commonly used; 29% employ the former, and 25% the latter. Sharp discrepancies between the several types of plans, in their respective use of a 1 or a 5 years' service period, are apparent. Group annuity plans utilize a 1 year service period in 45% of the cases, as against 9% for individual annuity plans. The latter utilize a 5 year period in 43% of the plans.

It also is to be observed that almost one-half the self-administered plans, 42%, have no service requirements for membership, while practically all group annuity and individual annuity plans stipulate them.

*Minimum Age.* In contrast to the high percentage of all plans which use a service requirement, 88%, only 44% of the plans carry a minimum age clause. Furthermore, such a clause is omitted in about two-thirds of the self-administered plans, in approximately 58% of group annuities, and 45% of individual annuity plans. 341 of the 612 plans carry no minimum age eligibility rule.

The most common minimum age requirement is 30, 105 plans; either age 25 or 35 is utilized more frequently in lieu of age 30. A small number utilize a different minimum age for men and women; usually women are made eligible at an age 5 years younger than men. This was found to be related to the fact that plans which so stipulated also made the normal retirement age for women five years earlier.

*Maximum Age.* The typical maximum age limitation beyond which an employee is ineligible for membership in the pension plan was found to be age 64. 205, or approximately 34%, of all plans utilize such an age limitation. There is no maximum age limitation imposed in 149, or 24%, of the plans. About 12% stipulate a different maximum age limitation for men and women. Where this is done, nearly all, 61 out of 74 plans, provide a maximum age of 64 for men, and of 59 for women.

Of the 205 plans using an age limitation of 64 this was most typical of group annuities. Whereas 48% of group annuity plans impose an age limit of 64, only 13% and 21% respectively of individual annuity and self-administered plans do so. Individual annuity plans are distinctive in that age 60 is employed in about 20% of such plans, while none of the self-administered and only 2 group annuity plans utilize an age limit of 60.

A further marked division is to be found among the 149 plans which impose no maximum age limitations. Over one-half of these, 77, are self-administered plans; thus 64% of the 121 self-administered plans omit a maximum age limitation, whereas this is so only in 14% and 18% respectively of the group annuity and individual annuity plans.

It is noticeable generally, with reference to the imposition either of a maximum age, or a minimum age, or a service requirement, that self-administered plans use such membership rules less frequently than insured plans.[7] In fact, in approximately 41 of the 121 self-administered plans all such membership rules are omitted, the sole condition for eligibility to membership being employment. This appears to be related to the fact that 35 of the 41 provide for no vesting or severance benefits. On the other hand, with reference to self-administered plans which are contributory, there appears a distinct tendency to impose eligibility rules of age or service for membership. Almost 80% of the contributory self-administered plans, as against 60% of the non-contributory ones, impose them.

---

[7] The more frequent use of membership rules of service and/or age by insured plans is partially explained by expense considerations. Under insured plans the calculations are made for, or the benefits are related to, the lives of particular employees. In other words, under either type of insured plan there is purchased on the life of each eligible employee an annuity benefit, which involves an expense to the employer. The use of service and/or age requirements for membership, particularly where turnover is high, tends to reduce such expense. A further reason is that insured plans more often vest some or all of the employer's contributions upon withdrawal from employment than do self-administered plans. Eligibility rules of service and/or age thus tend to reduce the costs which may arise from payment of withdrawal values.

## TABLE E

### Other Eligibility Rules for Membership

| Requirements for Eligibility | Total Companies | | Group Annuity | | Individual Annuity | | Self-Administered | | Combination and Others | |
|---|---|---|---|---|---|---|---|---|---|---|
| | Companies | Per Cent | Companies | Per Cent | Companies | Per Cent | Companies | Per Cent | Companies | Per Cent |
| **Service Requirements** | | | | | | | | | | |
| 1 month | 2 | 0.3 | 2 | 0.6 | — | — | — | — | — | — |
| 3 months | 5 | 0.8 | 5 | 1.6 | 1 | 0.7 | — | — | — | — |
| 6 months | 26 | 4.2 | 17 | 5.4 | 14 | 9.2 | 8 | 6.6 | 8 | 30.8 |
| 1 year | 180 | 29.4 | 141 | 45.0 | 22 | 14.5 | 17 | 14.0 | 3 | 11.5 |
| 2 years | 67 | 10.9 | 31 | 9.9 | 32 | 21.1 | 11 | 9.1 | 1 | 3.8 |
| 3 years | 70 | 11.4 | 30 | 9.6 | 7 | 4.6 | 7 | 5.8 | | |
| 4 years | 10 | 1.6 | 1 | 0.3 | 66 | 43.4 | 2 | 1.7 | 10 | 38.5 |
| 5 years | 155 | 25.3 | 59 | 18.8 | 4 | 2.6 | 20 | 16.5 | | |
| Others | 21 | 3.4 | 13 | 4.2 | 2 | 1.3 | 3 | 2.5 | 2 | 7.7 |
| No service requirement | 67 | 10.9 | 13 | 4.2 | 4 | 2.6 | 51 | 42.1 | 2 | 7.7 |
| Information not obtained | 9 | 1.5 | 1 | 0.3 | | | 2 | 1.7 | | |
| **Totals** | 612 | 100.0 | 313 | 100.0 | 152 | 100.0 | 121 | 100.0 | 26 | 100.0 |
| **Minimum Age Requirements** | | | | | | | | | | |
| Same for Men and Women | 240 | 39.2 | 112 | 35.8 | 78 | 51.3 | 39 | 32.2 | 11 | 42.3 |
| Aged 21 | 10 | 1.6 | 2 | 0.6 | 2 | 1.3 | 6 | 5.0 | — | — |
| Aged 24 | 2 | 0.3 | — | — | 2 | 1.3 | — | — | — | — |
| Aged 24½ | 3 | 0.5 | 2 | 0.6 | — | — | — | — | 1 | 3.8 |
| Aged 25 | 48 | 7.8 | 19 | 6.1 | 18 | 11.8 | 7 | 5.8 | 4 | 15.4 |
| Aged 27 | 1 | 0.2 | — | — | 1 | 0.7 | — | — | — | — |

Other Eligibility Rules for Membership

| Requirements for Eligibility | Total Companies | | Group Annuity | | Individual Annuity | | Self-Administered | | Combination and Others | |
|---|---|---|---|---|---|---|---|---|---|---|
| | Companies | Per Cent | Companies | Per Cent | Companies | Per Cent | Companies | Per Cent | Companies | Per Cent |
| Aged 29 | 1 | 0.2 | — | — | 1 | 0.7 | — | — | — | — |
| Aged 29½ | 5 | 0.8 | 1 | 0.3 | 4 | 2.6 | — | — | — | — |
| Aged 30 | 105 | 17.2 | 54 | 17.3 | 33 | 21.7 | 14 | 11.6 | 4 | 15.4 |
| Aged 34½ | 4 | 0.7 | 2 | 0.6 | 1 | 0.7 | — | — | 1 | 3.8 |
| Aged 35 | 54 | 8.8 | 29 | 9.3 | 12 | 7.9 | 12 | 9.9 | 1 | 3.8 |
| Aged 36 | 1 | 0.2 | — | — | 1 | 0.7 | — | — | — | — |
| Aged 39½ | 1 | 0.2 | — | — | 1 | 0.7 | — | — | — | — |
| Aged 40 | 4 | 0.7 | 3 | 1.0 | 1 | 0.7 | — | — | — | — |
| Aged 41 | 1 | 0.2 | — | — | 1 | 0.7 | — | — | — | — |
| Different for Men and Women | 17 | 2.8 | 10 | 3.2 | 3 | 2.0 | 2 | 1.7 | 2 | 7.7 |
| Men aged 25, women aged 30 | 2 | 0.3 | — | — | — | — | — | — | — | — |
| Men aged 30, women aged 25 | 6 | 1.0 | 3 | 1.0 | 1 | 0.7 | 2 | 1.7 | 2 | 7.7 |
| Men aged 35, women aged 30 | 4 | 0.7 | 4 | 1.3 | — | — | — | — | — | — |
| Men aged 36, women aged 31 | 1 | 0.2 | 1 | 0.3 | — | — | — | — | — | — |
| Men aged 40, women aged 35 | 2 | 0.3 | 2 | 0.6 | — | — | — | — | — | — |
| Men, no minimum age, women aged 30 | 2 | 0.3 | — | — | 2 | 1.3 | — | — | — | — |
| Others | 14 | 2.3 | 11 | 3.5 | 3 | 2.0 | — | — | — | — |
| No Minimum Age Requirement | 341 | 55.7 | 180 | 57.5 | 68 | 44.7 | 80 | 66.1 | 13 | 50.0 |
| Totals | 612 | 100.0 | 313 | 100.0 | 152 | 100.0 | 121 | 100.0 | 26 | 100.0 |

## TABLE E (Cont.)

### Other Eligibility Rules for Membership

| Requirements for Eligibility | Total Companies | | Group Annuity | | Individual Annuity | | Self-Administered | | Combination and Others | |
|---|---|---|---|---|---|---|---|---|---|---|
| | Companies | Per Cent | Companies | Per Cent | Companies | Per Cent | Companies | Per Cent | Companies | Per Cent |
| Maximum Age Limitations Same for Men and Women | 384 | 62.7 | 209 | 66.8 | 118 | 77.6 | 38 | 31.4 | 19 | 73.1 |
| Aged 74 | 1 | 0.2 | 1 | 0.3 | — | — | — | — | 1 | 3.8 |
| Aged 70½ | 1 | 0.2 | — | — | 1 | 0.7 | — | — | — | — |
| Aged 70 | 1 | 0.2 | 1 | 0.3 | — | — | — | — | — | — |
| Aged 69½ | 1 | 0.2 | 1 | 0.3 | — | — | — | — | — | — |
| Aged 69 | 9 | 1.5 | 5 | 1.6 | 4 | 2.6 | — | — | — | — |
| Aged 68½ | 1 | 0.2 | — | — | 1 | 0.7 | — | — | — | — |
| Aged 68 | 1 | 0.2 | — | — | 1 | 0.7 | — | — | — | — |
| Aged 66½ | 1 | 0.2 | — | — | 1 | 0.7 | — | — | — | — |
| Aged 66 | 3 | 0.5 | — | — | 2 | 1.3 | — | — | 1 | 3.8 |
| Aged 65½ | 13 | 2.1 | 2 | 0.6 | 11 | 7.2 | — | — | — | — |
| Aged 65 | 17 | 2.8 | 15 | 4.8 | 2 | 1.3 | — | — | — | — |
| Aged 64½ | 205 | 33.5 | 149 | 47.6 | 19 | 12.5 | 25 | 20.7 | 12 | 46.2 |
| Aged 64 | 15 | 2.5 | 11 | 3.5 | — | — | 3 | 2.5 | 1 | 3.8 |
| Aged 63 | 3 | 0.5 | 1 | 0.3 | 2 | 1.3 | — | — | — | — |
| Aged 62 | 1 | 0.2 | — | — | 1 | 0.7 | — | — | — | — |
| Aged 61 | 14 | 2.3 | 2 | 0.6 | 8 | 5.3 | — | — | 4 | 15.4 |
| Aged 60½ | 32 | 5.2 | 2 | 0.6 | 30 | 19.7 | — | — | — | — |
| Aged 60 | 3 | 0.5 | 1 | 0.3 | 2 | 1.3 | — | — | — | — |
| Aged 59½ | 24 | 3.9 | 13 | 4.2 | 6 | 3.9 | 5 | 4.1 | — | — |
| Aged 59 | 1 | 0.2 | — | — | 1 | 0.7 | — | — | — | — |
| Aged 58 | 1 | 0.2 | — | — | 1 | 0.7 | — | — | — | — |
| Aged 57½ | 1 | 0.2 | — | — | 1 | 0.7 | — | — | — | — |
| Aged 56 | 1 | 0.2 | — | — | 1 | 0.7 | — | — | — | — |

## TABLE E (Cont.)

### Other Eligibility Rules for Membership

| Requirements for Eligibility | Total Companies | | Group Annuity | | Individual Annuity | | Self-Administered | | Combination and Others | |
|---|---|---|---|---|---|---|---|---|---|---|
| | Companies | Per Cent | Companies | Per Cent | Companies | Per Cent | Companies | Per Cent | Companies | Per Cent |
| Aged 55½ | 5 | 0.8 | — | — | 5 | 3.3 | — | — | — | — |
| Aged 55 | 15 | 2.5 | 1 | 0.3 | 14 | 9.2 | — | — | — | — |
| Aged 54 | 7 | 1.1 | 4 | 1.3 | — | — | 3 | 2.5 | — | — |
| Aged 53 | 2 | 0.3 | — | — | 2 | 1.3 | — | — | — | — |
| Aged 51 | 1 | 0.2 | 1 | 0.3 | — | — | — | — | — | — |
| Aged 50 | 2 | 0.3 | — | — | 2 | 1.3 | — | — | — | — |
| Aged 45 | 1 | 0.2 | — | — | — | — | 1 | 0.8 | — | — |
| Aged 44 | 1 | 0.2 | — | — | — | — | 1 | 0.8 | — | — |
| *Different for Men and Women* | 74 | 12.1 | 59 | 18.8 | 6 | 3.9 | 4 | 3.3 | 5 | 19.2 |
| Men aged 65, women aged 55 | 1 | 0.2 | — | — | 1 | 0.7 | — | — | — | — |
| Men aged 64½, women aged 59½ | 3 | 0.5 | 3 | 1.0 | — | — | — | — | — | — |
| Men aged 64, women aged 59 | 61 | 10.0 | 52 | 16.6 | 1 | 0.7 | 3 | 2.5 | 5 | 19.2 |
| Men aged 64, women aged 54 | 1 | 0.2 | 1 | 0.3 | — | — | — | — | — | — |
| Men aged 63, women aged 58 | 2 | 0.3 | 2 | 0.6 | — | — | — | — | — | — |
| Men aged 65, women aged 59 | 1 | 0.2 | 1 | 0.3 | — | — | — | — | — | — |
| Men aged 60, women aged 55 | 3 | 0.5 | — | — | 3 | 2.0 | — | — | — | — |
| Men aged 59, women aged 54 | 1 | 0.2 | — | — | — | — | — | — | — | — |
| Men, no maximum age, women aged 54 | 1 | 0.2 | — | — | 1 | 0.7 | 1 | 0.8 | — | — |
| Others | 3 | 0.5 | 2 | 0.6 | 1 | 0.7 | — | — | — | — |
| No Maximum Age Provision | 149 | 24.3 | 43 | 13.7 | 27 | 17.8 | 77 | 63.6 | 2 | 7.7 |
| Information Not Obtained | 2 | 0.3 | — | — | — | — | 2 | 1.7 | — | — |
| Totals | 612 | 100.0 | 313 | 100.0 | 152 | 100.0 | 121 | 100.0 | 26 | 100.0 |

## E. Eligibility Rules for Receipt of Pension Allowance

Previously it was observed that under all pension plans certain conditions or eligibility rules must be satisfied to obtain pension benefits.[8] These conditions usually are that an employee attain the normal retirement age, and/or render a certain number of years of service. Under insured plans the attainment of the normal retirement age is the usual provision, the years of service to be rendered being dependent on the age at which an employee becomes eligible to the plan. Among 28 self-administered plans, however, eligibility rules for the receipt of a pension allowance are variously stipulated as follows:

*Age and Service.* 20 plans provide that, in addition to attainment of the normal retirement age, a specified number of years of service must have been rendered. The range is from 18 months to 25 years. 10 of the 20 are divided equally in their use either of 15 or 20 years. 2 plans call for 25 years of service, and the remaining 8 stipulate lesser periods of from 18 months to 10 years.

*Alternate Conditions.* The remaining 8 plans use a combination of eligibility rules for the receipt of pension benefits as follows: (1) 1 plan provides for retirement at 65 or 70, subject to a limitation that 20 years of service have been rendered. (2) 7 plans provide other alternate conditions. For example, 2 plans allow men to retire at ages 65, 60, 55, or under 55, with service of 20, 25, and 30 years, respectively; and women at 55, 50, or under 50, with like service of respectively 20, 25, and 30 years. One plan allows pension benefits at normal retirement age of 65, with completion of 20 years of service, or, in any case, after 25 years of service; another allows retirement at age 65, or upon the rendering of 15 years of service, whichever is the later event.

## F. Normal Retirement Ages

A provision for a normal retirement age is to be found in all modern pension plans. Of the 612 plans 469, or 77%, were found to provide a normal retirement age of 65 for all employees. 9 plans use age 60 for normal retirement of all employees, 1 age 55,[9] and 2 age 70. 111 plans retire men at 65, and women at 60. This earlier retirement provision for women, that is, 5 years in advance of men, is similarly true of the few other plans which make a differentiation; except, 7 plans retire women 10 years before men.

---

[8] See Chapter IX, pp. 197-198.
[9] A bank plan.

## TABLE F

### Normal Retirement Age

| Age | Total Companies | | Group Annuity | | Individual Annuity | | Self-Administered | | Combination and Others | |
|---|---|---|---|---|---|---|---|---|---|---|
| | Companies | Per Cent | Companies | Per Cent | Companies | Per Cent | Companies | Per Cent | Companies | Per Cent |
| **SAME FOR MEN AND WOMEN** | 481 | 78.6 | 229 | 73.2 | 139 | 91.4 | 94 | 77.7 | 19 | 73.1 |
| Aged 55 | 1 | 0.2 | — | — | — | — | 1 | 0.8 | — | — |
| Aged 60 | 9 | 1.5 | 1 | 0.3 | 3 | 2.0 | 5 | 4.1 | — | — |
| Aged 65 | 469 | 76.6 | 227 | 72.5 | 136 | 89.5 | 87 | 71.9 | 19 | 73.1 |
| Aged 70 | 2 | 0.3 | 1 | 0.3 | — | — | 1 | 0.8 | — | — |
| **DIFFERENT FOR MEN AND WOMEN** | 125 | 20.4 | 84 | 26.8 | 13 | 8.6 | 21 | 17.4 | 7 | 26.9 |
| Men aged 60, women aged 55 | 2 | 0.3 | — | — | 1 | 0.7 | 1 | 0.8 | — | — |
| Men aged 63, women aged 60 | 1 | 0.2 | 1 | 0.3 | — | — | — | — | — | — |
| Men aged 65, women aged 55 | 6 | 1.0 | 5 | 1.6 | — | — | 1 | 0.8 | — | — |
| Men aged 65, women aged 60 | 111 | 18.1 | 78 | 24.9 | 12 | 7.9 | 14 | 11.6 | 7 | 26.9 |
| Men aged 70, women aged 60 | 1 | 0.2 | — | — | — | — | 1 | 0.8 | — | — |
| Men aged 70, women aged 65 | 4 | 0.7 | — | — | — | — | 4 | 3.3 | — | — |
| **Information Not Obtained** | 6 | 1.0 | — | — | — | — | 6 | 5.0 | — | — |
| **TOTALS** | 612 | 100.0 | 313 | 100.0 | 152 | 100.0 | 121 | 100.0 | 26 | 100.0 |

Among the 469 plans using age 65 as a normal retirement age for all employees, individual annuity plans select this age in 90% of the cases, as against its employment in approximately 72% both in self-administered and group annuity plans. Use of a different retirement age for men and women is more common to group annuity plans, 27% of the cases; self-administered plans have a differentiation in 17%, and individual annuity plans in less than 9% of the respective plans. Table F gives the complete findings.

## G.  Early Retirement

Most pension plans make provision for retirement earlier than the stipulated normal retirement age. The analysis of early retirement provisions was made to determine generally, and in relation to the several major types (1) the number of plans which make provision for early retirement; (2) the *time* early retirement takes place, and the attached conditions of service, membership, or age, to be satisfied before allowed; (3) whether early retirement could occur *with* or *without* company consent; and (4) the benefits obtainable upon early retirement.

In examining the tabulation of these findings it should be recognized that provision for early retirement may be an indication of liberality in the terms of a plan, in contrast with plans which omit this provision. But as between plans which specifically provide for early retirement there exist important differences, such as the respective conditions to be satisfied for early retirement, whether company consent is required, and the amount of the benefits. Any comparisons or inferences must take account of all these factors.

### 1.  Number of Plans

As shown in Table G-1, 500, about 82% of the 612 plans, make specific provision for early retirement. A small number, 26, permit early retirement only for disability reasons; 8 others provide for early retirement but fail to mention when it will be allowed. 78, the remainder, make no provision for early retirement. It is noticeable that *specific* provision for early retirement is encountered in about 97% of the group annuity plans, but considerably less frequently in the self-administered and individual annuity plans.

### 2.  Time Permitted, and/or Conditions of Service, Membership, or Age to Be Satisfied

Under the 500 plans which make *specific* provision, early retirement is allowed either (1) a certain number of years prior to nor-

## TABLE G-1

### EARLY RETIREMENT

### Number of Plans with Early Retirement Provisions

| TYPE OF PROVISION | TOTAL COMPANIES | | GROUP ANNUITY | | INDIVIDUAL ANNUITY | | SELF-ADMINISTERED | | COMBINATION AND OTHERS | |
|---|---|---|---|---|---|---|---|---|---|---|
| | Companies | Per Cent | Companies | Per Cent | Companies | Per Cent | Companies | Per Cent | Companies | Per Cent |
| Plans having specific early retirement provisions | 500 | 81.7 | 303 | 96.8 | 94 | 61.8 | 81 | 66.9 | 22 | 84.6 |
| Plans having early retirement for disability only | 26 | 4.2 | 1 | 0.3 | 12 | 7.9 | 10 | 8.3 | 3 | 11.5 |
| Plans allowing early retirement, but no further information obtained | 8 | 1.3 | 2 | 0.6 | 3 | 2.0 | 3 | 2.5 | — | — |
| Plans having no early retirement provisions | 78 | 12.7 | 7 | 2.2 | 43 | 28.3 | 27 | 22.3 | 1 | 3.8 |
| TOTALS | 612 | 100.0 | 313 | 100.0 | 152 | 100.0 | 121 | 100.0 | 26 | 100.0 |

## TABLE G-2

### EARLY RETIREMENT

### Time Permitted and/or Conditions of Service, Membership or Age to Be Satisfied

| CONDITIONS | TOTAL COMPANIES | | GROUP ANNUITY | | INDIVIDUAL ANNUITY | | SELF-ADMINISTERED | | COMBINATION AND OTHERS | |
|---|---|---|---|---|---|---|---|---|---|---|
| | Companies | Per Cent | Companies | Per Cent | Companies | Per Cent | Companies | Per Cent | Companies | Per Cent |
| WITHIN 5 YEARS OF NORMAL RETIREMENT DATE | 36 | 7.2 | 4 | 1.3 | 9 | 9.6 | 21 | 25.9 | 2 | 9.1 |
| AND | | | | | | | | | | |
| 5 years' service | 2 | 0.4 | — | — | 1 | 1.1 | 1 | 1.2 | — | — |
| 10 years' service | 2 | 0.4 | — | — | — | — | 2 | 2.5 | — | — |
| 15 years' service | 6 | 1.2 | — | — | 2 | 2.1 | 4 | 4.9 | — | — |
| 20 years' service | 2 | 0.4 | — | — | — | — | 2 | 2.5 | — | — |
| 15 years' service, entry before age 55 | 1 | 0.2 | — | — | — | — | 1 | 1.2 | — | — |

TABLE G-2 (Cont.)

EARLY RETIREMENT

Time Permitted and/or Conditions of Service, Membership or Age to Be Satisfied

| CONDITIONS | TOTAL COMPANIES | | GROUP ANNUITY | | INDIVIDUAL ANNUITY | | SELF-ADMINISTERED | | COMBINATION AND OTHERS | |
|---|---|---|---|---|---|---|---|---|---|---|
| | Com-panies | Per Cent | Com-panies | Per Cent | Com-panies | Per Cent | Com-panies | Per Cent | Com-panies | Per Cent |
| 10 years of membership | 1 | 0.2 | — | — | 1 | 1.1 | — | — | — | — |
| Others | 1 | 0.2 | — | — | — | — | 1 | 1.2 | — | — |
| No service or membership conditions | 21 | 4.2 | 4 | 1.3 | 5 | 5.3 | 10 | 12.3 | 2 | 9.1 |
| WITHIN 10 YEARS OF NORMAL RETIREMENT DATE | 308 | 61.6 | 240 | 79.2 | 12 | 12.8 | 45 | 55.6 | 11 | 50.0 |
| AND | | | | | | | | | | |
| 5 years' service | 1 | 0.2 | 1 | 0.3 | — | — | 6 | 7.4 | 2 | 9.1 |
| 10 years' service | 13 | 2.6 | 5 | 1.7 | 1 | 1.1 | 4 | 4.9 | — | — |
| 15 years' service | 10 | 2.0 | 5 | 1.7 | 1 | 1.1 | 6 | 7.4 | — | — |
| 20 years' service | 16 | 3.2 | 9 | 3.0 | — | — | 1 | 1.2 | — | — |
| 25 years' service | 3 | 0.6 | 2 | 0.7 | — | — | 2 | 2.5 | — | — |
| 30 years' service | 2 | 0.4 | — | — | — | — | — | — | — | — |
| 20 years' service for men, 15 for women | 1 | 0.2 | 1 | 0.3 | — | — | — | — | — | — |
| 25 years' service for men, 20 for women | 1 | 0.2 | — | — | — | — | 1 | 1.2 | — | — |
| 30 years' service for men, 20 for women | 1 | 0.2 | 1 | 0.3 | — | — | — | — | — | — |
| 3 years of membership | 1 | 0.2 | 1 | 0.3 | — | — | — | — | — | — |
| 5 years of membership | 1 | 0.2 | 2 | 0.7 | — | — | — | — | — | — |
| 10 years of membership | 2 | 0.4 | 1 | 0.3 | — | — | — | — | 1 | 4.5 |
| 15 years' service, 5 years of membership | 2 | 0.4 | 1 | 0.3 | — | — | — | — | — | — |
| Others | 1 | 0.2 | 1 | 0.3 | — | — | 1 | 1.2 | — | — |
| No service or membership conditions | 253 | 50.6 | 211 | 69.6 | 10 | 10.6 | 24 | 29.6 | 8 | 36.4 |

## TABLE G-2 (Cont.)
### EARLY RETIREMENT
Time Permitted and/or Conditions of Service, Membership or Age to Be Satisfied

| Conditions | Total Companies | | Group Annuity | | Individual Annuity | | Self-Administered | | Combination and Others | |
|---|---|---|---|---|---|---|---|---|---|---|
| | Companies | Per Cent | Companies | Per Cent | Companies | Per Cent | Companies | Per Cent | Companies | Per Cent |
| WITHIN 15 YEARS OF NORMAL RETIREMENT DATE | 4 | | 3 | | — | | — | | 1 | |
| AND | | | | | | | | | | |
| No service or membership conditions | | 0.8 | | 1.0 | | — | | — | | 4.5 |
| WITHOUT REFERENCE TO NORMAL RETIREMENT DATE | 10 | 2.0 | 3 | 1.0 | 1 | 1.1 | 5 | 6.2 | 1 | 4.5 |
| 15 years' service | 2 | 0.4 | 1 | 0.3 | — | — | 1 | 1.2 | — | — |
| 20 years' service | 1 | 0.2 | — | — | — | — | 1 | 1.2 | — | — |
| 25 years' service | 1 | 0.2 | 1 | 0.3 | — | — | — | — | — | — |
| 10 years of membership | 1 | 0.2 | — | — | — | — | — | — | 1 | 4.5 |
| 20 years of membership | 1 | 0.2 | — | — | 1 | 1.1 | — | — | — | — |
| 15 years' service, 5 years of membership | 1 | 0.2 | 1 | 0.3 | — | — | — | — | — | — |
| Men aged 60, 20 years' service; women aged 55, 20 years of service | 1 | 0.2 | — | — | — | — | 1 | 1.2 | — | — |
| Upon attainment of age 50 | 2 | 0.4 | — | — | — | — | 2 | 2.5 | — | — |
| No Time, Service, Membership or Age Conditions Specified | 123 | 24.6 | 42 | 13.9 | 71 | 75.5 | 5 | 6.2 | 5 | 22.7 |
| Miscellaneous | 10 | 2.0 | 5 | 1.7 | 1 | 1.1 | 4 | 4.9 | — | — |
| Information Not Obtained | 9 | 1.8 | 6 | 2.0 | — | — | 1 | 1.2 | 2 | 9.1 |
| TOTAL PLANS WITH SPECIFIC EARLY RETIREMENT PROVISIONS | 500 | 100.0 | 303 | 100.0 | 94 | 100.0 | 81 | 100.0 | 22 | 100.0 |

mal retirement age, with or without attached conditions of service, membership, or age, or (2) simply upon satisfaction either of service, membership, or age conditions.

The time for early retirement most commonly provided is within 10 years prior to attainment of the normal retirement age; 308 of all plans so specify. It will be noted, however, that this figure is weighted heavily by group annuity plans, for, of the 308 plans, 240 are group annuities.

Of the total of 348 plans which provide a *time* for early retirement, that is, within 5, 10, or 15 years prior to normal retirement age, about 80% attach no service or membership requirements. Plans which specify as sole conditions either service, membership, or age, without reference to the *time,* are few in number. But the 123 plans which omit any and all conditions of time, service, membership, or age, constitute almost 25% of the 500 making specific provision for early retirement. These are concentrated heavily among individual annuity plans.

### 3. With or Without Company Consent

Over three-fourths of the plans with specific provision for early retirement require that an employee must have company consent to retire prior to normal retirement age, whether or not conditions of service, membership, or age are attached. As shown in Table G-3, 388, or 78% of the 500 plans specifically providing for early retirement, require company consent. In 83 plans, or 17%, early retirement is at the employee's election; in 14, or 3%, at the election either of the employer or the employee.

It is to be noted that there exists more or less uniformity among the several types of plans in the requirement of company consent for early retirement; except possibly in the case of self-administered plans, where retirement at the employee's election is more frequently encountered.

### 4. Benefits

The benefit which is payable upon early retirement usually is the actuarial equivalent of the normal retirement benefit. In general this means that a proportion of the normal retirement benefit will be payable, and thus that the early retirement benefit will be in a reduced amount. The technical process of determining this reduced benefit will differ as between the several types of plan, but under any type of plan, and in most instances, the early retire-

### EARLY RETIREMENT
#### With or Without Company's Consent

| PROVISION | TOTAL COMPANIES | | GROUP ANNUITY | | INDIVIDUAL ANNUITY | | SELF-ADMINISTERED | | COMBINATION AND OTHERS | |
|---|---|---|---|---|---|---|---|---|---|---|
| | Companies | Per Cent | Companies | Per Cent | Companies | Per Cent | Companies | Per Cent | Companies | Per Cent |
| With Company's Consent | 388 | 77.6 | 254 | 83.8 | 75 | 79.8 | 43 | 53.1 | 16 | 72.7 |
| At Employee's Election | 83 | 16.6 | 45 | 14.9 | 12 | 12.8 | 22 | 27.2 | 4 | 18.2 |
| At Election of Company or Employee | 14 | 2.8 | — | — | 7 | 7.4 | 14 | 17.3 | — | — |
| Information Not Obtained | 15 | 3.0 | 4 | 1.3 | — | — | 2 | 2.5 | 2 | 9.1 |
| TOTAL PLANS WITH SPECIFIC EARLY RETIREMENT PROVISIONS | 500 | 100.0 | 303 | 100.0 | 94 | 100.0 | 81 | 100.0 | 22 | 100.0 |

### TABLE G-4
### EARLY RETIREMENT
#### Pension Benefit Provided

| BENEFIT | TOTAL COMPANIES | | GROUP ANNUITY | | INDIVIDUAL ANNUITY | | SELF-ADMINISTERED | | COMBINATION AND OTHERS | |
|---|---|---|---|---|---|---|---|---|---|---|
| | Companies | Per Cent | Companies | Per Cent | Companies | Per Cent | Companies | Per Cent | Companies | Per Cent |
| Actuarial equivalent of normal pension, payment immediate | 446 | 89.2 | 293 | 96.7 | 83[a] | 88.3 | 48 | 59.3 | 22 | 100.0 |
| Actuarial equivalent of normal pension, payment immediate; or the pension accrued to early retirement date, payment deferred to normal retirement age; at the election of the employee | 37 | 7.4 | 9 | 3.0 | — | — | 28 | 34.6 | — | — |
| Others | 6 | 1.2 | 1 | 0.3 | 1 | 1.1 | 4 | 4.9 | — | — |
| Information Not Obtained | 11 | 2.2 | — | — | 10 | 10.6 | 1 | 1.2 | — | — |
| PLANS WITH SPECIFIC EARLY RETIREMENT PROVISIONS | 500 | 100.0 | 303 | 100.0 | 94 | 100.0 | 81 | 100.0 | 22 | 100.0 |

[a] The early retirement benefit of group annuity and self-administered plans normally will be an annuity in a reduced amount; this likewise may be the benefit under an individual annuity plan, but the latter alternatively may make available cash or income in installments for a limited time.

ment benefit will be in a sharply reduced amount relative to the normal retirement benefit.[10]

Provision for payment of an early retirement benefit may be made in several ways. A plan may provide for its immediate payment at the time of early retirement, or its deferment until the normal retirement age; or it may be immediate or deferred at the employee's election. Approximately 90% of the plans which provide for early retirement stipulate immediate payment. A small number, 37 out of 500, make it optional with the employee to receive immediate payment, or to postpone the time for receipt of the reduced pension benefit until attainment of the normal retirement age.

The standard procedure among group annuity plans is to make payment of the reduced early retirement benefit immediately upon early retirement; likewise is this true of individual annuity plans. In self-administered plans, however, 35% of the 81 plans permitting early retirement allow an employee the election of immediate or deferred payment of an adjusted pension benefit.

## H.　Retirement Benefits

In determining the pension benefits, most plans divide the benefits, or give credits for future and past service; 437 [11] of the 612 plans follow this practice, and the remaining 175 utilize other methods.

### 1. Future Service Benefits

As may be seen in Table H, future service benefits are calculated by giving an employee a percentage credit of his compensation for each year of future service to retirement. It will be noted, however, that there are considerable variations in the practical application of the principle. First of all, there are differences as between plans in the amount of compensation which will be considered as a basis for applying a percentage credit; and secondly, there are differing percentages used as between plans, and within the same plan, in relation to the amounts of compensation which

---

[10] The reasons for the reduction, of course, are that it is probable that payments will have to be made over a longer period to those employees who are granted early retirement benefits, and that several years of contributions, or accumulations, will not have been made for the employee's benefit. For example, as to contributions, where the normal retirement age is 65 and early retirement occurs at 55, ten years of contributions will not have been made.

[11] For classification purposes, there is included, in the 437, 66 money-purchase plans; these for the most part make no provision for a past service benefit.

are made a basis for pension credits. For example, one plan may base credits on all compensation received; another, only on compensation in excess of $3,000. In the use of percentages as applied to the compensation, one plan may use ¾ of 1% or 1%, another 1% or 2% of all or a portion of compensation. In the same plan the percentages may differ as applied to different amounts of compensation, such as ½ of 1% of the first $3,000, plus 1% on the amount in excess. The plans, therefore, have been classified, where possible, as to whether (1) the per cent of compensation granted for each year of service remains unchanged, that is, is applied uniformly to all or a portion of the compensation, (2) the per cent changes, or is a nonuniform per cent, when applied to all or a portion of the compensation.

The majority of the 437 plans, 263, use the entire amount of the compensation as a basis for computing the future service benefits; 170 of the 263, however, apply a different, nonuniform, per cent to all compensation, with 93 using a uniform per cent. In regard to the typical per cent used, of the 93 plans about one-half grant a uniform credit of 1% of all compensation for each year of future service; 22, of 1½%. Of the 170 plans using a nonuniform per cent of compensation, the typical formulas are either (1) ¾ of 1% of the first $3,000 and 1½% of the excess, 44 plans; (2) 1% of the first $3,000 and 1½% of excess, 20 plans; or (3) 1% of the first $3,000 and 2% of the excess, 44 plans.

Almost 44% of the group annuity plans make use of a nonuniform per cent applied to all compensation, with almost an equal percentage of self-administered plans doing likewise. Of the few individual annuity plans represented in this table the reverse is true; about 42% use a uniform per cent of all compensation.

It is notable that of the 313 group annuity plans represented in this study 99% base the pension benefits on credits for future and past service. 64% of self-administered plans do so; but in complete contrast, only 25% of the individual annuity plans follow this policy.

## 2. Past Service Benefits

Past service benefits, as in the case of future service, are provided in relation to some or all compensation; also, different per cents are applied as between plans, and in the same plans, to varying amounts of compensation.

As may be deduced from the tabulation in Table I, approximately

## TABLE H
### Future Service Benefit Formulas

| Per Cent (To be multiplied by years of future service) | Total Companies | | Group Annuity | | Individual Annuity | | Self-Administered | | Combination and Others | |
|---|---|---|---|---|---|---|---|---|---|---|
| | Companies | Per Cent | Companies | Per Cent | Companies | Per Cent | Companies | Per Cent | Companies | Per Cent |
| A Uniform Per Cent of Compensation | 93 | 21.3 | 45 | 14.5 | 16 | 42.1 | 28 | 36.4 | 4 | 33.3 |
| ⅛% | 1 | 0.2 | — | — | — | — | 1 | 1.3 | — | — |
| 4/10% | 1 | 0.2 | — | — | 1 | 2.6 | — | — | 1 | 8.3 |
| ½% | 2 | 0.5 | 1 | 0.3 | 1 | 2.6 | — | — | — | — |
| 7/10% | 1 | 0.2 | — | — | 1 | 2.6 | — | — | — | — |
| ¾% | 7 | 1.6 | 3 | 1.0 | 4 | 10.5 | 15 | 19.5 | 2 | 16.7 |
| 1% | 46 | 10.5 | 20 | 6.5 | 9 | 23.7 | — | — | — | — |
| 1⅓% | 1 | 0.2 | 1 | 0.3 | — | — | — | — | — | — |
| 1½% | 22 | 5.0 | 14 | 4.5 | 1 | 2.6 | 8 | 10.4 | — | — |
| 1⅔% | 1 | 0.2 | — | — | — | — | — | — | — | — |
| 2% | 11 | 2.5 | 6 | 1.9 | — | — | 4 | 5.2 | 1 | 8.3 |
| A Uniform Per Cent of Portion of Compensation | 40 | 9.2 | 26 | 8.4 | 5 | 13.2 | 7 | 9.1 | 2 | 16.7 |
| *Excess over $600* | | | | | | | | | | |
| 1¼% | 1 | 0.2 | 1 | 0.3 | — | — | — | — | — | — |
| 1½% | 2 | 0.5 | 2 | 0.6 | — | — | — | — | — | — |
| 1¾% | 1 | 0.2 | — | — | — | — | 1 | 1.3 | — | — |
| *Excess over $3,000* | | | | | | | | | | |
| 1% | 12 | 2.7 | 4 | 1.3 | 4 | 10.5 | 3 | 3.9 | 1 | 8.3 |
| 1¼% | 1 | 0.2 | 1 | 0.3 | — | — | — | — | — | — |
| 1¾% | 3 | 0.7 | 2 | 0.6 | 1 | 2.6 | — | — | — | — |
| 1½% | 19 | 4.3 | 15 | 4.8 | — | — | 3 | 3.9 | 1 | 8.3 |
| *First $3,000* | | | | | | | | | | |
| ¾% | 1 | 0.2 | 1 | 0.3 | — | — | — | — | — | — |

## TABLE H (*Cont.*)

### FUTURE SERVICE BENEFIT FORMULAS

| PER CENT (To be multiplied by years of future service) | TOTAL COMPANIES | | GROUP ANNUITY | | INDIVIDUAL ANNUITY | | SELF-ADMINISTERED | | COMBINATION AND OTHERS | |
|---|---|---|---|---|---|---|---|---|---|---|
| | *Companies* | *Per Cent* | *Companies* | *Per Cent* | *Companies* | *Per Cent* | *Companies* | *Per Cent* | *Companies* | *Per Cent* |
| A NONUNIFORM PER CENT OF COMPENSATION | 170 | 38.9 | 137 | 44.2 | 3 | 7.9 | 29 | 37.7 | 1 | 8.3 |
| *Per Cent Changes at $1,200* | | | | | | | | | | |
| 1% first $1,200, 1½% of excess | 1 | 0.2 | 1 | 0.3 | — | — | — | — | — | — |
| *Per Cent Changes at $3,000* | | | | | | | | | | |
| ¼% first $3,000, 1½% of excess | 1 | 0.2 | — | — | 1 | 2.6 | — | — | — | — |
| 3/10% first $3,000, 1 3/10% of excess | 1 | 0.2 | — | — | — | — | 1 | 1.3 | — | — |
| ½% first $3,000, ¾% of excess | 1 | 0.2 | 1 | 0.3 | — | — | — | — | — | — |
| ½% first $3,000, 1% of excess | 6 | 1.4 | 4 | 1.3 | — | — | 2 | 2.6 | — | — |
| ½% first $3,000, 1½% of excess | 6 | 1.4 | 5 | 1.6 | — | — | 1 | 1.3 | — | — |
| ⅔% first $3,000, 1⅓% of excess | 2 | 0.5 | 1 | 0.3 | — | — | 1 | 1.3 | — | — |
| ⅔% first $3,000, 1½% of excess | 3 | 0.7 | 2 | 0.6 | — | — | 1 | 1.3 | — | — |
| ⅔% first $3,000, 1⅔% of excess | 2 | 0.5 | 2 | 0.6 | — | — | — | — | — | — |
| ¾% first $3,000, 1% of excess | 1 | 0.2 | 1 | 0.3 | — | — | — | — | — | — |
| ¾% first $3,000, 1¼% of excess | 1 | 0.2 | — | — | — | — | 1 | 1.3 | — | — |
| ¾% first $3,000, 1½% of excess | 44 | 10.1 | 33 | 10.6 | 1 | 2.6 | 9 | 11.7 | 1 | 8.3 |
| ¾% first $3,000, 1¾% of excess | 2 | 0.5 | 2 | 0.6 | — | — | — | — | — | — |
| ¾% first $3,000, 2% of excess | 1 | 0.2 | — | — | — | — | 1 | 1.3 | — | — |
| 8/10% first $3,000, 1⅓% of excess | 1 | 0.2 | 1 | 0.3 | — | — | — | — | — | — |
| 8/10% first $3,000, 1½% of excess | 2 | 0.5 | 1 | 0.3 | — | — | 1 | 1.3 | — | — |
| 1% first $3,000, 1½% of excess | 20 | 4.6 | 18 | 5.8 | — | — | 2 | 2.6 | — | — |
| 1% first $3,000, 1 8/10% of excess | 1 | 0.2 | 1 | 0.3 | — | — | — | — | — | — |
| 1% first $3,000, 2% of excess | 44 | 10.1 | 37 | 11.9 | 1 | 2.6 | 6 | 7.8 | — | — |
| 1¼% first $3,000, 1¾% of excess | 1 | 0.2 | 1 | 0.3 | — | — | — | — | — | — |
| 1¼% first $3,000, 2% of excess | 2 | 0.5 | 1 | 0.3 | — | — | 1 | 1.3 | — | — |

TABLE H (*Cont.*)

FUTURE SERVICE BENEFIT FORMULAS

| PER CENT (To be multiplied by years of future service) | TOTAL COMPANIES | | GROUP ANNUITY | | INDIVIDUAL ANNUITY | | SELF-ADMINISTERED | | COMBINATION AND OTHERS | |
|---|---|---|---|---|---|---|---|---|---|---|
| | *Com-panies* | *Per Cent* | *Com-panies* | *Per Cent* | *Com-panies* | *Per Cent* | *Com-panies* | *Per Cent* | *Com-panies* | *Per Cent* |
| A NONUNIFORM PER CENT OF COMPENSATION (Cont.) | | | | | | | | | | |
| *Per Cent Changes at $3,000* (Cont.) | | | | | | | | | | |
| 1⅓% first $3,000, 1⅔% of excess........ | 1 | 0.2 | 1 | 0.3 | — | — | — | — | — | — |
| 1⅓% first $3,000, 2% of excess.......... | 1 | 0.2 | 1 | 0.3 | — | — | — | — | — | — |
| 1½% first $3,000, 2% of excess.......... | 3 | 0.7 | 3 | 1.0 | — | — | — | — | — | — |
| *Per Cent Changes at $600 and $3,000* | | | | | | | | | | |
| 3/10% first $600, 1 2/10% excess to $3,000, 1¾% of excess.................... | 1 | 0.2 | 1 | 0.3 | — | — | — | — | — | — |
| 3/10% first $600, 1 2/10% excess to $3,000, 2% of excess...................... | 1 | 0.2 | 1 | 0.3 | — | — | — | — | — | — |
| ½% first $600, 1½% excess to $3,000, 2% of excess...................... | 1 | 0.2 | 1 | 0.3 | — | — | — | — | — | — |
| ¾% first $600, 1¾% excess to $3,000, 2% of excess...................... | 1 | 0.2 | 1 | 0.3 | — | — | — | — | — | — |
| *Per Cent Changes at $600 and $10,000* | | | | | | | | | | |
| ½% first $600, 1% excess to $10,000, ⅞% of excess.......................... | 1 | 0.2 | 1 | 0.3 | — | — | — | — | — | — |
| *Per Cent Changes at $1,200 and $3,000* | | | | | | | | | | |
| 9/16% first $1,200, 1½% excess to $3,000, 2% of excess...................... | 1 | 0.2 | 1 | 0.3 | — | — | — | — | — | — |
| ½% first $1,200, ¾% excess to $3,000, 1½% of excess.................... | 1 | 0.2 | 1 | 0.3 | — | — | — | — | — | — |
| ¾% first $1,200, 1% excess to $3,000, 1½% of excess.................... | 4 | 0.9 | 3 | 1.0 | — | — | 1 | 1.3 | — | — |

## TABLE H (Cont.)

### FUTURE SERVICE BENEFIT FORMULAS

| PER CENT (To be multiplied by years of future service) | TOTAL COMPANIES | | GROUP ANNUITY | | INDIVIDUAL ANNUITY | | SELF-ADMINISTERED | | COMBINATION AND OTHERS | |
|---|---|---|---|---|---|---|---|---|---|---|
| | Companies | Per Cent | Companies | Per Cent | Companies | Per Cent | Companies | Per Cent | Companies | Per Cent |
| **A NONUNIFORM PER CENT OF COMPENSATION (Cont.)** | | | | | | | | | | |
| *Per Cent Changes at $1,200 and $3,000 (Cont.)* | | | | | | | | | | |
| ¾% first $1,200, 1% excess to $3,000, 2% of excess.... | 1 | 0.2 | 1 | 0.3 | | | | | — | — |
| 1% first $1,200, ¾% excess to $3,000, 1½% of excess.... | 1 | 0.2 | 1 | 0.3 | | | | | — | — |
| 1% first $1,200, 1½% excess to $3,000, 2% of excess.... | 1 | 0.2 | 1 | 0.3 | | | | | — | — |
| *Per Cent Changes at $1,500 and $3,000* | | | | | | | | | | |
| 6/10% first $1,500, 1% excess to $3,000, 1½% of excess.... | 1 | 0.2 | 1 | 0.3 | | | | | — | — |
| *Per Cent Changes at $1,800 and $3,000* | | | | | | | | | | |
| ¾% first $1,800, 1% excess to $3,000, 1½% of excess.... | 3 | 0.7 | 3 | 1.0 | | | | | — | — |
| *Per Cent Changes at $3,000 and $10,000* | | | | | | | | | | |
| ¾% first $3,000, 1½% excess to $10,000, ¾% of excess.... | 1 | 0.2 | 1 | 0.3 | | | | | — | — |
| 1% first $3,000, 1⅔% excess to $10,000, 1% of excess.... | 1 | 0.2 | 1 | 0.3 | | | | | — | — |
| 1% first $3,000, 2% excess to $10,000, 1½% of excess.... | 1 | 0.2 | 1 | 0.3 | | | | | — | — |
| *Per Cent Changes at $3,000 and $20,000* | | | | | | | | | | |
| ¾% first $3,000, 1¾% excess to $20,000, 1% of excess.... | 1 | 0.2 | — | — | | | 1 | 1.3 | — | — |

## TABLE H (*Cont.*)

### FUTURE SERVICE BENEFIT FORMULAS

| PER CENT (To be multiplied by years of future service) | TOTAL COMPANIES | | GROUP ANNUITY | | INDIVIDUAL ANNUITY | | SELF-ADMINISTERED | | COMBINATION AND OTHERS | |
|---|---|---|---|---|---|---|---|---|---|---|
| | Companies | Per Cent | Companies | Per Cent | Companies | Per Cent | Companies | Per Cent | Companies | Per Cent |
| A NONUNIFORM PER CENT OF PORTION OF COMPENSATION | 31 | 7.1 | 25 | 8.1 | — | — | 6 | 7.8 | — | — |
| *Per Cent Changes at $3,000, no Benefit on First $600* | | | | | | | | | | |
| 1% first $3,000, 1⅜% of excess | 1 | 0.2 | 1 | 0.3 | | | | | | |
| 1% first $3,000, 1½% of excess | 16 | 3.7 | 14 | 4.5 | | | | | | |
| 1% first $3,000, 2% of excess | 2 | 0.5 | 2 | 0.6 | | | | | | |
| 1 2/10% first $3,000, 1 8/10% of excess | 1 | 0.2 | 1 | 0.3 | | | | | | |
| 1¼% first $3,000, 1½% of excess | 2 | 0.5 | | | | | 2 | 2.6 | | |
| 1½% first $3,000, 2% of excess | 2 | 0.5 | 2 | 0.6 | | | 2 | 2.6 | | |
| *Per Cent Changes at $5,000, no Benefit on First $600* | | | | | | | | | | |
| 1% first $5,000, 1½% of excess | 1 | 0.2 | 1 | 0.3 | | | | | | |
| *Per Cent Changes at $1,800 and $3,000, no Benefit on First $600* | | | | | | | | | | |
| 4/10% first $1,800, 6/10% excess to $3,000, 1% of excess | 1 | 0.2 | | | | | 1 | 1.3 | | |
| *Per Cent Changes at $3,000 and $6,000, no Benefit on First $600* | | | | | | | | | | |
| 1% first $3,000, 1¼% excess to $6,000, 1% of excess | 1 | 0.2 | 1 | 0.3 | | | | | | |
| *Per Cent Changes at $3,000, no Benefit on First $1,000* | | | | | | | | | | |
| ¾% first $3,000, 1% of excess | 1 | 0.2 | 1 | 0.3 | | | | | | |
| 1% first $3,000, 1½% of excess | 1 | 0.2 | 1 | 0.3 | | | | | | |

## TABLE H (Cont.)

### FUTURE SERVICE BENEFIT FORMULAS

| PER CENT (To be multiplied by years of future service) | TOTAL COMPANIES | | GROUP ANNUITY | | INDIVIDUAL ANNUITY | | SELF-ADMINISTERED | | COMBINATION AND OTHERS | |
|---|---|---|---|---|---|---|---|---|---|---|
| | Companies | Per Cent | Companies | Per Cent | Companies | Per Cent | Companies | Per Cent | Companies | Per Cent |
| **A NONUNIFORM PER CENT OF PORTION OF COMPENSATION (Cont.)** | | | | | | | | | | |
| *Per Cent Changes at $10,000, no Benefit on First $3,000* | | | | | | | | | | |
| 1¾% first $10,000, 1½% of excess | 1 | 0.2 | 1 | 0.3 | — | — | — | | | |
| 2% first $10,000, 1% of excess | 1 | 0.2 | — | — | — | — | 1 | 1.3 | | |
| **A VARIABLE RATE** | 4 | 0.9 | 2 | 0.6 | — | — | 2 | 2.6 | — | — |
| Varies as to age at which service was rendered | 1 | 0.2 | 1 | 0.3 | — | — | — | | | |
| Varies as to occupation | 1 | 0.2 | 1 | 0.3 | — | — | — | | — | — |
| Varies as to earnings | 1 | 0.2 | — | — | — | — | 1 | 1.3 | | |
| Different rates after commencement of employee contributions | 1 | 0.2 | — | — | — | — | 1 | 1.3 | — | — |
| **MISCELLANEOUS** | 99 | 22.7 | 75 | 24.2 | 14 | 36.8 | 5 | 6.5 | 5 | 41.7 |
| Money-Purchase Plans | 66 | 15.1 | 49 | 15.8 | 9 | 23.7 | 4 | 5.2 | 4 | 33.3 |
| Others | 29 | 6.6 | 26 | 8.4 | 1 | 2.6 | 1 | 1.3 | 1 | 8.3 |
| Detailed Information Not Obtained | 4 | 0.9 | — | — | 4 | 10.5 | — | | — | — |
| **PLANS DIVIDED INTO FUTURE AND PAST SERVICE** | 437 | 100.0 | 310 | 100.0 | 38 | 100.0 | 77 | 100.0 | 12 | 100.0 |
| **PLANS BASING BENEFITS ON FUTURE AND PAST SERVICE** | 437 | 71.4 | 310 | 99.0 | 38 | 25.0 | 77 | 63.6 | 12 | 46.2 |
| **PLANS USING OTHER METHODS** | 175 | 28.6 | 3 | 1.0 | 114 | 75.0 | 44 | 36.4 | 14 | 53.8 |
| **TOTALS** | 612 | 100.0 | 313 | 100.0 | 152 | 100.0 | 121 | 100.0 | 26 | 100.0 |

75% of the plans which provide pension benefits based on future service, likewise offer past service benefits. Money-purchase plans are an exception, for only a few of this type also make provision for the purchase of past service benefits. It may be noted that in computing the past service benefits a relatively greater number of plans give credits as a uniform percentage of all compensation than do so in determining future service benefits. In so doing, however, the typical percentages are lower, with $\frac{1}{2}\%$, $\frac{3}{4}\%$, and 1% most frequently employed; or respectively one-half of the typical percentage credits granted for future service.

Under the majority of the plans, and under all types, the compensation specified as the basis for computation of past service benefits is the annual compensation received at the time of entrance or eligibility. A minority of plans specify, or define, compensation for past service benefits differently. For example, an average of the annual compensation received for 3, 5, or 10 years prior to becoming eligible to the plan is specified in some instances; the annual average of all compensation received prior to eligibility, in a few others. Again, in a small number of plans, self-administered, it is provided that the average of the final compensation received in the last 10 years preceding normal retirement date should be the basis for computing past service benefits.

### 3. Other Methods

Plans that make no division between future and past service are about 30% of the total. In this group, 175 plans, pension benefits are mainly provided as (1) a flat percentage of the annual compensation without direct reference to service, (2) a percentage of annual compensation multiplied by total years of service, (3) a flat benefit. Whenever either of the first two methods is employed all or a portion of compensation may be considered; to which, in turn, the same or different per cents are applied.

Under the flat percentage method the more common procedure is to take the annual compensation upon entrance into the plan as a base, and apply to it a flat per cent, to arrive at the pension benefit. This flat percentage method, as may be observed in Table J, is clearly associated with individual annuity plans, for it is employed in 89 plans, or over 50% of the 175 plans using other methods; only 7 self-administered and 2 group annuity plans do so.

The procedure of granting a percentage credit of some or all compensation for each year of service, on the other hand, is followed

TABLE I

## Past Service Benefit Formulas

| Per Cent (To be multiplied by years of allowed past service) | Total Companies | | Group Annuity | | Individual Annuity | | Self-Administered | | Combination and Others | |
|---|---|---|---|---|---|---|---|---|---|---|
| | Companies | Per Cent | Companies | Per Cent | Companies | Per Cent | Companies | Per Cent | Companies | Per Cent |
| A Uniform Per Cent of Compensation | 170 | 38.9 | 112 | 36.1 | 15 | 39.5 | 37 | 48.1 | 6 | 50.0 |
| 4/10% | 1 | 0.2 | — | — | — | — | — | — | 1 | 8.3 |
| 1/2% | 21 | 4.8 | 13 | 4.2 | 4 | 10.5 | 2 | 2.6 | 2 | 16.7 |
| 2/8% | 2 | 0.5 | 2 | 0.6 | — | — | — | — | — | — |
| 7/10% | 1 | 0.2 | — | — | 1 | 2.6 | — | — | — | — |
| 3/4% | 26 | 5.9 | 18 | 5.8 | 4 | 10.5 | 4 | 5.2 | — | — |
| 8/10% | 3 | 0.7 | 2 | 0.6 | — | — | 1 | 1.3 | — | — |
| 85/100% | 1 | 0.2 | 1 | 0.3 | — | — | — | — | — | — |
| 7/8% | 1 | 0.2 | 1 | 0.3 | 6 | 15.8 | 21 | 27.3 | 1 | 8.3 |
| 1% | 90 | 20.6 | 62 | 20.0 | — | — | — | — | — | — |
| 1 1/4% | 3 | 0.7 | 3 | 1.0 | — | — | 8 | 10.4 | 1 | 8.3 |
| 1 1/2% | 12 | 2.7 | 3 | 1.0 | — | — | 1 | 1.3 | 1 | 8.3 |
| 2% | 9 | 2.1 | 7 | 2.3 | — | — | — | — | — | — |
| A Uniform Per Cent of Portion of Compensation | 47 | 10.8 | 31 | 10.0 | 5 | 13.2 | 9 | 11.7 | 2 | 16.7 |
| First $3,000 | | | | | | | | | | |
| 1% | 2 | 0.5 | 2 | 0.6 | — | — | — | — | — | — |
| First $3,600 | | | | | | | | | | |
| 1% | 1 | 0.2 | 1 | 0.3 | — | — | — | — | — | — |
| Excess over $600 | | | | | | | | | | |
| 1/2% | 3 | 0.7 | 2 | 0.6 | — | — | 1 | 1.3 | — | — |
| 5/7% | 2 | 0.5 | 2 | 0.6 | — | — | — | — | — | — |
| 3/4% | 1 | 0.2 | 1 | 0.3 | — | — | — | — | — | — |
| 1% | 8 | 1.8 | 5 | 1.6 | — | — | 3 | 3.9 | — | — |

## TABLE I (Cont.)

### Past Service Benefit Formulas

| PER CENT (To be multiplied by years of allowed past service) | TOTAL COMPANIES | | GROUP ANNUITY | | INDIVIDUAL ANNUITY | | SELF-ADMINISTERED | | COMBINATION AND OTHERS | |
|---|---|---|---|---|---|---|---|---|---|---|
| | Companies | Per Cent | Companies | Per Cent | Companies | Per Cent | Companies | Per Cent | Companies | Per Cent |
| **A UNIFORM PER CENT OF PORTION OF COMPENSATION (Cont.)** | | | | | | | | | | |
| *Excess over $2,600* | | | | | | | | | | |
| 1% ............................. | 1 | 0.2 | 1 | 0.3 | | | | | | |
| *Excess over $3,000* | | | | | | | | | | |
| 3/8% ........................... | 2 | 0.5 | 2 | 0.6 | | | | | | |
| 3/4% ........................... | 18 | 4.1 | 9 | 2.9 | 5 | 13.2 | 3 | 3.9 | 1 | 8.3 |
| 1% ............................. | 8 | 1.8 | 6 | 1.9 | | | 2 | 2.6 | | |
| 1½% ........................... | 1 | 0.2 | | | | | | | 1 | 8.3 |
| **A NONUNIFORM PER CENT OF COMPENSATION** ............ | 65 | 14.9 | 43 | 13.9 | 3 | 7.9 | 18 | 23.4 | 1 | 8.3 |
| *Per Cent Changes at $1,200* | | | | | | | | | | |
| 6/10% first $1,200, 3/4% of excess.... | 1 | 0.2 | 1 | 0.3 | | | | | | |
| 1% first $1,200, 1½% of excess.... | 1 | 0.2 | 1 | 0.3 | | | | | | |
| *Per Cent Changes at $1,500* | | | | | | | | | | |
| 1/3% first $1,500, 1/2% of excess.... | 1 | 0.2 | 1 | 0.3 | | | | | | |
| *Per Cent Changes at $3,000* | | | | | | | | | | |
| 1/4% first $3,000, 3/4% of excess.... | 1 | 0.2 | 1 | 0.3 | | | 1 | 1.3 | | |
| 1/4% first $3,000, 1% of excess.... | 1 | 0.2 | 1 | 0.3 | | | | | | |
| 1/2% first $3,000, 3/4% of excess.... | 1 | 0.2 | 1 | 0.3 | | | | | | |
| 1/2% first $3,000, 1% of excess.... | 14 | 3.2 | 7 | 2.3 | 2 | 5.3 | 5 | 6.5 | | |
| 3/4% first $3,000, 3/4% of excess.... | 1 | 0.2 | 1 | 0.3 | | | | | | |
| 6/10% first $3,000, 8/10% of excess.... | 2 | 0.5 | 2 | 0.6 | | | | | | |
| 6/10% first $3,000, 1% of excess.... | 1 | 0.2 | | | | | 1 | 1.3 | | |

## TABLE I (*Cont.*)

### Past Service Benefit Formulas

| Per Cent (To be multiplied by years of allowed past service) | Total Companies | | Group Annuity | | Individual Annuity | | Self-Administered | | Combination and Others | |
|---|---|---|---|---|---|---|---|---|---|---|
| | *Companies* | *Per Cent* | *Companies* | *Per Cent* | *Companies* | *Per Cent* | *Companies* | *Per Cent* | *Companies* | *Per Cent* |
| A Nonuniform Per Cent of Compensation (Cont.) | | | | | | | | | | |
| *Per Cent Changes at $3,000* (Cont.) | | | | | | | | | | |
| 6/10% first $3,000, 1 2/10% of excess | 1 | 0.2 | — | — | — | — | 1 | 1.3 | — | — |
| ⅔% first $3,000, ⅓% of excess | 1 | 0.2 | — | — | — | — | 1 | 1.3 | — | — |
| ⅔% first $3,000, 1⅓% of excess | 2 | 0.5 | 2 | 0.6 | — | — | — | — | — | — |
| ⅔% first $3,000, 1⅔% of excess | 1 | 0.2 | 1 | 0.3 | — | — | — | — | — | — |
| 7/10% first $3,000, 1 4/10% of excess | 1 | 0.2 | 1 | 0.3 | — | — | — | — | — | — |
| ¾% first $3,000, 1% of excess | 4 | 0.9 | 4 | 1.3 | — | — | — | — | — | — |
| ¾% first $3,000, 1¼% of excess | 2 | 0.5 | 1 | 0.3 | — | — | — | — | 1 | 8.3 |
| ¾% first $3,000, 1½% of excess | 8 | 1.8 | 5 | 1.6 | 1 | 2.6 | 2 | 2.6 | — | — |
| 1% first $3,000, ½% of excess | 1 | 0.2 | 1 | 0.3 | — | — | — | — | — | — |
| 1% first $3,000, ¾% of excess | 1 | 0.2 | — | — | — | — | 1 | 1.3 | — | — |
| 1% first $3,000, 1½% of excess | 1 | 0.2 | 1 | 0.3 | — | — | — | — | — | — |
| 1% first $3,000, 1¾% of excess | 1 | 0.2 | — | — | — | — | 1 | 1.3 | — | — |
| 1% first $3,000, 2% of excess | 4 | 0.9 | 4 | 1.3 | — | — | — | — | — | — |
| 1¼% first $3,000, 2% of excess | 1 | 0.2 | — | — | — | — | 1 | 1.3 | — | — |
| 1½% first $3,000, 2% of excess | 1 | 0.2 | — | — | — | — | 1 | 1.3 | — | — |
| *Per Cent Changes at $4,000* | | | | | | | | | | |
| 1% first $4,000, ¾% of excess | 2 | 0.5 | 1 | 0.3 | — | — | 1 | 1.3 | — | — |
| *Per Cent Changes at $600 and $3,000* | | | | | | | | | | |
| 3/10% first $600, 1% excess to $3,000, 1¼% of excess | 1 | 0.2 | 1 | 0.3 | — | — | — | — | — | — |
| *Per Cent Changes at $600 and $10,000* | | | | | | | | | | |
| ½% first $600, 1% excess to $10,000, ⅞% of excess | 1 | 0.2 | 1 | 0.3 | — | — | — | — | — | — |

TABLE I (Cont.)

PAST SERVICE BENEFIT FORMULAS

| PER CENT (To be multiplied by years of allowed past service) | TOTAL COMPANIES | | GROUP ANNUITY | | INDIVIDUAL ANNUITY | | SELF-ADMINISTERED | | COMBINATION AND OTHERS | |
|---|---|---|---|---|---|---|---|---|---|---|
| | Companies | Per Cent | Companies | Per Cent | Companies | Per Cent | Companies | Per Cent | Companies | Per Cent |
| **A NONUNIFORM PER CENT OF COMPENSATION (Cont.)** | | | | | | | | | | |
| *Per Cent Changes at $1,200 and $3,000* | | | | | | | | | | |
| ½% first $1,200, ¾% excess to $3,000, 1½% of excess..... | 1 | 0.2 | 1 | 0.3 | | | | | | |
| ¾% first $1,200, 1% excess to $3,000, 1½% of excess..... | 2 | 0.5 | 1 | 0.3 | | | 1 | 1.3 | | |
| 1% first $1,200, 1½% excess to $3,000, 2% of excess..... | 1 | 0.2 | 1 | 0.3 | | | | | | |
| *Per Cent Changes at $1,500 and $2,500* | | | | | | | | | | |
| 1½% first $1,500, 1¼% excess to $2,500, 1% of excess..... | 1 | 0.2 | 1 | 0.3 | | | | | | |
| *Per Cent Changes at $3,000 and $10,000* | | | | | | | | | | |
| 1% first $3,000, 2% excess to $10,000, 1½% of excess..... | 1 | 0.2 | 1 | 0.3 | | | | | | |
| *Per Cent Changes at $3,000 and $20,000* | | | | | | | | | | |
| 55/100% first $3,000, 1 3/10% excess to $20,000, 1% of excess..... | 1 | 0.2 | | | | | 1 | 1.3 | | |
| **A NONUNIFORM PER CENT OF PORTION OF COMPENSATION..... ** | 12 | 2.7 | 11 | 3.5 | — | — | 1 | 1.3 | — | — |
| *Per Cent Changes at $3,000, no Benefit on First $600* | | | | | | | | | | |
| ⅔% first $3,000, 1% of excess..... | 1 | 0.2 | 1 | 0.3 | | | | | | |
| ¾% first $3,000, 1% of excess..... | 4 | 0.9 | 3 | 1.0 | | | 1 | 1.3 | | |

## TABLE I (Cont.)

### Past Service Benefit Formulas

| Per Cent (To be multiplied by years of allowed past service) | Total Companies | | Group Annuity | | Individual Annuity | | Self-Administered | | Combination and Others | |
|---|---|---|---|---|---|---|---|---|---|---|
| | Companies | Per Cent | Companies | Per Cent | Companies | Per Cent | Companies | Per Cent | Companies | Per Cent |
| **A Nonuniform Per Cent of Portion of Compensation (Cont.)** | | | | | | | | | | |
| *Per Cent Changes at $3,000, no Benefit on First $600 (Cont.)* | | | | | | | | | | |
| 1% first $3,000, ¾% of excess.......... | 2 | 0.5 | 2 | 0.6 | | | | | | |
| 1% first $3,000, 1⅓% of excess.......... | 1 | 0.2 | 1 | 0.3 | | | | | — | — |
| 1% first $3,000, 1½% of excess.......... | 1 | 0.2 | 1 | 0.3 | | | | | — | — |
| *Per Cent Changes at $5,000, no Benefit on First $600* | | | | | | | | | | |
| ½% first $5,000, 1½% of excess......... | 1 | 0.2 | 1 | 0.3 | | | | | — | — |
| *Per Cent Changes at $3,000, no Benefit on First $1,000* | | | | | | | | | | |
| ¾% first $3,000, 1% of excess.......... | 1 | 0.2 | 1 | 0.3 | | | | | — | — |
| *Per Cent Changes at $10,000, no Benefit on First $3,000* | | | | | | | | | | |
| 1½% first $10,000, 1% of excess......... | 1 | 0.2 | 1 | 0.3 | | | | | — | — |
| **A Variable Rate............** | 37 | 8.5 | 30 | 9.7 | — | — | 4 | 5.2 | 3 | 25.0 |
| Varies as to age when past service was rendered............ | 18 | 4.1 | 16 | 5.2 | | | 1 | 1.3 | 1 | 8.3 |
| Varies as to age when past service was rendered and sex......... | 1 | 0.2 | 1 | 0.3 | | | | | — | — |
| Varies as to dates when past service was rendered......... | 5 | 1.1 | 3 | 1.0 | | | 1 | 1.3 | 1 | 8.3 |
| Varies as to age at retirement............ | 1 | 0.2 | 1 | 0.3 | | | | | — | — |

## TABLE I (Cont.)

### Past Service Benefit Formulas

| PER CENT (To be multiplied by years of allowed past service) | TOTAL COMPANIES | | GROUP ANNUITY | | INDIVIDUAL ANNUITY | | SELF-ADMINISTERED | | COMBINATION AND OTHERS | |
|---|---|---|---|---|---|---|---|---|---|---|
| | Companies | Per Cent | Companies | Per Cent | Companies | Per Cent | Companies | Per Cent | Companies | Per Cent |
| **A Variable Rate (Cont.)** | | | | | | | | | | |
| Varies as to age at retirement and sex | 1 | 0.2 | 1 | 0.3 | — | — | — | — | — | — |
| Varies as to age at date of establishment | 1 | 0.2 | 1 | 0.3 | — | — | — | — | — | — |
| Varies as to date of employment | 2 | 0.5 | 1 | 0.3 | — | — | 1 | 1.3 | — | — |
| Varies as to occupation | 3 | 0.7 | 3 | 1.0 | — | — | — | — | — | — |
| Varies as to amount of past service | 5 | 1.1 | 3 | 1.0 | — | — | 1 | 1.3 | 1 | 8.3 |
| Miscellaneous | 106 | 24.3 | 83 | 26.8 | 15 | 39.5 | 8 | 10.4 | — | — |
| No Past Service Benefit | 97 | 22.2 | 79 | 25.5 | 11 | 28.9 | 7 | 9.1 | — | — |
| Others | 2 | 0.5 | 1 | 0.3 | — | — | 1 | 1.3 | — | — |
| Information Not Obtained | 7 | 1.6 | 3 | 1.0 | 4 | 10.5 | — | — | — | — |
| **PLANS DIVIDED INTO PAST AND FUTURE SERVICE** | 437 | 100.0 | 310 | 100.0 | 38 | 100.0 | 77 | 100.0 | 12 | 100.0 |
| **PLANS DIVIDED INTO PAST AND FUTURE SERVICE BENEFITS** | 437 | 71.4 | 310 | 99.0 | 38 | 25.0 | 77 | 63.6 | 12 | 46.2 |
| PLANS USING OTHER METHODS | 175 | 28.6 | 3 | 1.0 | 114 | 75.0 | 44 | 36.4 | 14 | 53.8 |
| **TOTALS** | 612 | 100.0 | 313 | 100.0 | 152 | 100.0 | 121 | 100.0 | 26 | 100.0 |

by self-administered plans; for 27, or about 60% of the 44 self-administered plans using other methods, employ it.

A few plans, 4, simply give a flat benefit without reference to compensation or service; 2 provide a flat benefit but make it subject to years of service.

Finally, it was found that among the self-administered plans using other methods, about 50%, 22 plans, define compensation as the average of final compensation received in the last years of service. For example, 6 companies use the average of final compensation in the 10 years of service prior to retirement; 12, in the last 5 years. Four plans use the annual compensation received *at* retirement.

## I. Contribution Schemes

### 1. All Contributory Plans

Pension plans may be contributory or non-contributory, whether of a definite-benefit or money-purchase character. Of the 612 plans, 385 are contributory, or about 63%. As between the several types, however, differences appear. About 86% of group annuity plans are contributory, but only 41% of self-administered and less than 32% of individual annuity plans.

The detailed contribution schemes employed are shown in Table K-1. The methods mainly used for determining contributions are analogous to those used in computing future service benefits; that is, contributions are obtained either as a uniform or as a nonuniform per cent of some or all of compensation. The large majority of the plans, 249, base the contributions on the entire compensation; but in applying the percentage a nonuniform per cent, such as 2% of the first $3,000, 4% of the excess, is the more common practice. This is largely true of group annuity plans, as might be expected; for as the table on future service benefits shows (Table H), group annuity plans largely provide benefits as a nonuniform per cent of compensation. It will be recalled that contributory group annuity (definite-benefit) plans usually fix employee contributions in relation to benefits. For example, if the annuity credit or benefit is 1% of compensation, the contribution is 2%;[12] or if contributions are 2% of the first $3,000, and 4% of the excess, then the benefits are 1% and 2% respectively.

The more common contribution scheme, where all compensation

---

[12] See pp. 107-109 for discussion.

## TABLE J

### Other Methods of Computing Pension Benefits

| Benefit Formulas | Total Companies | | Group Annuity | | Individual Annuity | | Self-Administered | | Combination and Others | |
|---|---|---|---|---|---|---|---|---|---|---|
| | Com-panies | Per Cent | Com-panies | Per Cent | Com-panies | Per Cent | Com-panies | Per Cent | Com-panies | Per Cent |
| A—Flat Percentage of Compensation.. | 101 | 57.7 | 2 | 66.7 | 89 | 78.1 | 7 | 15.9 | 3 | 21.4 |
| Uniform Per Cent of Compensation.. | 41 | 23.4 | — | — | 38 | 33.3 | 3 | 6.8 | — | — |
| 12½%................ | 1 | 0.6 | — | | 1 | 0.9 | — | | — | |
| 20%................ | 3 | 1.7 | — | | 3 | 2.6 | — | | — | |
| 24%................ | 2 | 1.1 | — | | 2 | 1.8 | — | | — | |
| 25%................ | 13 | 7.4 | — | | 11 | 9.6 | 2 | 4.5 | — | |
| 30%................ | 7 | 4.0 | — | | 7 | 6.1 | — | | — | |
| 33⅓%............... | 4 | 2.3 | — | | 4 | 3.5 | — | | — | |
| 35%................ | 4 | 2.3 | — | | 4 | 3.5 | — | | — | |
| 40%................ | 5 | 2.9 | — | | 4 | 3.5 | 1 | 2.3 | — | |
| 50%................ | 2 | 1.1 | — | | 2 | 1.8 | — | | — | |
| Uniform Per Cent of Portion of Compensation.............. | 12 | 6.9 | — | — | 8 | 7.0 | 2 | 4.5 | 2 | 14.3 |
| First $3,000 | | | | | | | | | | |
| 30%............... | 1 | 0.6 | | | — | | 1 | 2.3 | | |
| Excess over $500 | | | | | | | | | | |
| 25%............... | 1 | 0.6 | | | 1 | 0.9 | | | | |
| Excess over $600 | | | | | | | | | | |
| 40%............... | 1 | 0.6 | | | 1 | 0.9 | | | | |
| Excess over $1,200 | | | | | | | | | | |
| 30%............... | 1 | 0.6 | | | 1 | 0.9 | | | | |
| Excess over $2,400 | | | | | | | | | | |
| 30%............... | 1 | 0.6 | | | 1 | 0.9 | | | | |

## TABLE J (Cont.)

### Other Methods of Computing Pension Benefits

| Benefit Formulas | Total Companies | | Group Annuity | | Individual Annuity | | Self-Administered | | Combination and Others | |
|---|---|---|---|---|---|---|---|---|---|---|
| | Com-panies | Per Cent | Com-panies | Per Cent | Com-panies | Per Cent | Com-panies | Per Cent | Com-panies | Per Cent |
| **Uniform Per Cent of Portion of Compensation (Cont.)** | | | | | | | | | | |
| *Excess over $3,000* | | | | | | | | | | |
| 20%............... | 1 | 0.6 | — | — | | | | | 1 | 7.1 |
| 25%............... | 2 | 1.1 | — | — | 1 | 0.9 | — | | 1 | 7.1 |
| 30%............... | 4 | 2.3 | — | — | 3 | 2.6 | 1 | 2.3 | | |
| **Nonuniform Per Cent of Compensation** | 22 | 12.6 | 2 | 66.7 | 19 | 16.7 | — | — | 1 | 7.1 |
| *Per Cent Changes at $1,200* | | | | | | | | | | |
| 20% first $1,200, 30% of excess......... | 1 | 0.6 | | | 1 | 0.9 | | | | |
| *Per Cent Changes at $1,500* | | | | | | | | | | |
| 16% first $1,500, 24% of excess......... | 2 | 1.1 | | | 2 | 1.8 | | | | |
| *Per Cent Changes at $3,000* | | | | | | | | | | |
| 6% first $3,000, 25% of excess......... | 1 | 0.6 | | | 1 | 0.9 | | | | |
| 10% first $3,000, 30% of excess......... | 1 | 0.6 | | | 1 | 0.9 | | | | |
| 14% first $3,000, 10% of excess......... | 1 | 0.6 | | | 1 | 0.9 | | | | |
| 15% first $3,000, 30% of excess......... | 2 | 1.1 | | | 2 | 1.8 | | | | |
| 20% first $3,000, 15% of excess......... | 1 | 0.6 | | | 1 | 0.9 | | | | |
| 20% first $3,000, 30% of excess......... | 2 | 1.1 | | | 1 | 0.9 | | | 1 | 7.1 |
| 25% first $3,000, 50% of excess......... | 3 | 1.7 | 1 | 33.3 | 2 | 1.8 | | | | |
| 30% first $3,000, 20% of excess......... | 1 | 0.6 | | | 1 | 0.9 | | | | |
| 33⅓% first $3,000, 50% of excess..... | 1 | 0.6 | | | 1 | 0.9 | | | | |
| 40% first $3,000, 30% of excess......... | 1 | 0.6 | | | 1 | 0.9 | | | | |
| 50% first $3,000, 30% of excess......... | 1 | 0.6 | | | 1 | 0.9 | | | | |

## Other Methods of Computing Pension Benefits

| Benefit Formulas | Total Companies | | Group Annuity | | Individual Annuity | | Self-Administered | | Combination and Others | |
|---|---|---|---|---|---|---|---|---|---|---|
| | Companies | Per Cent | Companies | Per Cent | Companies | Per Cent | Companies | Per Cent | Companies | Per Cent |
| Nonuniform Per Cent of Compensation (Cont.) | | | | | | | | | | |
| *Per Cent Changes at $1,200 and $3,000* 25% first $1,200, 30% excess to $3,000, 45% of excess......... | 1 | 0.6 | | | 1 | 0.9 | | | — | — |
| *Per Cent Changes at $1,500, and $3,000* 12% first $1,500, 24% excess to $3,000, 40% of excess......... | 1 | 0.6 | | | 1 | 0.9 | | | — | — |
| 16% first $1,500, 24% excess to $3,000, 30% of excess......... | 1 | 0.6 | | | 1 | 0.9 | | | — | — |
| *Per Cent Changes at $3,000 and $6,000* 15% first $3,000, 22½% excess to $6,000, 30% of excess......... | 1 | 0.6 | 1 | 33.3 | — | — | — | | — | — |
| Nonuniform Per Cent of Portion of Compensation... | 3 | 1.7 | — | — | 3 | 2.6 | — | — | — | — |
| *Per Cent Changes at $3,000, no Benefit on First $1,800* 20% first $3,000, 30% excess......... | 3 | 1.7 | — | — | 3 | 2.6 | — | — | — | — |
| Variable Rate......... | 6 | 3.4 | — | — | 6 | 5.3 | — | — | — | — |
| Varies as to years of service......... | 2 | 1.1 | — | — | 2 | 1.8 | — | — | — | — |
| Varies as to age at entry......... | 1 | 0.6 | — | — | 1 | 0.9 | — | — | — | — |
| Varies as to earnings......... | 2 | 1.1 | — | — | 2 | 1.8 | — | — | — | — |
| Varies as to sex......... | 1 | 0.6 | — | — | 1 | 0.9 | — | — | — | — |
| Miscellaneous......... | 17 | 9.7 | — | — | 15 | 13.2 | 2 | 4.5 | — | — |

## OTHER METHODS OF COMPUTING PENSION BENEFITS

| Benefit Formulas | Total Companies | | Group Annuity | | Individual Annuity | | Self-Administered | | Combination and Others | |
|---|---|---|---|---|---|---|---|---|---|---|
| | Companies | Per Cent | Companies | Per Cent | Companies | Per Cent | Companies | Per Cent | Companies | Per Cent |
| B—Percentage of Compensation Multiplied by Total Service | 39 | 22.3 | — | — | 10 | 8.8 | 27 | 61.4 | 2 | 14.3 |
| Uniform Per Cent of Compensation | 26 | 14.9 | — | — | 7 | 6.1 | 18 | 40.9 | 1 | 7.1 |
| 1/2% | 1 | 0.6 | — | — | | | — | — | 1 | 7.1 |
| 4/10% | 1 | 0.6 | — | — | 1 | 0.9 | | | | |
| 3/4% | 2 | 1.1 | — | — | 1 | 0.9 | 1 | 2.3 | | |
| 7/8% | 1 | 0.6 | — | — | | | 1 | 2.3 | | |
| 1% | 13 | 7.4 | — | — | 4 | 3.5 | 9 | 20.5 | | |
| 1 1/4% | 1 | 0.6 | — | — | 1 | 0.9 | | | | |
| 1 1/2% | 6 | 3.4 | — | — | | | 6 | 13.6 | | |
| 2% | 1 | 0.6 | — | — | | | 1 | 2.3 | | |
| Uniform Per Cent of Portion of Compensation | 3 | 1.7 | — | — | 2 | 1.8 | 1 | 2.3 | — | — |
| *First $3,000* | | | | | | | | | | |
| 1% | 1 | 0.6 | — | — | | | 1 | 2.3 | | |
| *Excess over $3,000* | | | | | | | | | | |
| 1 1/2% | 2 | 1.1 | — | — | 2 | 1.8 | | | | |
| Nonuniform Per Cent of Compensation | 2 | 1.1 | — | — | 1 | 0.9 | 1 | 2.3 | — | — |
| *Per Cent Changes at $3,000* | | | | | | | | | | |
| 1/2% first $3,000, 1 1/4% excess | 1 | 0.6 | — | — | 1 | 0.9 | | | | |
| 1/2% first $3,000, 1 1/2% excess | 1 | 0.6 | — | — | | | 1 | 2.3 | | |

## TABLE J (Cont.)

### Other Methods of Computing Pension Benefits

| Benefit Formulas | Total Companies | | Group Annuity | | Individual Annuity | | Self-Administered | | Combination and Others | |
|---|---|---|---|---|---|---|---|---|---|---|
| | Companies | Per Cent | Companies | Per Cent | Companies | Per Cent | Companies | Per Cent | Companies | Per Cent |
| Nonuniform Per Cent of Portion of Compensation | — | — | — | — | — | — | — | — | — | — |
| Variable Rate | 4 | 2.3 | — | — | — | — | 4 | 9.1 | — | — |
| Varies as to date of employment | 1 | 0.6 | — | — | — | — | 1 | 2.3 | — | — |
| Varies if over 15 years' service | 1 | 0.6 | — | — | — | — | 1 | 2.3 | — | — |
| Varies if over 20 years' service | 1 | 0.6 | — | — | — | — | 1 | 2.3 | — | — |
| Varies if over 25 years' service | 1 | 0.6 | — | — | — | — | 1 | 2.3 | — | — |
| Miscellaneous | 4 | 2.3 | — | — | — | — | 3 | 6.8 | 1 | 7.1 |
| C—Flat Benefit | 6 | 3.4 | — | — | 3 | 2.6 | 3 | 6.8 | — | — |
| $480 | 1 | 0.6 | — | — | — | — | 1 | 2.3 | — | — |
| $600 | 2 | 1.1 | — | — | 2 | 1.8 | — | — | — | — |
| $1,200 | 1 | 0.6 | — | — | 1 | 0.9 | — | — | — | — |
| Varies as to years of service | 2 | 1.1 | — | — | — | — | 2 | 4.5 | — | — |
| D—Combined Forms | 29 | 16.6 | 1 | 33.3 | 12 | 10.5 | 7 | 15.9 | 9 | 64.3 |
| Future plus past plus flat percentage | 7 | 4.0 | — | — | 1 | 0.9 | 1 | 2.3 | 5 | 35.7 |
| Future plus past plus per cent of compensation times total service | 1 | 0.6 | — | — | — | — | — | — | — | — |
| Future plus flat percentage | 14 | 8.0 | 1 | 33.3 | 10 | 8.8 | 2 | 4.5 | 1 | 7.1 |
| Future plus percentage of compensation times total service | 1 | 0.6 | — | — | — | — | — | — | 1 | 7.1 |

## TABLE J (Cont.)

### OTHER METHODS OF COMPUTING PENSION BENEFITS

| BENEFIT FORMULAS | TOTAL COMPANIES | | GROUP ANNUITY | | INDIVIDUAL ANNUITY | | SELF-ADMINISTERED | | COMBINATION AND OTHERS | |
|---|---|---|---|---|---|---|---|---|---|---|
| | Com-panies | Per Cent | Com-panies | Per Cent | Com-panies | Per Cent | Com-panies | Per Cent | Com-panies | Per Cent |
| **D—COMBINED FORMS (Cont.)** | | | | | | | | | | |
| Flat percentage plus percentage of compensation times service.......... | 2 | 1.1 | — | | | | 1 | 2.3 | 1 | 7.1 |
| Flat percentage plus flat benefit.......... | 1 | 0.6 | — | | — | | 1 | — | 1 | 7.1 |
| Others.......... | 3 | 1.7 | — | | 1 | 0.9 | 2 | 4.5 | — | |
| TOTAL PLANS USING OTHER METHODS...... | 175 | 100.0 | 3 | 100.0 | 114 | 100.0 | 44 | 100.0 | 14 | 100.0 |
| PLANS USING OTHER METHODS......... | 175 | 28.6 | 3 | 1.0 | 114 | 75.0 | 44 | 36.4 | 14 | 53.8 |
| PLANS DIVIDED INTO FUTURE AND PAST SERVICE BENEFITS.......... | 437 | 71.4 | 310 | 99.0 | 38 | 25.0 | 77 | 63.6 | 12 | 46.2 |
| TOTALS.......... | 612 | 100.0 | 313 | 100.0 | 152 | 100.0 | 121 | 100.0 | 26 | 100.0 |

is used as a base and a uniform per cent applied thereto, is to obtain either 2% or 3% of it; and if contributions are based on only a portion of compensation, such as the excess over $3,000, then 3% or 5%.

If a nonuniform per cent of all compensation is the method, the typical contribution schemes are designed to obtain 2% of the first $3,000 and 4% of the excess; or 2% and 5%; or 2½% of the first $3,000 and 5% of the excess. Only a few plans are based on obtaining contributions as a nonuniform per cent of a portion of compensation.

### 2. Money-Purchase Plans

Money-purchase plans are included in Table K-1 for the purpose of distinguishing the number of contributory plans. That table, however, does not show the employer-employee contribution schemes which are used in money-purchase plans. In Table K-2, therefore, the several methods employed are set forth.

It will be noted that there are 73 money-purchase plans: 12% of the entire 612 plans, and about 20% of the 385 contributory plans. Of the 73 money-purchase plans, 57, or about 80%, are group annuities; the remaining 16 divide almost evenly between individual, self-administered, and combination and other plans.

The contribution scheme most commonly used under money-purchase plans, as shown in Table K-2, calls for a *nonuniform* percentage of all compensation to be contributed by employees, with the employer *matching*, or contributing an amount equal to the employee's.

### J.   Withdrawal (Severance) Benefits

### 1. Number of Plans

The granting of a withdrawal or severance benefit to an employee, that is, the vesting of an interest or share of the employer's contributions toward the cost of an employee's pension benefits, was found to be provided for in 461, or 79% of 586 [13] plans. 98 of the 586 plans have no vesting provisions, and definite information as to vesting in the remaining 27 was not obtained. As between the several types, vesting provisions were found in 90% of the group annuity, 93% of individual annuity plans. In contrast, only 32% of self-administered plans allow any vesting.

---

[13] Only 586 of the 612 plans were analyzed for vesting provisions. (See footnote, Table L-1.)

## TABLE K-1

### Contribution Schemes
### All Contributory Plans

| Contribution | Total Companies | | Group Annuity | | Individual Annuity | | Self-Administered | | Combination and Others | |
|---|---|---|---|---|---|---|---|---|---|---|
| | Companies | Per Cent | Companies | Per Cent | Companies | Per Cent | Companies | Per Cent | Companies | Per Cent |
| **I—A Uniform Per Cent of Compensation** | 60 | 15.6 | 34 | 12.6 | 13 | 27.1 | 9 | 18.4 | 4 | 21.1 |
| 1% | 3 | 0.8 | 1 | 0.4 | 1 | 2.1 | — | — | 1 | 5.3 |
| 1½% | 1 | 0.3 | 1 | 0.4 | — | — | — | — | — | — |
| 2% | 13 | 3.4 | 8 | 3.0 | 2 | 4.2 | 2 | 4.1 | 1 | 5.3 |
| 2¼% | 1 | 0.3 | 1 | 0.4 | — | — | — | — | — | — |
| 2½% | 1 | 0.3 | 1 | 0.4 | — | — | — | — | — | — |
| 2⅔% | 2 | 0.5 | 1 | 0.4 | — | — | — | — | — | — |
| 3% | 21 | 5.5 | 10 | 3.7 | 6 | 12.5 | 5 | 10.2 | 1 | 5.3 |
| 3⅓% | 1 | 0.3 | 1 | 0.4 | — | — | — | — | — | — |
| 3½% | 1 | 0.3 | 1 | 0.4 | — | — | — | — | — | — |
| 3¾% | 2 | 0.5 | 2 | 0.7 | — | — | — | — | — | — |
| 4% | 7 | 1.8 | 5 | 1.9 | 1 | 2.1 | 2 | 4.1 | — | — |
| 5% | 6 | 1.6 | 2 | 0.7 | 2 | 4.2 | 2 | 4.1 | 1 | 5.3 |
| 6% | 1 | 0.3 | — | — | 1 | 2.1 | — | — | — | — |
| **II—A Uniform Per Cent of Portion of Compensation** | 62 | 16.1 | 31 | 11.5 | 14 | 29.2 | 10 | 20.4 | 7 | 36.8 |
| *First $3,000* | | | | | | | | | | |
| ¾% | 1 | 0.3 | — | — | — | — | 1 | 2.0 | — | — |
| 2% | 2 | 0.5 | 2 | 0.7 | — | — | — | — | — | — |
| 2¼% | 1 | 0.3 | — | — | 1 | 2.1 | — | — | — | — |
| 5% | 1 | 0.3 | 1 | 0.4 | — | — | — | — | — | — |
| *Excess over $3,000* | | | | | | | | | | |
| 2% | 1 | 0.3 | — | — | — | — | 1 | 2.0 | — | — |
| 3½% | 1 | 0.3 | 1 | 0.4 | — | — | — | — | — | — |
| 4% | 1 | 0.3 | 1 | 0.4 | — | — | — | — | — | — |

## TABLE K-1 (Cont.)

### CONTRIBUTION SCHEMES
### All Contributory Plans

| CONTRIBUTION | Total Companies | | Group Annuity | | Individual Annuity | | Self-Administered | | Combination and Others | |
|---|---|---|---|---|---|---|---|---|---|---|
| | Companies | Per Cent | Companies | Per Cent | Companies | Per Cent | Companies | Per Cent | Companies | Per Cent |
| **II—A Uniform Per Cent of Portion of Compensation (Cont.)** | | | | | | | | | | |
| *Excess over $1,000* | | | | | | | | | | |
| 5% | 1 | 0.3 | | | 1 | 2.1 | | | | |
| *Excess over $1,200* | | | | | | | | | | |
| 3% | 1 | 0.3 | | | 1 | 2.1 | | | | |
| *Excess over $1,500* | | | | | | | | | | |
| 6% | 1 | 0.3 | | | | | 1 | 2.0 | | |
| *Excess over $3,000* | | | | | | | | | | |
| 3% | 13 | 3.4 | 3 | 1.1 | 4 | 8.3 | 4 | 8.2 | 2 | 10.5 |
| 3¼% | 1 | 0.3 | 1 | 0.4 | | | | | | |
| 3½% | 1 | 0.3 | | | | | | | 1 | 5.3 |
| 4% | 9 | 2.3 | 6 | 2.2 | 1 | 2.1 | | | 2 | 10.5 |
| 4½% | 2 | 0.5 | | | | | 1 | 2.0 | 1 | 5.3 |
| 5% | 20 | 5.2 | 14 | 5.2 | 5 | 10.4 | 1 | 2.0 | | |
| 5¼% | 1 | 0.3 | | | | | | | 1 | 5.3 |
| 6% | 4 | 1.0 | 2 | 0.7 | 1 | 2.1 | 1 | 2.0 | | |
| **III—A Nonuniform Per Cent of Compensation** | 189 | 49.1 | 161 | 59.9 | 10 | 20.8 | 14 | 28.6 | 4 | 21.1 |
| *Per Cent Changes at $1,200* | | | | | | | | | | |
| 3% first $1,200, 3⅓% of excess | 1 | 0.3 | 1 | 0.4 | | | | | | |
| 3% first $1,200, 4½% of excess | 1 | 0.3 | 1 | 0.4 | | | | | | |
| *Per Cent Changes at $3,000* | | | | | | | | | | |
| 2½% first $3,000, 3% of excess | 1 | 0.3 | | | 1 | 2.1 | | | | |
| 2⅓% first $3,000, 4% of excess | 1 | 0.3 | 1 | 0.4 | | | | | | |

TABLE K–1 (*Cont.*)

CONTRIBUTION SCHEMES

All Contributory Plans

| Contribution | Total Companies | | Group Annuity | | Individual Annuity | | Self-Administered | | Combination and Others | |
|---|---|---|---|---|---|---|---|---|---|---|
| | *Companies* | *Per Cent* | *Companies* | *Per Cent* | *Companies* | *Per Cent* | *Companies* | *Per Cent* | *Companies* | *Per Cent* |
| III—A NONUNIFORM PER CENT OF COMPENSATION (Cont.) | | | | | | | | | | |
| *Per Cent Changes at $3,000* (Cont.) | | | | | | | | | | |
| ⅔% first $3,000, 4½% of excess | 1 | 0.3 | 1 | 0.4 | — | — | — | — | — | — |
| 1% first $3,000, 1½% of excess | 1 | 0.3 | 1 | 0.4 | — | — | — | — | — | — |
| 1% first $3,000, 3% of excess | 1 | 0.3 | 1 | 0.4 | — | — | — | — | — | — |
| 1% first $3,000, 3½% of excess | 1 | 0.3 | 1 | 0.4 | — | — | — | — | — | — |
| 1% first $3,000, 3¾% of excess | 1 | 0.3 | — | — | — | — | 1 | 2.0 | — | — |
| 1% first $3,000, 4% of excess | 1 | 0.3 | 1 | 0.4 | — | — | — | — | — | — |
| 1% first $3,000, 6% of excess | 1 | 0.3 | — | — | 1 | 2.1 | — | — | — | — |
| 1¼% first $3,000, 3½% of excess | 1 | 0.3 | 1 | 0.4 | — | — | — | — | — | — |
| 1½% first $3,000, 3% of excess | 3 | 0.8 | 2 | 0.7 | 1 | 2.1 | — | — | — | — |
| 1½% first $3,000, 3½% of excess | 4 | 1.0 | 4 | 1.5 | — | — | — | — | — | — |
| 1½% first $3,000, 4½% of excess | 2 | 0.5 | 2 | 0.7 | — | — | — | — | — | — |
| 1⅔% first $3,000, 5% of excess | 1 | 0.3 | 1 | 0.4 | — | — | — | — | — | — |
| 1⅞% first $3,000, 4% of excess | 1 | 0.3 | 1 | 0.4 | — | — | — | — | — | — |
| 2% first $3,000, 3% of excess | 8 | 2.1 | 8 | 3.0 | — | — | — | — | — | — |
| 2% first $3,000, 3⅓% of excess | 2 | 0.5 | 2 | 0.7 | — | — | — | — | — | — |
| 2% first $3,000, 3½% of excess | 2 | 0.5 | 2 | 0.7 | — | — | — | — | — | — |
| 2% first $3,000, 4% of excess | 30 | 7.8 | 28 | 10.4 | — | — | 2 | 4.1 | — | — |
| 2% first $3,000, 4½% of excess | 5 | 1.3 | 4 | 1.5 | — | — | 1 | 2.0 | — | — |
| 2% first $3,000, 4⅔% of excess | 1 | 0.3 | 1 | 0.4 | — | — | — | — | — | — |
| 2% first $3,000, 5% of excess | 16 | 4.2 | 12 | 4.5 | 1 | 2.1 | 2 | 4.1 | 1 | 5.3 |
| 2% first $3,000, 5½% of excess | 1 | 0.3 | 1 | 0.4 | — | — | — | — | — | — |
| 2¼% first $3,000, 4½% of excess | 5 | 1.3 | 3 | 1.1 | — | — | 2 | 4.1 | — | — |
| 2¼% first $3,000, 6% of excess | 2 | 0.5 | 1 | 0.4 | — | — | — | — | 1 | 5.3 |

TABLE K-1 (*Cont.*)

CONTRIBUTION SCHEMES

All Contributory Plans

| CONTRIBUTION | TOTAL COMPANIES | | GROUP ANNUITY | | INDIVIDUAL ANNUITY | | SELF-ADMINISTERED | | COMBINATION AND OTHERS | |
|---|---|---|---|---|---|---|---|---|---|---|
| | Companies | Per Cent | Companies | Per Cent | Companies | Per Cent | Companies | Per Cent | Companies | Per Cent |
| **III—A NONUNIFORM PER CENT OF COMPENSATION (Cont.)** | | | | | | | | | | |
| *Per Cent Changes at $3,000 (Cont.)* | | | | | | | | | | |
| 2½% first $3,000, 3½% of excess.... | 4 | 1.0 | 4 | 1.5 | | | | | | |
| 2½% first $3,000, 4% of excess.... | 2 | 0.5 | 2 | 0.7 | | | | | | |
| 2½% first $3,000, 4½% of excess.... | 2 | 0.5 | 2 | 0.7 | | | | | | |
| 2½% first $3,000, 5% of excess.... | 25 | 6.5 | 17 | 6.3 | 3 | 6.3 | 5 | 10.2 | | |
| 2⅔% first $3,000, 5⅓% of excess.... | 1 | 0.3 | 1 | 0.4 | | | | | | |
| 3% first $3,000, 4% of excess.... | 2 | 0.5 | 2 | 0.7 | | | | | | |
| 3% first $3,000, 4½% of excess.... | 2 | 0.5 | 2 | 0.7 | | | | | | |
| 3% first $3,000, 5% of excess.... | 9 | 2.3 | 7 | 2.6 | 1 | 2.1 | 1 | 2.0 | | |
| 3% first $3,000, 5⅓% of excess.... | 1 | 0.3 | 1 | 0.4 | | | | | | |
| 3% first $3 000, 6% of excess.... | 6 | 1.6 | 6 | 2.2 | | | | | | |
| 3½% first $3,000, 5½% of excess.... | 2 | 0.5 | 2 | 0.7 | | | | | | |
| 3½% first $3,000, 7% of excess.... | 1 | 0.3 | 1 | 0.4 | | | | | | |
| 4% first $3,000, 5% of excess.... | 1 | 0.3 | 1 | 0.4 | | | | | | |
| 4% first $3,000, 5½% of excess.... | 1 | 0.3 | 1 | 0.4 | | | | | | |
| 4½% first $3,000, 6% of excess.... | 1 | 0.3 | 1 | 0.4 | | | | | | |
| *Per Cent Changes at $600 and $3,000* | | | | | | | | | | |
| ¾% first $600, 3% excess to $3,000, 4⅜% of excess.... | 1 | 0.3 | 1 | 0.4 | | | | | | |
| ¾% first $600, 3% excess to $3,000, 5% of excess.... | 1 | 0.3 | 1 | 0.4 | | | | | | |
| 1¼% first $600, 3½% excess to $3,000, 4% of excess.... | 1 | 0.3 | 1 | 0.4 | | | | | | |
| 1½% first $600, 3¾% excess to $3,000, 5% of excess.... | 1 | 0.3 | 1 | 0.4 | | | | | | |

## TABLE K-1 (Cont.)

### Contribution Schemes
### All Contributory Plans

| Contribution | Total Companies | | Group Annuity | | Individual Annuity | | Self-Administered | | Combination and Others | |
|---|---|---|---|---|---|---|---|---|---|---|
| | Companies | Per Cent | Companies | Per Cent | Companies | Per Cent | Companies | Per Cent | Companies | Per Cent |
| **III—A Nonuniform Per Cent of Compensation (Cont.)** | | | | | | | | | | |
| *Per Cent Changes at $1,200 and $3,000* | | | | | | | | | | |
| 2% first $1,200, 2½% excess to $3,000, 3¾% of excess...... | 1 | 0.3 | 1 | 0.4 | | | | | | |
| 2% first $1,200, 3% excess to $3,000, 5% of excess...... | 3 | 0.8 | 3 | 1.1 | | | | | | |
| *Per Cent Changes at $1,500 and $3,000* | | | | | | | | | | |
| 8/10% first $1,500, 2% excess to $3,000, 4% of excess...... | 1 | 0.3 | 1 | 0.4 | | | | | | |
| 1% first $1,500, 1½% excess to $3,000, 3½% of excess...... | 1 | 0.3 | 1 | 0.4 | | | | | | |
| 1½% first $1,500, 2½% excess to $3,000, 3¾% of excess...... | 1 | 0.3 | 1 | 0.4 | | | | | | |
| 2% first $1,500, 3% excess to $3,000, 4% of excess...... | 1 | 0.3 | 1 | 0.4 | | | | | | |
| 2% first $1,500, 3% excess to $3,000, 6% of excess...... | 1 | 0.3 | | — | 1 | 2.1 | | | | |
| *Per Cent Changes at $1,800 and $3,000* | | | | | | | | | | |
| 1½% first $1,800, 2% excess to $3,000, 3% of excess...... | 1 | 0.3 | 1 | 0.4 | | | | | | |
| 2% first $1,800, 4% excess to $3,000, 6% of excess...... | 10 | 2.6 | 8 | 3.0 | | | | | 2 | 10.5 |
| 2% first $1,800, 2⅔% excess to $3,000, 4% of excess...... | 1 | 0.3 | 1 | 0.4 | | | | | | |
| 2¼% first $1,800, 3% excess to $3,000, 4½% of excess...... | 1 | 0.3 | 1 | 0.4 | | | | | | |

## Contribution Schemes
### All Contributory Plans

| Contribution | Total Companies | | Group Annuity | | Individual Annuity | | Self-Administered | | Combination and Others | |
|---|---|---|---|---|---|---|---|---|---|---|
| | Companies | Per Cent | Companies | Per Cent | Companies | Per Cent | Companies | Per Cent | Companies | Per Cent |
| *Per Cent Changes at $3,000 and $12,000* 1% first $3,000, 2% excess to $12,000, 3% of excess | 1 | 0.3 | — | — | 1 | 2.1 | | | — | |
| *Per Cent Changes at $2,000 and $3,000* 1½% first $2,000, 3% excess to $3,000, 4½% of excess | 1 | 0.3 | 1 | 0.4 | — | | — | | — | |
| *Per Cent Changes at $2,000 and $4,000* 3% first $2,000, 5% excess to $4,000, 6% of excess | 1 | 0.3 | 1 | 0.4 | — | | — | | — | |
| *Per Cent Changes at $2,000, $3,000 and $6,000* 2% first $2,000, 3% excess to $3,000, 4% excess to $6,000, 5% of excess | 2 | 0.5 | 2 | 0.7 | — | | — | | — | |
| *Per Cent Changes at $1,000, $2,000 and $3,000* 2% first $1,000, 3% excess to $2,000, 4% excess to $3,000, 5% of excess | 1 | 0.3 | 1 | 0.4 | — | | — | | — | |
| *Per Cent Changes at $3,000 and $5,000* 2% first $3,000, 9% excess to $5,000, 4½% of excess | 1 | 0.3 | 1 | 0.4 | — | | — | | — | |
| *Per Cent Changes at $3,000 and $10,000* 2½% first $3,000, 5% excess to $10,000, 2½% of excess | 1 | 0.3 | 1 | 0.4 | — | | — | | — | |

## TABLE K-1 (*Cont.*)

### Contribution Schemes
### All Contributory Plans

| Contribution | Total Companies | | Group Annuity | | Individual Annuity | | Self-Administered | | Combination and Others | |
|---|---|---|---|---|---|---|---|---|---|---|
| | Com-panies | Per Cent | Com-panies | Per Cent | Com-panies | Per Cent | Com-panies | Per Cent | Com-panies | Per Cent |
| IV—A Nonuniform Per Cent of Portion of Compensation... | 28 | 7.3 | 25 | 9.3 | 1 | 2.1 | 1 | 2.0 | 1 | 5.3 |
| *Per Cent Changes at $3,000, No Contribution on First $500* | | | | | | | | | | |
| 2% first $3,000, 3% of excess... | 1 | 0.3 | | — | | | | | | |
| *Per Cent Changes at $3,000, No Contribution on First $600* | | | | | 1 | 2.1 | | | | |
| 2% first $3,000, 3% of excess... | 3 | 0.8 | 3 | 1.1 | | | | | | |
| 2% first $3,000, 4% of excess... | 4 | 1.0 | 3 | 1.1 | | | | | 1 | 5.3 |
| 2% first $3,000, 5% of excess... | 1 | 0.3 | 1 | 0.4 | | | | | | |
| 2½% first $3,000, 3½% of excess... | 1 | 0.3 | 1 | 0.4 | | | | | | |
| 2½% first $3,000, 4½% of excess... | 1 | 0.3 | 1 | 0.4 | | | | | | |
| 2½% first $3,000, 5% of excess... | 1 | 0.3 | 1 | 0.4 | | | | | | |
| 3% first $3,000, 4½% of excess... | 3 | 0.8 | 2 | 0.7 | | | 1 | 2.0 | | |
| 3% first $3,000, 6% of excess... | 1 | 0.3 | 1 | 0.4 | | | | | | |
| 3½% first $3,000, 5¼% of excess... | 1 | 0.3 | 1 | 0.4 | | | | | | |
| 3¾% first $3,000, 5% of excess... | 1 | 0.3 | 1 | 0.4 | | | | | | |
| 4% first $3,000, 6% of excess... | 2 | 0.5 | 2 | 0.7 | | | | | | |
| *Per Cent Changes at $3,000, and $6,000, No Contribution on First $600* | | | | | | | | | | |
| 2% first $3,000, 2½% excess to $6,000, 4% of excess... | 1 | 0.3 | 1 | 0.4 | | | | | | |
| *Per Cent Changes at $1,800 and $3,000, No Contribution on First $600* | | | | | | | | | | |
| 2% first $1,800, 3% excess to $3,000, 4½% of excess... | 2 | 0.5 | 2 | 0.7 | | | | | | |

## TABLE K-1 (*Cont.*)

### CONTRIBUTION SCHEMES

#### All Contributory Plans

| CONTRIBUTION | TOTAL COMPANIES | | GROUP ANNUITY | | INDIVIDUAL ANNUITY | | SELF-ADMINISTERED | | COMBINATION AND OTHERS | |
|---|---|---|---|---|---|---|---|---|---|---|
| | Com-panies | Per Cent | Com-panies | Per Cent | Com-panies | Per Cent | Com-panies | Per Cent | Com-panies | Per Cent |
| **IV–A NONUNIFORM PER CENT OF PORTION OF COMPENSATION** (Cont.) | | | | | | | | | | |
| *Per Cent Changes at $3,000, No Contribution on First $1,200* | | | | | | | | | | |
| 4% first $3,000, 6% of excess......... | 1 | 0.3 | 1 | 0.4 | | | | | | |
| 4½% first $3,000, 6% of excess...... | 1 | 0.3 | 1 | 0.4 | | | | | | |
| *Per Cent Changes at $3,000, No Contribution on First $1,000* | | | | | | | | | | |
| 2% first $3,000, 3% of excess......... | 1 | 0.3 | 1 | 0.4 | | | | | | |
| 2¼% first $3,000, 4% of excess...... | 1 | 0.3 | 1 | 0.4 | | | | | | |
| *Per Cent Changes at $10,000, No Contribution on First $3,000* | | | | | | | | | | |
| 5% first $10,000, 4½% of excess...... | 1 | 0.3 | 1 | 0.4 | | | | | | |
| **V–A VARIABLE RATE**............... | 37 | 9.6 | 18 | 6.7 | 4 | 8.3 | 12 | 24.5 | 3 | 15.8 |
| *Varies as to Age at Entry and Other Factors* | | | | | | | | | | |
| Age at entry only............. | 10 | 2.6 | 4 | 1.5 | 2 | 4.2 | 1 | 2.0 | 3 | 15.8 |
| Age at entry and sex.......... | 2 | 0.5 | — | — | 1 | 2.1 | 1 | 2.0 | | |
| Age at entry, rate increasing for compensation over $3,000...... | 10 | 2.6 | 7 | 2.6 | 1 | 2.1 | 2 | 4.1 | | |
| Age at entry and earnings class.. | 1 | 0.3 | — | — | — | — | 1 | 2.0 | | |
| Others................. | 2 | 0.5 | — | — | — | — | 2 | 4.1 | | |
| Periodically adjusted........ | 4 | 1.0 | — | — | — | — | 4 | 8.2 | | |
| Varies as to compensation...... | 2 | 0.5 | 2 | 0.7 | — | — | — | — | | |
| Varies as to Social Security coverage...... | 3 | 0.8 | 2 | 0.7 | — | — | 1 | 2.0 | | |
| Varies as to occupation......... | 3 | 0.8 | 3 | 1.1 | — | — | — | — | | |

## TABLE K-1 (*Cont.*)
### CONTRIBUTION SCHEMES
#### All Contributory Plans

| CONTRIBUTION | TOTAL COMPANIES | | GROUP ANNUITY | | INDIVIDUAL ANNUITY | | SELF-ADMINISTERED | | COMBINATION AND OTHERS | |
|---|---|---|---|---|---|---|---|---|---|---|
| | Com-panies | Per Cent | Com-panies | Per Cent | Com-panies | Per Cent | Com-panies | Per Cent | Com-panies | Per Cent |
| VI—A FLAT CONTRIBUTION | 2 | 0.5 | — | — | — | — | 2 | 4.1 | — | — |
| $36 annually | 1 | 0.3 | — | — | — | — | 1 | 2.0 | — | — |
| $48 annually | 1 | 0.3 | — | — | — | — | 1 | 2.0 | — | — |
| VII—MISCELLANEOUS BASIS | 7 | 1.8 | — | — | 6 | 12.5 | 1 | 2.0 | — | — |
| *As a Percentage of Premiums* | | | | | | | | | | |
| 10% | 1 | 0.3 | | | 1 | 2.1 | | | | |
| 20% | 1 | 0.3 | | | 1 | 2.1 | | | | |
| 25% | 1 | 0.3 | | | 1 | 2.1 | | | | |
| 33⅓% | 1 | 0.3 | | | 1 | 2.1 | | | | |
| 50% | 2 | 0.5 | | | 2 | 4.2 | | | | |
| *As a Percentage of Cost* | | | | | | | | | | |
| 50% | 1 | 0.3 | | | — | — | 1 | 2.0 | | |
| TOTAL CONTRIBUTORY PLANS | 385 | 100.0 | 269 | 100.0 | 48 | 100.0 | 49 | 100.0 | 19 | 100.0 |
| TOTAL CONTRIBUTORY PLANS | 385 | 62.9 | 269 | 85.9 | 48 | 31.6 | 49 | 40.5 | 19 | 73.1 |
| TOTAL NON-CONTRIBUTORY PLANS | 227 | 37.1 | 44 | 14.1 | 104 | 68.4 | 72 | 59.5 | 7 | 26.9 |
| TOTAL PLANS | 612 | 100.0 | 313 | 100.0 | 152 | 100.0 | 121 | 100.0 | 26 | 100.0 |

## TABLE K-2

### Contribution Schemes
### Money-Purchase Plans

| Employee's Contribution | Employer's Contribution | Total Companies | Group Annuity | Individual Annuity | Self-Administered | Combination and Others |
|---|---|---|---|---|---|---|
| | | Companies | Companies | Companies | Companies | Companies |
| A UNIFORM PER CENT OF COMPENSATION | | 7 | 4 | 2 | 1 | — |
| 2% | Equal | 1 | — | — | 1 | — |
| 2% | 1½ times employee's contribution | 1 | 1 | — | — | — |
| 2% | 2½ times employee's contribution | 1 | 1 | — | — | — |
| 3% | Equal | 1 | — | 1 | — | — |
| 4% | Equal | 1 | 1 | — | — | — |
| 5% | 2 times employee's contribution | 1 | 1 | — | — | — |
| 5% | Equal | 1 | — | 1 | — | — |
| A UNIFORM PER CENT OF PORTION OF COMPENSATION | | 3 | 2 | — | 1 | — |
| *First $3,000* | | | | | | |
| 2% | Equal | 1 | 1 | — | — | — |
| 5% | Equal | 1 | 1 | — | — | — |
| *Excess over $3,000* | | | | | | |
| 6% | ½ of employee's contribution | 1 | — | — | 1 | — |
| A NONUNIFORM PER CENT OF COMPENSATION | | 39 | 34 | — | 2 | 3 |
| *Per Cent Changes at $3,000* | | | | | | |
| 1% first $3,000, 4% of excess | 4% first $3,000, 8% of excess | 1 | 1 | — | — | — |
| 2% first $3,000, 3⅓% of excess | 2 times employee's contribution | 1 | 1 | — | — | — |

CONTRIBUTION SCHEMES

Money-Purchase Plans

| EMPLOYEE'S CONTRIBUTION | EMPLOYER'S CONTRIBUTION | TOTAL COMPANIES | GROUP ANNUITY | INDIVIDUAL ANNUITY | SELF-ADMINISTERED | COMBINATION AND OTHERS |
|---|---|---|---|---|---|---|
| | | Companies | Companies | Companies | Companies | Companies |
| **A NONUNIFORM PER CENT OF COMPENSATION (Cont.)** | | | | | | |
| *Per Cent Changes at $3,000 (Cont.)* | | | | | | |
| 2% first $3,000, 4% of excess | Equal | 2 | 2 | — | — | — |
| 2% first $3,000, 4% of excess | 1½ times employee's contribution | 1 | 1 | — | — | — |
| 2% first $3,000, 4% of excess | 2 times employee's contribution | 1 | 1 | — | — | 1 |
| 2% first $3,000, 5% of excess | Equal | 6 | 4 | — | 1 | — |
| 2% first $3,000, 5% of excess | 1½ times employee's contribution | 2 | 2 | — | 1 | — |
| 2½% first $3,000, 5% of excess | Equal | 3 | 3 | — | — | — |
| 3% first $3,000, 5% of excess | Equal | 4 | 4 | — | — | — |
| 3% first $3,000, 5% of excess | 5% of compensation | 1 | — | — | 1 | — |
| 4% first $3,000, 5% of excess | Equal | 1 | 1 | — | — | — |
| *Per Cent Changes at $1,200 and $3,000* | | | | | | |
| 2% first $1,200, 3% excess to $3,000, 5% of excess | Equal | 3 | 3 | — | — | — |
| *Per Cent Changes at $1,500 and $3,000* | | | | | | |
| 8/10% first $1,500, 2% excess to $3,000, 4% of excess | 2½% first $1,500, remainder equal | 1 | 1 | — | — | — |
| *Per Cent Changes at $1,800 and $3,000* | | | | | | |
| 2% first $1,800, 4% excess to $3,000, 6% of excess | Equal | 6 | 5 | — | — | 1 |

CONTRIBUTION SCHEMES

Money-Purchase Plans

| EMPLOYEE'S CONTRIBUTION | EMPLOYER'S CONTRIBUTION | TOTAL COMPANIES | GROUP ANNUITY | INDIVIDUAL ANNUITY | SELF-ADMINISTERED | COMBINATION AND OTHERS |
|---|---|---|---|---|---|---|
| | | Companies | Companies | Companies | Companies | Companies |
| **A NONUNIFORM PER CENT OF COMPENSATION** (Cont.) | | | | | | |
| *Per Cent Changes at $1,800 and $3,000* (Cont.) | | | | | | |
| 2% first $1,800, 4% excess to $3,000, 6% of excess | 1¼ times employee's contribution.... | 2 | 1 | — | — | 1 |
| 2% first $1,800, 4% excess to $3,000, 6% of excess | 1½ times employee's contribution.... | 2 | 2 | — | — | — |
| *Per Cent Changes at $2,000, $3,000, $6,000* | | | | | | |
| 2% first $2,000, 3% excess to $3,000, 4% excess to $6,000, 5% of excess | 3% first $2,000, 3½% excess to $3,000, remainder equal........ | 2 | 2 | — | — | — |
| **A NONUNIFORM PER CENT OF PORTION OF COMPENSATION** | | 1 | 1 | — | — | — |
| *Per Cent Changes at $3,000, No Contribution on First $1,200* | | | | | | |
| 4% first $3,000, 6% of excess | Equal, plus $48 annually for those earning under $1,200............ | 1 | 1 | — | — | — |

## TABLE K-2 (Cont.)
### CONTRIBUTION SCHEMES
### Money-Purchase Plans

| EMPLOYEE'S CONTRIBUTION | EMPLOYER'S CONTRIBUTION | TOTAL COMPANIES | GROUP ANNUITY | INDIVIDUAL ANNUITY | SELF-ADMINISTERED | COMBINATION AND OTHERS |
|---|---|---|---|---|---|---|
| | | Companies | Companies | Companies | Companies | Companies |
| A VARIABLE RATE | | 9 | 7 | 1 | 1 | — |
| Varies as to age at entry only | Equal | 1 | 1 | — | — | — |
| Varies as to age at entry, rate increasing for compensation over $3,000 | Equal | 5 | 3 | 1 | 1 | — |
| Varies as to age at entry, rate increasing for compensation over $3,000 | ½ times employee's contribution | 1 | 1 | — | — | — |
| Varies as to compensation | Equal | 1 | 1 | — | — | — |
| Varies as to compensation | Minimum to produce benefit of ¼% times future service | 1 | 1 | — | — | — |
| MISCELLANEOUS | | 14 | 9 | 4 | — | 1 |
| 25% of premiums | 75% of premiums | 1 | — | 1 | — | — |
| Non-contributory | 5% of compensation | 1 | — | 1 | — | — |
| Non-contributory | ¾% of average compensation times past service, plus 1% of present compensation times future service | 1 | 1 | — | — | — |
| Non-contributory | 4% first $3,000, 8% of excess | 1 | 1 | — | — | — |
| Others | | 10 | 7 | 2 | — | 1 |
| TOTAL MONEY-PURCHASE PLANS | | 73 | 57 | 7 | 5 | 4 |

311

Of the 461 plans which make provision for vesting, 424 of them stipulate deferred vesting, and 37 immediate vesting. As between types, those which provide for immediate vesting are largely individual annuity plans, for of the 37 which allow immediate vesting, 29 are such. The tabulation appears in Table L-1.[13a]

## 2. Conditions to Be Satisfied to Obtain Withdrawal (Severance) Benefits

Among plans which provide for *deferred* vesting there are to be found, of course, conditions to be satisfied before a withdrawal benefit is allowed. These conditions may involve requirements of service, participation (membership), age and service, or age and participation, as shown in Table L-2.

Of the 424 plans with deferred vesting, service is the more common requirement, 146, or 34%, so providing; years of participation in the plan, or age *and* service, are in the order named, the other conditions most frequently used in lieu of service. As between the several types, individual annuity plans largely make use of either conditions of service or participation in the plan; group annuities tend to do likewise, except that the latter employ a combined condition of age *and* service, as often as service alone. The self-administered plans, in this respect, are similar to the group annuities.

In relation to the three most commonly used conditions for deferred vesting, that is, service, participation, and age *and* service, the typical service requirements are 5, 10, or 15 years; the participation periods are 1, 5, or 10 years; and the age *and* service require-

---

[13a] A study of vesting provisions in pension plans must be approached from at least three aspects: the *time,* the *amount,* and the *form* of vesting. In relation to time, the terms *immediate* and *deferred* are used to distinguish whether an employee upon becoming eligible to a plan initially is granted an interest in the employer's contributions upon withdrawal, or whether such interest is postponed. These terms, however, do not reveal the amount of the employer's contributions which will be vested, or the form of the vesting. For example, as to amount, a plan said to provide immediate vesting may grant only a portion of the employer's contributions upon withdrawal by an employee in the first few years of participation, the remainder being made subject to satisfaction of service conditions. To be more exact, therefore, a plan which allows the full amount of the employer's contributions, if withdrawal occurs at any time after becoming eligible to a plan, is more accurately described as one with immediate *full* vesting; if an employee is entitled only to a portion of the employer's contribution, then as a plan with immediate *partial* vesting. Deferred vesting likewise might be deferred *full,* or deferred *partial.* With reference to the form of vesting, while it is more or less standardized under group annuity plans, through the allowance of a paid-up deferred life annuity, it may take different forms in individual annuity and self-administered plans. In either of the latter cash might be payable, an income in installments for a limited time, and so forth.

## WITHDRAWAL (SEVERANCE) BENEFITS

### TABLE L-1

#### NUMBER OF PLANS PROVIDING WITHDRAWAL BENEFITS

| TYPE OF PROVISION | TOTAL COMPANIES | | GROUP ANNUITY | | INDIVIDUAL ANNUITY | | SELF-ADMINISTERED | |
|---|---|---|---|---|---|---|---|---|
| | Com-panies | Per Cent | Com-panies | Per Cent | Com-panies | Per Cent | Com-panies | Per Cent |
| PLANS WITH DEFERRED VESTING | 424 | 72.4 | 275 | 87.9 | 113 | 74.3 | 36 | 29.8 |
| PLANS WITH IMMEDIATE VESTING | 37 | 6.3 | 5 | 1.6 | 29 | 19.1 | 3 | 2.5 |
| PLANS WITH NO VESTING | 98 | 16.7 | 33 | 10.5 | 5 | 3.3 | 81 | 66.9 |
| INFORMATION NOT OBTAINED | 27 | 4.6 | — | — | 5 | 3.3 | 1 | 0.8 |
| TOTALS | 586[a] | 100.0 | 313 | 100.0 | 152 | 100.0 | 121 | 100.0 |

[a] The twenty-six combination plans have not been used in this table. Percentages, therefore, have been computed on the basis of 586 plans.

### WITHDRAWAL (SEVERANCE) BENEFITS

### TABLE L-2

#### CONDITIONS TO BE SATISFIED TO OBTAIN WITHDRAWAL (SEVERANCE) BENEFITS

| CONDITIONS | TOTAL COMPANIES | | GROUP ANNUITY | | INDIVIDUAL ANNUITY | | SELF-ADMINISTERED | |
|---|---|---|---|---|---|---|---|---|
| | Com-panies | Per Cent | Com-panies | Per Cent | Com-panies | Per Cent | Com-panies | Per Cent |
| I—SERVICE | 146 | 34.4 | 75 | 27.3 | 58 | 51.3 | 13 | 36.1 |
| 1 year | 5 | 1.2 | 2 | 0.7 | 2 | 1.8 | 1 | 2.8 |
| 2 years | 2 | 0.5 | — | — | 2 | 1.8 | — | — |

# WITHDRAWAL (SEVERANCE) BENEFITS

## TABLE L-2 (Cont.)

### CONDITIONS TO BE SATISFIED TO OBTAIN WITHDRAWAL (SEVERANCE) BENEFITS

| Conditions | Total Companies | | Group Annuity | | Individual Annuity | | Self-Administered | |
|---|---|---|---|---|---|---|---|---|
| | Companies | Per Cent | Companies | Per Cent | Companies | Per Cent | Companies | Per Cent |
| **I—Service (Cont.)** | | | | | | | | |
| 3 years | 3 | 0.7 | 2 | 0.7 | — | — | 1 | 2.8 |
| 5 years | 46 | 10.8 | 14 | 5.1 | 30 | 26.5 | 2 | 5.6 |
| 6 years | 1 | 0.2 | — | — | 1 | 0.9 | — | — |
| 10 years | 47 | 11.1 | 28 | 10.2 | 18 | 15.9 | 1 | 2.8 |
| 11 years | 2 | 0.5 | — | — | 2 | 1.8 | — | — |
| 13 years | 1 | 0.2 | 1 | 0.4 | — | — | — | — |
| 15 years | 23 | 5.4 | 17 | 6.2 | 2 | 1.8 | 4 | 11.1 |
| 16 years | 1 | 0.2 | — | — | 1 | 0.9 | — | — |
| 20 years | 11 | 2.6 | 8 | 2.9 | — | — | 3 | 8.3 |
| 25 years | 1 | 0.2 | 1 | 0.4 | — | — | — | — |
| 30 years | 2 | 0.5 | 1 | 0.4 | — | — | 1 | 2.8 |
| Men 20 years, women 15 years | 1 | 0.2 | 1 | 0.4 | — | — | — | — |
| **II—Participation** | 102 | 24.1 | 57 | 20.7 | 42 | 37.2 | 3 | 8.3 |
| 1 year | 10 | 2.4 | — | — | 10 | 8.8 | — | — |
| 2 years | 5 | 1.2 | — | — | 5 | 4.4 | — | — |
| 3 years | 4 | 0.9 | — | — | 4 | 3.5 | — | — |
| 4 years | 2 | 0.5 | — | — | 2 | 1.8 | — | — |
| 5 years | 48 | 11.3 | 31 | 11.3 | 16 | 14.2 | 1 | 2.8 |
| 8 years | 2 | 0.5 | 2 | 0.7 | — | — | — | — |
| 10 years | 26 | 6.1 | 20 | 7.3 | 5 | 4.4 | 1 | 2.8 |
| 11 years | 1 | 0.2 | — | — | — | — | 1 | 2.8 |
| 15 years | 3 | 0.7 | 3 | 1.1 | — | — | — | — |
| 20 years | 1 | 0.2 | 1 | 0.4 | — | — | — | — |

# WITHDRAWAL (SEVERANCE) BENEFITS

## TABLE L–2 (Cont.)

### CONDITIONS TO BE SATISFIED TO OBTAIN WITHDRAWAL (SEVERANCE) BENEFITS

| CONDITIONS | TOTAL COMPANIES | | GROUP ANNUITY | | INDIVIDUAL ANNUITY | | SELF-ADMINISTERED | |
|---|---|---|---|---|---|---|---|---|
| | Companies | Per Cent | Companies | Per Cent | Companies | Per Cent | Companies | Per Cent |
| III—AGE AND SERVICE.......... | 87 | 20.5 | 72 | 26.2 | 2 | 1.8 | 13 | 36.1 |
| Aged 25 and 1 year's service......... | 1 | 0.2 | — | — | 1 | 0.9 | — | — |
| Aged 35 and 10 years' service...... | 2 | 0.5 | 1 | 0.4 | — | — | 1 | 2.8 |
| Aged 40 and 10 years' service...... | 10 | 2.4 | 10 | 3.6 | — | — | — | — |
| Aged 40 and 15 years' service...... | 2 | 0.5 | 2 | 0.7 | — | — | — | — |
| Aged 45 and 10 years' service...... | 20 | 4.7 | 18 | 6.5 | — | — | 2 | 5.6 |
| Aged 45 and 15 years' service...... | 8 | 1.9 | 8 | 2.9 | — | — | — | — |
| Aged 45 and 20 years' service...... | 2 | 0.5 | 2 | 0.7 | — | — | — | — |
| Aged 45 and 30 years' service...... | 1 | 0.2 | — | — | — | — | 1 | 2.8 |
| Aged 50 and 10 years' service...... | 10 | 2.4 | 9 | 3.3 | — | — | 1 | 2.8 |
| Aged 50 and 15 years' service...... | 11 | 2.6 | 10 | 3.6 | — | — | 1 | 2.8 |
| Aged 50 and 20 years' service...... | 1 | 0.2 | 1 | 0.4 | — | — | — | — |
| Aged 55 and 10 years' service...... | 5 | 1.2 | 3 | 1.1 | — | — | 2 | 5.6 |
| Aged 55 and 15 years' service...... | 2 | 0.5 | 2 | 0.7 | — | — | — | — |
| Aged 55 and 20 years' service...... | 4 | 0.9 | 2 | 0.7 | 1 | 0.9 | 1 | 2.8 |
| Aged 55 and 25 years' service...... | 2 | 0.5 | — | — | — | — | 2 | 5.6 |
| Aged 60 and 15 years' service...... | 1 | 0.2 | 1 | 0.4 | — | — | — | — |
| Aged under 55 and 10 years' service..... | 1 | 0.2 | — | — | — | — | 1 | 2.8 |
| Men aged 40, women aged 35 and 10 years' service..... | 1 | 0.2 | 1 | 0.4 | — | — | — | — |
| Men aged 50, women aged 45 and 10 years' service..... | 1 | 0.2 | 1 | 0.4 | — | — | — | — |
| Men aged 55, women aged 50 and 10 years' service..... | 1 | 0.2 | — | — | — | — | 1 | 2.8 |
| Men aged 55, women aged 50 and 25 years' service..... | 1 | 0.2 | 1 | 0.4 | — | — | — | — |

# WITHDRAWAL (SEVERANCE) BENEFITS

## TABLE L-2 (Cont.)

### CONDITIONS TO BE SATISFIED TO OBTAIN WITHDRAWAL (SEVERANCE) BENEFITS

| CONDITIONS | TOTAL COMPANIES | | GROUP ANNUITY | | INDIVIDUAL ANNUITY | | SELF-ADMINISTERED | |
|---|---|---|---|---|---|---|---|---|
| | Companies | Per Cent | Companies | Per Cent | Companies | Per Cent | Companies | Per Cent |
| IV—AGE AND PARTICIPATION | 20 | 4.7 | 15 | 5.5 | 4 | 3.5 | 1 | 2.8 |
| Aged 40 and 5 years' participation | 2 | 0.5 | 1 | 0.4 | 1 | 0.9 | — | — |
| Aged 40 and 10 years' participation | 2 | 0.5 | 1 | 0.4 | 1 | 0.9 | — | — |
| Aged 45 and 5 years' participation | 9 | 2.1 | 9 | 3.3 | — | — | — | — |
| Aged 45 and 15 years' participation | 2 | 0.5 | 1 | 0.4 | 1 | 0.9 | — | — |
| Aged 50 and 10 years' participation | 1 | 0.2 | 1 | 0.4 | — | — | — | — |
| Aged 55 and 1 year's participation | 1 | 0.2 | — | — | — | — | 1 | 2.8 |
| Aged 60 and 10 years' participation | 1 | 0.2 | — | — | 1 | 0.9 | — | — |
| Men aged 50, women aged 45 and 5 years' participation | 1 | 0.2 | 1 | 0.4 | — | — | — | — |
| Men aged 50, women aged 45 and 10 years' participation | 1 | 0.2 | 1 | 0.4 | — | — | — | — |
| V—AGE | 10 | 2.4 | 5 | 1.8 | 2 | 1.8 | 3 | 8.3 |
| 40 | 2 | 0.5 | 1 | 0.4 | 1 | 0.9 | — | — |
| 45 | 1 | 0.2 | — | — | 1 | 0.9 | — | — |
| 50 | 1 | 0.2 | 1 | 0.4 | — | — | 1 | 2.8 |
| 55 | 2 | 0.5 | 1 | 0.4 | — | — | 2 | 5.6 |
| 60 | 2 | 0.5 | — | — | — | — | — | — |
| Men 55, women 50 | 1 | 0.2 | 1 | 0.4 | — | — | — | — |
| Men 60, women 55 | 1 | 0.2 | 1 | 0.4 | — | — | — | — |
| VI—SERVICE AND PARTICIPATION | 23 | 5.4 | 19 | 6.9 | 3 | 2.7 | 1 | 2.8 |
| 5 years' service and 5 years' participation | 1 | 0.2 | — | — | 1 | 0.9 | — | — |
| 6 years' service and 1 year's participation | 1 | 0.2 | — | — | — | — | — | — |

# WITHDRAWAL (SEVERANCE) BENEFITS

## TABLE L–2 (Cont.)

### CONDITIONS TO BE SATISFIED TO OBTAIN WITHDRAWAL (SEVERANCE) BENEFITS

| CONDITIONS | TOTAL COMPANIES | | GROUP ANNUITY | | INDIVIDUAL ANNUITY | | SELF-ADMINISTERED | |
|---|---|---|---|---|---|---|---|---|
| | Com-panies | Per Cent | Com-panies | Per Cent | Com-panies | Per Cent | Com-panies | Per Cent |
| **VI—SERVICE AND PARTICIPATION (Cont.)** | | | | | | | | |
| 10 years' service and 2 years' participation | 1 | 0.2 | 1 | 0.4 | | | | |
| 10 years' service and 3 years' participation | 1 | 0.2 | 1 | 0.4 | | | | |
| 10 years' service and 5 years' participation | 6 | 1.4 | 5 | 1.8 | 1 | 0.9 | | |
| 10 years' service and 7 years' participation | 1 | 0.2 | | | | | 1 | 2.8 |
| 10 years' service and 8 years' participation | 1 | 0.2 | 1 | 0.4 | | | | |
| 15 years' service and 5 years' participation | 6 | 1.4 | 5 | 1.8 | 1 | 0.9 | | |
| 20 years' service and 5 years' participation | 4 | 0.9 | 4 | 1.5 | | | | |
| 20 years' service and 10 years' participation | 1 | 0.2 | 1 | 0.4 | | | | |
| **VII—AGE, SERVICE, AND PARTICIPATION** | 1 | 0.2 | 1 | 0.4 | — | — | — | — |
| Aged 50, 15 years' service and 5 years' participation | 1 | 0.2 | 1 | 0.4 | — | — | — | — |
| **VIII—PROXIMITY TO NORMAL RETIREMENT AGE AND SERVICE** | 1 | 0.2 | — | — | — | — | 1 | 2.8 |
| 10 years before normal retirement age and 5 years' service | 1 | 0.2 | — | — | — | — | 1 | 2.8 |
| **IX—ALTERNATES** | 34 | 8.0 | 31 | 11.3 | 2 | 1.8 | 1 | 2.8 |
| *Service or Participation* | | | | | | | | |
| 10 years' service OR 5 years' participation | 2 | 0.5 | 1 | 0.4 | 1 | 0.9 | 1 | 2.8 |
| 15 years' service OR 2 years' participation | 1 | 0.2 | 1 | 0.4 | | | | |
| 15 years' service OR 10 years' participation | 1 | 0.2 | 1 | 0.4 | | | | |

## WITHDRAWAL (SEVERANCE) BENEFITS

### TABLE L-2 (Cont.)

CONDITIONS TO BE SATISFIED TO OBTAIN WITHDRAWAL (SEVERANCE) BENEFITS

| CONDITIONS | TOTAL COMPANIES | | GROUP ANNUITY | | INDIVIDUAL ANNUITY | | SELF-ADMINISTERED | |
|---|---|---|---|---|---|---|---|---|
| | Companies | Per Cent | Companies | Per Cent | Companies | Per Cent | Companies | Per Cent |
| **IX—ALTERNATES (Cont.)** | | | | | | | | |
| *Age or Service* | | | | | | | | |
| Men aged 55, women aged 50 OR 5 years' service........ | 1 | 0.2 | 1 | 0.4 | | | | |
| *Age and Service or Service* | | | | | | | | |
| Aged 40 and 5 years' service OR 15 years' service...... | 1 | 0.2 | 1 | 0.4 | | | | |
| Aged 45 and 10 years' service OR 15 years' service..... | 4 | 0.9 | 4 | 1.5 | | | | |
| Aged 45 and 15 years' service OR 20 years' service...... | 1 | 0.2 | 1 | 0.4 | | | | |
| Aged 45 and 20 years' service OR 25 years' service...... | 2 | 0.5 | 2 | 0.7 | | | | |
| Aged 50 and 15 years' service OR 20 years' service...... | 6 | 1.4 | 6 | 2.2 | | | | |
| *Age and Participation or Service* | | | | | | | | |
| Aged 50 and 5 years' participation OR 20 years' service.... | 1 | 0.2 | 1 | 0.4 | | | | |
| Aged 50 and 10 years' participation OR 20 years' service.... | 1 | 0.2 | 1 | 0.4 | | | | |
| Aged 60 and 5 years' participation OR 20 years' service.... | 1 | 0.2 | 1 | 0.4 | | | | |
| *Proximity to Normal Retirement Age or Service* | | | | | | | | |
| 10 years before normal retirement age OR 10 years' service | 1 | 0.2 | | | | | 1 | 2.8 |
| *Participation or Age and Service* | | | | | | | | |
| 5 years' participation OR aged 45 and 15 years' service.... | 1 | 0.2 | 1 | 0.4 | | | | |
| 5 years' participation OR aged 50 and 10 years' service.... | 1 | 0.2 | 1 | 0.4 | | | | |
| *Participation or Age and Participation* | | | | | | | | |
| 10 years' participation OR aged 50 and 5 years' participation | 1 | 0.2 | | | 1 | 0.9 | | |
| 20 years' participation OR aged 50 and 10 years' participation........ | 1 | 0.2 | 1 | 0.4 | | | | |
| *Participation or Service and Participation* | | | | | | | | |
| 10 years' participation OR 20 years' service and 5 years' participation........ | 1 | 0.2 | 1 | 0.4 | | | | |

# WITHDRAWAL (SEVERANCE) BENEFITS

## TABLE L-2 (Cont.)

### CONDITIONS TO BE SATISFIED TO OBTAIN WITHDRAWAL (SEVERANCE) BENEFITS

| CONDITIONS | TOTAL COMPANIES | | GROUP ANNUITY | | INDIVIDUAL ANNUITY | | SELF-ADMINISTERED | |
|---|---|---|---|---|---|---|---|---|
| | Companies | Per Cent | Companies | Per Cent | Companies | Per Cent | Companies | Per Cent |
| **IX—ALTERNATES (Cont.)** | | | | | | | | |
| *Age or Service and Participation* | | | | | | | | |
| Aged 55 OR 15 years' service and 10 years' participation... | 1 | 0.2 | 1 | 0.4 | — | | — | |
| *Service and Participation OR Age, Service, and Participation* | | | | | | | | |
| 15 years' service and 10 years' participation OR aged 50, 15 years' service and 3 years' participation... | 1 | 0.2 | 1 | 0.4 | — | | — | |
| 20 years' service and 10 years' participation OR aged 50, 15 years' service and 10 years' participation... | 1 | 0.2 | 1 | 0.4 | | | | |
| *Age and Participation or Age and Service* | | | | | | | | |
| Aged 45 and 5 years' participation OR aged 45 and 15 years' service... | 1 | 0.2 | 1 | 0.4 | | | | |
| *Age and Participation or Service and Participation* | | | | | | | | |
| Aged 45 and 5 years' participation OR 25 years' service and 5 years' participation... | 1 | 0.2 | 1 | 0.4 | — | | — | |
| *Others* | | | | | | | | |
| 15 years' service and attainment of an age 5 years less than normal retirement age or 25 years' service... | 1 | 0.2 | 1 | 0.4 | — | | — | |
| PLANS WITH DEFERRED VESTING | 424 | 100.0 | 275 | 100.0 | 113 | 100.0 | 36 | 100.0 |
| PLANS WITH DEFERRED VESTING | 424 | 72.4 | 275 | 87.9 | 113 | 74.3 | 36 | 29.8 |
| PLANS WITH IMMEDIATE VESTING | 37 | 6.3 | 5 | 1.6 | 29 | 19.1 | 3 | 2.5 |
| PLANS WITH NO VESTING | 98 | 16.7 | 33 | 10.5 | 5 | 3.3 | 81 | 66.9 |
| INFORMATION NOT OBTAINED | 27 | 4.6 | — | | 5 | 3.3 | 1 | 0.8 |
| TOTALS | 586 | 100.0 | 313 | 100.0 | 152 | 100.0 | 121 | 100.0 |

ments are the attainment of age 40 and 10 years of service, 45 and
10 years of service, 45 and 15 years of service, or age 50 after 10 or
15 years of service.

This discussion of the conditions imposed in plans which provide
for deferred vesting has been in relation to the *time,* or when vesting of the employer's contributions is allowed. It has not given
consideration to the relative amounts of employer contributions
which might be vested after conditions have been satisfied, nor has
it indicated the form of vesting. To illustrate the procedures under plans with deferred vesting including those aspects mentioned
in the footnote on page 312, there has been prepared a table giving
examples of deferred vesting schemes and showing conditions to be
satisfied, the amounts of the employer's contribution then vested,
and the form of the vesting. These will be found in Table 1,
Appendix A.

## K.  Death Benefits

It was stated in Chapter IX that death benefits prior to retirement are rarely provided as an integral part of group annuity or
self-administered pension plans,[14] as contrasted to the procedure of
individual annuity plans, where the use of retirement income or
retirement annuity contracts automatically makes provision for a
death benefit.[15] Employers who establish group annuity or self-
administered plans, and wish to provide death benefits, normally
employ some form of group life insurance. In this survey, no
group annuity plans were found which provide a death benefit[16]
as an integral part of the pension plan. Of the self-administered
plans, 31, or about 25% so provide. A substantial number of employers, however, who use either group annuity or self-administered plans carry group life insurance to provide death benefits.
Of the 313 corporations with group annuity plans, it was *definitely
established* that at least 235, or about 75% of them carry group life
insurance to provide death benefits; and of the 121 corporations

---

[14] Employee contributions, under contributory pension plans, when death occurs
prior to retirement, are normally refunded to a beneficiary or his estate, and are
sometimes referred to as the death benefit. (See Table, p. 113.) By death benefits
in this discussion, however, there is meant those benefits which arise from the
*employer's* contributions, whether the pension plan is contributory or non-contributory.

[15] No individual annuity plan which makes use of *individual* level premium, or
individual single-premium, deferred life annuity contracts was uncovered in this
survey. These contracts do not make provision for a death benefit, for they are
issued with a discount for mortality. (See Table, p. 155.)

[16] That is, no full cash refund group annuity as described on p. 121.

with self-administered plans at least 91, or likewise about 75%, carry such insurance.

Five of the 152 individual annuity plans and 18 self-administered plans, which provide a death benefit in the pension plan itself, make payment of the death benefits conditional. In other words, vesting of the death benefits is deferred. For example, of the few individual annuity plans which defer the vesting of death benefits, one allows them after 5 years' service; 2 others make payments after participation of 1 and 10 years respectively. These limitations and similar ones in the self-administered plans may be seen in Table M. In this table, for the reason given above, group annuity plans are not represented.

Where death benefits are provided for either in an individual annuity or in a self-administered plan the amounts payable will vary, whether or not there is immediate or deferred vesting of such benefits. For example, under an individual annuity plan, notwith-

TABLE M

CONDITIONS TO BE SATISFIED FOR DEATH BENEFITS TO VEST

| CONDITIONS | INDIVIDUAL ANNUITY | | SELF-ADMINISTERED | |
|---|---|---|---|---|
| | Com-panies | Per Cent | Com-panies | Per Cent |
| Service Only............................ | 1 | 0.7 | 13 | 10.7 |
| 6 months............................. | — | — | 1 | 0.8 |
| 1 year............................... | — | — | 1 | 0.8 |
| 2 years.............................. | — | — | 4 | 3.3 |
| 3 years.............................. | — | — | 1 | 0.8 |
| 5 years.............................. | 1 | 0.7 | — | — |
| 10 years............................. | — | — | 2 | 1.7 |
| 15 years............................. | — | — | 3 | 2.5 |
| 25 years............................. | — | — | 1 | 0.8 |
| Participation Only...................... | 2 | 1.3 | 2 | 1.7 |
| 1 year............................... | 1 | 0.7 | 2 | 1.7 |
| 10 years............................. | 1 | 0.7 | — | — |
| Age and Service........................ | — | — | 3 | 2.5 |
| Aged 60, 20 years' service............. | — | — | 1 | 0.8 |
| Aged 60 to 65, 25 years' service........ | — | — | 1 | 0.8 |
| Aged 55, 15 years' service or aged 50, 20 years' service...................... | — | — | 1 | 0.8 |
| Other Conditions....................... | 2 | 1.3 | — | — |
| PLANS HAVING CONDITIONS—DEFERRED VESTING............................ | 5 | 3.3 | 18 | 14.9 |
| NO CONDITIONS—IMMEDIATE VESTING.... | 145 | 95.4 | 13 | 10.7 |
| PLANS OFFERING NO DEATH BENEFITS... | 2 | 1.3 | 90 | 74.4 |
| TOTALS.............................. | 152 | 100.0 | 121 | 100.0 |

standing the fact that the use of retirement income contracts carry an insurance feature of $1,000 for each $10.00 monthly pension benefit, there may be stipulated that there will be payable to an employee as a death benefit only the premiums paid on the contract. The insurance proceeds less such premiums, therefore, will revert to a trust or suspense fund, to be used to reduce future employer contributions to the pension plan. This is the exceptional procedure; nevertheless it is employed. Again, whereas under self-administered plans death benefits technically are provided for in a different fashion than under individual annuity plans, the amounts payable may differ similarly from plan to plan. All the various death benefit schemes which were found in either type of plan will not be enumerated, but examples are given in Table 2, Appendix A.

## L.  Disability Benefits

Benefits payable on the occurrence of total and permanent disability may be provided in pension plans either directly or indirectly. Under plans which make *direct* provision it usually is found that there is specific provision for the payment of disability benefits, that the cost of such benefits has been anticipated in the valuation, and that the benefits will be more or less definite in amount. An example of direct provision may be seen most clearly in the disability contracts once widely issued by insurance companies, in which the usual benefit was $10.00 a month per $1,000 of insurance coverage. Plans which make *indirect* provision for disability benefits, whether or not specific reference is made to them, are those which allow the payment of the employer's contributions to an employee in one form or another, through the operation of the early retirement and/or vesting provisions.[17] Under pension plans that make indirect provision for disability, the benefits, however, will be indefinite in amount.[18] This distinction of direct and

---

[17] The early retirement provision is sometimes referred to as a vesting provision. But a vesting provision is one which provides that withdrawal benefits shall vest *absolutely* after the conditions necessary to obtain them have been satisfied by an employee. As was disclosed in the analysis of early retirement provisions, consent of the company is necessary in the great majority of the plans before early retirement is permitted. Thus, while an early retirement provision under some plans might be of such a nature as to justify a description of it as a vesting provision, it usually would be inaccurate to describe it as such.

[18] Stated differently, pension plans which indirectly provide disability benefits through the use of early retirement or vesting clauses, might be said to have *money-purchase* disability provisions; meaning that if total disability coincides with the right to early retirement, or to withdrawal benefits, or if specific provision is made

indirect provision for disability benefits is a broad one and non-technical, but should serve generally to distinguish the several ways in which provision for the payment of disability benefits may be made.

## 1. Group Annuity

Of the 313 group annuity plans only 14 make reference to payment of disability benefits. In 9 of the 14, provision is made that an employee may retire if disabled and receive the actuarial equivalent of the normal pension. This is an example of the indirect method mentioned above, and the actual benefit an employee would receive cannot be accurately predicted. It would vary, dependent on such factors as the pension benefits provided under the terms of the plan, the age at which an employee becomes eligible, the age at which he becomes disabled, and so forth. In 3 of the 14 there are created separate disability funds, from which disability benefits may be payable. These disability funds are apart from the group annuity plan itself, and essentially constitute self-administered disability funds. One of the 14 purchases disability insurance separately.[19] These four companies, with group annuity plans, therefore, do make provision for a definite disability benefit, but by methods apart from the pension plan. Finally, one company vests the employer's contributions to the group annuity plan, that is, 96% of the employer's contributions, immediately upon disability, payable in cash. This again, however, is indirect provision.

## 2. Individual Annuity

Of the individual annuity plans, 58, or almost 40%, make reference to disability. The disability benefits provided are those which result from full vesting of the cash value of any contracts on an employee's life, such benefits to be payable either in cash or in installments, or as a reduced annuity income benefit purchased by the cash value.[20] Again, however, the method is indirect, for the

---

for *full* vesting upon disability, the amounts then accumulated for the account of the employee can be distributed to him in some form. In contrast, plans with a direct provision, where the disability benefit is in a prearranged and specific amount, may be said to have *definite-benefit* disability provisions.

[19] This company, through its group life insurance, provides a disability benefit equal to the amount of group insurance carried on an employee's life.

[20] It may be noted in the individual annuity plans that there are several forms in which disability payments may be payable as distinguished from the procedure of a group annuity. In the latter, an employee would normally be offered a reduced annuity income benefit.

benefits an employee could expect to receive on the occurrence of disability would be indefinite in amount.

### 3. Self-Administered

About 50%, or 61 of the self-administered plans, make reference to disability benefits, and for their payment one way or another. In most of them, however, the procedure is akin to that used in insured plans, that is, indirect provision. Moreover, through the use of age and service conditions in self-administered plans, the effect in a considerable number is to approximate the operation of the typical early retirement provision encountered in group annuity plans. In short, 54 of the 61 plans provide a disability benefit equal essentially to the actuarial equivalent of the normal pension with the consequent uncertainty as to the amount of the benefit, but in addition attach service and/or age conditions for its receipt. The most typical service requirements are 10, 15, or 20 years; and where age *and* service are conditions, the attainment of age 50 or 55 with 10 or 15 years of service is stipulated. A small number of the 54, 10 plans, while providing as do the others for a disability benefit equal essentially to the actuarial equivalent of the normal pension, make the benefits available immediately; that is, without conditions of service and/or age attached.

Of the remaining plans, 7 make direct provision for the payment of relatively definite amounts of disability benefit. Of these, 2 plans allow 90% of the normal pension, one after 15 years' service, the other after 5 years' service; one uses the actuarial equivalent of the normal pension, but provides for a minimum pension of 25% of the average annual compensation, after 10 years of service; one allows 66⅔% of current compensation for the first year of disability, but not to exceed $1,600, 50% of such current compensation the second year of disability, not to exceed $1,200, and thereafter graduates the amounts in relation to years of service or participation; two plans provide a flat benefit of $40 a month after 10 and 15 years of service respectively; finally one plan has a composite scheme.

## II. BANK PLANS

The 92 bank plans in this survey, as pointed out earlier, constitute a rather large proportion of the 612 plans, about 15%. A complete analysis of the basic provisions of these plans no doubt would disclose interesting differences in detail from the findings for the entire 612 plans, but such an analysis was not attempted. There is shown for bank plans, however, in Table BB, the findings by date of establishment.[21]   It may be mentioned, although no tabulation is given, that bank plans for the most part make all employees eligible to membership; moreover, earnings tests for eligibility, such as $3,000, are seldom employed.

## A.  Date of Establishment

As was found for the entire group of plans, approximately 80% of the bank plans in this survey were established in the period 1940-45.   Also paralleling the general findings, the peak years for the establishment of plans were 1941, 18 plans, and 1944, 33 plans.[22]

There is evidence in Table BB of an increasing use by banks of individual annuity and self-administered plans in 1944, as compared with the previous years.   Whereas in 1941, of the 18 plans established, 14, or about 78% are group annuity plans, less than 37% of the 33 created in 1944 are such.

Only one combination plan was encountered among bank plans, as shown in the table.   This is a combination of a self-administered plan, to provide the past service benefits, and of a group annuity to provide future service benefits.

## III.  OTHER FINDINGS

*Compulsory Participation.*   In contributory pension plans it is sometimes provided that employees who are eligible shall be obliged to participate.   Stated differently, participation in the pension plan is made a condition of employment.   It is the exception rather than the rule that contributory plans require compulsory participation, and there exists a difference of opinion as to the advisability of this procedure.   Briefly, on the one hand, it is felt

---

[21] For the table showing parallel findings for the entire 612 plans, see Table B, p. 257.

[22] In examining either Table BB or B, it will be noted that in 1942 there was a sharp drop in the number of plans established as measured against 1941.   This phenomenon is not believed to be accidental to this survey, that is, a result influenced by the methods used in obtaining the plans.   The explanation undoubtedly is to be found in the fact that in 1942 the Federal law governing the establishment of pension and profit sharing plans was amended, but not before considerable uncertainty had developed as to the taxable status of pension plans.   The enactment in 1942 of the revised law, Section 165, of the Internal Revenue Code, however, did not entirely clarify matters.   Many employers, therefore, thought it wise to await the issuance of regulations by the Treasury Department before establishing a new plan.   It was not until July 8th, 1943, however, that the Treasury Department issued the first of its regulations under the new law, relating to the establishment and operation of pension and profit-sharing plans.

TABLE BB

Date of Establishment

Bank Plans

| Year Established | Total Companies | | Group Annuity | | Individual Annuity | | Self-Administered | | Combination and Others | |
|---|---|---|---|---|---|---|---|---|---|---|
| | Companies | Per Cent | Companies | Per Cent | Companies | Per Cent | Companies | Per Cent | Companies | Per Cent |
| 1945ᵃ | 9 | 9.8 | — | — | 5 | 27.8 | 4 | 17.4 | — | — |
| 1944 | 33 | 35.9 | 12 | 24.0 | 11 | 61.1 | 10 | 43.5 | — | — |
| 1943 | 7 | 7.6 | 4 | 8.0 | 2 | 11.1 | 1 | 4.3 | — | — |
| 1942 | 6 | 6.5 | 5 | 10.0 | — | — | 1 | 4.3 | — | — |
| 1941 | 18 | 19.6 | 14 | 28.0 | — | — | 3 | 13.0 | 1 | 100.0 |
| 1940 | 2 | 2.2 | 1 | 2.0 | — | — | 1 | 4.3 | — | — |
| 1938 | 4 | 4.3 | 4 | 8.0 | — | — | — | — | — | — |
| 1937 | 3 | 3.3 | 3 | 6.0 | — | — | — | — | — | — |
| 1936 | 2 | 2.2 | 2 | 4.0 | — | — | — | — | — | — |
| 1935 | 2 | 2.2 | 2 | 4.0 | — | — | — | — | — | — |
| 1934 | 1 | 1.1 | — | — | — | — | 1 | 4.3 | — | — |
| 1933 | 2 | 2.2 | 2 | 4.0 | — | — | — | — | — | — |
| 1932 | 1 | 1.1 | 1 | 2.0 | — | — | — | — | — | — |
| 1928 | 1 | 1.1 | — | — | — | — | 1 | 4.3 | — | — |
| 1914 | 1 | 1.1 | — | — | — | — | 1 | 4.3 | — | — |
| Totals | 92 | 100.0 | 50 | 100.0 | 18 | 100.0 | 23 | 100.0 | 1 | 100.0 |

ᵃ Includes first half of 1945 only.

that, if participation is not made compulsory, the employees who refuse to participate may be the very ones to reach normal retirement age with no funds accumulated with which to effect their retirement. On the other hand, a compulsory participation provision may be unsatisfactory in terms of its effects on employee morale; or it may create practical difficulties where employees, for one reason or another, feel they can no longer afford to make contributions.

Among the 385 contributory plans found in this survey, 62 plans, or about 16%, provide for compulsory participation. 29 of the 62 plans, however, make participation compulsory only for future employees, that is, employees who were employed after the pension plan was established.

It was noticeable that of the 62 plans, compulsory participation was found chiefly in the group annuity and self-administered plans; for 36 are of the former, and 22 of the latter type. Only 3 contributory individual annuity plans make participation compulsory.

*Guarantee of the Pension Benefits.* Under fully insured plans, the pension benefits provided for employees are payable by the insurance carrier, and are guaranteed by the latter. The employer is relieved of, or assumes no direct responsibility for the pension payments. Under self-administered plans the pension payments are made from the accumulated pension funds, and likewise the employer assumes no direct responsibility for the pension payments. Only one self-administered plan was encountered in the survey, which was an exception to the rule; thereunder, the employer, a large building materials company, agrees to guarantee payment of the pension benefits.

*Competitor Clause.* The phrase *competitor clause* is used here to describe a provision frequently found in self-administered plans, which may result in an employee forfeiting his pension benefit after its commencement. The following is a typical example of a competitor clause.

Anything herein contained to the contrary notwithstanding, if the Board of Directors finds that any retired member is engaged or employed in any occupation which is in competition with the company, and if after due notice such retired member continues to be engaged or be employed in such occupation the Retirement Board shall suspend his retirement allowance, which suspension shall continue until revoked by notice of the Board of Directors, and after such suspension has continued for one year the Retirement Board shall cancel such member's retirement allowance.

Of the 121 self-administered plans 41, or about 39%, were found to contain a competitor clause, more or less worded as the above provision.

*Minimum Pensions.* Provision for a minimum pension benefit, payable in the event the pension formula used under the plan does not produce a given minimum, was found in 134, or about 22% of the 612 plans. Individual annuity plans make greater relative use of this provision, for almost 41% of the 152 plans provide for a minimum pension; 28% of self-administered plans do so, but less than 8% of group annuity plans.

In practically all plans which make provision for minimum pensions the benefit is granted as a flat amount, but a few stipulate the minimum as a percentage of compensation. The flat amounts most frequently provided are $120, $240, or $360 a year, or monthly, $10, $20, and $30 respectively. The tabulations of minimum pension provisions, as found in the several types of plans, may be seen in Table 3, Appendix A.

*Maximum Pensions.* There are 244, or about 40% of all plans, which stipulate a maximum pension; almost twice the number that make provision for a minimum. This general average of 40% was approximated as between the several types of plans; group annuity plans using a maximum pension provision in 36%, individual annuity in 39%, and self-administered in 48% of the cases. Again, flat amounts are the usual stipulation, with a small number expressing the maximum pension as a percentage of compensation. The detailed maximum pension provisions are to be found in Table 4, Appendix A.

*Investments of Trustees.* Under a group annuity plan the management and investment of the pension funds is in the hands of an insurance company. This is also largely true of individual annuity plans, notwithstanding the fact that use may be made of a trustee or trustees. For, while in this type funds may come to the hands of the trustees from death or withdrawals which may require temporary investment, normally such amounts will be used shortly thereafter for future premium payments. It is the investment powers of the trustees in self-administered plans, therefore, which were analyzed and are reported on here.

In only about one-half, 59 of the 121 self-administered plans, was information obtained as to the investment powers of the trustees. In 17 plans there are no limitations placed on the trustee, who thus receives full discretion as to investment of the pension funds. 26 plans permit investment only in securities legal for life insurance companies, savings banks, and trust funds. 6 plans likewise stipulate the foregoing limitation, but also further provide that no more than 10% of the pension funds may be invested in the securities of any one issuer, but without limitation in United States Government securities. 8 plans allow the trustees complete discretion as to the type of securities selected but provide that no more than 5% (1 plan), 10% (5 plans), or 25% (1 plan) of the pension funds can be invested in the securities of any one issuer, but, again, without limitation in United States Government securities. Finally, one plan provides that the trustee may make investments upon instructions from the retirement committee; the other, after approval of the Board of Directors of the company.

# Appendixes

## TABLE 1

### Examples of Frequently Encountered Deferred Vesting (Severance) Schemes[a]

| Group Annuity<br>I. Service Only | | Individual Annuity<br>I. Service Only | | Self-Administered<br>I. Service Only | |
|---|---|---|---|---|---|
| 5 years' service, paid-up deferred life annuity. | 3 | 5 to 10 years' service, 25% of cash value; 10 to 15 years, 50%; 15 to 20 years, 75%; 20 years or more, 100%. | 10 | 20 years' service, the pension accrued to termination date, payment deferred to normal retirement age. | 2 |
| 10 years' service, paid-up deferred life annuity. | 17 | 5 years' service, 25% of cash value, plus 7½% for each additional year of service. | 2 | 10 years' service, actuarial equivalent of normal pension, payment immediate; or the pension accrued to termination date, payment deferred to normal retirement age; at the employee's election. | 1 |
| 10 years' service, paid-up deferred life annuity for future service only. | 2 | 5 to 10 years' service, 33⅓% of cash value; 10 to 15 years, 66⅔%; 15 or more years, 100%. | 4 | 15 years' service, after age 30, actuarial equivalent of normal pension, payment immediate (1 plan); actuarial equivalent of normal pension, payment immediate, or the pension accrued to termination date, payment deferred to normal retirement age; at the employee's election (1 plan). | 2 |
| 15 years' service, paid-up deferred life annuity. | 14 | 10 to 15 years' service, 33⅓% of cash value; 15 to 20 years, 66⅔%; 20 years or more, 100%. | 6 | 30 years' service, the pension accrued to termination date, payment deferred to normal retirement age. | 1 |
| 20 years' service, paid-up deferred life annuity. | 6 | 10 years' service, 50% of cash value, plus 5% for each additional year of service over 10 years. | 2 | 20 years' service, if discharged, actuarial equivalent of normal pension, payment immediate, or the pension accrued to termination date, payment deferred to normal retirement age; at the employee's election. | 1 |

333

TABLE 1 (*Cont.*)

EXAMPLES OF FREQUENTLY ENCOUNTERED DEFERRED VESTING (SEVERANCE) SCHEMES[a]

| | GROUP ANNUITY | | INDIVIDUAL ANNUITY | | SELF-ADMINISTERED |
|---|---|---|---|---|---|
| | *I. Service Only (Cont.)* | | *I. Service Only (Cont.)* | | *I. Service Only (Cont.)* |
| 2 | 3 years' service, 30% of paid-up deferred life annuities, plus 10% for each additional year. | 4 | 10 to 15 years, 25% of cash value; 15 to 20 years, 50%; 20 to 25 years, 75%; 25 or more years, 100%. | 1 | 5 years' service, 25% of employer's contributions. Additional 5% for each additional year of service. |
| 4 | 10 to 15 years' service, 25% of paid-up deferred life annuities; 15 to 20 years, 50%; 20 to 25 years, 75%; 25 years or more, 100%. | 2 | 10 to 15 years, 50% of cash value; 15 to 20 years, 75%; 20 or more years, 100%. | 1 | 5 years' service, 25% of employer's contributions. Additional 25% for each added 5 year period up to a maximum of 90% at 20 years. |
| 7 | 5 to 10 years' service, 25% of paid-up deferred life annuities; 10 to 15 years, 50%; 15 to 20 years, 75%; 20 years or more, 100%. | | | 1 | 15 years' service, election of $1,000, or the pension accrued to termination date, payment deferred to normal retirement age. |
| 2 | 10 to 15 years' service, 33⅓% of paid-up deferred life annuities; 15 to 20 years, 66⅔%; 20 years or more, 100%. | | | 1 | 3 to 5 years' service, 50% of employer's contributions. 5 to 10 years, 75%; 10 years or more, 100%. |
| | | | | 1 | 1 year of service, 10% of total contributions. Additional 10% for each additional year. |
| | | | | 1 | 15 years' service, involuntary severance (not for cause), actuarial equivalent of normal pension, payment immediate, or the pension accrued to termination date, payment deferred to normal retirement age; at the employee's election. |

## TABLE 1 (*Cont.*)

### EXAMPLES OF FREQUENTLY ENCOUNTERED DEFERRED VESTING (SEVERANCE) SCHEMES[a]

| GROUP ANNUITY — *II. Participation Only* | | INDIVIDUAL ANNUITY — *II. Participation Only* | | SELF-ADMINISTERED — *II. Participation Only* | |
| --- | --- | --- | --- | --- | --- |
| 5 years' participation, paid-up deferred life annuity. | 12 | 1 year's participation, 10% of cash value, plus 10% for each additional year of participation. | 2 | 10 years' participation, 50% of employer's contributions; 15 years, 75%; 20 years, 100%. | 1 |
| 5 years' participation, paid-up deferred life annuity for future service only. (In 6 companies, paid-up annuities for past service vest upon satisfaction of further conditions.) | 9 | 5 years' participation, 25% of cash value, plus 5% for each additional year of participation. | 3 | 5 years' participation, 50% of the actuarial equivalent of normal pension. Additional 10% for each added year of participation. | 1 |
| 10 years' participation, a paid-up deferred life annuity. | 15 | 5 years' participation, 20% of cash value. Additional 20% for each additional 5 year period. 25 years or more, 100%. | 2 | 11 years' participation, 10% of normal pension, plus 10% for each additional year of participation. (If aged 60, 20 years' service, full normal pension vests, but payment deferred to normal retirement age.) | 1 |
| 15 years' participation, a paid-up deferred life annuity. | 3 | 4 years' participation, 10% of cash value, plus 10% for each additional year of participation up to 100% for 13 years. | 2 | | |
| | | 5 years' participation, 50% of employer's contributions. (One company vests 100% if aged 55, and 5 years' participation.) | 2 | | |

## TABLE 1 (*Cont.*)

### Examples of Frequently Encountered Deferred Vesting (Severance) Schemes[a]

| Group Annuity[b] | | Individual Annuity[c] | | Self-Administered | |
|---|---|---|---|---|---|
| *III. Age Only* | | *III. Age Only* | | *III. Age Only* | |
| Men aged 55, women aged 50, a paid-up deferred life annuity. | 1 | Aged 45, 6⅔% of cash value for each year of service. | 1 | Aged 55, the pension accrued to termination date, payment deferred to normal retirement age. | 1 |
| | | | | Aged 60, termination without cause, actuarial equivalent of normal pension, payment immediate, or the pension accrued to termination date, payment deferred to normal retirement age; at the election of the employee. | 1 |
| *IV. Age and Service* | | *IV. Age and Service*[c] | | *IV. Age and Service* | |
| Aged 50, 10 years' service, a paid-up deferred life annuity. | 8 | Aged 55, 20 years' service, the cash value. | 1 | Aged 55, 25 years' service, actuarial equivalent of normal pension, payment immediate (1 plan); the pension accrued to termination date, payment deferred to normal retirement age (1 plan). | 2 |
| Aged 50, 15 years' service, a paid-up deferred life annuity. | 7 | | | Men aged 55, women aged 50, 10 years' service, the pension accrued to termination date, payment deferred to normal retirement age. | 1 |
| Aged 40, 10 years' service, a paid-up deferred life annuity. | 7 | | | Aged 50, 15 years' service, the pension accrued to termination date, payment deferred to normal retirement age. | 1 |

TABLE 1 (*Cont.*)

EXAMPLES OF FREQUENTLY ENCOUNTERED DEFERRED VESTING (SEVERANCE) SCHEMES[a]

| GROUP ANNUITY (Cont.)<br>IV. *Age and Service* | | INDIVIDUAL ANNUITY[c] (Cont.)<br>IV. *Age and Service* | | SELF-ADMINISTERED (Cont.)<br>IV. *Age and Service* | |
|---|---|---|---|---|---|
| Aged 55, 10 years' service, a paid-up deferred life annuity. | 2 | | | Aged 55, 20 years' service, **actuarial equivalent of normal pension, payment immediate.** | 1 |
| Aged 45, 10 years' service, a paid-up deferred life annuity. | 13 | | | Aged 55, 10 years' service, **actuarial equivalent of normal pension, payment immediate, or the pension accrued to termination date, payment deferred to normal retirement age; at the employee's election.** | 1 |
| Aged 45, 15 years' service, a paid-up deferred life annuity. | 8 | | | Aged 50, 10 years' service, **actuarial equivalent of normal pension, payment immediate, or the pension accrued to termination date, payment deferred to normal retirement age; at the employee's election.** | 1 |
| Aged 40, 15 years' service, a paid-up deferred life annuity. | 2 | | | Aged 45, 30 years' service, **actuarial equivalent of normal pension, payment immediate, or the pension accrued to termination date, payment deferred to normal retirement age; at the employee's election.** | 1 |
| Aged 45, 20 years' service, a paid-up deferred life annuity. | 2 | | | Aged 35, 10 years' service, **not discharged for cause, 4% of employer's contributions for each year age exceeds 35.** | 1 |

## TABLE 1 (Cont.)

### Examples of Frequently Encountered Deferred Vesting (Severance) Schemes[a]

| Group Annuity IV. Age and Service (Cont.) | Individual Annuity IV. Age and Service (Cont.) | Self-Administered IV. Age and Service (Cont.) | |
|---|---|---|---|
| | | Under age 55, 10 years' service, released without cause, actuarial equivalent of normal pension, payment immediate, or the pension accrued to termination date, payment deferred to normal retirement age; at the employee's election. In either case, there is a deduction of one-half of the primary Social Security benefit. | 1 |
| | | Aged 55, 15 years' service, the pension accrued to termination date, payment deferred to normal retirement age. | 1 |
| | | Aged 45, 10 years' service, "annuity income or other equitable settlement." | 1 |
| | | Aged 55, 10 years' service, the pension accrued to termination date, payment deferred to normal retirement age. If aged 60, 10 years' service, actuarial equivalent of normal pension, payment immediate, or the pension accrued to termination date, payment deferred to normal retirement age; at the employee's election. | 1 |

## TABLE 1 (*Cont.*)

### EXAMPLES OF FREQUENTLY ENCOUNTERED DEFERRED VESTING (SEVERANCE) SCHEMES[a]

| GROUP ANNUITY (Cont.) | | INDIVIDUAL ANNUITY[b] (Cont.) | | SELF-ADMINISTERED (Cont.) | |
|---|---|---|---|---|---|
| *IV. Age and Service (Cont.)* | | *IV. Age and Service (Cont.)* | | *IV. Age and Service (Cont.)* | |
| | | | | Aged 45, 10 years' service, actuarial equivalent of normal pension arising from future service; aged 55, 10 years' service, actuarial equivalent of normal pension arising from both future and past service; in either case, payment immediate. | 1 |
| *V. Age and Participation* | | *V. Age and Participation*[c] | | *V. Age and Participation* | |
| Aged 45, 5 years' participation, a paid-up deferred life annuity. | 7 | Aged 40, 5 years' participation, the cash value. | 1 | 1 year's participation, aged 55, 100% of employer's contributions. If under 55, a percentage of employer's contributions, graduated from 6% for 3 years' service, to 100% for 30 years or more service. | 1 |
| Aged 45, 5 years' participation, a paid-up deferred life annuity for future service only. | 2 | | | | |
| *VI. Service and Participation* | | *VI. Service and Participation* | | *VI. Service and Participation* | |
| 20 years' service, 5 years' participation, a paid-up deferred life annuity. | 4 | 5 years' service, 5% of cash value for each year of participation. | 2 | 10 years' service, 7 years' participation, actuarial equivalent of normal pension, payment immediate; or the pension accrued to termination date, payment deferred to normal retirement age; at the election of the employee. | 1 |

## TABLE 1 (Cont.)

### EXAMPLES OF FREQUENTLY ENCOUNTERED DEFERRED VESTING (SEVERANCE) SCHEMES[a]

| GROUP ANNUITY VI. Service and Participation (Cont.) | | INDIVIDUAL ANNUITY VI. Service and Participation (Cont.) | | SELF-ADMINISTERED VI. Service and Participation (Cont.) | |
|---|---|---|---|---|---|
| 10 years' service, 5 years' participation, a paid-up deferred life annuity. | 4 | 5% of cash value (after return of employee's contributions) for each year of past service up to 10, plus 5% for each year of participation. | 2 | | |
| 15 years' service, 5 years' participation, a paid-up deferred life annuity. | 5 | | | | |

[a] Practically every self-administered plan which provides for deferred vesting imposes a different set of conditions. Under group annuity and individual annuity plans, unless otherwise noted, examples of vesting schemes are given only where more than one of the respective types were found to use the same scheme.

[b] No two group annuity plans were found to use the same vesting scheme under this classification, but one example is given for illustrative purposes.

[c] No two individual annuity plans were found to use the same vesting scheme under this classification, but one example is given for illustrative purposes.

## TABLE 2

Examples of Frequently Encountered Death Benefit Schemes[a]

| Individual Annuity | | Self-Administered | |
|---|---|---|---|
| Total proceeds of policy.[b] | 107 | Full amount of employer's contribution allocated to decedent's account. | 4 |
| Greater of total premiums paid or cash value. | 17 | One-half compensation of year preceding death. | 3 |
| Total company contributions. | 3 | Actuarial equivalent of normal pension, computed as of date of death, or a stipulated minimum. | 5 |
| Greater of (1) 50% of total premiums or (2) the amount which would have been payable if severance of employment otherwise occurred. | 3 | One to ten years' participation, one-half average annual compensation not to exceed $10,000; over ten years' participation, full average annual compensation. | 2 |

[a] For the conditions to be satisfied to obtain death benefits, see Table M, p. 321.

[b] The annuity contracts on the lives of insurable employees normally provide for a minimum death benefit of $1,000 for each $10.00 of monthly pension benefit, or the cash value of the contract if greater than $1,000; annuity contracts on the lives of uninsurable employees normally provide a death benefit equal to the premiums paid thereon, or the cash value of the contract, whichever is the greater.

## TABLE 3

### MINIMUM ANNUAL PENSION

| AMOUNT | TOTAL COMPANIES | | GROUP ANNUITY | | INDIVIDUAL ANNUITY | | SELF-ADMINISTERED | | COMBINATION AND OTHERS | |
|---|---|---|---|---|---|---|---|---|---|---|
| | Companies | Per Cent | Companies | Per Cent | Companies | Per Cent | Companies | Per Cent | Companies | Per Cent |
| FLAT AMOUNTS | | | | | | | | | | |
| $60 | 1 | 0.2 | — | — | — | — | 1 | 0.8 | — | — |
| $90 | 1 | 0.2 | — | — | — | — | 1 | 0.8 | 8 | 30.8 |
| $120 | 28 | 4.6 | 1 | 0.3 | 16 | 10.5 | 3 | 2.5 | 1 | 3.8 |
| $144 | 2 | 0.3 | — | — | 1 | 0.7 | — | — | — | — |
| $180 | 8 | 1.3 | 2 | 0.6 | 6 | 3.9 | — | — | — | — |
| $240 | 44 | 7.2 | 7 | 2.2 | 25 | 16.4 | 6 | 5.0 | 6 | 23.1 |
| $300 | 8 | 1.3 | 2 | 0.6 | 4 | 2.6 | 2 | 1.7 | — | — |
| $360 | 12 | 2.0 | 1 | 0.3 | 6 | 3.9 | 5 | 4.1 | — | — |
| $420 | 1 | 0.2 | — | — | — | — | 1 | 0.8 | — | — |
| $480 | 2 | 0.3 | — | — | — | — | 1 | 0.8 | — | — |
| $500 | 2 | 0.3 | 1 | 0.3 | 2 | 1.3 | 2 | 1.7 | — | — |
| $600 | 3 | 0.5 | — | — | — | — | 1 | 0.8 | — | — |
| $660 | 2 | 0.3 | 2 | 0.6 | — | — | — | — | — | — |
| $720 | 1 | 0.2 | — | — | — | — | 1 | 0.8 | — | — |
| $900 | 1 | 0.2 | 1 | 0.3 | 1 | 0.7 | — | — | — | — |
| $1,200 | 2 | 0.3 | — | — | — | — | 1 | 0.8 | — | — |
| PERCENTAGE OF COMPENSATION | | | | | | | | | | |
| 6% | 1 | 0.2 | — | — | 1 | 0.7 | — | — | — | — |
| 30% | 2 | 0.3 | — | — | — | — | 2 | 1.7 | — | — |
| PERCENTAGE OF COMPENSATION EXCEEDING $3,000 | | | | | | | | | | |
| 30% | 2 | 0.3 | 2 | 0.6 | — | — | — | — | — | — |
| OTHERS | 11 | 1.8 | 4 | 1.3 | — | — | 7 | 5.8 | — | — |
| PLANS WITH MINIMUM PENSION PROVISIONS | 134 | 21.9 | 23 | 7.3 | 62 | 40.8 | 34 | 28.1 | 15 | 57.7 |
| NO MINIMUM PENSION PROVISIONS | 478 | 78.1 | 290 | 92.7 | 90 | 59.2 | 87 | 71.9 | 11 | 42.3 |
| TOTALS | 612 | 100.0 | 313 | 100.0 | 152 | 100.0 | 121 | 100.0 | 26 | 100.0 |

## TABLE 4

### MAXIMUM ANNUAL PENSION

| AMOUNT | Total Companies | | Group Annuity | | Individual Annuity | | Self-Administered | | Combination and Others | |
|---|---|---|---|---|---|---|---|---|---|---|
| | Companies | Per Cent | Companies | Per Cent | Companies | Per Cent | Companies | Per Cent | Companies | Per Cent |
| FLAT AMOUNTS | 214 | 35.0 | 113 | 36.1 | 46 | 30.3 | 46 | 38.0 | 9 | 34.6 |
| $600 | 1 | 0.2 | — | — | — | — | 1 | 0.8 | — | — |
| $720 | 1 | 0.2 | — | — | 1 | 0.7 | — | — | — | — |
| $780 | 1 | 0.2 | — | — | 1 | 0.7 | — | — | — | — |
| $900 | 2 | 0.3 | — | — | 2 | 1.3 | — | — | — | — |
| $960 | 1 | 0.2 | — | — | 1 | 0.7 | — | — | — | — |
| $1,200 | 3 | 0.5 | 1 | 0.3 | 2 | 1.3 | — | — | — | — |
| $1,800 | 1 | 0.2 | — | — | 1 | 0.7 | — | — | — | — |
| $2,000 | 1 | 0.2 | 1 | 0.3 | — | — | — | — | — | — |
| $2,400 | 1 | 0.2 | — | — | 1 | 0.7 | — | — | — | — |
| $3,000 | 6 | 1.0 | 1 | 0.3 | 4 | 2.6 | — | — | 1 | 3.8 |
| $3,600 | 4 | 0.7 | — | — | 3 | 2.0 | 1 | 0.8 | — | — |
| $4,000 | 1 | 0.2 | 1 | 0.3 | — | — | — | — | — | — |
| $4,200 | 4 | 0.7 | — | — | 2 | 1.3 | 1 | 0.8 | 1 | 3.8 |
| $4,800 | 6 | 1.0 | — | — | 4 | 2.6 | 1 | 0.8 | — | — |
| $5,000 | 16 | 2.6 | 11 | 3.5 | — | — | 4 | 3.3 | 1 | 3.8 |
| $5,200 | 2 | 0.3 | — | — | — | — | 1 | 0.8 | 1 | 3.8 |
| $5,400 | 1 | 0.2 | — | — | 1 | 0.7 | — | — | — | — |
| $6,000 | 37 | 6.0 | 15 | 4.8 | 7 | 4.6 | 12 | 9.9 | 3 | 11.5 |
| $6,500 | 1 | 0.2 | 1 | 0.3 | — | — | — | — | — | — |
| $6,600 | 1 | 0.2 | — | — | 1 | 0.7 | — | — | — | — |
| $7,000 | 4 | 0.7 | 4 | 1.3 | — | — | — | — | — | — |
| $7,200 | 8 | 1.3 | 4 | 1.3 | 4 | 2.6 | — | — | — | — |
| $7,350 | 1 | 0.2 | — | — | — | — | 1 | 0.8 | — | — |

### TABLE 4 (Cont.)
### Maximum Annual Pension

| Amount | Total Companies | | Group Annuity | | Individual Annuity | | Self-Administered | | Combination and Others | |
|---|---|---|---|---|---|---|---|---|---|---|
| | Companies | Per Cent | Companies | Per Cent | Companies | Per Cent | Companies | Per Cent | Companies | Per Cent |
| **Flat Amounts (Cont.)** | | | | | | | | | | |
| $7,500 | 5 | 0.8 | 2 | 0.6 | 2 | 1.3 | 1 | 0.8 | — | — |
| $8,000 | 1 | 0.2 | — | — | — | — | 1 | 0.8 | — | — |
| $8,500 | 7 | 1.1 | 7 | 2.2 | — | — | — | — | — | — |
| $9,000 | 6 | 1.0 | 5 | 1.6 | 1 | 0.7 | — | — | — | — |
| $9,600 | 1 | 0.2 | 1 | 0.3 | — | — | — | — | — | — |
| $10,000 | 29 | 4.7 | 21 | 6.7 | 3 | 2.0 | 5 | 4.1 | 1 | 3.8 |
| $12,000 | 16 | 2.6 | 9 | 2.9 | 1 | 0.7 | 5 | 4.1 | — | — |
| $12,500 | 11 | 1.8 | 10 | 3.2 | — | — | 1 | 0.8 | 1 | 3.8 |
| $15,000 | 15 | 2.5 | 8 | 2.6 | — | — | 6 | 5.0 | — | — |
| $17,500 | 5 | 0.8 | 3 | 1.0 | — | — | 1 | 0.8 | — | — |
| $18,000 | 3 | 0.5 | 2 | 0.6 | 1 | 0.7 | — | — | — | — |
| $20,000 | 4 | 0.7 | 3 | 1.0 | 1 | 0.7 | 1 | 0.8 | — | — |
| $21,600 | 1 | 0.2 | — | — | — | — | — | — | — | — |
| $25,000 | 2 | 0.3 | 1 | 0.3 | 1 | 0.7 | — | — | — | — |
| $35,000 | 1 | 0.2 | 1 | 0.3 | — | — | 1 | 0.8 | — | — |
| $37,500 | 1 | 0.2 | — | — | — | — | — | — | — | — |
| $49,700 | 1 | 0.2 | — | — | — | — | 1 | 0.8 | — | — |
| *Different for Men and Women* | | | | | | | | | | |
| Men $720, women $480 | 1 | 0.2 | — | — | — | — | 1 | 0.8 | — | — |

TABLE 4 (*Cont.*)

MAXIMUM ANNUAL PENSION

| AMOUNT | TOTAL COMPANIES | | GROUP ANNUITY | | INDIVIDUAL ANNUITY | | SELF-ADMINISTERED | | COMBINATION AND OTHERS | |
|---|---|---|---|---|---|---|---|---|---|---|
| | Companies | Per Cent | Companies | Per Cent | Companies | Per Cent | Companies | Per Cent | Companies | Per Cent |
| PERCENTAGE OF COMPENSATION | 15 | 2.5 | 1 | 0.3 | 6 | 3.9 | 8 | 6.6 | — | — |
| 20%. | 2 | 0.3 | | | 1 | 0.7 | 1 | 0.8 | | |
| 30%. | 1 | 0.2 | | | 1 | 0.7 | — | — | | |
| 33⅓%. | 1 | 0.2 | | | — | — | 1 | 0.8 | | |
| 40%. | 1 | 0.2 | | | — | — | 1 | 0.8 | | |
| 45%. | 1 | 0.2 | | | 1 | 0.7 | 1 | 0.8 | | |
| 50%. | 2 | 0.3 | | | — | — | 1 | 0.8 | | |
| 60%. | 2 | 0.3 | | | 1 | 0.7 | 2 | 1.7 | | |
| 65%. | 1 | 0.2 | | | — | — | — | — | | |
| 66⅔%. | 1 | 0.2 | 1 | 0.3 | — | — | — | — | | |
| 75%. | 1 | 0.2 | | | — | — | 1 | 0.8 | | |
| *Percentage of Compensation Exceeding $3,000* | | | | | | | | | | |
| 25% plus ¼% times future service after 1941. | 1 | 0.2 | | | 1 | 0.7 | | | | |
| 30%. | 1 | 0.2 | | | 1 | 0.7 | | | | |
| OTHERS. | 15 | 2.5 | — | — | 7 | 4.6 | 4 | 3.3 | 4 | 15.4 |
| INFORMATION NOT OBTAINED. | 2 | 0.3 | 2 | 0.6 | — | — | — | — | — | — |
| PLANS WITH MAXIMUM PENSION PROVISIONS. | 244 | 39.9 | 114 | 36.4 | 59 | 38.8 | 58 | 47.9 | 13 | 50.0 |
| PLANS WITH NO MAXIMUM PENSION PROVISIONS. | 366 | 59.8 | 197 | 62.9 | 93 | 61.2 | 63 | 52.1 | 13 | 50.0 |
| TOTALS. | 612 | 100.0 | 313 | 100.0 | 152 | 100.0 | 121 | 100.0 | 26 | 100.0 |

# APPENDIX B
## Mortality Tables

AMERICAN EXPERIENCE TABLE

| Age | Number Living | Number Dying | Yearly Probability of Dying | Complete Expectation of Life |
|-----|---------------|--------------|------------------------------|------------------------------|
| 10 | 100,000 | 749 | .007490 | 48.72 |
| 11 | 99,251 | 746 | .007516 | 48.08 |
| 12 | 98,505 | 743 | .007543 | 47.45 |
| 13 | 97,762 | 740 | .007569 | 46.80 |
| 14 | 97,022 | 737 | .007596 | 46.16 |
| 15 | 96,285 | 735 | .007634 | 45.50 |
| 16 | 95,550 | 732 | .007661 | 44.85 |
| 17 | 94,818 | 729 | .007688 | 44.19 |
| 18 | 94,089 | 727 | .007727 | 43.53 |
| 19 | 93,362 | 725 | .007765 | 42.87 |
| 20 | 92,637 | 723 | .007805 | 42.20 |
| 21 | 91,914 | 722 | .007855 | 41.53 |
| 22 | 91,192 | 721 | .007906 | 40.85 |
| 23 | 90,471 | 720 | .007958 | 40.17 |
| 24 | 89,751 | 719 | .008011 | 39.49 |
| 25 | 89,032 | 718 | .008065 | 38.81 |
| 26 | 88,314 | 718 | .008130 | 38.12 |
| 27 | 87,596 | 718 | .008197 | 37.43 |
| 28 | 86,878 | 718 | .008264 | 36.73 |
| 29 | 86,160 | 719 | .008345 | 36.03 |
| 30 | 85,441 | 720 | .008427 | 35.33 |
| 31 | 84,721 | 721 | .008510 | 34.63 |
| 32 | 84,000 | 723 | .008607 | 33.92 |
| 33 | 83,277 | 726 | .008718 | 33.21 |
| 34 | 82,551 | 729 | .008831 | 32.50 |
| 35 | 81,822 | 732 | .008946 | 31.78 |
| 36 | 81,090 | 737 | .009089 | 31.07 |
| 37 | 80,353 | 742 | .009234 | 30.35 |
| 38 | 79,611 | 749 | .009408 | 29.62 |
| 39 | 78,862 | 756 | .009586 | 28.90 |
| 40 | 78,106 | 765 | .009794 | 28.18 |
| 41 | 77,341 | 774 | .010008 | 27.45 |
| 42 | 76,567 | 785 | .010252 | 26.72 |
| 43 | 75,782 | 797 | .010517 | 26.00 |
| 44 | 74,985 | 812 | .010829 | 25.27 |
| 45 | 74,173 | 828 | .011163 | 24.54 |
| 46 | 73,345 | 848 | .011562 | 23.81 |
| 47 | 72,497 | 870 | .012000 | 23.08 |
| 48 | 71,627 | 896 | .012509 | 22.36 |
| 49 | 70,731 | 927 | .013106 | 21.63 |
| 50 | 69,804 | 962 | .013781 | 20.91 |
| 51 | 68,842 | 1,001 | .014541 | 20.20 |
| 52 | 67,841 | 1,044 | .015389 | 19.49 |
| 53 | 66,797 | 1,091 | .016333 | 18.79 |
| 54 | 65,706 | 1,143 | .017396 | 18.09 |

| Age | Number Living | Number Dying | Yearly Probability of Dying | Complete Expectation of Life |
|---|---|---|---|---|
| 55 | 64,563 | 1,199 | .018571 | 17.40 |
| 56 | 63,364 | 1,260 | .019885 | 16.72 |
| 57 | 62,104 | 1,325 | .021335 | 16.05 |
| 58 | 60,779 | 1,394 | .022936 | 15.39 |
| 59 | 59,385 | 1,468 | .024720 | 14.74 |
| 60 | 57,917 | 1,546 | .026693 | 14.10 |
| 61 | 56,371 | 1,628 | .028880 | 13.47 |
| 62 | 54,743 | 1,713 | .031292 | 12.86 |
| 63 | 53,030 | 1,800 | .033943 | 12.26 |
| 64 | 51,230 | 1,889 | .036873 | 11.67 |
| 65 | 49,341 | 1,980 | .040129 | 11.10 |
| 66 | 47,361 | 2,070 | .043707 | 10.54 |
| 67 | 45,291 | 2,158 | .047647 | 10.00 |
| 68 | 43,133 | 2,243 | .052002 | 9.47 |
| 69 | 40,890 | 2,321 | .056762 | 8.97 |
| 70 | 38,569 | 2,391 | .061993 | 8.48 |
| 71 | 36,178 | 2,448 | .067665 | 8.00 |
| 72 | 33,730 | 2,487 | .073733 | 7.55 |
| 73 | 31,243 | 2,505 | .080178 | 7.11 |
| 74 | 28,738 | 2,501 | .087028 | 6.68 |
| 75 | 26,237 | 2,476 | .094371 | 6.27 |
| 76 | 23,761 | 2,431 | .102311 | 5.88 |
| 77 | 21,330 | 2,369 | .111064 | 5.49 |
| 78 | 18,961 | 2,291 | .120827 | 5.11 |
| 79 | 16,670 | 2,196 | .131734 | 4.74 |
| 80 | 14,474 | 2,091 | .144466 | 4.39 |
| 81 | 12,383 | 1,964 | .158605 | 4.05 |
| 82 | 10,419 | 1,816 | .174297 | 3.71 |
| 83 | 8,603 | 1,648 | .191561 | 3.39 |
| 84 | 6,955 | 1,470 | .211359 | 3.08 |
| 85 | 5,485 | 1,292 | .235552 | 2.77 |
| 86 | 4,193 | 1,114 | .265681 | 2.47 |
| 87 | 3,079 | 933 | .303020 | 2.18 |
| 88 | 2,146 | 744 | .346692 | 1.91 |
| 89 | 1,402 | 555 | .395863 | 1.66 |
| 90 | 847 | 385 | .454545 | 1.42 |
| 91 | 462 | 246 | .532468 | 1.19 |
| 92 | 216 | 137 | .634259 | .98 |
| 93 | 79 | 58 | .734177 | .80 |
| 94 | 21 | 18 | .857143 | .64 |
| 95 | 3 | 3 | 1.000000 | .50 |

## Male

| Age | Number Living | Number Dying | Yearly Probability of Dying | Complete Expectation of Life |
|---|---|---|---|---|
| 25 | 100,000 | 431 | .00431 | 41.71 |
| 26 | 99,569 | 440 | .00442 | 40.89 |
| 27 | 99,129 | 451 | .00455 | 40.07 |
| 28 | 98,678 | 462 | .00468 | 39.25 |
| 29 | 98,216 | 474 | .00483 | 38.44 |
| 30 | 97,742 | 488 | .00499 | 37.62 |
| 31 | 97,254 | 502 | .00516 | 36.81 |
| 32 | 96,752 | 518 | .00535 | 35.99 |
| 33 | 96,234 | 534 | .00555 | 35.18 |
| 34 | 95,700 | 551 | .00576 | 34.37 |
| 35 | 95,149 | 571 | .00600 | 33.57 |
| 36 | 94,578 | 592 | .00626 | 32.77 |
| 37 | 93,986 | 615 | .00654 | 31.98 |
| 38 | 93,371 | 639 | .00684 | 31.18 |
| 39 | 92,732 | 664 | .00716 | 30.40 |
| 40 | 92,068 | 691 | .00751 | 29.61 |
| 41 | 91,377 | 722 | .00790 | 28.83 |
| 42 | 90,655 | 753 | .00831 | 28.06 |
| 43 | 89,902 | 788 | .00877 | 27.29 |
| 44 | 89,114 | 823 | .00924 | 26.53 |
| 45 | 88,291 | 863 | .00978 | 25.77 |
| 46 | 87,428 | 904 | .01034 | 25.02 |
| 47 | 86,524 | 949 | .01097 | 24.27 |
| 48 | 85,575 | 997 | .01165 | 23.54 |
| 49 | 84,578 | 1,045 | .01236 | 22.81 |
| 50 | 83,533 | 1,098 | .01315 | 22.09 |
| 51 | 82,435 | 1,154 | .01400 | 21.38 |
| 52 | 81,281 | 1,214 | .01493 | 20.67 |
| 53 | 80,067 | 1,274 | .01591 | 19.98 |
| 54 | 78,793 | 1,340 | .01701 | 19.29 |
| 55 | 77,453 | 1,407 | .01817 | 18.62 |
| 56 | 76,046 | 1,478 | .01944 | 17.95 |
| 57 | 74,568 | 1,552 | .02081 | 17.30 |
| 58 | 73,016 | 1,628 | .02230 | 16.66 |
| 59 | 71,388 | 1,706 | .02390 | 16.02 |
| 60 | 69,682 | 1,788 | .02566 | 15.40 |
| 61 | 67,894 | 1,869 | .02753 | 14.80 |
| 62 | 66,025 | 1,952 | .02956 | 14.20 |
| 63 | 64,073 | 2,035 | .03176 | 13.62 |
| 64 | 62,038 | 2,119 | .03415 | 13.05 |

Male

| Age | Number Living | Number Dying | Yearly Probability of Dying | Complete Expectation of Life |
|---|---|---|---|---|
| 65 | 59,919 | 2,201 | .03673 | 12.49 |
| 66 | 57,718 | 2,280 | .03950 | 11.95 |
| 67 | 55,438 | 2,356 | .04250 | 11.42 |
| 68 | 53,082 | 2,430 | .04577 | 10.91 |
| 69 | 50,652 | 2,496 | .04927 | 10.41 |
| 70 | 48,156 | 2,555 | .05305 | 9.92 |
| 71 | 45,601 | 2,607 | .05716 | 9.45 |
| 72 | 42,994 | 2,646 | .06155 | 8.99 |
| 73 | 40,348 | 2,675 | .06631 | 8.55 |
| 74 | 37,673 | 2,692 | .07145 | 8.12 |
| 75 | 34,981 | 2,693 | .07698 | 7.70 |
| 76 | 32,288 | 2,679 | .08296 | 7.30 |
| 77 | 29,609 | 2,645 | .08933 | 6.92 |
| 78 | 26,964 | 2,595 | .09625 | 6.55 |
| 79 | 24,369 | 2,527 | .10370 | 6.19 |
| 80 | 21,842 | 2,439 | .11165 | 5.85 |
| 81 | 19,403 | 2,333 | .12023 | 5.52 |
| 82 | 17,070 | 2,209 | .12939 | 5.21 |
| 83 | 14,861 | 2,069 | .13925 | 4.91 |
| 84 | 12,792 | 1,917 | .14985 | 4.63 |
| 85 | 10,875 | 1,752 | .16112 | 4.35 |
| 86 | 9,123 | 1,580 | .17322 | 4.09 |
| 87 | 7,543 | 1,403 | .18606 | 3.85 |
| 88 | 6,140 | 1,227 | .19977 | 3.61 |
| 89 | 4,913 | 1,054 | .21445 | 3.39 |
| 90 | 3,859 | 888 | .23004 | 3.17 |
| 91 | 2,971 | 733 | .24675 | 2.97 |
| 92 | 2,238 | 591 | .26397 | 2.78 |
| 93 | 1,647 | 466 | .28272 | 2.60 |
| 94 | 1,181 | 357 | .30207 | 2.43 |
| 95 | 824 | 266 | .32306 | 2.27 |
| 96 | 558 | 192 | .34426 | 2.12 |
| 97 | 366 | 134 | .36667 | 1.97 |
| 98 | 232 | 91 | .39035 | 1.81 |
| 99 | 141 | 59 | .41727 | 1.66 |
| 100 | 82 | 37 | .45679 | 1.50 |
| 101 | 45 | 23 | .50000 | 1.32 |
| 102 | 22 | 12 | .54545 | 1.18 |
| 103 | 10 | 6 | .60000 | 1.00 |
| 104 | 4 | 3 | .75000 | .75 |
| 105 | 1 | 1 | 1.00000 | .50 |

COMBINED ANNUITY TABLE

| Age | | Number Living | Number Dying | Yearly Probability of Dying | Complete Expectation of Life |
|---|---|---|---|---|---|
| Male | Female | | | | |
| 10 | 14 | 100,000 | 153 | .00153 | 58.10 |
| 11 | 15 | 99,847 | 157 | .00157 | 57.19 |
| 12 | 16 | 99,690 | 161 | .00162 | 56.28 |
| 13 | 17 | 99,529 | 164 | .00165 | 55.37 |
| 14 | 18 | 99,365 | 168 | .00169 | 54.46 |
| 15 | 19 | 99,197 | 173 | .00174 | 53.55 |
| 16 | 20 | 99,024 | 177 | .00179 | 52.64 |
| 17 | 21 | 98,847 | 183 | .00185 | 51.74 |
| 18 | 22 | 98,664 | 188 | .00191 | 50.83 |
| 19 | 23 | 98,476 | 194 | .00197 | 49.93 |
| 20 | 24 | 98,282 | 201 | .00205 | 49.02 |
| 21 | 25 | 98,081 | 207 | .00211 | 48.12 |
| 22 | 26 | 97,874 | 210 | .00215 | 47.22 |
| 23 | 27 | 97,664 | 213 | .00218 | 46.32 |
| 24 | 28 | 97,451 | 214 | .00220 | 45.42 |
| 25 | 29 | 97,237 | 216 | .00222 | 44.52 |
| 26 | 30 | 97,021 | 216 | .00223 | 43.62 |
| 27 | 31 | 96,805 | 217 | .00224 | 42.72 |
| 28 | 32 | 96,588 | 219 | .00227 | 41.81 |
| 29 | 33 | 96,369 | 223 | .00231 | 40.91 |
| 30 | 34 | 96,146 | 227 | .00236 | 40.00 |
| 31 | 35 | 95,919 | 234 | .00244 | 39.09 |
| 32 | 36 | 95,685 | 244 | .00255 | 38.19 |
| 33 | 37 | 95,441 | 257 | .00269 | 37.28 |
| 34 | 38 | 95,184 | 274 | .00288 | 36.28 |
| 35 | 39 | 94,910 | 294 | .00310 | 35.49 |
| 36 | 40 | 94,616 | 318 | .00336 | 34.60 |
| 37 | 41 | 94,298 | 343 | .00364 | 33.71 |
| 38 | 42 | 93,955 | 371 | .00395 | 32.83 |
| 39 | 43 | 93,584 | 401 | .00428 | 31.96 |
| 40 | 44 | 93,183 | 432 | .00464 | 31.10 |
| 41 | 45 | 92,751 | 467 | .00503 | 30.24 |
| 42 | 46 | 92,284 | 503 | .00545 | 29.39 |
| 43 | 47 | 91,781 | 542 | .00590 | 28.55 |
| 44 | 48 | 91,239 | 583 | .00639 | 27.71 |
| 45 | 49 | 90,656 | 628 | .00693 | 26.89 |
| 46 | 50 | 90,028 | 676 | .00751 | 26.07 |
| 47 | 51 | 89,352 | 727 | .00814 | 25.27 |
| 48 | 52 | 88,625 | 782 | .00882 | 24.47 |
| 49 | 53 | 87,843 | 839 | .00955 | 23.68 |
| 50 | 54 | 84,004 | 900 | .01035 | 22.91 |
| 51 | 55 | 86,104 | 965 | .01121 | 22.14 |
| 52 | 56 | 85,139 | 1,034 | .01215 | 21.39 |
| 53 | 57 | 84,105 | 1,107 | .01316 | 20.64 |
| 54 | 58 | 82,998 | 1,184 | .01426 | 19.91 |

| Age | | Number Living | Number Dying | Yearly Probability of Dying | Complete Expectation of Life |
|---|---|---|---|---|---|
| Male | Female | | | | |
| 55 | 59 | 81,814 | 1,264 | .01545 | 19.19 |
| 56 | 60 | 80,550 | 1,348 | .01673 | 18.49 |
| 57 | 61 | 79,202 | 1,435 | .01812 | 17.79 |
| 58 | 62 | 77,767 | 1,527 | .01963 | 17.11 |
| 59 | 63 | 76,240 | 1,621 | .02126 | 16.44 |
| 60 | 64 | 74,619 | 1,718 | .02302 | 15.79 |
| 61 | 65 | 72,901 | 1,817 | .02493 | 15.15 |
| 62 | 66 | 71,084 | 1,919 | .02700 | 14.52 |
| 63 | 67 | 69,165 | 2,022 | .02923 | 13.91 |
| 64 | 68 | 67,143 | 2,124 | .03164 | 13.32 |
| 65 | 69 | 65,019 | 2,227 | .03425 | 12.74 |
| 66 | 70 | 62,792 | 2,328 | .03707 | 12.17 |
| 67 | 71 | 60,464 | 2,426 | .04012 | 11.62 |
| 68 | 72 | 58,038 | 2,519 | .04341 | 11.08 |
| 69 | 73 | 55,519 | 2,608 | .04697 | 10.56 |
| 70 | 74 | 52,911 | 2,688 | .05081 | 10.06 |
| 71 | 75 | 50,223 | 2,760 | .05495 | 9.57 |
| 72 | 76 | 47,463 | 2,821 | .05943 | 9.10 |
| 73 | 77 | 44,642 | 2,868 | .06425 | 8.64 |
| 74 | 78 | 41,774 | 2,901 | .06945 | 8.20 |
| 75 | 79 | 38,873 | 2,918 | .07506 | 7.78 |
| 76 | 80 | 35,955 | 2,916 | .08109 | 7.37 |
| 77 | 81 | 33,039 | 2,894 | .08759 | 6.97 |
| 78 | 82 | 30,145 | 2,851 | .09458 | 6.60 |
| 79 | 83 | 27,294 | 2,787 | .10210 | 6.23 |
| 80 | 84 | 24,507 | 2,700 | .11018 | 5.88 |
| 81 | 85 | 21,807 | 2,592 | .11886 | 5.55 |
| 82 | 86 | 19,215 | 2,463 | .12817 | 5.23 |
| 83 | 87 | 16,752 | 2,314 | .13814 | 4.93 |
| 84 | 88 | 14,438 | 2,149 | .14883 | 4.64 |
| 85 | 89 | 12,289 | 1,970 | .16027 | 4.36 |
| 86 | 90 | 10,319 | 1,780 | .17249 | 4.10 |
| 87 | 91 | 8,539 | 1,584 | .18553 | 3.85 |
| 88 | 92 | 6,955 | 1,387 | .19944 | 3.61 |
| 89 | 93 | 5,568 | 1,193 | .21425 | 3.39 |
| 90 | 94 | 4,375 | 1,006 | .22999 | 3.18 |
| 91 | 95 | 3,369 | 831 | .24669 | 2.97 |
| 92 | 96 | 2,538 | 671 | .26439 | 2.79 |
| 93 | 97 | 1,867 | 529 | .28310 | 2.61 |
| 94 | 98 | 1,338 | 405 | .30285 | 2.44 |
| 95 | 99 | 933 | 302 | .32364 | 2.28 |
| 96 | 100 | 631 | 218 | .34548 | 2.13 |
| 97 | 101 | 413 | 152 | .36835 | 2.00 |
| 98 | 102 | 261 | 102 | .39225 | 1.87 |
| 99 | 103 | 159 | 66 | .41712 | 1.75 |

| Age | | Number Living | Number Dying | Yearly Probability of Dying | Complete Expectation of Life |
|---|---|---|---|---|---|
| Male | Female | | | | |
| 100 | 104 | 93 | 41 | .44294 | 1.63 |
| 101 | 105 | 52 | 24 | .46963 | 1.52 |
| 102 | 106 | 28 | 14 | .49712 | 1.39 |
| 103 | 107 | 14 | 7 | .52613 | 1.29 |
| 104 | 108 | 7 | 4 | .55409 | 1.07 |
| 105 | 109 | 3 | 2 | .58331 | .83 |
| 106 | 110 | 1 | 1 | 1.00000 | .50 |

| Age | | Number Living | Number Dying | Yearly Probability of Dying | Complete Expectation of Life |
|---|---|---|---|---|---|
| Male | Female | | | | |
| 5 | 10 | 1,000,000 | 1,234 | .001234 | 65.08 |
| 6 | 11 | 998,766 | 1,241 | .001243 | 64.16 |
| 7 | 12 | 997,525 | 1,247 | .001250 | 63.24 |
| 8 | 13 | 996,278 | 1,250 | .001255 | 62.32 |
| 9 | 14 | 995,028 | 1,250 | .001256 | 61.40 |
| 10 | 15 | 993,778 | 1,249 | .001257 | 60.48 |
| 11 | 16 | 992,529 | 1,247 | .001257 | 59.55 |
| 12 | 17 | 991,282 | 1,246 | .001257 | 58.63 |
| 13 | 18 | 990,036 | 1,244 | .001257 | 57.70 |
| 14 | 19 | 988,792 | 1,245 | .001259 | 56.77 |
| 15 | 20 | 987,547 | 1,246 | .001262 | 55.84 |
| 16 | 21 | 986,301 | 1,250 | .001267 | 54.91 |
| 17 | 22 | 985,051 | 1,258 | .001277 | 53.98 |
| 18 | 23 | 983,793 | 1,269 | .001290 | 53.05 |
| 19 | 24 | 982,524 | 1,285 | .001308 | 52.12 |
| 20 | 25 | 981,239 | 1,306 | .001331 | 51.18 |
| 21 | 26 | 979,933 | 1,333 | .001360 | 50.25 |
| 22 | 27 | 978,600 | 1,368 | .001398 | 49.32 |
| 23 | 28 | 977,232 | 1,409 | .001442 | 48.39 |
| 24 | 29 | 975,823 | 1,460 | .001496 | 47.46 |
| 25 | 30 | 974,363 | 1,521 | .001561 | 46.53 |
| 26 | 31 | 972,842 | 1,590 | .001634 | 45.60 |
| 27 | 32 | 971,252 | 1,672 | .001721 | 44.67 |
| 28 | 33 | 969,580 | 1,767 | .001822 | 43.75 |
| 29 | 34 | 967,813 | 1,874 | .001936 | 42.83 |
| 30 | 35 | 965,939 | 1,995 | .002065 | 41.91 |
| 31 | 36 | 963,944 | 2,132 | .002212 | 41.00 |
| 32 | 37 | 961,812 | 2,286 | .002377 | 40.19 |
| 33 | 38 | 959,526 | 2,458 | .002562 | 39.18 |
| 34 | 39 | 957,068 | 2,644 | .002763 | 38.28 |
| 35 | 40 | 954,424 | 2,845 | .002981 | 37.38 |
| 36 | 41 | 951,579 | 3,060 | .003216 | 36.49 |
| 37 | 42 | 948,519 | 3,291 | .003470 | 35.61 |
| 38 | 43 | 945,228 | 3,537 | .003742 | 34.73 |
| 39 | 44 | 941,691 | 3,802 | .004037 | 33.86 |
| 40 | 45 | 937,889 | 4,085 | .004356 | 33.00 |
| 41 | 46 | 933,804 | 4,388 | .004699 | 32.14 |
| 42 | 47 | 929,416 | 4,710 | .005068 | 31.29 |
| 43 | 48 | 924,706 | 5,056 | .005468 | 30.44 |
| 44 | 49 | 919,650 | 5,424 | .005898 | 29.61 |
| 45 | 50 | 914,226 | 5,816 | .006362 | 28.78 |
| 46 | 51 | 908,410 | 6,234 | .006863 | 27.96 |
| 47 | 52 | 902,176 | 6,679 | .007403 | 27.15 |
| 48 | 53 | 895,497 | 7,149 | .007983 | 26.35 |
| 49 | 54 | 888,348 | 7,651 | .008613 | 25.56 |

| Age | | Number Living | Number Dying | Yearly Probability of Dying | Complete Expectation of Life |
|---|---|---|---|---|---|
| Male | Female | | | | |
| 50 | 55 | 880,697 | 8,180 | .009288 | 24.78 |
| 51 | 56 | 872,517 | 8,741 | .010018 | 24.01 |
| 52 | 57 | 863,776 | 9,333 | .010805 | 23.24 |
| 53 | 58 | 854,443 | 9,957 | .011653 | 22.49 |
| 54 | 59 | 844,486 | 10,612 | .012566 | 21.75 |
| 55 | 60 | 833,874 | 11,302 | .013554 | 21.02 |
| 56 | 61 | 822,572 | 12,021 | .014614 | 20.30 |
| 57 | 62 | 810,551 | 12,774 | .015760 | 19.60 |
| 58 | 63 | 797,777 | 13,556 | .016992 | 18.90 |
| 59 | 64 | 784,221 | 14,368 | .018321 | 18.22 |
| 60 | 65 | 769,853 | 15,207 | .019753 | 17.55 |
| 61 | 66 | 754,646 | 16,072 | .021297 | 16.90 |
| 62 | 67 | 738,574 | 16,956 | .022958 | 16.25 |
| 63 | 68 | 721,618 | 17,859 | .024749 | 15.62 |
| 64 | 69 | 703,759 | 18,773 | .026675 | 15.01 |
| 65 | 70 | 684,986 | 19,694 | .028751 | 14.40 |
| 66 | 71 | 666,292 | 20,615 | .030986 | 13.81 |
| 67 | 72 | 644,677 | 21,526 | .033390 | 13.24 |
| 68 | 73 | 623,151 | 22,420 | .035978 | 12.68 |
| 69 | 74 | 600,731 | 23,286 | .038763 | 12.14 |
| 70 | 75 | 577,445 | 24,113 | .041758 | 11.60 |
| 71 | 76 | 553,332 | 24,889 | .044980 | 11.09 |
| 72 | 77 | 528,443 | 25,600 | .048444 | 10.59 |
| 73 | 78 | 502,843 | 26,232 | .052167 | 10.10 |
| 74 | 79 | 476,611 | 26,770 | .056167 | 9.63 |
| 75 | 80 | 449,841 | 27,199 | .060464 | 9.17 |
| 76 | 81 | 422,642 | 27,506 | .065081 | 8.73 |
| 77 | 82 | 395,136 | 27,672 | .070032 | 8.30 |
| 78 | 83 | 367,464 | 27,688 | .075349 | 7.89 |
| 79 | 84 | 339,776 | 27,539 | .081050 | 7.49 |
| 80 | 85 | 312,237 | 27,215 | .087161 | 7.11 |
| 81 | 86 | 285,022 | 26,709 | .093709 | 6.74 |
| 82 | 87 | 258,313 | 26,018 | .100723 | 6.39 |
| 83 | 88 | 232,295 | 25,141 | .108229 | 6.05 |
| 84 | 89 | 207,154 | 24,083 | .116257 | 5.72 |
| 85 | 90 | 183,071 | 22,854 | .124837 | 5.41 |
| 86 | 91 | 160,217 | 21,469 | .134000 | 5.11 |
| 87 | 92 | 138,748 | 19,950 | .143786 | 4.82 |
| 88 | 93 | 118,798 | 18,320 | .154211 | 4.54 |
| 89 | 94 | 100,478 | 16,611 | .165320 | 4.28 |
| 90 | 95 | 83,867 | 14,856 | .177138 | 4.03 |
| 91 | 96 | 69,011 | 13,092 | .189709 | 3.79 |
| 92 | 97 | 55,919 | 11,355 | .203062 | 3.56 |
| 93 | 98 | 44,564 | 9,680 | .217216 | 3.34 |
| 94 | 99 | 34,884 | 8,100 | .232198 | 3.13 |

| Age | | Number Living | Number Dying | Yearly Probability of Dying | Complete Expectation of Life |
|---|---|---|---|---|---|
| Male | Female | | | | |
| 95 | 100 | 26,784 | 6,644 | .248059 | 2.92 |
| 96 | 101 | 20,140 | 5,333 | .264796 | 2.72 |
| 97 | 102 | 14,807 | 4,198 | .283515 | 2.52 |
| 98 | 103 | 10,609 | 3,244 | .305778 | 2.32 |
| 99 | 104 | 7,365 | 2,444 | .331840 | 2.12 |
| 100 | 105 | 4,921 | 1,782 | .362122 | 1.93 |
| 101 | 106 | 3,139 | 1,248 | .397579 | 1.74 |
| 102 | 107 | 1,891 | 830 | .438921 | 1.55 |
| 103 | 108 | 1,061 | 517 | .487276 | 1.37 |
| 104 | 109 | 544 | 295 | .542279 | 1.20 |
| 105 | 110 | 249 | 152 | .610442 | 1.04 |
| 106 | 111 | 97 | 67 | .690722 | .88 |
| 107 | 112 | 30 | 24 | .800000 | .73 |
| 108 | 113 | 6 | 5 | .833333 | .67 |
| 109 | 114 | 1 | 1 | 1.000000 | .50 |
| 110 | 115 | 0 | | | |

| Age | Number Living | Number Dying | Yearly Probability of Dying | Complete Expectation of Life |
|---|---|---|---|---|
| 1 | 1,000,000 | 5,770 | .00577 | 62.76 |
| 2 | 994,230 | 4,116 | .00414 | 62.12 |
| 3 | 990,114 | 3,347 | .00338 | 61.37 |
| 4 | 986,767 | 2,950 | .00299 | 60.58 |
| 5 | 983,817 | 2,715 | .00276 | 59.76 |
| 6 | 981,102 | 2,561 | .00261 | 58.92 |
| 7 | 978,541 | 2,417 | .00247 | 58.08 |
| 8 | 976,124 | 2,255 | .00231 | 57.22 |
| 9 | 973,869 | 2,065 | .00212 | 56.35 |
| 10 | 971,804 | 1,914 | .00197 | 55.47 |
| 11 | 969,890 | 1,852 | .00191 | 54.58 |
| 12 | 968,038 | 1,859 | .00192 | 53.68 |
| 13 | 966,179 | 1,913 | .00198 | 52.78 |
| 14 | 964,266 | 1,996 | .00207 | 51.89 |
| 15 | 962,270 | 2,069 | .00215 | 50.99 |
| 16 | 960,201 | 2,103 | .00219 | 50.10 |
| 17 | 958,098 | 2,156 | .00225 | 49.21 |
| 18 | 955,942 | 2,199 | .00230 | 48.32 |
| 19 | 953,743 | 2,260 | .00237 | 47.43 |
| 20 | 951,483 | 2,312 | .00243 | 46.54 |
| 21 | 949,171 | 2,382 | .00251 | 45.66 |
| 22 | 946,789 | 2,452 | .00259 | 44.77 |
| 23 | 944,337 | 2,531 | .00268 | 43.88 |
| 24 | 941,806 | 2,609 | .00277 | 43.00 |
| 25 | 939,197 | 2,705 | .00288 | 42.12 |
| 26 | 936,492 | 2,800 | .00299 | 41.24 |
| 27 | 933,692 | 2,904 | .00311 | 40.36 |
| 28 | 930,788 | 3,025 | .00325 | 39.49 |
| 29 | 927,763 | 3,154 | .00340 | 38.61 |
| 30 | 924,609 | 3,292 | .00356 | 37.74 |
| 31 | 921,317 | 3,437 | .00373 | 36.88 |
| 32 | 917,880 | 3,598 | .00392 | 36.01 |
| 33 | 914,282 | 3,767 | .00412 | 35.15 |
| 34 | 910,515 | 3,961 | .00435 | 34.29 |
| 35 | 906,554 | 4,161 | .00459 | 33.44 |
| 36 | 902,393 | 4,386 | .00486 | 32.59 |
| 37 | 898,007 | 4,625 | .00515 | 31.75 |
| 38 | 893,382 | 4,878 | .00546 | 30.91 |
| 39 | 888,504 | 5,162 | .00581 | 30.08 |
| 40 | 883,342 | 5,459 | .00618 | 29.25 |
| 41 | 877,883 | 5,785 | .00659 | 28.43 |
| 42 | 872,098 | 6,131 | .00703 | 27.62 |
| 43 | 865,967 | 6,503 | .00751 | 26.81 |
| 44 | 859,464 | 6,910 | .00804 | 26.01 |
| 45 | 852,554 | 7,340 | .00861 | 25.21 |

| Age | Number Living | Number Dying | Yearly Probability of Dying | Complete Expectation of Life |
|---|---|---|---|---|
| 46 | 845,214 | 7,801 | .00923 | 24.43 |
| 47 | 837,413 | 8,299 | .00991 | 23.65 |
| 48 | 829,114 | 8,822 | .01064 | 22.88 |
| 49 | 820,292 | 9,392 | .01145 | 22.12 |
| 50 | 810,900 | 9,990 | .01232 | 21.37 |
| 51 | 800,910 | 10,628 | .01327 | 20.64 |
| 52 | 790,282 | 11,301 | .01430 | 19.91 |
| 53 | 778,981 | 12,020 | .01543 | 19.19 |
| 54 | 766,961 | 12,770 | .01665 | 18.48 |
| 55 | 754,191 | 13,560 | .01798 | 17.78 |
| 56 | 740,631 | 14,390 | .01943 | 17.10 |
| 57 | 726,241 | 15,251 | .02100 | 16.43 |
| 58 | 710,990 | 16,147 | .02271 | 15.77 |
| 59 | 694,843 | 17,072 | .02457 | 15.13 |
| 60 | 677,771 | 18,022 | .02659 | 14.50 |
| 61 | 659,749 | 18,988 | .02878 | 13.88 |
| 62 | 640,761 | 19,979 | .03118 | 13.27 |
| 63 | 620,782 | 20,958 | .03376 | 12.69 |
| 64 | 599,824 | 21,942 | .03658 | 12.11 |
| 65 | 577,882 | 22,907 | .03964 | 11.55 |
| 66 | 554,975 | 23,842 | .04296 | 11.01 |
| 67 | 531,133 | 24,730 | .04656 | 10.48 |
| 68 | 506,403 | 25,553 | .05046 | 9.97 |
| 69 | 480,850 | 26,302 | .05470 | 9.47 |
| 70 | 454,548 | 26,955 | .05930 | 8.99 |
| 71 | 427,593 | 27,481 | .06427 | 8.52 |
| 72 | 400,112 | 27,872 | .06966 | 8.08 |
| 73 | 372,240 | 28,104 | .07550 | 7.64 |
| 74 | 344,136 | 28,154 | .08181 | 7.23 |
| 75 | 315,982 | 28,009 | .08864 | 6.82 |
| 76 | 287,973 | 27,651 | .09602 | 6.44 |
| 77 | 260,322 | 27,071 | .10399 | 6.07 |
| 78 | 233,251 | 26,262 | .11259 | 5.72 |
| 79 | 206,989 | 25,224 | .12186 | 5.38 |
| 80 | 181,765 | 23,966 | .13185 | 5.06 |
| 81 | 157,799 | 22,502 | .14260 | 4.75 |
| 82 | 135,297 | 20,857 | .15416 | 4.46 |
| 83 | 114,440 | 19,062 | .16657 | 4.18 |
| 84 | 95,378 | 17,157 | .17988 | 3.91 |
| 85 | 78,221 | 15,185 | .19413 | 3.66 |
| 86 | 63,036 | 13,198 | .20937 | 3.42 |
| 87 | 49,838 | 11,245 | .22563 | 3.19 |
| 88 | 38,593 | 9,378 | .24300 | 2.98 |
| 89 | 29,215 | 7,638 | .26144 | 2.77 |
| 90 | 21,577 | 6,063 | .28099 | 2.58 |

| Age | Number Living | Number Dying | Yearly Probability of Dying | Complete Expectation of Life |
|-----|------|------|--------|------|
| 91 | 15,514 | 4,681 | .30173 | 2.39 |
| 92 | 10,833 | 3,506 | .32364 | 2.21 |
| 93 | 7,327 | 2,540 | .34666 | 2.03 |
| 94 | 4,787 | 1,776 | .37100 | 1.84 |
| 95 | 3,011 | 1,193 | .39621 | 1.63 |
| 96 | 1,818 | 813 | .44719 | 1.37 |
| 97 | 1,005 | 551 | .54826 | 1.08 |
| 98 | 454 | 329 | .72467 | .78 |
| 99 | 125 | 125 | 1.00000 | .50 |

| Age | Number Living | Number Dying | Yearly Probability of Dying | Complete Expectation of Life |
|-----|--------------|--------------|-----------------------------|------------------------------|
| 15 | 100,000 | 346 | .00346 | 50.06 |
| 16 | 99,654 | 352 | .00353 | 49.23 |
| 17 | 99,302 | 360 | .00363 | 48.40 |
| 18 | 98,942 | 367 | .00371 | 47.58 |
| 19 | 98,575 | 376 | .00381 | 46.75 |
| 20 | 98,199 | 385 | .00392 | 45.93 |
| 21 | 97,814 | 393 | .00402 | 45.11 |
| 22 | 97,421 | 401 | .00412 | 44.29 |
| 23 | 97,020 | 406 | .00418 | 43.47 |
| 24 | 96,614 | 411 | .00425 | 42.65 |
| 25 | 96,203 | 415 | .00431 | 41.83 |
| 26 | 95,788 | 417 | .00435 | 41.01 |
| 27 | 95,371 | 419 | .00439 | 40.18 |
| 28 | 94,952 | 419 | .00441 | 39.36 |
| 29 | 94,533 | 419 | .00443 | 38.53 |
| 30 | 94,114 | 420 | .00446 | 37.70 |
| 31 | 93,694 | 420 | .00448 | 36.87 |
| 32 | 93,274 | 421 | .00451 | 36.03 |
| 33 | 92,853 | 426 | .00459 | 35.19 |
| 34 | 92,427 | 433 | .00468 | 34.35 |
| 35 | 91,994 | 440 | .00478 | 33.51 |
| 36 | 91,554 | 452 | .00494 | 32.67 |
| 37 | 91,102 | 466 | .00512 | 31.83 |
| 38 | 90,636 | 482 | .00532 | 30.99 |
| 39 | 90,154 | 501 | .00556 | 30.15 |
| 40 | 89,653 | 524 | .00584 | 29.32 |
| 41 | 89,129 | 549 | .00616 | 28.49 |
| 42 | 88,580 | 579 | .00654 | 27.66 |
| 43 | 88,001 | 611 | .00694 | 26.84 |
| 44 | 87,390 | 648 | .00742 | 26.03 |
| 45 | 86,742 | 689 | .00794 | 25.22 |
| 46 | 86,053 | 733 | .00852 | 24.41 |
| 47 | 85,320 | 783 | .00918 | 23.62 |
| 48 | 84,537 | 836 | .00989 | 22.83 |
| 49 | 83,701 | 896 | .01070 | 22.06 |
| 50 | 82,805 | 959 | .01158 | 21.29 |
| 51 | 81,846 | 1,026 | .01254 | 20.53 |
| 52 | 80,820 | 1,101 | .01362 | 19.79 |
| 53 | 79,719 | 1,178 | .01478 | 19.05 |
| 54 | 78,541 | 1,263 | .01608 | 18.33 |
| 55 | 77,278 | 1,350 | .01747 | 17.62 |
| 56 | 75,928 | 1,444 | .01902 | 16.93 |
| 57 | 74,484 | 1,541 | .02069 | 16.25 |
| 58 | 72,943 | 1,642 | .02251 | 15.58 |
| 59 | 71,301 | 1,746 | .02449 | 14.93 |

| Age | Number Living | Number Dying | Yearly Probability of Dying | Complete Expectation of Life |
|---|---|---|---|---|
| 60 | 69,555 | 1,856 | .02668 | 14.29 |
| 61 | 67,699 | 1,965 | .02903 | 13.67 |
| 62 | 65,734 | 2,076 | .03158 | 13.06 |
| 63 | 63,658 | 2,188 | .03437 | 12.47 |
| 64 | 61,470 | 2,298 | .03738 | 11.90 |
| 65 | 59,172 | 2,406 | .04066 | 11.34 |
| 66 | 56,766 | 2,508 | .04418 | 10.80 |
| 67 | 54,258 | 2,606 | .04803 | 10.28 |
| 68 | 51,652 | 2,694 | .05216 | 9.77 |
| 69 | 48,958 | 2,773 | .05664 | 9.28 |
| 70 | 46,185 | 2,839 | .06147 | 8.81 |
| 71 | 43,346 | 2,891 | .06670 | 8.35 |
| 72 | 40,455 | 2,926 | .07233 | 7.91 |
| 73 | 37,529 | 2,942 | .07839 | 7.49 |
| 74 | 34,587 | 2,937 | .08492 | 7.08 |
| 75 | 31,650 | 2,910 | .09194 | 6.69 |
| 76 | 28,740 | 2,860 | .09951 | 6.32 |
| 77 | 25,880 | 2,786 | .10765 | 5.96 |
| 78 | 23,094 | 2,686 | .11631 | 5.62 |
| 79 | 20,408 | 2,565 | .12569 | 5.30 |
| 80 | 17,843 | 2,422 | .13574 | 4.99 |
| 81 | 15,421 | 2,258 | .14642 | 4.69 |
| 82 | 13,163 | 2,078 | .15787 | 4.41 |
| 83 | 11,085 | 1,885 | .17005 | 4.14 |
| 84 | 9,200 | 1,685 | .18315 | 3.89 |
| 85 | 7,515 | 1,481 | .19707 | 3.65 |
| 86 | 6,034 | 1,278 | .21180 | 3.42 |
| 87 | 4,756 | 1,081 | .22729 | 3.21 |
| 88 | 3,675 | 897 | .24408 | 3.00 |
| 89 | 2,778 | 727 | .26170 | 2.81 |
| 90 | 2,051 | 575 | .28035 | 2.63 |
| 91 | 1,476 | 442 | .29946 | 2.46 |
| 92 | 1,034 | 332 | .32108 | 2.30 |
| 93 | 702 | 240 | .34188 | 2.15 |
| 94 | 462 | 168 | .36364 | 2.01 |
| 95 | 294 | 114 | .38776 | 1.87 |
| 96 | 180 | 74 | .41111 | 1.74 |
| 97 | 106 | 47 | .44340 | 1.61 |
| 98 | 59 | 27 | .45763 | 1.50 |
| 99 | 32 | 16 | .50000 | 1.34 |
| 100 | 16 | 9 | .56250 | 1.19 |
| 101 | 7 | 4 | .57143 | 1.07 |
| 102 | 3 | 2 | .66667 | .83 |
| 103 | 1 | 1 | 1.00000 | .50 |

# APPENDIX C

## Interest Tables

AMOUNT OF ONE DOLLAR PRINCIPAL WITH COMPOUND INTEREST AT VARIOUS RATES

| Years | 1.5% | 2% | 2.5% | 3% | 3.5% | 4% | 4.5% | 5% | 6% |
|-------|------|------|------|------|------|------|------|------|------|
| 1 | 1.0150 | 1.0200 | 1.0250 | 1.0300 | 1.0350 | 1.0400 | 1.0450 | 1.0500 | 1.0600 |
| 2 | 1.0302 | 1.0404 | 1.0506 | 1.0609 | 1.0712 | 1.0816 | 1.0920 | 1.1025 | 1.1236 |
| 3 | 1.0457 | 1.0612 | 1.0769 | 1.0927 | 1.1087 | 1.1249 | 1.1412 | 1.1576 | 1.1910 |
| 4 | 1.0614 | 1.0824 | 1.1038 | 1.1255 | 1.1475 | 1.1699 | 1.1925 | 1.2155 | 1.2625 |
| 5 | 1.0773 | 1.1041 | 1.1314 | 1.1593 | 1.1877 | 1.2167 | 1.2462 | 1.2763 | 1.3382 |
| 6 | 1.0934 | 1.1262 | 1.1597 | 1.1941 | 1.2293 | 1.2653 | 1.3023 | 1.3401 | 1.4185 |
| 7 | 1.1098 | 1.1487 | 1.1887 | 1.2299 | 1.2723 | 1.3159 | 1.3609 | 1.4071 | 1.5036 |
| 8 | 1.1265 | 1.1717 | 1.2184 | 1.2668 | 1.3168 | 1.3686 | 1.4221 | 1.4775 | 1.5938 |
| 9 | 1.1434 | 1.1951 | 1.2489 | 1.3048 | 1.3629 | 1.4233 | 1.4861 | 1.5513 | 1.6895 |
| 10 | 1.1605 | 1.2190 | 1.2801 | 1.3439 | 1.4106 | 1.4802 | 1.5530 | 1.6289 | 1.7908 |
| 11 | 1.1779 | 1.2434 | 1.3121 | 1.3842 | 1.4600 | 1.5395 | 1.6229 | 1.7103 | 1.8983 |
| 12 | 1.1956 | 1.2682 | 1.3449 | 1.4258 | 1.5111 | 1.6010 | 1.6959 | 1.7959 | 2.0122 |
| 13 | 1.2136 | 1.2936 | 1.3785 | 1.4685 | 1.5640 | 1.6651 | 1.7722 | 1.8856 | 2.1329 |
| 14 | 1.2318 | 1.3195 | 1.4130 | 1.5126 | 1.6187 | 1.7317 | 1.8519 | 1.9799 | 2.2609 |
| 15 | 1.2502 | 1.3459 | 1.4483 | 1.5580 | 1.6753 | 1.8009 | 1.9353 | 2.0789 | 2.3966 |
| 16 | 1.2690 | 1.3728 | 1.4845 | 1.6047 | 1.7340 | 1.8730 | 2.0224 | 2.1829 | 2.5404 |
| 17 | 1.2880 | 1.4002 | 1.5216 | 1.6528 | 1.7947 | 1.9479 | 2.1134 | 2.2920 | 2.6928 |
| 18 | 1.3073 | 1.4282 | 1.5597 | 1.7024 | 1.8575 | 2.0258 | 2.2085 | 2.4066 | 2.8543 |
| 19 | 1.3270 | 1.4568 | 1.5987 | 1.7535 | 1.9225 | 2.1068 | 2.3079 | 2.5270 | 3.0256 |
| 20 | 1.3469 | 1.4859 | 1.6386 | 1.8061 | 1.9898 | 2.1911 | 2.4117 | 2.6533 | 3.2071 |
| 21 | 1.3671 | 1.5157 | 1.6796 | 1.8603 | 2.0594 | 2.2788 | 2.5202 | 2.7860 | 3.3996 |
| 22 | 1.3876 | 1.5460 | 1.7216 | 1.9161 | 2.1315 | 2.3699 | 2.6337 | 2.9253 | 3.6035 |
| 23 | 1.4084 | 1.5769 | 1.7646 | 1.9736 | 2.2061 | 2.4647 | 2.7522 | 3.0715 | 3.8197 |
| 24 | 1.4295 | 1.6084 | 1.8087 | 2.0328 | 2.2833 | 2.5633 | 2.8760 | 3.2251 | 4.0489 |
| 25 | 1.4509 | 1.6406 | 1.8539 | 2.0938 | 2.3632 | 2.6658 | 3.0054 | 3.3864 | 4.2919 |
| 26 | 1.4727 | 1.6734 | 1.9003 | 2.1566 | 2.4460 | 2.7725 | 3.1407 | 3.5557 | 4.5494 |
| 27 | 1.4948 | 1.7069 | 1.9478 | 2.2213 | 2.5316 | 2.8834 | 3.2820 | 3.7335 | 4.8223 |
| 28 | 1.5172 | 1.7410 | 1.9965 | 2.2879 | 2.6202 | 2.9987 | 3.4297 | 3.9201 | 5.1117 |
| 29 | 1.5400 | 1.7758 | 2.0464 | 2.3566 | 2.7119 | 3.1187 | 3.5840 | 4.1161 | 5.4184 |
| 30 | 1.5631 | 1.8114 | 2.0976 | 2.4273 | 2.8068 | 3.2434 | 3.7453 | 4.3219 | 5.7435 |
| 31 | 1.5865 | 1.8476 | 2.1500 | 2.5001 | 2.9050 | 3.3731 | 3.9139 | 4.5380 | 6.0881 |
| 32 | 1.6103 | 1.8845 | 2.2038 | 2.5751 | 3.0067 | 3.5081 | 4.0900 | 4.7649 | 6.4534 |
| 33 | 1.6345 | 1.9222 | 2.2589 | 2.6523 | 3.1119 | 3.6484 | 4.2740 | 5.0032 | 6.8406 |
| 34 | 1.6590 | 1.9607 | 2.3153 | 2.7319 | 3.2209 | 3.7943 | 4.4664 | 5.2533 | 7.2510 |
| 35 | 1.6839 | 1.9999 | 2.3732 | 2.8139 | 3.3336 | 3.9461 | 4.6673 | 5.5160 | 7.6861 |
| 36 | 1.7091 | 2.0399 | 2.4325 | 2.8983 | 3.4503 | 4.1039 | 4.8774 | 5.7918 | 8.1473 |
| 37 | 1.7348 | 2.0807 | 2.4933 | 2.9852 | 3.5710 | 4.2681 | 5.0969 | 6.0814 | 8.6361 |
| 38 | 1.7608 | 2.1223 | 2.5557 | 3.0748 | 3.6960 | 4.4388 | 5.3262 | 6.3855 | 9.1543 |
| 39 | 1.7872 | 2.1647 | 2.6196 | 3.1670 | 3.8254 | 4.6164 | 5.5659 | 6.7048 | 9.7035 |
| 40 | 1.8140 | 2.2080 | 2.6851 | 3.2620 | 3.9593 | 4.8010 | 5.8164 | 7.0400 | 10.2857 |
| 41 | 1.8412 | 2.2522 | 2.7522 | 3.3599 | 4.0978 | 4.9931 | 6.0781 | 7.3920 | 10.9029 |
| 42 | 1.8688 | 2.2972 | 2.8210 | 3.4607 | 4.2413 | 5.1928 | 6.3516 | 7.7616 | 11.5570 |
| 43 | 1.8969 | 2.3432 | 2.8915 | 3.5645 | 4.3897 | 5.4005 | 6.6374 | 8.1497 | 12.2505 |
| 44 | 1.9253 | 2.3901 | 2.9638 | 3.6715 | 4.5433 | 5.6165 | 6.9361 | 8.5572 | 12.9855 |
| 45 | 1.9542 | 2.4379 | 3.0379 | 3.7816 | 4.7024 | 5.8412 | 7.2482 | 8.9850 | 13.7646 |
| 46 | 1.9835 | 2.4866 | 3.1139 | 3.8950 | 4.8669 | 6.0748 | 7.5744 | 9.4343 | 14.5905 |
| 47 | 2.0133 | 2.5363 | 3.1917 | 4.0119 | 5.0373 | 6.3178 | 7.9153 | 9.9060 | 15.4659 |
| 48 | 2.0435 | 2.5871 | 3.2715 | 4.1323 | 5.2136 | 6.5705 | 8.2715 | 10.4013 | 16.3939 |
| 49 | 2.0741 | 2.6388 | 3.3533 | 4.2562 | 5.3961 | 6.8333 | 8.6437 | 10.9213 | 17.3775 |
| 50 | 2.1052 | 2.6916 | 3.4371 | 4.3839 | 5.5849 | 7.1067 | 9.0326 | 11.4674 | 18.4202 |

| Years | 1.5% | 2% | 2.5% | 3% | 3.5% | 4% | 4.5% | 5% | 6% |
|---|---|---|---|---|---|---|---|---|---|
| 1 | 1.0150 | 1.0200 | 1.0250 | 1.0300 | 1.0350 | 1.0400 | 1.0450 | 1.0500 | 1.0600 |
| 2 | 2.0452 | 2.0604 | 2.0756 | 2.0909 | 2.1062 | 2.1216 | 2.1370 | 2.1525 | 2.1836 |
| 3 | 3.0909 | 3.1216 | 3.1525 | 3.1836 | 3.2149 | 3.2465 | 3.2782 | 3.3101 | 3.3746 |
| 4 | 4.1523 | 4.2040 | 4.2563 | 4.3091 | 4.3625 | 4.4163 | 4.4707 | 4.5256 | 4.6371 |
| 5 | 5.2296 | 5.3081 | 5.3877 | 5.4684 | 5.5502 | 5.6330 | 5.7169 | 5.8019 | 5.9753 |
| 6 | 6.3230 | 6.4343 | 6.5474 | 6.6625 | 6.7794 | 6.8993 | 7.0192 | 7.1420 | 7.3938 |
| 7 | 7.4328 | 7.5830 | 7.7361 | 7.8923 | 8.0517 | 8.2142 | 8.3800 | 8.5491 | 8.8975 |
| 8 | 8.5593 | 8.7546 | 8.9545 | 9.1591 | 9.3685 | 9.5828 | 9.8021 | 10.0266 | 10.4913 |
| 9 | 9.7027 | 9.9497 | 10.2034 | 10.4639 | 10.7314 | 11.0061 | 11.2882 | 11.5779 | 12.1808 |
| 10 | 10.8633 | 11.1687 | 11.4835 | 11.8078 | 12.1420 | 12.4864 | 12.8412 | 13.2068 | 13.9716 |
| 11 | 12.0412 | 12.4121 | 12.7956 | 13.1920 | 13.6020 | 14.0258 | 14.4650 | 14.9171 | 15.8699 |
| 12 | 13.2368 | 13.6803 | 14.1404 | 14.6178 | 15.1130 | 15.6268 | 16.1599 | 16.7130 | 17.8821 |
| 13 | 14.4504 | 14.9739 | 15.5190 | 16.0863 | 16.6770 | 17.2919 | 17.9321 | 18.5986 | 20.0151 |
| 14 | 15.6821 | 16.2934 | 16.9319 | 17.5989 | 18.2957 | 19.0236 | 19.7841 | 20.5786 | 22.2760 |
| 15 | 16.9324 | 17.6393 | 18.3802 | 19.1569 | 19.9710 | 20.8245 | 21.7193 | 22.6575 | 24.6725 |
| 16 | 18.2014 | 19.0121 | 19.8647 | 20.7616 | 21.7050 | 22.6975 | 23.7417 | 24.8404 | 27.2129 |
| 17 | 19.4894 | 20.4123 | 21.3863 | 22.4144 | 23.4997 | 24.6454 | 25.8551 | 27.1324 | 29.9057 |
| 18 | 20.7967 | 21.8406 | 22.9460 | 24.1169 | 25.3572 | 26.6712 | 28.0636 | 29.5390 | 32.7600 |
| 19 | 22.1237 | 23.2974 | 24.5447 | 25.8704 | 27.2797 | 28.7781 | 30.3714 | 32.0660 | 35.7856 |
| 20 | 23.4705 | 24.7833 | 26.1833 | 27.6765 | 29.2695 | 30.9692 | 32.7831 | 34.7193 | 38.9927 |
| 21 | 24.8376 | 26.2990 | 27.8629 | 29.5368 | 31.3289 | 33.2480 | 35.3034 | 37.5052 | 42.3923 |
| 22 | 26.2251 | 27.8450 | 29.5844 | 31.4529 | 33.4604 | 35.6179 | 37.9370 | 40.4305 | 45.9958 |
| 23 | 27.6335 | 29.4219 | 31.3490 | 33.4265 | 35.6665 | 38.0826 | 40.6892 | 43.5020 | 49.8156 |
| 24 | 29.0630 | 31.0303 | 33.1578 | 35.4593 | 37.9499 | 40.6459 | 43.5652 | 46.7271 | 53.8645 |
| 25 | 30.5140 | 32.6709 | 35.0117 | 37.5530 | 40.3131 | 43.3117 | 46.5706 | 50.1135 | 58.1564 |
| 26 | 31.9867 | 34.3443 | 36.9120 | 39.7096 | 42.7591 | 46.0842 | 49.7113 | 53.6691 | 62.7058 |
| 27 | 33.4815 | 36.0512 | 38.8598 | 41.9309 | 45.2906 | 48.9676 | 52.9933 | 57.4026 | 67.5281 |
| 28 | 34.9987 | 37.7922 | 40.8563 | 44.2189 | 47.9108 | 51.9663 | 56.4230 | 61.3227 | 72.6398 |
| 29 | 36.5387 | 39.5681 | 42.9027 | 46.5754 | 50.6227 | 55.0849 | 60.0071 | 65.4388 | 78.0582 |
| 30 | 38.1018 | 41.3794 | 45.0003 | 49.0027 | 53.4295 | 58.3283 | 63.7524 | 69.7608 | 83.8017 |
| 31 | 39.6883 | 43.2270 | 47.1503 | 51.5028 | 56.3345 | 61.7015 | 67.6662 | 74.2988 | 89.8898 |
| 32 | 41.2986 | 45.1116 | 49.3540 | 54.0778 | 59.3412 | 65.2095 | 71.7562 | 79.0638 | 96.3432 |
| 33 | 42.9331 | 47.0338 | 51.6129 | 56.7302 | 62.4532 | 68.8579 | 76.0303 | 84.0670 | 103.1838 |
| 34 | 44.5921 | 48.9945 | 53.9282 | 59.4621 | 65.6740 | 72.6522 | 80.4966 | 89.3203 | 110.4348 |
| 35 | 46.2760 | 50.9944 | 56.3014 | 62.2759 | 69.0076 | 76.5983 | 85.1640 | 94.8363 | 118.1209 |
| 36 | 47.9851 | 53.0343 | 58.7339 | 65.1742 | 72.4579 | 80.7022 | 90.0413 | 100.6281 | 126.2681 |
| 37 | 49.7199 | 55.1149 | 61.2273 | 68.1594 | 76.0289 | 84.9703 | 95.1382 | 106.7095 | 134.9042 |
| 38 | 51.4807 | 57.2372 | 63.7830 | 71.2342 | 79.7249 | 89.4091 | 100.4644 | 113.0950 | 144.0585 |
| 39 | 53.2679 | 59.4020 | 66.4026 | 74.4013 | 83.5503 | 94.0255 | 106.0303 | 119.7998 | 153.7620 |
| 40 | 55.0819 | 61.6100 | 69.0876 | 77.6633 | 87.5095 | 98.8265 | 111.8467 | 126.8398 | 164.0477 |
| 41 | 56.9231 | 63.8622 | 71.8398 | 81.0232 | 91.6074 | 103.8196 | 117.9248 | 134.2318 | 174.9505 |
| 42 | 58.7920 | 66.1595 | 74.6608 | 84.4839 | 95.8486 | 109.0124 | 124.2764 | 141.9933 | 186.5076 |
| 43 | 60.6889 | 68.5027 | 77.5523 | 88.0484 | 100.2383 | 114.4129 | 130.9138 | 150.1430 | 198.7580 |
| 44 | 62.6142 | 70.8927 | 80.5161 | 91.7199 | 104.7817 | 120.0294 | 137.8500 | 158.7002 | 221.7435 |
| 45 | 64.5684 | 73.3306 | 83.5540 | 95.5015 | 109.4840 | 125.8706 | 145.0982 | 167.6852 | 225.5081 |
| 46 | 66.5519 | 75.8172 | 86.6679 | 99.3965 | 114.3510 | 131.9454 | 152.6726 | 177.1194 | 240.0986 |
| 47 | 68.5652 | 78.3535 | 89.8596 | 103.4084 | 119.3883 | 138.2632 | 160.5879 | 187.0254 | 255.5645 |
| 48 | 70.6087 | 80.9406 | 93.1311 | 107.5406 | 124.6018 | 144.8337 | 168.8594 | 197.4267 | 271.9584 |
| 49 | 72.6828 | 83.5794 | 96.4843 | 111.7969 | 129.9979 | 151.6671 | 177.5030 | 208.3480 | 289.3359 |
| 50 | 74.7881 | 86.2710 | 99.9215 | 116.1808 | 135.5828 | 158.7738 | 186.5357 | 219.8154 | 307.7561 |

| Years | 1.5% | 2% | 2.5% | 3% | 3.5% | 4% | 4.5% | 5% | 6% |
|---|---|---|---|---|---|---|---|---|---|
| 1 | .9852 | .9804 | .9756 | .9709 | .9662 | .9615 | .9569 | .9524 | .9434 |
| 2 | .9707 | .9612 | .9518 | .9426 | .9335 | .9246 | .9157 | .9070 | .8900 |
| 3 | .9563 | .9423 | .9286 | .9151 | .9019 | .8890 | .8763 | .8638 | .8396 |
| 4 | .9422 | .9238 | .9060 | .8885 | .8714 | .8548 | .8386 | .8227 | .7921 |
| 5 | .9283 | .9057 | .8839 | .8626 | .8420 | .8219 | .8025 | .7835 | .7473 |
| 6 | .9145 | .8880 | .8623 | .8375 | .8135 | .7903 | .7679 | .7462 | .7050 |
| 7 | .9010 | .8706 | .8413 | .8131 | .7860 | .7599 | .7348 | .7107 | .6651 |
| 8 | .8877 | .8535 | .8207 | .7894 | .7594 | .7307 | .7032 | .6768 | .6274 |
| 9 | .8746 | .8368 | .8007 | .7664 | .7337 | .7026 | .6729 | .6446 | .5919 |
| 10 | .8617 | .8203 | .7812 | .7441 | .7089 | .6756 | .6439 | .6139 | .5584 |
| 11 | .8489 | .8043 | .7621 | .7224 | .6849 | .6496 | .6162 | .5847 | .5268 |
| 12 | .8364 | .7885 | .7436 | .7014 | .6618 | .6246 | .5897 | .5568 | .4970 |
| 13 | .8240 | .7730 | .7254 | .6810 | .6394 | .6006 | .5643 | .5303 | .4688 |
| 14 | .8118 | .7579 | .7077 | .6611 | .6178 | .5775 | .5400 | .5051 | .4423 |
| 15 | .7999 | .7430 | .6905 | .6419 | .5969 | .5553 | .5167 | .4810 | .4173 |
| 16 | .7880 | .7284 | .6736 | .6232 | .5767 | .5339 | .4945 | .4581 | .3936 |
| 17 | .7764 | .7142 | .6572 | .6050 | .5572 | .5134 | .4732 | .4363 | .3714 |
| 18 | .7649 | .7002 | .6412 | .5874 | .5384 | .4936 | .4528 | .4155 | .3503 |
| 19 | .7536 | .6864 | .6255 | .5703 | .5202 | .4746 | .4333 | .3957 | .3305 |
| 20 | .7425 | .6730 | .6103 | .5537 | .5026 | .4564 | .4146 | .3769 | .3118 |
| 21 | .7315 | .6598 | .5954 | .5375 | .4856 | .4388 | .3968 | .3589 | .2942 |
| 22 | .7207 | .6468 | .5809 | .5219 | .4692 | .4220 | .3797 | .3418 | .2775 |
| 23 | .7100 | .6342 | .5667 | .5067 | .4533 | .4057 | .3634 | .3256 | .2618 |
| 24 | .6995 | .6217 | .5529 | .4919 | .4380 | .3901 | .3477 | .3101 | .2470 |
| 25 | .6892 | .6095 | .5394 | .4776 | .4231 | .3751 | .3327 | .2953 | .2330 |
| 26 | .6790 | .5976 | .5262 | .4637 | .4088 | .3607 | .3184 | .2812 | .2198 |
| 27 | .6690 | .5859 | .5134 | .4502 | .3950 | .3468 | .3047 | .2678 | .2074 |
| 28 | .6591 | .5744 | .5009 | .4371 | .3817 | .3335 | .2916 | .2551 | .1956 |
| 29 | .6494 | .5631 | .4887 | .4243 | .3687 | .3207 | .2790 | .2429 | .1846 |
| 30 | .6398 | .5521 | .4767 | .4120 | .3563 | .3083 | .2670 | .2314 | .1741 |
| 31 | .6303 | .5412 | .4651 | .4000 | .3442 | .2965 | .2555 | .2204 | .1643 |
| 32 | .6210 | .5306 | .4538 | .3883 | .3326 | .2851 | .2445 | .2099 | .1550 |
| 33 | .6118 | .5202 | .4427 | .3770 | .3213 | .2741 | .2340 | .1999 | .1462 |
| 34 | .6028 | .5100 | .4319 | .3660 | .3105 | .2636 | .2239 | .1904 | .1379 |
| 35 | .5939 | .5000 | .4214 | .3554 | .3000 | .2534 | .2143 | .1813 | .1301 |
| 36 | .5851 | .4902 | .4111 | .3450 | .2898 | .2437 | .2050 | .1727 | .1227 |
| 37 | .5764 | .4806 | .4011 | .3350 | .2800 | .2343 | .1962 | .1644 | .1158 |
| 38 | .5679 | .4712 | .3913 | .3252 | .2706 | .2253 | .1878 | .1566 | .1092 |
| 39 | .5595 | .4619 | .3817 | .3158 | .2614 | .2166 | .1797 | .1491 | .1031 |
| 40 | .5513 | .4529 | .3724 | .3066 | .2526 | .2083 | .1719 | .1420 | .0972 |
| 41 | .5431 | .4440 | .3633 | .2976 | .2440 | .2003 | .1645 | .1353 | .0917 |
| 42 | .5351 | .4353 | .3545 | .2890 | .2358 | .1926 | .1574 | .1288 | .0865 |
| 43 | .5272 | .4268 | .3458 | .2805 | .2278 | .1852 | .1507 | .1227 | .0816 |
| 44 | .5194 | .4184 | .3374 | .2724 | .2201 | .1780 | .1442 | .1169 | .0770 |
| 45 | .5117 | .4102 | .3292 | .2644 | .2127 | .1712 | .1380 | .1113 | .0727 |
| 46 | .5042 | .4022 | .3211 | .2567 | .2055 | .1646 | .1320 | .1060 | .0685 |
| 47 | .4967 | .3943 | .3133 | .2493 | .1985 | .1583 | .1263 | .1009 | .0647 |
| 48 | .4894 | .3865 | .3057 | .2420 | .1918 | .1522 | .1209 | .0961 | .0610 |
| 49 | .4821 | .3790 | .2982 | .2350 | .1853 | .1463 | .1157 | .0916 | .0575 |
| 50 | .4750 | .3715 | .2909 | .2281 | .1791 | .1407 | .1107 | .0872 | .0543 |

| Years | 1.5% | 2% | 2.5% | 3% | 3.5% | 4% | 4.5% | 5% | 6% |
|---|---|---|---|---|---|---|---|---|---|
| 1 | .9852 | .9804 | .9756 | .9709 | .9662 | .9615 | .9569 | .9524 | .9434 |
| 2 | 1.9559 | 1.9416 | 1.9274 | 1.9135 | 1.8997 | 1.8861 | 1.8727 | 1.8594 | 1.8334 |
| 3 | 2.9122 | 2.8839 | 2.8560 | 2.8286 | 2.8016 | 2.7751 | 2.7490 | 2.7232 | 2.6730 |
| 4 | 3.8544 | 3.8077 | 3.7620 | 3.7171 | 3.6731 | 3.6299 | 3.5875 | 3.5460 | 3.4651 |
| 5 | 4.7826 | 4.7135 | 4.6458 | 4.5797 | 4.5151 | 4.4518 | 4.3900 | 4.3295 | 4.2124 |
| 6 | 5.6972 | 5.6014 | 5.5081 | 5.4172 | 5.3286 | 5.2421 | 5.1579 | 5.0757 | 4.9173 |
| 7 | 6.5982 | 6.4720 | 6.3494 | 6.2303 | 6.1145 | 6.0021 | 5.8927 | 5.7864 | 5.5824 |
| 8 | 7.4859 | 7.3255 | 7.1701 | 7.0197 | 6.8740 | 6.7327 | 6.5959 | 6.4632 | 6.2098 |
| 9 | 8.3605 | 8.1622 | 7.9709 | 7.7861 | 7.6077 | 7.4353 | 7.2688 | 7.1078 | 6.8017 |
| 10 | 9.2222 | 8.9826 | 8.7521 | 8.5302 | 8.3166 | 8.1109 | 7.9127 | 7.7217 | 7.3601 |
| 11 | 10.0711 | 9.7868 | 9.5142 | 9.2526 | 9.0016 | 8.7605 | 8.5289 | 8.3064 | 7.8869 |
| 12 | 10.9075 | 10.5753 | 10.2578 | 9.9540 | 9.6633 | 9.3851 | 9.1186 | 8.8633 | 8.3838 |
| 13 | 11.7315 | 11.3484 | 10.9832 | 10.6350 | 10.3027 | 9.9856 | 9.6829 | 9.3936 | 8.8527 |
| 14 | 12.5434 | 12.1062 | 11.6909 | 11.2961 | 10.9205 | 10.5631 | 10.2228 | 9.8986 | 9.2950 |
| 15 | 13.3432 | 12.8493 | 12.3814 | 11.9379 | 11.5174 | 11.1184 | 10.7395 | 10.3797 | 9.7122 |
| 16 | 14.1313 | 13.5777 | 13.0550 | 12.5611 | 12.0941 | 11.6523 | 11.2340 | 10.8378 | 10.1059 |
| 17 | 14.9076 | 14.2919 | 13.7122 | 13.1661 | 12.6513 | 12.1657 | 11.7072 | 11.2741 | 10.4773 |
| 18 | 15.6726 | 14.9920 | 14.3534 | 13.7535 | 13.1897 | 12.6593 | 12.1600 | 11.6896 | 10.8276 |
| 19 | 16.4262 | 15.6785 | 14.9789 | 14.3238 | 13.7098 | 13.1339 | 12.5933 | 12.0853 | 11.1581 |
| 20 | 17.1686 | 16.3514 | 15.5892 | 14.8775 | 14.2124 | 13.5903 | 13.0079 | 12.4622 | 11.4699 |
| 21 | 17.9001 | 17.0112 | 16.1845 | 15.4150 | 14.6980 | 14.0292 | 13.4047 | 12.8212 | 11.7641 |
| 22 | 18.6208 | 17.6580 | 16.7654 | 15.9369 | 15.1671 | 14.4511 | 13.7844 | 13.1630 | 12.0416 |
| 23 | 19.3309 | 18.2922 | 17.3321 | 16.4436 | 15.6204 | 14.8568 | 14.1478 | 13.4886 | 12.3034 |
| 24 | 20.0304 | 18.9139 | 17.8850 | 16.9355 | 16.0584 | 15.2470 | 14.4955 | 13.7986 | 12.5504 |
| 25 | 20.7196 | 19.5235 | 18.4244 | 17.4131 | 16.4815 | 15.6221 | 14.8282 | 14.0939 | 12.7834 |
| 26 | 21.3986 | 20.1210 | 18.9506 | 17.8768 | 16.8904 | 15.9828 | 15.1466 | 14.3752 | 13.0032 |
| 27 | 22.0676 | 20.7069 | 19.4640 | 18.3270 | 17.2854 | 16.3296 | 15.4513 | 14.6430 | 13.2105 |
| 28 | 22.7267 | 21.2813 | 19.9649 | 18.7641 | 17.6670 | 16.6631 | 15.7429 | 14.8981 | 13.4062 |
| 29 | 23.3761 | 21.8444 | 20.4535 | 19.1885 | 18.0358 | 16.9837 | 16.0219 | 15.1411 | 13.5907 |
| 30 | 24.0158 | 22.3965 | 20.9303 | 19.6004 | 18.3920 | 17.2920 | 16.2889 | 15.3725 | 13.7648 |
| 31 | 24.6461 | 22.9377 | 21.3954 | 20.0004 | 18.7363 | 17.5885 | 16.5444 | 15.5928 | 13.9291 |
| 32 | 25.2671 | 23.4683 | 21.8492 | 20.3888 | 19.0689 | 17.8736 | 16.7889 | 15.8027 | 14.0840 |
| 33 | 25.8790 | 23.9886 | 22.2919 | 20.7658 | 19.3902 | 18.1476 | 17.0229 | 16.0025 | 14.2302 |
| 34 | 26.4817 | 24.4986 | 22.7238 | 21.1318 | 19.7007 | 18.4112 | 17.2468 | 16.1929 | 14.3681 |
| 35 | 27.0756 | 24.9986 | 23.1452 | 21.4872 | 20.0007 | 18.6646 | 17.4610 | 16.3742 | 14.4982 |
| 36 | 27.6607 | 25.4888 | 23.5563 | 21.8323 | 20.2905 | 18.9083 | 17.6660 | 16.5469 | 14.6210 |
| 37 | 28.2371 | 25.9695 | 23.9573 | 22.1672 | 20.5705 | 19.1426 | 17.8622 | 16.7113 | 14.7368 |
| 38 | 28.8051 | 26.4406 | 24.3486 | 22.4925 | 20.8411 | 19.3679 | 18.0500 | 16.8679 | 14.8460 |
| 39 | 29.3646 | 26.9026 | 24.7303 | 22.8082 | 21.1025 | 19.5845 | 18.2297 | 17.0170 | 14.9491 |
| 40 | 29.9158 | 27.3555 | 25.1028 | 23.1148 | 21.3551 | 19.7928 | 18.4016 | 17.1591 | 15.0463 |
| 41 | 30.4590 | 27.7995 | 25.4661 | 23.4124 | 21.5991 | 19.9931 | 18.5661 | 17.2944 | 15.1380 |
| 42 | 30.9941 | 28.2348 | 25.8206 | 23.7014 | 21.8349 | 20.1856 | 18.7235 | 17.4232 | 15.2245 |
| 43 | 31.5212 | 28.6616 | 26.1664 | 23.9819 | 22.0627 | 20.3708 | 18.8742 | 17.5459 | 15.3062 |
| 44 | 32.0406 | 29.0800 | 26.5038 | 24.2543 | 22.2828 | 20.5488 | 19.0184 | 17.6628 | 15.3832 |
| 45 | 32.5523 | 29.4902 | 26.8330 | 24.5187 | 22.4955 | 20.7200 | 19.1563 | 17.7741 | 15.4558 |
| 46 | 33.0565 | 29.8923 | 27.1542 | 24.7754 | 22.7009 | 20.8847 | 19.2884 | 17.8801 | 15.5244 |
| 47 | 33.5532 | 30.2866 | 27.4675 | 25.0247 | 22.8994 | 21.0429 | 19.4147 | 17.9810 | 15.5890 |
| 48 | 34.0426 | 30.6731 | 27.7732 | 25.2667 | 23.0912 | 21.1951 | 19.5356 | 18.0772 | 15.6500 |
| 49 | 34.5247 | 31.0521 | 28.0714 | 25.5017 | 23.2766 | 21.3415 | 19.6513 | 18.1687 | 15.7076 |
| 50 | 34.9997 | 31.4236 | 28.3623 | 25.7298 | 23.4556 | 21.4822 | 19.7620 | 18.2559 | 15.7619 |

# Selected Pension Bibliography

........................................................................

## GENERAL

Cloud, Arthur David, *Pensions in Modern Industry*, Hawkins and Loomis Co., Chicago, 1930, 531 pp.

Conant, Luther, Jr., *A Critical Analysis of Industrial Pension Systems*, The Macmillan Co., New York, 1922, 262 pp.

Hohaus, Reinhard A., "Reinsurance of Retirement Plans," *Transactions*, Actuarial Society of America, October, 1925, New York, Vol. 26, Part 2, No. 74, pp. 480-506.

Journal of Commerce, The, *Employee Retirement Plans*, New York, July 15, 1943, 60 pp.

————, *Practical Pension Planning*, New York, May 15, 1944, 60 pp.

————, *Approval of Pension and Profit Sharing Plans*, New York, May 15, 1945, 52 pp.

————, *Pension and Profit Sharing Plan Expansion*, New York, May 29, 1946, 40 pp.

Latimer, Murray Webb, *Industrial Pension Systems in the United States and Canada*, Vols. I and II, Industrial Relations Counselors, Inc., New York, 1932, 1,195 pp.

Latimer, Murray Webb, and Tufel, Karl, *Trends in Industrial Pensions*, Industrial Relations Counselors, Inc., New York, 1940, 88 pp.

Myers, Robert J., "Some Considerations in Pension Fund Valuation," *Transactions*, Actuarial Society of America, May, 1945, New York, Vol. 46, Part I, No. 113, pp. 51-58.

National Industrial Conference Board, Inc., *Industrial Pensions in the United States*, New York, 1929, 157 pp.

————, *Elements of Industrial Pension Plans*, New York, 1931, 48 pp.

————, *Trends in Company Pension Plans*, New York, 1944, 52 pp.

Prentice-Hall, Inc., *Pension and Profit Sharing Service*, New York (published as a continuous loose-leaf service).

Report of the Subcommittee of the Committee on Finance, United States Senate, pursuant to S. Res. 215 (75th Congress): *Survey of Experiences in Profit Sharing and Possibilities of Incentive Taxation*, Senate, Report No. 610, 76th Congress, 1st Session, U. S. Government Printing Office, Washington, 1939, 351 pp.

Robbins, Rainard B., *College Plans for Retirement Income*, Columbia University Press, New York, 1940, 253 pp.

Winslow, C. Morton, and Clark, K. Raymond, *Profit Sharing and Pension Plans*, Commerce Clearing House, Chicago, 1939, 192 pp.

Wyatt, Birchard E., *Private Group Retirement Plans*, Graphic Arts Press, Inc., Washington, D. C., 1936, 145 pp.

TECHNICAL

King, George, "On Staff Pension Funds," *Journal*, Institute of Actuaries, April, 1905, London, Vol. 39, pp. 129-209.

Maclean, Joseph B., "Notes on Problems of Small Pension Funds," *Transactions*, Actuarial Society of America, May 20 and 21, 1920, New York, Vol. 21, Part I, No. 63, pp. 77-94.

Manly, Henry W., "On Staff Pension Funds," *Journal*, Institute of Actuaries, April, 1911, London, Vol. 45, pp. 149-229.

M'Lauchlan, James J., "The Fundamental Principles of Pension Funds," *Transactions*, Faculty of Actuaries, 1909, London, Vol. 4, Part 7, No. 41, pp. 195-228.

————, "On the Construction of Salary Scales for Use in the Valuation of Pension Funds, and . . . ," *Transactions*, Faculty of Actuaries, 1915, London, Vol. 7, No. 68.

Porteous, D. A., *Pension and Widows' and Orphans' Funds*, Cambridge University Press, London (published for the Institute of Actuaries Students' Society), 1936, 111 pp.

# List of Tables

.......................................................................

# Index